GUERNEVILLE EARLY DAYS

A History of the Lower Russian River

BY

JOHN C. SCHUBERT

GUERNEVILLE EARLY DAYS

A History of the Lower Russian River - Third Edition

ISBN 13: 9781943359417

Library of Congress Control Number: 2016949303

Copyright © 2016, John C. Schubert

All rights reserved.

No part of this book may be reproduced in any form without express permission of the copyright holder.

Printed in the United States by Chapbook Press.

Schuler Books
2660 28th Street SE
Grand Rapids, MI 49512
(616) 942-7330
www.schulerbooks.com

Other books by John C. Schubert:

Then & Now Russian River, published 2011 with Valerie A. Munthe
Red Slide Magnesite Mines and Railroad, published 2012
Stumptown Stories: Tales of the Russian River, published 2013

Acknowledgements:

Cover designed by Valerie A. Munthe
Cover photos from John C. Schubert Collection
Front & Back Cover images, courtesy of John C. Schubert Collection
Back cover photo of John C. Schubert by Jeff Lee
Etching of Stump and Axes contributed by Mike Capitani (pg. iii)

Dedicated
to my grandchildren,
Jasmine, Sabrina,
Johnna, Heather, & Doran

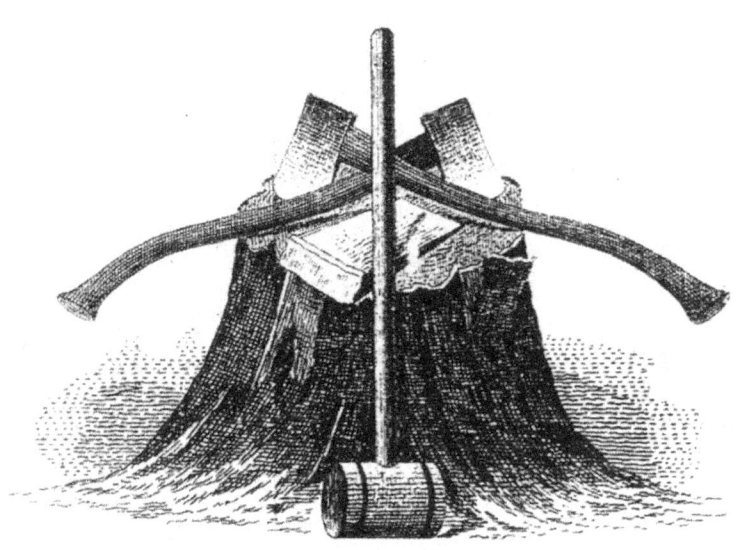

About the Author

John C. Schubert was born in 1938 in San Francisco. During his childhood, although living in various northern and southern California communities during the winter, he spent his summers on the Guerneville property his grandfather acquired in 1920. He has lived permanently in the Guerneville area since 1956.

The author received a B.A. degree in anthropology at Sonoma State College. He has been known as the Russian River historian since 1960 and has written for several Guerneville newspapers with his column "Stumptown Stories." He has received several literary awards for his poetry and historical articles. A Sonoma County deputy sheriff for 32 years, he is also a past president of the Sonoma County Historical Society and a former Marine. He has three sons, Keith, Hilmar, and Preston.

Foreward

By Valerie A. Munthe

It's 2016 and as I walk amongst the tourists down the crowded sidewalk in Guerneville on a hot summer day, I can't help but imagine what this small town was like 140 years ago. I imagine the sights of horse-drawn wagons, steam engines and massive redwood trees and stumps; the sound of the steam whistle from the mill; the smell of wood chips, roasted redwood duff and horse manure. It would, indeed, be a far cry from the Guerneville we know today. In his own way, John Schubert takes you back in time with his methodical, staccato-like manner of spewing facts, mixed in with occasional story-like rhetoric, painting a perfect picture of an ancient town when life was challenging, dangerous and yet much simpler. Without realizing it, John has transformed Guerneville's story, making it significant amongst those of larger townships, such as Santa Rosa, Healdsburg and even San Francisco. Guerneville Early Days is more than just a biographical text of a small town; it's a gift that John has entrusted to the community. Just as John Washington Bagley deserves the title of being Guerneville's founding father, John Schubert has earned the title of Guerneville's Historic Steward due to his tireless efforts of collecting data for over 50 years, writing and compiling countless articles and stories (some not included in this book) and being the go-to person of all things history.

Guerneville Early Days is a legacy masterpiece. It tells the story of small, humble beginnings and how human innovation can develop and transform the environment, wherever they may be. But we must remember that history is an organic material; constantly changing and adjusting to new discoveries. This third edition is a manifestation of this process, with updated facts and imagery. The stories in the following pages will shed new and improved light on this small river town. And for those budding historians, when in need of any facts, historic or otherwise, of Guerneville, just remember what John would say:
"IT'S IN THE BOOK!"

Table of Contents

1. Introduction..1
2. Lay of the Land & Run of the River 5
3. The First Occupiers...9
4. Kashaya Texts...11
5. Russians, Spaniards, Englishmen & Few French...19
6. Pioneers, Homesteaders & Squatters...................25
7. Beginnings of a Village.....................................33
8. Steamship Enterprise.......................................41
9. Trees & Stumps — the Green Legions................45
10. Lumber Mills — 1870 – 1875...........................55
11. Guerneville 1872 – 1875...................................67
12. Lumber Mills 1876 – 1880................................75
13. Guerneville 1876 – 1880...................................85
14. Quicksilver — Part 1.......................................99
15. Whites vs Chinese — Part 1...........................107
16. Lumber Mills — 1881 – 1885..........................115
17. Guerneville — 1881 – 1885............................121
18. Arson...135
19. Lumber Mills — 1886 – 1890..........................139
20. Guerneville — 1886 – 1890............................147
21. Whites vs Chinese — Part 2...........................157
22. Bricks..161
23. Lumber Mills — 1891 – 1895..........................165
24. Guerneville — 1891 – 1895............................169
25. Phoenix...179
26. Lumber Mills — 1895 to end..........................189
27. Quicksilver — Part 2.....................................195
28. Religion...201
29. Past Organizations..209
30. Tobacco...215
31. Agriculture..223
32. Guerneville — 1896 – 1900............................229
33. Earthquake..247
34. Armstrong Park..255
35. John Washington Bagley................................267
36. In Closing..269

APPENDICES

I. Pioneers & Early Settlers to 1870....................271
II. Asian Residents to 1900.................................277
III. Postmasters of Guerneville............................279
VI. Redwood Township Post Offices....................280
V. Redwood Township Justices of the Peace.......281
VI. Redwood Township Constables.....................281
VII. Roadmasters of Redwood Road District........282
VIII. Agents of Wells, Fargo & Co. Express..........282
VX. Incorporations...283
X. Registered Partnerships.................................283
XI. Biographies..284
XII. Bibliography..286

Guerneville circa 1873

GUERNEVILLE EARLY DAYS

Chapter 1

INTRODUCTION

WELCOME!

Some of you readers are visiting these pages out of curiosity about Guerneville; others are students of history. There are chapters here to satisfy all. Of course, of the many facts included, not all are stimulating, but they are the foundation of Guerneville's history. Some chapters are colorful anecdotes that reflect the character of the times and area.

I wrote this book for three reasons. The first was to satisfy my own curiosity about the beginnings and subsequent stories of the Lower Russian River. The second was to debunk or substantiate the traditional tales of the "old timer" about the town. Out of these two reasons came the third: to preserve the past for the future.

During the 20-plus years that have passed while gathering the Guerneville story, a book by C. Raymond Clar, *Out of the River Mist*, was printed. It is an enjoyable publication of Clar's reminiscences of growing up in Guerneville during the first part of the 20th century as a modern-day Tom Sawyer. Because of his book, a fourth cause emerged for writing this history — to complement his book.

But as Ray Clar, pen pal, constant critic and friend told me, " . . . written history is the interpretation of cause and effect, not just the recording of chronological events." In some cases I fulfilled the cause and effect, other times all that could be done was to compose a statistical record; both are valid.

I have attempted to discover every aspect of Guerneville, from flora and geography to commercial enterprise and racial disturbances; from fire and flood to epidemics and elections. My quest for the earthly remains of "old" Guerneville has taken me from this village to Los Angeles, from 1000 feet below sea level in the Sonoma Quicksilver Mine to the fifth floor of the California State Library and to many locations in between.

Much of the town's record has been disposed of, destroyed, or just vanished. The Sonoma County government literally hauled old records, papers and letters to the dumps and burned them. I witnessed this when the courts, county clerk's office and sheriff's office moved into the County's Hall of Justice on the north side of Santa Rosa.

Many inquiries garnered nothing. Letters to the Library of Congress and National Archives were at times extremely fruitful and, on occasion, for naught: They had destroyed records also.

In collecting information, some facts could not be proven or refuted for any number of reasons. Because of these occurrences (not many), I propose the challenge to any and all persons to prove me wrong. Propagating misinformation only leads to confusion. I welcome any and all corrections to this volume.

As the title states, Guerneville Early Days, the time span covers from about 3000 B.C. to 1900 A.D. and a little after. Though most of the community's recorded history is of recent origin (the last 160 years), the attempts to discover events prior to this small span have been manifold, but with little result.

The reader must remember that human occupation of this area, though sparse, extends over several millenia. The end product is a few chapters pertaining to the Pomo peoples of Western Sonoma County. It is an imbalance, true, between distant and recent histories, but this inequity has not passed unobserved and has been corrected as best as information could provide.

Some chapters are composed from many sources and others are almost totally constructed from interviewees and data in their possession, as in the case of Jack Hetzel and the chapter "Tobacco."

Present and former residents of the Russian River area contributed a large amount to this book. The name came from a small album by the town's photographer, Laddie Hasek.

With the exceptions of a few photographs from libraries, all are copies of those owned by residents. It is surprising how many pictures survived the first century of Guerneville's existence; as the reader will discover, the town was completely burned to the ground on four occasions, flooded in five instances, and damaged by earthquake once. Whenever possible, I give credit to the owners for use of their pictures.

The story of maps and engravings is similar to that of photographs. They were discovered in old bookstores, libraries, homes and drawers of companies and government agencies. The best source was the federal government with their Sanborn maps and original survey plots of the 1860s. The county has a good collection of original road surveys with notes. The state depositories had nothing to offer that I did not recover elsewhere.

Now I come to the acknowledgments and credits. I am putting them here as the people who helped me; they are part of the story and not separate, regardless of how it is done in other books. Some deserve special thanks for their assistance:

C. Raymond Clar and Jack Hetzel, as already noted; Anne Stroberger, county librarian, for her unhesitating assistance in filling requests and directing me to new sources or how to find them; Jim Huston, Sonoma State College librarian, for charging me with enthusiasm when I lagged and for opening college archives. And to those who provided pieces of the puzzle, their names are in alphabetical order, placed here in the text of the history because each illuminates some facet of the Guerneville story in his or her own particular way:

Derrick Andrews	Maud Laws
Chris Baagoe	June Lewek
Rhoda Bean	Alta Starret Lutrell
Vivian Beck	Jack Lutrell
Gretchen "Pet" Belden	Gordon Maguire
Anna Bever	Cliff Marshall
J.V. "Pete" Bever	Ken McKitrick
Ann Birkhofer	Lenabelle Miller
Laura Ayres Birkhofer	Paul Mitchell
Alice Blue	Gertrude Joost Moore
Sal Bonelli	David Myrick
Diana Broberg	Keith Neeley
Douglas Broberg	John "Shorty" Parkins
Joe Buttner, Jr.	Essie Parrish
Clarence Clar	Otis Parrish
George Clar	Sid Parrish
John Crump	Charles Peck
George Denise	David W. Peri
Ben Drake	Mable Peter
Margaret Drake	Robert Ridenhour
Viola French	Judge Jesse Robertson
Frank Gianoli	Gary Rodgers
Frank Gori	Ernest Schulte
Gladys Bagley Goselyn	Gertrude L. Schulte
Dale Haskins	Edson Smith
Amy Bagley Hatch	Ina Stephenson
Gary Heck	Noel Stephenson
Rasperson Jensen	Lincoln Stewart
Wendell Joost	Andrew "Andy" Strode
Tom King Jr.	Clara Strode Smith
Joseph L. "Red" Kerr	Jeanette Sutton
Inza Lambert	Elmer Sam Tomblinson
Ed Langhart	Harold "Cap" Trine
Margaret Laughlin	R. Noel Tunstall
Harold Laws	Mary Edgar Westcott

Offices of:
- Russian River Chamber of Commerce
- Guerneville District School
- Healdsburg City Archives

County Offices of Sonoma:
- Assessor
- County Clerk
- Recorder
- Supervisors
- Superintendent of Schools
- Law Library
- Public Works

California State Offices:
- Archives
- Library
- Division of Mines & Geology

U.S. Federal Departments:
- Dept. of Nat'l. Archives
- Library of Congress
- Department of Agriculture
- Department of Interior

Libraries:
- Sonoma County
- Santa Rosa Junior College
- Sonoma State University
- University of California (Bancroft Library)
- California Historical Society
- Society of California Pioneers
- Wells Fargo Bank
- Pacific Telephone

Bookstores:
- Argonaut Bookshop of San Francisco
- Cipriano's Book Store of Santa Rosa
- Treehorn Book of Santa Rosa

There is one family that made history, recorded it, and saved it for over a century, passing it on from generation to generation: the Bagleys. If there is to be declared a nucleus in Guerneville history, it would be the records, surveys, photographs and newspaper articles of John W. and Ellen D. Bagley. They are an outstanding example of a pioneer people that literally laid the foundation of a town, lived and created its history, then recorded and preserved it. This was done not with thoughts of the future, but upon seeing to a job that needed to be done, they did it. Over astronomical numbers of obstacles as well as surviving catastrophes, their records endure.

To add importance to the Bagley contributions, it should be stated that John Bagley was the original millwright and one of the original owners of the Guerne mill; he was the town's first sexton, first surveyor, first merchant, first postmaster, second in commercial river freight, later district school clerk and Board of Trustees' member for 16 years.

Ellen Downing Bagley was the first correspondent (bimonthly) to newspapers for 16 years and consequently saved all her columns and articles. She was the town's first chronicler of all events, large and small, in effect, the historian. Her cousin, Joseph P. Downing, was the first photographer of the settlement, occasionally visiting from Healdsburg. His views, panoramas and portraits of Guerneville were kept by Ellen. Because Ellen saved her 16 years' worth of articles, I have deviated from the normal citing in footnotes. Ordinarily, the date of publication is given in the notes. But since her scrapbook contains only her letters with her dates, and not publication dates, I have used hers. Why? Each page of the scrapbook contained four or five letters. A letter was written every two weeks. Consequently, I was saved hours — days — of reading newspaper microfilm. This deviation extends only to Healdsburg newspapers.

If it were not for this couple and their succeeding generations, these records of Guerneville would not have survived to the present (and again saved this writer untold hundreds of research hours). The story of Guerneville without the Bagley records would be like looking at the countryside with one eye.

For the scholar's information, I placed the footnotes at the end of the chapter, as I find footnotes at the bottom of a page disrupting to the flow of the text by constant glancing at them, and was done out of courtesy to the casual reader. Footnotes at the end of the book are too cumbersome to search through and locate a specific entry. And so, they are appened to each chapter. The bibliography is situated in its usual location — beyond the end of the text.

George E. Guerne and his granddaughter, Geraldine Peugh, perched on a redwood stump, 1912. Courtesy Sonoma County Library

Chapter 2

Lay of the Land & Run of the River

The Oxbow Cutoff at Guerneville[1]

Wherever loops occur in a meandering river there is a tendency for erosion on the outside of the curves to cut away the intervening land in the narrowest part of the loop. This creates an oxbow cutoff, so familiar in the streams of flat alluvian plains. With a river deeply entrenched in a

Aerial photo of Guerneville, May 1961, showing the old river bed looping north. County of Sonoma.

plateau such instances of the cutting through of the loop are rare and when found are interesting to study. There has been only one such case on the Russian River, but that one instance furnishes an example. It occurs in the highland midway from Santa Rosa Valley to the ocean at the town of Guerneville. From the northwestern edge of town, Lone Mountain rises to a height of 230 feet with a broad, flat-bottomed horseshoe valley sweeping around it. The curving ridge of the hill bears corroborative evidence of the genesis of the topography in the undercut bluffs and slipoff slopes which fit the bends of the horseshoe valley. Starting northward from the bridge at Guerneville the three-mile trip around the aggraded horseshoe valley to the river again is full of interest to the observing student of topography. The northern bank of the river at Guerneville at the opening of the two ends of the horseshoe is really the top of a broad natural levee which slopes gently away from the river. Undoubtedly it was built up gradually during floods by depositing of sediment as the high water spread northward with slackening current. At the northwest end of the horseshoe valley there is found a small marsh with cattails and other swamp life, the vanishing remnants of the lake that once filled the oxbow cutoff. In the time of great floods the river still spreads through the village streets and sets back into the old valley. In the western curve of the horseshoe on top of one of the great redwood stumps there used to be seen another stump which floated to its position during the flood of January 1895. The significance of the stranded stump lies in the fact it shows that the land within the oxbow is lower than the banks of the town where the depth of

Top: Redwood stump deposited by flooding, located on the south end of Willet's timber claim, today's Korbel vineyard west of town. Jack Hetzel Collection. Above: the stump after the waters receded. JCS Collection.

the flood water was not over two feet.

Age of the Cutoff

When first visited by white men, the horseshoe bend was one dense redwood forest which later furnished the lumber during the early days of San Francisco. The highest flood plain or lowest terrace of the Lower River is practically continuous with the filled-in surface of the old oxbow. The lumbermen report some of the trees that were cut showed 2,400 rings of annual growth. The stumps are so weathered a recount is difficult. But, also, it was common practice in clearing agricultural land in a field of stumps to pile debris around the stumps and burn it, thus causing most stumps to have a surface of black charcoal. The diameter of some of the stumps still standing is 18 feet, exclusive of the bark. The fact is also vouched for that in removing one of the stumps in making an excavation, the prostrate trunk of a large redwood was found below. The age of the cutoff must be considerably greater than the age of the redwoods, for the period of aggrading necessary to make the lake into good forest land probably exceeded the time for the growth of the forest. Five thousand years or possibly more may not be an unreasonable time limit for the period since the cutoff, yet it is one of the recent events in the history of the canyon.

Domestic Piracy at Bohemian Grove

A peculiar result of the cutting on the outward curve of a meander loop is found opposite the point of Northwood. Formerly, a branch of the railroad crossed on a rather high bridge at this point. Looking across the river from Northwood, one sees what are apparently two valleys meeting at the old site of the bridge and tributary to the river. Actual inspection reveals a stream on the left — Smith's Creek — joining the river through a very short, youthful gully; but looking to the right, one is surprised to find that the floor of the branch valley slopes gently away from the banks of the Russian River, which on this side are nearly 60 feet high above low water. Continuing down this branch valley, the noted Bohemian Grove of redwoods is found. Here the little valley bends sharply to the right and in half a mile or more opens into the Russian River. The Bohemian Valley is a narrow, flat-bottomed valley with steep sides rising 400 to 500 feet. Formerly, Smith's Creek did not flow into the river where it does at present, but turned to the left and flowed through Bohemian Grove joining the river just above Monte Rio. The Russian River in its bend at Northwood, in the process of undercutting, finally broke through the ridge separating it from the bend in Smith's Creek and thus captured the headwaters of that stream, leaving the lower part practically as it is found today. The grade of Smith's Creek is so much greater than that of the river that at the point of capture, the floor of the abandoned portion of Smith's Creek Valley is too high for the flood waters of the river to be diverted even in part to the longer channel through Bohemian Grove.

1. R.S. Holway, University of California Publication in Geography, (Berkeley, 1913).

While the Kashaya Pomo lived along the Sonoma Coast, other Pomo groups lived inland in Sonoma, Mendocino and Lake Counties. This photo shows the ceremonial decoration common to Pomo dancers. Hearst Museum, University of California at Berkeley Collection.

Chapter 3

THE FIRST OCCUPIERS

Along almost the entire length of the coast between the mouths of Gualala River and Salmon Creek, near Bodega Bay, the redwood forest begins almost at the shoreline; nowhere does the open land extend for more than a mile back from the cliffs. Redwood continues as a solid belt of timber with but few open areas for many miles inland. This belt of timber was not inhabited except in these small open areas by the people of either the Kashaya of the Sonoma Coast (Southwestern Pomo) or the Southern Pomo dialects;[1] portions of it seem to have been virtually unclaimed by either people. This is particularly the case in the southern part of the area and, in part at least, accounts for the fact it was impossible to determine the exact territorial boundary from Salmon Creek to the head of Austin Creek. As evidence that a great part of this forested area was but little known to Indians, it may be noted some of the Kashaya claim the site of the present town of Guerneville was unknown to them until after the coming of the lumber mills to the region. It was then named "moko'cpeulu," from moko'c, stump, and peulu, a corruption of the Spanish pueblo, on account of the many huge redwood stumps left after the felling of the trees for milling purposes. The people of the Southern dialectic area seem to have known the site, at least using it as a camp if not a village. Their name for this site, ciyo'le,[2] signifying shady place, seems to have been derived from the denseness of the forest.[3]

Another old village site was that of bu'dutchilan, on the north bank of the Russian River at a point probably about five and a half miles upstream from Guerneville. This village was located on the ranch owned by Mr. Thomas Hill and was but a short distance downstream from the confluence of Mark West Creek with the Russian River.[4]

The houses in the coast region were built chiefly of slabs of redwood bark and wood which were leaned together against a vertical center pole to produce a building of conical form, 10 to 15 feet in diameter, and a little more than half as high. True planks were not used, and there was no covering of earth. The construction prevented any considerable size from being attained, but the huts were very warm and serviceable and each dwelling seems to have been occupied by a single household.[5]

The only settled portions of the coast region were the more open parts of the mountains and the few valleys along the eastern border of the belt. The Indians inhabiting these valleys usually built houses of the same sort as those of the Coast Pomo and, in other respects, their mode of life resembled that of the coast people.[6]

Sonoma Coast village. Charles Nordhoff, Northern California, Oregon and the Sandwich Islands, 1874.

The native peoples were hunters; they preferred the snare to the bow and arrow. The Pomo ate bear, deer, elk, wildcats, raccoons, otter, beaver, mink, skunk, rabbits, cottontails, squirrels, wood rats, field mice and gophers. They also ate the mountain lion. The coyote, fox and wolf were never eaten. No domesticated dog was kept by any of the divisions of the Pomo before its introduction by the Spanish.[7]

The Russian River is not navigable except in the last few lower miles of its course, and tule balsas were not used as watercraft in its drainage except in the Laguna de Santa Rosa. Southern Pomo dialect called the Russian River "Shabaikai" or "Shahaikai."[8] Today Kashaya call it "sho-ga-wi," south water place.[9]

1. S.A. Barrett, The Ethno-Geography of the Pomo Indians, p. 213, 1908, The University Press of California, Berkeley.
2. Op. Cit., p. 215.
3. A.L. Kroeber, Handbook of Indians of California, (California Book Co., Berkeley, 1953), p. 241.
4. Ibid.
5. Hubert H. Bancroft, Native Races, Vol. 1, p. 336 (hereinafter cited as "Bancroft").
6. Loeb, Pomo Folkways (U. of Calif. Pubs., in American Archaeology and Ethnology, 1926), Vol. 19, p. 170.
7. Op. Cit., p. 182.
8. Bancroft, History of California, Vol. II, p. 297, San Francisco, 1885.
9. Tikkemeneff (Compiler), Historical Review of the Origin of the Russ-Amer. Co. Russian-American MSS, translated, (Bancroft Library 1, i, pp.203-204.)

Chapter 4

Kashaya Texts

As far as is recorded, the first contact of the Kashaya[1] with white men was with the Russians, who, after reconnoitering the coast, founded Fort Ross in 1811.[2] The Russians came to exploit the area, to collect sea otter pelts, and to grow what food they could for their Alaskan colony. They did not come to convert or civilize the Indians. The Kashaya were not pressed into forced labor nor confined in missions; they were thus unaffected by a major cause of the decimation of most Indians in the missionized areas.

The Russians hired the Indians to do various unskilled jobs at Fort Ross and in the surrounding gardens. As a consequence, the Kashaya gradually became accustomed to the idea of working for wages and grew to like the articles — beads, clothing, tools — they could acquire in that way. The majority of the natives continued a nomadic existence, making Fort Ross only one more stop in their seasonal round. However, towards the end of the Russian occupancy, it is recorded (Laplace, 1864:173) that more and more Indian families were settling permanently at Fort Ross.

The Russians left in the fall and winter of 1841-42, after having sold their possessions to John A. Sutter. He transferred the movable stock and equipment to his headquarters in Sacramento. Subsequently, Mexican and American settlers began moving in, although not so overwhelmingly as in the richer agricultural lands to the east. Since their food-gathering territory was being occupied by ranchers, the Indians soon found they had to work for wages in order to buy sufficient food. Almost every landowner along the coast had a small Indian rancheria attached to his holdings, providing him with a convenient labor force. The unwarlike nature of the Kashaya and their economic usefulness doubtless contributed to their preservation during this period. There was no demand for their removal to a confining reservation; nor were there any massacres.

From soon after the sale of Fort Ross until the late 1860s, William Benitz ranched the lands that had been under the Russians, and the largest group of Kashayas remained with him. He worked them hard, but apparently treated them with benevolence. It was from him, his family and his Mexican cowboys that the Kashaya learned to speak Spanish — roughly 150 Spanish loan words remain in the Kashaya language from that era, five times as many as there are from Russian.

The owner at Fort Ross after Benitz seems to have been unwilling to have the natives around, and about 1870, they began to concentrate at the Haupt Ranch (pronounced "hop"). Charlie Haupt had married a Kashaya woman, and he made the Indians welcome at his place. A few family groups remained on scattered ranches, but the two villages on his land, Potol and Abaloneville, became, with Danak'a at Stewart's Point, the chief Kashaya settlements. They remained the more or less permanently occupied places for over 40 years, although even in them, the population was constantly in flux as the people followed various types of seasonal employment, moving to the Russian River Valley to pick crops as they ripened, moving back to work in lumber camps.

In 1914, the State bought the Kashaya a small 40-acre plot, now called the Kashaya Reservation, and by 1919, most of the group had moved to their new home. It soon proved to be inadequate for their numbers; the water supply gave out every summer, and the Indians hauled in by car any water needed for drinking or washing. In accord with a new policy of settling Indians on land which could make them partly self-supporting and which would locate them near a labor market, the Indian Bureau offered to buy agricultural land in the Russian River Valley; the Bureau would not purchase more acreage near the existing reservation because it did not meet the requirements. The offer was made in 1916, repeated in 1939, and then withdrawn because the Kashayas, under the influence of their spiritual leader, would not agree to move from their isolated homeland. Their domination by a succession of such retention of Indian beliefs has been the prime factor in their being so culturally preserved as a distinct group.

The chain of events leading to this nativistic movement began in 1872, when a representative of the Earth Lodge cult of the Ghost Dance religion arrived and summoned the Indians to Clear Lake to meet the end of the world. All of the Kashaya went. The congregation of so many Indians worried the white settlers, who feared an uprising was imminent. Soldiers came and were about to attack when the matriarch, Kukaria, went up to them and showed a paper from an employer stating they were peaceable people and had steady work with him. That crisis passed, but another arrived when the Kashaya came to realize that the end of the world was not at hand. They set out for home, but being unprepared for the long trek, they suffered many hardships and starvation, and the weaker ones succumbed. This episode is known to all the adult Kashaya at the present time.

In conjunction with their disillusionment in the prediction of the end of the world, in a development of the Ghost Dance known as the Bole-Maru, the Kashaya produced prophets of their own. A succession of the spiritual leaders, through revelation, has guided the community from that time to the present. It should be emphasized that the Kashaya were not alone in this movement; the other Pomo had their own revivalist prophets, too. However, the Kashaya produced an individual who proved to be significantly stronger and more effective — Annie Jarvis — who held sway from 1912 to 1943. She banned gambling and drinking; forbade intermarriage with non-Indians, favoring unions with the Central Pomo of Point Arena if suitable matches could not be made within the group; barred sending the children away to boarding school; and discouraged any association with white people other than the minimum necessary in the course of work.

This era came to an end in 1943 with the death of Annie Jarvis and concurrent disruption brought by the Second World War. The shortage of local work, the availability of war jobs elsewhere, the draft, and gasoline rationing led to temporary abandonment of the reservation. When the reservation was reopened after the war, things were not the same; there was greater acceptance of the values of the white man and no longer so great a desire for self-segregation.

The spiritual head since 1943 has been Essie Parrish, who, while encouraging the preservation of Kashaya traditions, dropped the isolationism of her predecessor. She advocated as much school education as possible for the children. Under her leadership the majority of the people have entered an organized American church, that of the Latter Day Saints, while still retaining many of their older beliefs.

Only about a third of the population now lives on the reservation the year round. The rest live in scattered spots in the Russian River Valley, from Healdsburg to Sebastopol, near their sources of employment. However, all who can do so return to the home reservation for major celebrations, such as the barbecue on the Fourth of July and the associated four-night dance preceding it.

Like other Indian groups, the Kashaya were much reduced in numbers by disease after contact with white men. Nevertheless, the Kashaya and their language and culture have been preserved to a greater degree than have those of neighboring Indians. The significant factors in this relative preservation were their freedom from forced labor, confinement, and massacre, and a less drastic acculturation pressure; this has allowed them to adopt the material things of the white man — clothing, housing, food, money, the automobile — while retaining, under their own spiritual leaders, much of the non-material; that is, beliefs, traditions, language, attitude toward real and private property, and self-identification as a group. Now that the group is scattering, the children are receiving more schooling, and the majority have joined an outside church. The retarding effect of the nativistic movement is in decline, and the assimilation into the dominant culture of the Kashaya is proceeding more rapidly.

FOLK HISTORY

The following stories were told by the Kashaya elders and are translated from their language.

The tellers are identified by their English names as their Kashaya names are private and are only divulged to chosen friends.

"THE FIRST SAIL BOAT"

(by Essie Parrish)

In the old days, before the white people came up here, there was a boat sailing on the ocean from the south. Because before that they had never seen a boat, they said, "Our world must be coming to an end. Couldn't we do something? This big bird floating on the ocean is from somewhere, probably from up high. Let us plan a feast. Let us have a dance." They followed its course with their eyes to see what it would do. Having done so, they promised Our Father a feast saying that destruction was upon them.

When they had done so, they watched the ship sail away to the north and disappear. They thought that the ship had not done anything but sail northwards because of the feast they had promised. They were saying that nothing had happened to them — the big bird person had sailed northward without doing anything — because of the promise of a feast, because of that they thought it had not done anything. Consequently, they had a feast and a big dance.

A long time afterwards, when white men had come up and they saw their boats, they then found out that what they had thought was a big bird was otherwise. It wasn't a bird they had seen; they had spied a sailboat. From then on we knew that they hadn't seen a big bird.

This is the end.

"HUNTING SEA OTTER AND FARMING"

(by Herman James)

I am going to tell about what the undersea people[3] did. When they first came up, they lived at Metini. They lived there a long time.

After a while, it turned out that they had sailed out and found a land up north.[4] After sailing a while, they arrived during what we call leafing-out time or early spring; the land was already starting to warm up. When they had been traveling for six months, they sailed south from there. Sailing along, they were long overdue. They must have found what we call otter — otter skin is valuable; they sell one skin for a lot. When they arrived back they told about it — their own people, the undersea people — the Indians didn't know about that yet.

After a while they filled a slightly larger boat with everything—food, guns, ammunition. Having gotten everything ready, they sailed off at pinole (seed gathering) time, being summer. They sailed for a while — it was perhaps one month that they were sailing towards that place. At that time the ships moved around by sail only. There were no motors at that time operating to propel boats.

Then they sailed up to that place. That land in the north was a cold place. We Indians called it Ice Country, now Alaska. After staying a while, they sailed southward. They were transporting south many skins — many otter skins. They say it was six months before they showed up.

Once in a while they ran out of food; they saw hard times. Many times that happened to them, but they didn't listen, or profit from their mistakes. They sailed off for long periods and sold those skins. Loading up the boats, they sent them off to some other place. When they sold the skins they made quite a lot of money. Other things they didn't do much. They only did that work. They went collecting in the north.

One time many young men sailed out in two boats. Still others had already sailed on ahead. One of the two boats sailed off after them. That one didn't find the others, but the second one did sail up to the north to the Ice Country. Nowadays that has become a big town known as Sitka. But at that time it was a wild country; there was no one there — only a lot of wild animals.

The other was absent for a long time; it turned out to be lost; it had sailed a little off course. They set out to search for it and unexpectedly found it way off somewhere else. The lost ship accompanied the others now, when they sailed off, they followed. They landed over there. They were starving, having run out of food. For a while, for a week perhaps, they had been starving. Some had become very weak; only a few of the stronger ones could walk around.

When the two crews had landed there, rested a while, become a little stronger, then they went out hunting. They found a lot of sea otter; they are said to have killed quite a few in one day — about 20 or 30. Some of the men skinned them, dried them, put them in sacks and loaded them in the boats. There were many, about two or three hundred skins, when they returned. That is what they did.

They did that for a long time. With that money they lived there — the undersea people. They didn't grow anything; they didn't even keep cattle. They only did that one thing. With that they a made money for food to eat and clothes to wear and food to feed their wives and children. They did that for a long time.

After a while it got so that they couldn't sail up there because of the ice. They say that in that country the ice was like houses floating around, it was so cold. It was like mountains rising from the sea. Once in a while when a boat was bumped by one, it was smashed to pieces. When that happened the people drowned and froze stiff from the cold. One time when that must have happened to a boat, the undersea people — there were perhaps 20 in the boat — were all drowned. They were never found, never heard from again; they were never to return again.

They still didn't listen, but still sailed off to gather and shoot the otter, and, having loaded up the boats with them, sailed off to their home — which was Metini. One time, after a while, as I said before, the route where they were accustomed to sailing up turned out to be closed off by ice rearing up like mountains. It was blocked where they usually went, it having really begun to turn cold. It got so that they couldn't return; there was no way to sail forward. When that happened, they said, "Let's go back; it's too hard for us to break a way through," and, having turned around, they started back. When they were sailing along the way, they, too, ran out of food — the food ran short. Starving, they sailed along.

When they didn't show up from there, the other undersea people from Metini set out to search; they already knew what had happened to them when they didn't show up for so long. Now they set sail. They found the lost ship when it had sailed about halfway back. Some of the men had already died — starved — only the few stronger ones were sailing the ship. The ship that had sailed out from Metini was carrying a lot of food, for they had known that the others would be starving. They gave them a lot of food. After a while the others or rescuers took over the operation of the ship, letting them relax and just live on the boat while being fed. They became stronger. They sailed along. They sailed on without anything.

They had just turned back on the way without otter skins. They didn't even catch one.

They say that it was on the last trip that that happened to them. "Let's quit. We can't sail up there any more," they said to the commander. At first the commander didn't agree. "It's true," they said. "These sick people are sick from starvation," said the captain of the expedition. While speaking he announced that he wasn't going to sail off any more. The commander then said, "We'll find something else to do."

Then they sold the skins and got a lot of money for them. With that they bought what they could grow for food (seeds), because they couldn't sail off northwards any more. With that they bought wheat to plant where the fields stretch out at Metini. The whole land was covered; that was their business now. By growing they learned how to grow food, all the things they are. They lived there a long time. That was the only way they prospered.

Other people didn't do that work that they had discovered — of valuable otter skins. When they sold those, everywhere they prepared clothes — made expensive coats. Poor people, however, couldn't buy them; they were so expensive then. But they made their own coats, everything for their women and for the children. They sewed them for wearing in winter. That's what they say they did. Poor people, however, couldn't buy them; they were so expensive then. But they made their own coats, everything for their women and for wearing in winter. That's what they say they did, realizing they couldn't get them any more, couldn't find otter skins any more.

This, too, is true; this, too, my grandmother saw and told about. She had remembered well everything they did. Then she told it to me. I have remembered it for a long time. It was 65 years ago that my grandmother told me that. I still remember it and have told it true. She also said that it was true about how they first landed and made money for food to eat, and did those things. This is all.

"GRAIN FOODS"

(by Herman James)

My grandmother told me this, too, about what the undersea people did. What I am going to tell about now is how they ground their flour when they raised and gathered wheat.

Where the land lies stretched out, where all the land is at Metini, they raised wheat which blanketed the land. When it was ripe everywhere, then the people, by hand, cut it down, tied it up, and laid it there. Then, in a sea lion skin, they dragged it to their houses.

They had made a big place there, with the earth packed down hard by wetting — there they threw down what they had tied up. Next they drove horses down there. The person who drove the horses around there in a circle was one man who took turns with various others. When it was that way (threshed), when it had become food along, they put it in sacks. While loading it in sacks, they hauled it off in stages to where their storehouse was. They filled that place up with lots — many sacks.

In order to make it turn into flour, they had something that spun around for them in the wind — they called it a "flour grinder." When they got ready to grind with that, they poured the wheat down in there to be ground, while tossing the sacks up — that they did all day long. They then filled the sacks up with flour and, hauling it away as before, they piled it up in a building. There was a lot for them to eat in winter.

Once, while a woman was walking around there, she happened to get too close while the wind was turning the grindstone. At that time, women's hair was long. The woman's hair got caught and turned with it. The woman, too, was spun around, all of her hair was chewed off, and she was thrown off dead.

They picked her up, carried her home, and cremated her — at that time they still cremated. That is the way it happened; the flour grinder snared the woman and she died.

They also used to tell that the Indians in

their different fashion also gathered grain when it was ripe by taking a tightly woven packing basket and knocking the grain so that it would fall into that. When they filled the baskets they, too, would store that at their houses. They, too, had a lot, a lot like that for winter, and pinole, too.

Then they found out; they saw how they, the undersea people, stored their own kind of food. At that time, the Indians didn't yet know much about flour. Later on, when the Russians had lived there a while, the Indians ate flour, too. And they also still ate pinole in their own way.

This had been a true story that our grandmother used to tell me, one that she saw herself — at that time when she saw those things, she was still a young woman. When she had grown old, she told me that true story. That is what I have told, the true story that our grandmother told. This is all.

"TALE OF FORT ROSS"

(by Herman James)

This, too, my grandmother told me. She also really saw this herself. I am going to tell about the land at Metini. They lived there. Where they originated, where our ancestors originated, at Metini, is the place where they first lived. They lived there for a long time.

Then unexpectedly, they detected something white sailing on the water. It later proved to be a boat, but they didn't know what it was — the Indians hadn't seen anything like that before. Then it came closer and closer, and unexpectedly it landed, and it proved to be a boat. They turned out to be the undersea people — we Indians named those people that.

Having landed, they built their houses close to where the Indians were. After staying for a while, they got acquainted with them. They stayed with them. The Indians started to work for them. They lived there quite a while; having lived there for 30 years, they returned home.

Then the white people (literally, "miracles") arrived. They, the white people, took over the land where all the Indians had been living. But the Indians still stayed.

Then they put them (the Indians) to work. The womenfolk, too, worked for the wives of the white men. My grandmother washed clothes for a white woman there in her house. They lived there a long time.

Then many white men arrived on horseback. But the boss or owner of the ranch watched them closely. At first, they could only ride up secretly. Then one time two white men rode up to where a mother and her daughter were, and there they were halted.

The mother and child couldn't get out; the men were blocking the door of the house with the horses' bodies. My mother's younger sister happened to be there at that time. She crawled out underneath the horses and ran off over to her home and told her mother, my grandmother.

Meanwhile, the mother was trying to protect the child from those two. When she did so, they beat her up, they stabbed her with their spurs so that she was unable to get up. Then grabbing the girl's hair, they wrapped it around the saddle horn, and dragged her off, dragged her across a ravine.

At that time my grandmother worked inside the house for the white woman and happened to see that from there. Having gone outside, she yelled from there. She screamed for a long time.

The white man dragging the child wanted to shoot the screaming woman. "She must be a tough woman," he said. "I'm going to shoot her." The other one dissuaded him. "Don't shoot; that's a lady."

After a while they let the child drop and released her. Then the child ran off. Over at her home she arrived running. Now they stayed there inside.

When they had recovered, they moved in closer, next to the boss. That white man guarded them there, driving the strangers away from there at first. They were too afraid of him to ride up to there.

When he lived there for a while, the boss led his Indians off to dig the gold — he had discovered gold at a place in the south. It took three weeks to go there. Then they arrived where the gold was.

At that time, they didn't dig, they dipped the gold out from under the water, poured it out in a certain place and gathered it up. Then, having loaded it all into sacks, they lifted it up onto a mule and returned. It took three more weeks to come back — tired out.

Then they set it down — set down the gold at Metini. Having done so, they spread it out to take the dampness off. Then the boss had the Indians guard it, knowing that the Indians wouldn't steal it — they wouldn't put even one nugget in their pockets. They just guarded it.

Then he shipped it off southwards to his home. When he had done so, when he had gotten everything ready, having lived there a long time, he returned, sailing away. Having sold everything, all of his cattle, having become rich, he returned home to South America.

My grandmother still lived there at Metini. I remember that the wife of the former ranch owner came from there and visited my grandmother. She must have remembered her

Living History Day at Fort Ross State Historic Park, 1990. Photo by Simone Wilson.

(my grandmother) for quite a while.

Then my mother and grandmother moved there and lived in a place named Much Gravel. I was there, too. I grew up there. We lived there.

This is a story she told me of the old days. It, too, is a true happening that she saw, herself. This is all.

1. Robert L. Oswalt (University of California Press, University of California Publications in Linguistics, September 1, 1964), Vol. 36.
2. Bancroft, Vol. II, p. 298, called by the natives "Mad-Shui–Nui."
3. The "undersea people" were the Russians of Fort Ross and Bodega.
4. Herman James was under the impression that the undersea people came to Fort Ross first and then discovered Alaska from there, rather than the reverse, which is the true sequence.

Engraving showing the stockade and surrounding buildings at Fort Ross, 1843.

Chapter 5

Russians, Spaniards, Englishmen & a Few French

In November of 1811, a second official party set out from the northern Russian base of Sitka, Alaska, with the definite determination to settle a Russian outpost somewhere on the shores of New Albion (Marin-Sonoma counties).[1] This group was made up of 95 Russians and the Aleut crews to man 40 bidarkas (kayaks). Kuskof's favorable report on the north bay coastline guided the location of this proposed permanent venture to the vicinity of the Russian River. After navigating the channel of this stream for about 50 Russian versts, approximately 25 miles[2] without coming upon a suitable site, they returned to the coast. Probably the shallowness of the river during the dry season, as is November, is one reason, and the remoteness of tillable land another, for not settling inland. The Russian mechanics could not produce or did not have the machinery to handle the immensely forested area, so they remained in the same open areas as the Indian.

Two establishments were set up on the ocean shore. One was a place which they named Fort Ross, 16 miles above the mouth of the Russian River and, according to their observations, in latitude 38° 33' and longitude 123° 15'. This became the citadel and permanent center of the colony. The second group of buildings was erected at Bodega Bay for the purpose of utilizing to the fullest advantage the exceptionally fertile soil in the vicinity.[3] Bodega Bay was a very important seaport and warehousing center — more so by far than Ross.

On September 10, 1812, Ross was formally dedicated. From that day dates the first permanent occupancy of Sonoma County by a non-Indian.[4]

The Russian River looking upstream toward Guernewood Beach. This is what the first explorers saw: no roads, no structures, but taller trees. JCS Collection.

The convenience of both the fort and Bodega to the river is made clear in this description of the situation by a contemporary writer:[5]

> About halfway between the fort and little Bodega the Slavianka (Russian River) empties, which is called 'She-hai-kai' by the natives. It springs from a large lake, but its mouth is obstructed by a bar, the sand washing down the

river in such quantity as to form a temporary barrier between the current of the river and the tide of the ocean.

It is perhaps significant to note that the lands taken up by the Russian establishments encompassed the mouth of the river. Their interest in it had not ended by their failure to settle upon its banks or to successfully navigate its mouth with their ships. This situation was strategic: The river was the most convenient and logical highway into the unexplored interior. Thus, surrounded by Russian settlement, it became a Russian highway.

About June-July 1827, a Frenchman, du Haut-Chilly, visited the Russians during a tour of California. He wrote:

> It (the Russian River) is too deep, even in summer, to be forded; and in the winter it becomes terrible.[6]

On this trip from Bodega to Fort Ross, he, his small party and guides crossed in bidarkas or kayaks and let the horses swim. Two years before an American captain had drowned there.[7]

During the occupation of the coast lands by the Russians, and which the Russians had claimed as their own during their tenancy, the Mexicans were getting an impression that the Russians would expand and possess more territory south and inland towards Yerba Buena (San Francisco). In June 1827, Echeandia, Mexican governor of California, was sent orders from Mexico to build a fort on the northern frontier facing the Russians. The object was not only to protect the villages of San Rafael and Sonoma, but chiefly to prevent Russian expansion. But his reply to the orders was he could not build the desired fort due to a lack of materials.[8]

The Russians were not the only intruders in Northern California. The English had a solid claim in the Oregon Territory and enforced it with the Hudson's Bay Company on the Columbia River. The company's trappers were working their trap lines in San Joaquin Valley in 1827 on a regular basis. By the end of the same decade, American trappers and mountain men were up and down the Great Central Valley, trapping and exploring. The Hudson's Bay Company so dominated California from the Straits of Carquinez north and inland that they had possession more or less physically, if not by claim of title. The company had a trading post by agreement with the Mexican government in Yerba Buena by fall 1829.[9]

In 1830, the Russians began to penetrate inland for tillable land. Their choice became the rich river soil found in the triangle formed by the Russian River and Mark West Creek, which is now called the Wohler Ranch. In Spring 1831, the Russians had made some plantings at Tamalanica, this being the Wohler Ranch.[10]

To counteract this movement, the Mexicans made grants of land to those who were or would become citizens of Mexico and form a buffer zone of grants between Mexican California and the Russian settlements. These surrounding grants were the Estero Americano, Canada de la Jonive, Canada de Pogolimi, El Molino and Sotoyome.[11]

The Mexicans also maintained surveillance of Ross by sending soldiers and men in consort with the Mexicans under the guise of traders or carriers of official documents and postings. They were to report in detail the number of men, armament of their various settlements, and what could be learned of the Russians' future plans.[12]

For the "caravans" and messengers to traverse from the Mexican lands to Ross, the most common way to go was by way of Bodega (Corners) and up the coast to Fort Ross. Other trail ways from the environs of Tamalanica to the fort were the Russian River during the dry season, as already stated, and the Indian trail that skirted Mt. Jackson. The eastern end of the Mt. Jackson-Indian trail to Ross passed over an earthen causeway from the higher ground of the Santa Rosa Valley through the site of the Indian village of Tamalanica, on through the Wohler Ranch, and across Russian River

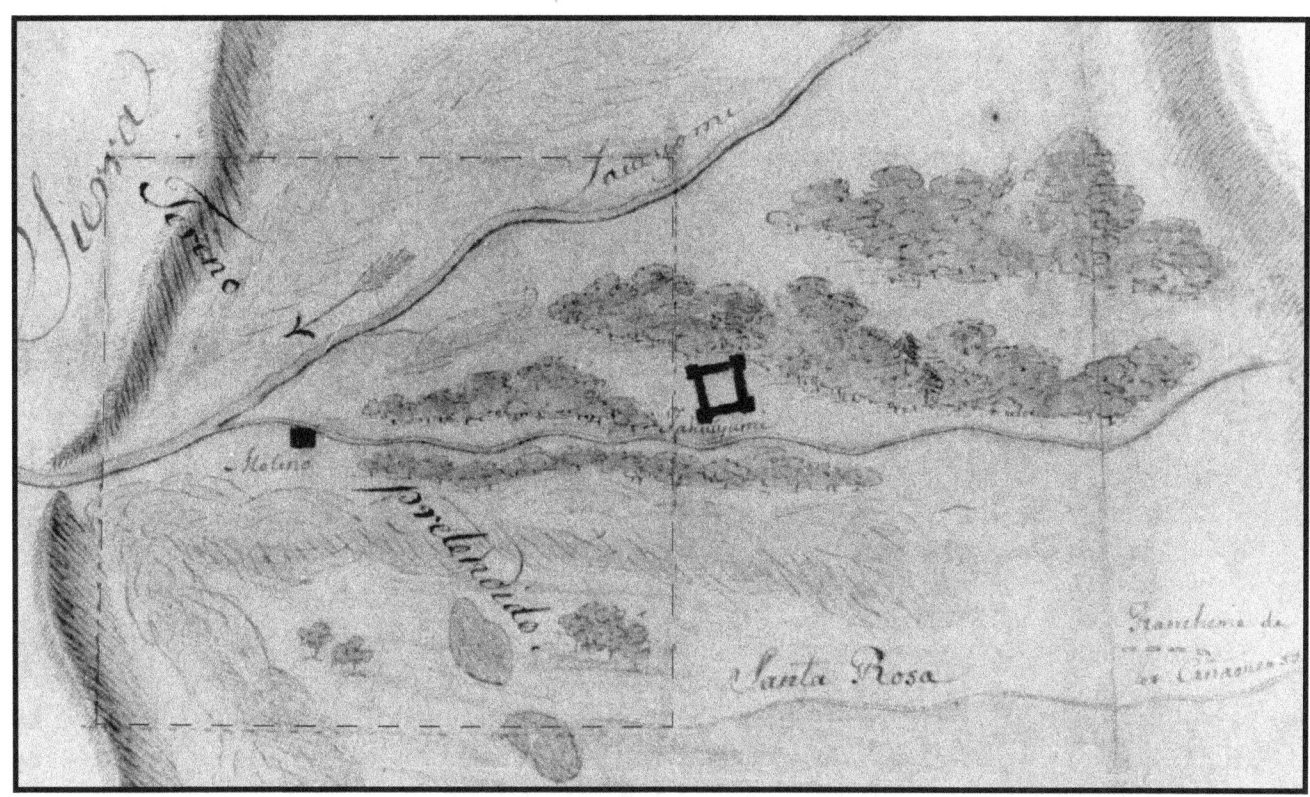

Land claim of El Molino Rancho (Terreno Pretendido). The broken line indicates the boundaries of the rancho; the dark square near its center is the mill location. Original map in Bancroft Library.

near where the Lafayette School stood. This was part of the Indian and, later, Russian trail from Ross to the river and the interior.[13] This trail could still be found as late as 1926.[14]

The author does not think it too extreme to conjecture that at least during the late spring, summer and fall, there was some traffic originating from Ross and going through the Guerneville area to the planting sites of Tamalanica during the early 1830s. But the Russians did not have sole possession by 1834.

In 1833, the Mexican military commandant, Mariano Vallejo, and his brother-in-law, Juan Bautista Rogers Cooper, constructed California's first known power-operated commercial sawmill at a cost of $10,000, and it was probably fortified. The building of a small community began in April 1833. The first structure was a home, the second, a blacksmith shop. Sometime in the late summer or early fall, construction began on the sawmill. Redwood timbers and crudely sawed boards were used.

There were 16 or more workmen building the mill and its companion dam in Mark West Creek, and it is reasonable to assume that this could have been accomplished in a matter of weeks or, at most, a few months. Combined with the fact that the season's first rains would probably be needed to provide the water necessary to turn the wheel buckets, the first product of the Cooper mill would in all likelihood have been cut in November or December of 1833.

The few hundred logs that Cooper's men each year laboriously chewed up with sash saws were dragged to mill by horses, mules and oxen, or floated down Mark West Creek and the Russian River.

No certain evidence has come to light as to how much lumber was actually produced before the mill was destroyed by flood during the winter of 1841-42.

In addition to sawing redwood lumber, the mill and settlement served as a barrier to Russian encroachment from the west.[15] However, Mexican presence did not intimidate the

Russians.

A cavalcade left Ross on September 10, 1834, with two mules packed with road provisions or supplies for about four days. The party, including Baron von Wrangell, the director of all Russia's American operations, consisted of 21 horsemen. In that number were six Aleuts, four American Vaqueros and two Indian interpreters with quivers filled with arrows.

The Baron wrote in his journal:[16]

> Crossing the River Slavianka near her mouth, now washed up with sand, we turned to the left, to the mountains, leaving the sea behind our backs, and made our way through cavities, forests, and thickets to places more even and less overgrown, and though we rode by trail beaten out by the savages, who traveled by it from the valley to the seashore to collect the testaceans for food, however, we did not meet any of them. At last, and coming to a large, overgrown with grass valley, we heard loud singing voices. The interpreters hurried away in advance to recognize friend or enemy to meet us. Our own impatience to see the inhabitants of these lonely places made us speed after our advance guard, and in full gallop we all surprised an old lady of these American tribes, gathering some kind of herb corns in her basket, plaited from fine roots. From fear she was stupified. Not without difficulty we ascertained that behind the nearest thicket there are living several families of Americans, who, without doubt, had already noticed us at this time and concealed themselves, fearing to fall into the hands of the Spaniards, not seldom riding out to catch the savages to convert them to the Christian faith, and that gathering the corns for food, sung out of her full throat, to disperse and drive off the evil spirits, always obeying the voice, repelling a hundred times in the mountains. Assuring the old woman that her voice did not attract evil-intended people we left her in peace and continued on our way. The first night we stopped on a considerable collected plain valley between several hills, on the shore of a litttle river falling in the Slavianka under branched oaks.[17] The warm, mild air, the clear sky, the moonlit night, the bivouac fires, and herding of the horses in this high grass, all this presented a picture agreeable to the imagination and the feeling. The piercing and shrill howls of the jackals disturbed the harmony of nature, but with the beginning of daylight all became quiet, and we hurried forward with impatience to reach the famous valleys spoken of in Ross and to meet their inhabitants. Soon the places became wider, and enlarged, extended fields with rich vegetable earth, covered with fat grasses, opened themselves, one after another, but nowhere even a trace of inhabitants. Suddenly we perceived on the far edge of the valley a winding stream of smoke; the interpreters and vaqueros concluded that there must be a village of many American natives, and with some fear communicated to us this information. The smoothness and spaciousness of the place permitted our whole army out of five nations to unroll by front and gallop with loose bridles ...

It appears rather unusual that the Baron did not make a passing mention of the Cooper mill at Mark West Creek in his travels, or of the supposed plantings made by his Russians at Tamalanica.

By 1841, the Russian colony was literally "dying on the vine" and in the fields. The colony could not support itself and Sitka, both. The Russians were casting about for a buyer of their establishment in 1841 when another Frenchman, Duflot de Mofras, made a visit to Bodega and Ross. His report of his visit is probably the most complete of the colony in its last ten years of existence. He reported there were two other settlements (actually, farms) besides Bodega and Ross. One was at Salmon Creek and the farm of Kostromitinoff on the south side of Russian River near its mouth. He described the river and farm thus:[18]

> "San Sebastian River (the Spanish name) has a width during the rainy season of 600 meters at its mouth, yet in summer it is dry and then it is possible to walk in comfort along its shore."

The farm here had:

1. Barracks: 3 rooms and 2 covered corridors, 16 by 6 meters.

2. Store: 14 by 6 meters with lofts for storing grain and a wooden flume for sliding the grain to the brook that runs at the foot of the hill.

3. A house 6 by 4 meters.

4. 2 wooden platforms for threshing wheat, one 20 meters and the other 8 meters square.
5. A wooden platform for winnowing the wheat, 24 meters wide.
6. A wooden house for the Indians, 14 meters long by 5 meters wide.
7. A kitchen with 2 ovens.
8. A Russian bath 6 by 4 meters.
9. A large fenced enclosure for livestock.
10. A boat for traveling on the Slawinska River.
11. This farm contains approximately 40 hectares of agricultural land adequate to plant 140 hectolitres of wheat.[19]

He further wrote that, "The houses which the Russians call isbas, resemble those found in Muscovite villages."

The Russians finally found a buyer of their stock at Fort Ross by the name of John A. Sutter. The sale was completed in late 1841, and some Russian caretakers remained until the end of the 1841-42 winter.

The Hudson's Bay Company was still trapping about Northern California at this time. In 1842, two parties led by LaFramboise and Ermatingzer were hunting under provisional permits from Vallejo and were allowed a company ship to land supplies at Bodega.[20] One party came south via the coast, and the other came via an inland route. There is a strong possibility that they trapped their way down Russian River, just as there is a possibility that they took the usual trail through Bodega Corners.

Nothing more has been found regarding the travels and exploring by foreign powers or independent parties, specifically so with the area in and about Russian River from Tamalanica to its mouth, from 1842 to American occupation, about 1855.

Fort Ross as it looks today. JCS photo

1. The first voyage was to Bodega in spring 1809 by Kuskoff to found an agricultural and commercial supply station and to support Sitka in Alaska. Bancroft, *History of California*, Vol. II, p. 294.
2. Bancroft states 50 miles. *Op. Cit.*, p. 295.
3. Russian claims to the lands were based upon the right of first occupancy and an asserted purchase from the Indians. Russian-American MSS (Bancroft Library) II, ii, 202; iii, 258; and III, iv, 75.
4. *Sonoma County History*, 1889, p. 15, (hereafter cited as Son. Co. Hist).
5. Russian-American MSS, I, i, pp. 203-04, Bancroft Library.
6. *California Historical Society Quarterly* (1929), Vol. 8, p. 324.
7. *Ibid.*
8. Bancroft, Vol. III, pp. 114-15, p. 257, footnote 30.
9. See Clarence E. Pearsall, et al, *The Quest for Qual-a-wa-loo*.
10. *Son. Co. Hist.*, 1926, pp. 400-01, and Bancroft, Vol. III, p. 160, footnote.
11. The following information is given not to cloud up the facts, but to be read and taken for what it is worth. I think it dubious:

Map of the land granted by Spain in the year 1812 to the Russian American Fur Company known as the Russian or Fort Ross Grant. Subdivided by George H. Goddard, civil engineer. The Russian or Fort Ross Grant extends from Point Drake, now called Point Reyes, to Cape Mendocino and back into the interior, a distance of 3 Spanish leagues equivalent to 7 miles 72 chs. 31 lks. Filed at request of Wm. Muldrow, Jan. 6th, 1859 at 9 1/4 o'clock a.m.

The map can be found in Book 8, pages 9A-OC in the Sonoma County Recorder's Office, Book of Maps.

12. *Son. Co. Hist.*, 1937, p. 65.
13. *Son Co. Hist.*, 1926, p. 455
14. *Op Cit.*, p. 401.
15. *Santa Rosa Press Democrat*, Jan. 31, 1970 (hereafter cited as *P.D.*).
16. This is an account by von Wrangell, head of the Russian-American operations. He made this visit from Sitka to Fort Ross in 1834. River Slavianka is the Russians' name for Russian River.
17. The "collected plain" could be the large field north of the Casini Ranch and south of the mouth of Austin Creek. Austin Creek could be the "little river falling into the Slavianka." Several days later they came to another that some writer/historians think to be Dry Creek.
18. Duflot de Mofras, *Travels on the Pacific Coast*, 1845, Paris. p. 6-7. Translated by Marguerite Wilbur, The Fine Arts Press, Santa Ana, California, 1937.
19. *Op Cit.*, p. 253.
20. Engelson, Lester. *Interests & Activities of the Hudson's Bay Company in California*, 1939. Master's Thesis, University of California, Berkeley.

View of Fort Ross, 1827; engraving from 1841 Italian translation of A. Duhaut-Cilly's account of his journey in California. California Historical Society.

Chapter 6

Pioneers, Homesteaders & Squatters

The years between the Russian exit in 1841-42 and the first Anglo-American residence established in 1855 are void of any information pertaining to any person traveling or inhabiting the lower, westward arm of the Russian River. But in surveying the histories of the surrounding areas, we can surmise certain possible events.

Between 1842 and 1855, the Americans were arriving in California in increasing numbers. The signficant events were the Bear Flag Revolt, Mexican-American War, the Gold Rush, and California's admission to the Union.

Up to 1855, Sonoma County was in a condition of confused transition from almost native wilds to permanent civilized occupancy. The county was largely covered by Spanish (or, more specifically, Mexican) grants. Yet with a few exceptions the holders of such had not yet acquired flocks and herds to occupy most of their broad acres, and the adventurous Americans very often located within the lines of such grants with as little reverence as though settling upon government land. The grant holders had little idea of rising land value, and many of them were willing to accept from settlers on their domains very moderate prices for the land. Many, if not most, of the settlers got their land at prices not much above what they would have had to pay had it been United States government public domain. There were exceptions to this rule, and in a few instances there was considerable friction and trouble between new settlers and original land grantees or their legitimate heirs and assignees.

To help settle these land problems, the U.S. government sent out surveyors in 1855 to map and measure the canyon lands of the redwood forests. One of the first surveyors to come into the future site of Guerneville was John C. Hudspeth, under a contract to the government.[1]

About 1855 a wave of immigration seemed to sweep over the country and soon every nook and cranny of the county available for farming or grazing was bought out and occupied. The steep ravines, canyons and heavily forested areas were bypassed. Some took up residence on the Spanish grants without permission or making just compensation to the owners of the lands first. They did at times pay for the land — not to the proper parties, but to a third-party claimant. In some cases they refused to pay again to the proper grant owners or to vacate the premises. These cases often ended up in conflicts between the involved factions. Luckily, or otherwise, no blood was shed in these altercations, though they did gain some notoriety. One, in June 1859, was called "The Bodega War," and another, in July 1862, was called "The Healdsburg War."[2]

The total acreage of the county's 23 Mexican land grants amounted to 400,143, or approximately two-fifths of the county's 992,000 acres. The grants were located on the best of land, but some of those desirous of owning their land without any legal entanglements acquired government lands under the Homestead Act.

Surveying 1850s-1860s style was hard, hard work. The team, usually three men, had to traverse country where few trails existed, if any. After days and weeks at a time of going up and down canyons, cliffs, through "buck" brush and sage brush, poison oak and nettles,

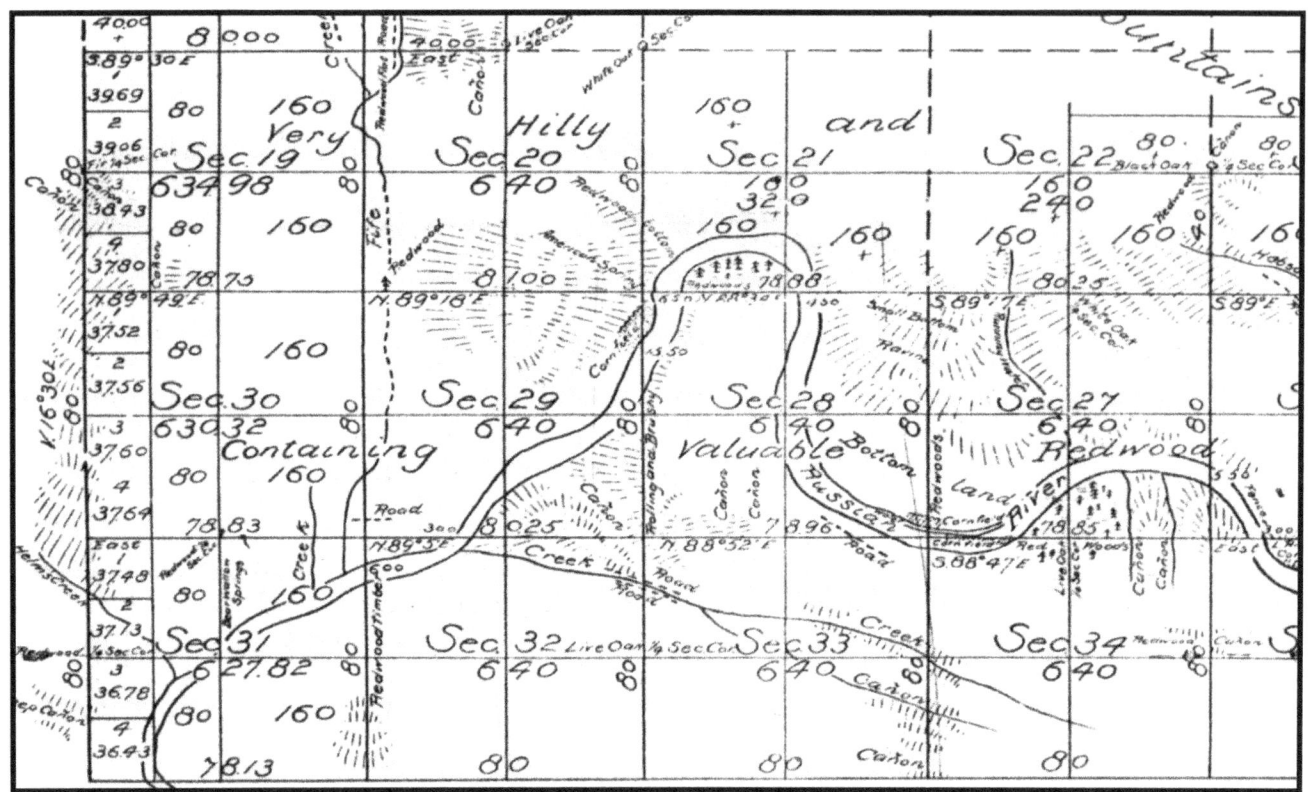

U.S. Government map surveyed from June 1855 to July 1860; Helm's Creek on the left is now Hulbert Creek in Guernewood Park. At the top of the river's upper bow is today's Rio Nido. Library of Congress, Archives Map Division.

their bodies ached and tempers were short. Some surveyors would write in their field notes:

> N. bet. secs. 5 & 6
>
> descend NE slope
>
> 1900 brook crs west
>
> 4000 redwood 38 in. dia 1/4 sec cor
>
> country ahead rough
>
> I quit.

Some surveyors never measured or even tramped the country they said they worked in. One surveyor commented about the veracity of another's notes: [3]

> this Cor[ner] is Fals [sic] as Hell....as he was never at the Corner nor at the sec[tion] Cor's E W S N of it.

The plots (160 acres) acquired were near population centers, main transportation routes, or industrial areas. As the sections were purchased, new landseekers were progressively forced to buy proper private land or homestead more remote public land areas. In the case of the Russian River between Mark West Creek and the mouth of the river, the lands were occupied from both ends toward the area void of human occupation, being Dutch Bill Creek, Big Bottom and Smith Creek. Besides farm homesteading, industry in the form of lumbering moved into the heavily timbered canyons slowly.

Of those people occupying the lands to the west of Big Bottom, one was James Sheridan. In 1856 he bought 400 acres that were partly cleared at Duncan's Mill. In 1860 he moved to two miles west of Dutch Bill Creek where the Sheridan Ranch is still located.[4]

Two others were Samuel Duncan and his brother, Alexander. In 1854 they located a lumber mill at Salt Point. In 1860 they moved their mill to a site on the Russian River now known as Bridge Haven. In early histories of Sonoma County this site was called Duncan

Mills or Duncanville. In 1877 they relocated again, due to the exhausted supply of trees, to the present community of Duncans' Mills on Highway 116, not to be confused with the first site at Bridge Haven.[5]

The area to the east of Big Bottom was being homesteaded about 1853. In that year Lewis W. Ridenhour came from Placerville and acquired a quarter section under the Homestead Act. The Ridenhour home is still located on this property, one-quarter mile east of Korbel Winery on River Road.[6]

Two years later, D.B. English came from Napa to Cosmo, today's Hacienda, though at the time there was no name for that location, and purchased a section of land from the government. He and Ridenhour, both in their twenties, were instrumental in the development of the area which had an effect on Guerneville, which will be later described.

One of the first mills erected in the lower Russian River watershed, excluding "El Molino" at the river and Mark West Creek, was the Pocket Mill. It was located at the intersecting canyons of Pocket and Oregon. In 1858 Messrs. Segley and Miller moved it down Pocket Canyon, one mile, near B.F. Alden's home. A second mill near Pocket Mill was Howland's, probably operating in 1855 or sooner, definitely in 1856.[7]

Another mill was located this same year of 1858 on the Russian River, one mile below Mark West Creek. It as called the Tuscadora Mills, possibly named for the nearby Atascadero Creek, which drained Green Valley.[8]

In the spring of 1856, S.H. Torrance bought a ranch, but discovered it was on the Spanish grant "Walla."[9] He gave it up, and that fall he could be found across the river from Big Bottom, where he built a cabin. This is the first recorded incident of a person making residence in the immediate area of Guerneville. The gap was finally being occupied.

Succeeding 1856, Torrance engaged in trapping beaver and hunting. After a time he made shingles, and in 1860, he brought ma-

S.H. Torrance, Guerneville Pioneer

chinery from San Francisco and put up the first sawmill in the Big Bottom area.[10] Since it is doubtful he built it by himself, who were the others? This mill was a small, water-powered operation on the river, and was still located there in 1861-63.[11]

In 1857 Henry Hulbert, his wife and three-year-old son, Hiram, arrived in this vicinity. He located downstream from Torrance one-half mile on a forest-covered flat. The Hulberts resided in the area long enough to have a creek named after them — Hulbert Creek — in today's Guernewood Park.[12]

At this time the redwoods in the close vicinity of the mill were being felled, but the forest still dominated the scene. The biggest trees were not being felled as yet for the lack of space to move and handle them.

W.H. Willets filed a claim on a quarter section of forest in the choicest area of Big Bottom. He subsequently made his residence there in 1858. About ten years later, he moved to the infant village of Stumptown, a quarter mile to the southeast.

The redwoods, crowding each other for

Miriam School District, April 1873, located at today's Veterans Memorial Building, southeast corner of Church and First Sts. Ellis T. Crane, teacher at far left. JCS Collection

sunlight, cast acre upon acre of shade except during those few hours near noon. The Big Bottom was an outstanding example of this. The trees did not occupy the whole ground, but permitted laurel, dogwood, ferns and other shade-tolerant flora their places amongst the fallen branches and prostrate trunks.[13]

On the few wagon roads, drag or log roads, there was a good deal of dust, but it was, as they said, "clean dirt," and washed off easily. On a journey through the country one element was its somewhat haphazard nature. The traveler did not travel over beaten ground, in a contemporary description, "you may sleep in a house today, in the woods tomorrow, you dine one day in a logging camp, and another in a farmhouse."[14]

A correspondent (*for Harpers Monthly Magazine*) in 1861 described the coast redwood forests thusly:[15]

> The large timber grew thicker as I advanced, so that it was soon impossible to determine the direction of the sun in consequence of the dense shade overhead, and I could only rely upon the faint indications of north perceptible on the trunks of the trees.
>
> There is something profoundly awesome in the solitude of a great forest, when one becomes conscious of being lost within its vast shades and utterly cut off from every trace of human fellowship. What power can cope with unseen enemies that may be hidden in every jungle, and how weak and puny one feels beside those gigantic trees which have grown and battled with the elements for centuries, and tower to such a dizzy height above his head.

In 1860 three more men came to Big Bottom. Richard E. Lewis located and obtained a state patent on 200 acres of timberland (as it all was) where Guerneville proper now stands. Another man was R.B. Lundsford, who, on May 1 of this year, took up residence there. The third was Andrew Fife, who gave his name to the creek in town. He may have been here earlier.[16]

Meanwhile, upstream, English, Ridenhour and others[17] petitioned the Board of Supervisors for a school district on August 6, 1860, to be called "Miriam."[18] It was granted that day. This is significant in that it indicates a sufficient population with children in the area as to warrant a school. This district included Big Bottom, although there were probably few, if any, school-age children there at that date.

Probably the location of this school, judging by the names of the trustees of that year and the next, and those involved was near the English and/or Ridenhour homestead, that is, near Hilton. In 1867 it was on a McPeak's property across the river from today's Korbel Winery. In 1877 the school was located on the Ridenhour property in School House Canyon.[19]

The day following the granting of the school petition, August 7, 1860, R.H. Hayes was appointed the first member of the board of trustees of the school.[20] On May 25, 1861, F.S. Dunhill was the first school teacher hired, at a monthly salary of thirty dollars.[21] Between 1861 and 1865, comments and records are few.

The early school board of trustees was in a constant state of flux, as were the teachers, with a frequent changing of personnel in both.

The juvenile population by name and number is unknown. It is not unreasonable to believe that children were born in the area. The earliest discovered birth was that of Silvester Florence Faudre, October 31, 1860, on the Fred Bond place.[22] The mother, Martha C. (Jose) Faudre, is the second earliest known arrival of a woman in this area, that is not to say she and Mrs. Hulbert were the first. Many times when a name appeared on these records, it was the first recording of that person being in the area.

The Big Bottom and the immediate area surrounding it was still sparsely populated, but of that population, 21 men presented a petition to the Board of Supervisors praying for the "Old Pocket Mill Road to go by way of the new Pocket Mill, two miles further, to the River," in April 1861.[23] The petition was granted, as a map, circa 1863, shows the "road crossing Russian River below Torrance's mill and leading to a point near Healdsburg Road."[24]

Again it is not too presumptuous to believe the area was not all that sparsely inhabited. Surely more than here recorded were present to sign the petition in sufficient numbers so as to have it granted. In 1862, three men appeared.[25] The year 1863 records show no immigrants. In 1864, the school's papers shed more light: William H. Willets became the first board member to come from Big Bottom. His claim was located on the Laughlin Ranch and fields.[26] In this same year, records show eight more people moved to the area.[27]

In one rare instance, we have evidence as to when and how a new family arrived. William Beaver, son of Henry Beaver, wrote:[28]

> In 1864, my father, Henry Beaver, and family landed with an ox team at the road at Powers' sawmill [now Summer Home Park]. After a short stay here we proceeded on down the river, in a flat boat, about five miles to where Guerneville now stands. They built our cabin just west, about Main and Mill Streets. My father, in the spring of '65, started his freight wagons drawn by oxen, going out Pocket Canyon, which was the main route in and out of Big Bottom, to Petaluma, the nearest shipping point.

Even though William Beaver wrote he arrived in Guerneville in 1864 or '65, his death certificate states he was born in Guerneville December 1863 to Henry and Mary Beaver.[29]

Another family, by the name of Strode, moved to the area. At that time Maggie Strode was pregnant. On October 20, 1864, C.E. Strode became the father of a boy, named John Morgan.[30] This is the second recorded birth in Big Bottom. The mother is also the second wom-

John Morgan Strode, born 1864 in Guerneville (photographed 1930), and C.E. Strode, his mother, one of the first white women in the area.

an on record residing here, but the author and possibly the reader should not doubt that other women were present with their families as was Martha Faudre.

Most of the people in the lower Russian River area were not settlers, but, rather, "timber tramps," a catchall phrase for loggers, suglers, snipers, and anybody in general connected with logging. These men were like most men of almost all trades of this era: transient workers. They went where the work was or to where the mill would move — hence the problem of trying to make a guess, educated and reasonable, as to the population of Big Bottom.

As can be seen, families and men of productive and monetary minds were immigrating to the area in greater numbers as the years progressed. An indication of increase of population is the number of children in the whole of the Miriam School District, not just in Big Bottom, being 117 in 1864, 153 in 1865, and 170 in 1866.[31]

1. John W. Bagley, Survey Notes, Book 1, p. 44; John C. Hudspeth, U.S. Gov't. Map, signed; *Son. Co. Hist.*, 1889,

2. These events are covered to a greater extent in Son. Co. Hist., 1889, pp. 133-137; *Son Co. Hist.*, 1926, pp. 426-427.

3. John W. Bagley, *Field Notes of Government Surveys*, Book 1, pp. 74 & 110, handwritten, Guerneville. Last Comment was JWB's own.

4. On Highway 116, on the north side of Russian River *S.D.*, November 4, 1858.

5. Present-day Bridge Haven on the south side of Russian River, one mile from its mouth. *Son. Co. Hist.*, 1880.

6. Robert Ridenhour, interview, March 5, 1967.

7. *Pacific Rural Press*, San Francisco, October 30, 1875.

8. *S.D.*, Santa Rosa, November 4, 1858.

9. *Son. Co. Hist.*, 1889, p. 573. A check of all California Mexican and Spanish grants shows no name of "Walla" or in Spanish spelling "guala." It could be "Gualala," but the grant name of that area is "German Grant" or "Muniz."

10. *Ibid.; Pacific Rural Press*, October 30, 1875. S.T. Powers had a water power mill at the Laguna de Santa Rosa in 1857, produced 4,000 bd. ft./day (*State Registry & Book of Facts*, Langley & Matthews, 1857.)

11. *The Hist. of State of Calif. Biog. Rec. Coast Co.'s*, Chicago, 1904, Guinn Co., p. 642; Son. Co. Rec., Road Record, p. 21.

12. Also called Helm's Creek; see map, page 26.*Cloverdale Reveille*, July 29, 1927.

13. The only remnant of the Big Bottom Forest is Armstrong State Park. It serves as an example, though not as good as the old forest closer to Guerneville, of a local redwood environment.

14. Charles Nordhoff, *Northern Calif. Oregon & the Sandwich Islands*, Harper Bros., Publ., New York, 1874, p. 151.

15. J. Ross Browne, "The Coast Rangers," *Harper's New Monthly Magazine*, Vol. XXIII, New York, Harper Bros. Publ., 1861), p. 604.

16. R.A. Thompson, *Sonoma County Atlas*, Oakland, 1877, p. 24; and Board of Supervisors' Minutes, Vol. 4, p. 290 (hereafter cited as Bd. Supvrs. Mins.).

17. See Appendix pioneers

18. Bd. Supvrs. Mins., Vol. 4, p. 240.

19. See Appendix, "Board of Trustees." R.A. Thompson, *Sonoma County Atlas*, Oakland, 1877, p. 35; and Bower's Map of 1867 Sonoma County.

20. The small amount of information and names regarding the Miriam School District was gained from county records too numerous to cite. See Appendix: "Teachers, Board of Trustees, and Miriam School Dist." Records - papers and books - are in Sonoma County Archives.

21. *Ibid.*

22. Pauline Olson and Edith Olson Merritt, *Sonoma County Cemetery Records* (Santa Rosa, 1950). I have been unable to locate this property though source says "in Guerneville District."

23. Bd. Supvrs. petition #224 (86).

24. Bd. Supvrs. Road Rec., Book A, p. 21. See Index.

25. Samuel Blakley, George Peterson, William Chormicle.

26. Book A of Patents, p. 563, Sonoma County Records; J.R. Watson, *Guerneville*, undated, eight-page manuscript, "Willits and Richard Lewis first look at Guerneville timber region and recognized commercial value. Land unsurveyed by U.S., cross river landed where Church Street in Guerneville. Agreed one man should have all timber to right of it and the other to the left. Hired Cap Eliason of Santa Rosa to make prelim. survey so they might

gain possessory title to land."

27. Henry Beaver, wife, Mary, and son, William Beaver; G.E. Strode, wife, Maggie, and infant, John; James Greenwood; John Ungewitter.
28. William J. Beaver, letter to *Guerneville Times*, February 27, [1933?]
29. Sonoma County Recorder's Office, death certificate #443.
30. *Son. Co. Hist.*, 1911, p. 908.
31. Superintendent of Schools, *Records* (for Miriam School District), respective years.

Addendeum:

1. First Marriage in Guerneville, David B. English to Emily Beaver, 1866.
2. First house built in Guerneville by David B. English for R.E. Lewis, Sonoma Co. History, 1911, pg. 861

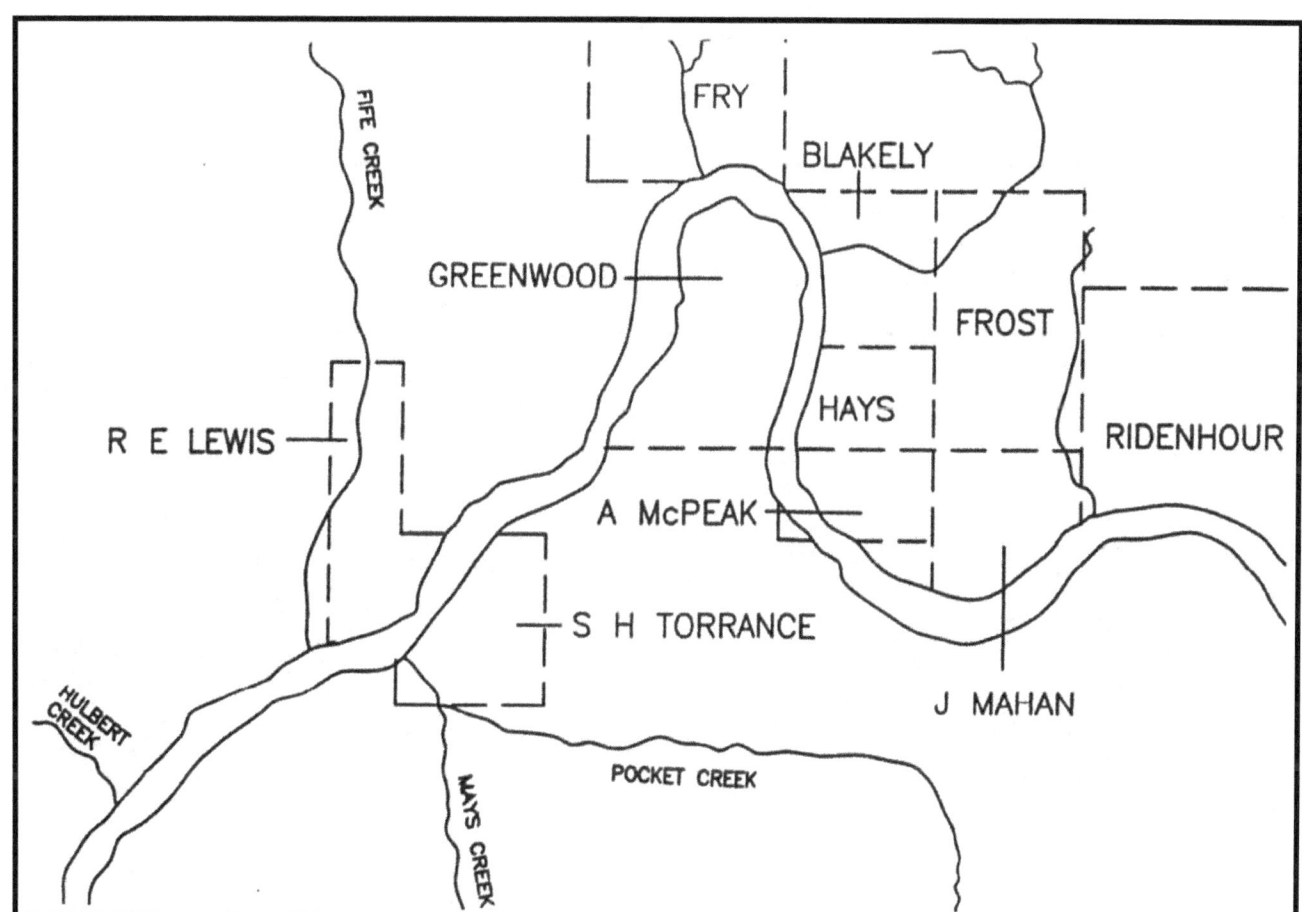

Property owners in 1864, from Sonoma County Tax records, JCS Collection

Looking east up 1st Street toward Bagley's store with men on the porch. Buildings left to right: first two unkonwn; Guerneville Hotel in background; across the street school in background, Lunsford's home; Bagley's store and post office; Bagley's home on far right. Mabel Peter Collection.

View of Guerneville from the second floor porch of Bagley's Post Office, looking east up 1st Street, 1873. The two-story building on the right is today's Riverland Resort. Healdsburg Museum.

Chapter 7

BEGINNINGS OF A VILLAGE

In the last chapter, it was mentioned Torrance had a waterpowered sawmill put up in 1860. The mill was located on the Russian River approximately 400 yards upstream from the present Guerneville bridge on the south bank.[1] He operated his mill for four or five years, then sold a portion of the machinery to the Meeker Brothers and the remainder to Guerne and Bagley. Torrance's buildings and dam were still standing in 1875.[2] The sale by Torrance was in August 1865, and the buyers were the firm of Guerne, Bagley, Heald and Willets.[3] Mr. Willets transferred his interest to Heald and Guerne. Mr. Bagley also withdrew from the partnership.[4] Other information states the origin of the Heald and Guerne mill a little differently:[5]

> Mr. Bagley came in with the machinery to build the very first mill that was ever operated here, and literally making a road upon which to travel. The firm was Bagley, Heald, and Willets. Mr. Willets transferred his interest to George E. Guerne and later Mr. Bagley withdrew also.

Bagley resided in Healdsburg and was well known in the area. He had a mill on Mill Creek from 1858 to 1865. He ran for Justice of the Peace in the early 1860s. Bagley probably knew Thomas T. Heald (brother of Hiram Heald, namesake of Healdsburg). Tom's home was on the trail from Healdsburg to Ridenhour's, across the river from Mirabel Park.

Bagley probably dismantled his mill and with Heald, and possibly with Willets, moved the machinery to Big Bottom, widening and carving a road out of the trail.

Willets naturally could see profits coming his way with a mill, steam at that, in the immediate area of his timber, among the best in the world. How Guerne teamed up with this trio is wanting for an answer.

These men constructed their mill in Big Bottom in that area bordered by Fife Creek, Main Street and Mill Street, and just southeast of the Beaver residence of 1864.

For clarification and easier identification of various locations about town, the current (1980) street names will be used.

First Street was known as Front Street, Main Street, and now its present name. Second Street was first called Polly Ann Street, next Railroad Avenue, presently Main Street. Third, Fourth and Fifth Streets have remained unchanged.

Cross-streets, those running north and south, are Mill Street at the west end of town, then Church Street in the middle. The names have not changed. The street at the east end has had different names. In town it was called Cinnabar Avenue, and where it left town, was called the Mines Road. Later, Cinnabar and Mines were changed to Armstrong Woods Road.

The year following the founding of Heald & Guerne, another mill was located near the junction of May's and Pocket Canyons, called the Sonoma Mill, and owned by C.W. Holland or Howland.[6] This could be Howland's Mill, written on the U.S. Government Maps Survey of the 1860's.

In the winter of 1866-67, the original structure of Heald & Guerne was carried away by the overflowing of the Russian River.[7]

They rebuilt the structure, the workmanship of Messrs. Bagley and Goddart, with a capacity of producing 20,000 feet of lumber per day. It was powered by a 48-horsepower engine, 14-inch cylinders and an 18-inch stroke, and ran a double circle saw (the lower one 62-inch diameter, and the upper one 72-inch

Left: Ellen Antoinette Bagley and John Washington Bagley, courtesy Mabel Peter. Above: George E. Guerne circa 1912, courtesy Mabel Peugh White

diameter), plus an edger and planer.[8] Though its capacity was 20,000 board feet a day, it was generally cutting only 12,000.

There were five sawmills in Mendocino Township, of which Big Bottom area was a part, in 1868. These were Power's Mill, near Cosmo[9], Peel's Mill and Alexander's, up by Healdsburg, and Heald & Guerne's Mill.[10] The fifth mill is unknown by name, but probably was Hewlett's Mill, located roughly in the area of today's Korbel Winery.

It appears lumbermen generated much thirst from their work, so to relieve them of this frustration (and their cash), Ruben Williams established a saloon in 1868, located roughly at the intersection of Armstrong Woods Road and First Street. He had to haul the lumber from two miles distant to build it, the town's first saloon, because Heald & Guerne refused to sell lumber for that purpose.[11] This was the only saloon in town until 1872. About 1871-72, a new saloon was erected for the disbursement of more spirits by Williams.

The number of men, sober or otherwise, in the Miriam School District increased enough for the Board of Supervisors to create, in mid-1867, the Miriam Election District in the Mendocino Township.[12] The first general election was held September 9, 1867 for Mendocino Township. The polls were at Bagley's store, and 58 votes were cast. The second election to be held in the new district took place October 16, 1867, for Justice or the Peace of the same township. The results were 36 votes for Samuel P. Hayes, and 35 for John Price, both men of Healdsburg.[13]

Healdsburg was the "seat" of Mendocino Township; therefore, Miriam was in that jurisdiction.

Another indication of a growing population was the schools. Throughout the county, schools sprung up around population centers, urban and rural. About 1867-69, the Miriam School District had more than one school and as many as four.[14] No locations are given in the records, so we have to rely on information describing industrial/population centers; these could have a population of around 50 to have all the trappings of a full-fledged community. The concentrations of people in Miriam District were in Pocket Canyon, along Russian River at present-day Korbel Winery, and Heald & Guerne's Mill. The fourth possible area could be anybody's guess.

It would be safe to assume that by 1868 a schoolhouse was erected at Heald's Mill. S.H. Torrance built the first schoolhouse and supported it for the first three months at his own

Left: Eliza Gibson Montgomery Guerne with her children Julia, on lap, and Marie, 1870; Julia Guerne Collection. Right: Bagley's house behind the post office. The woman at left is Lula Bagley; woman in the doorway is Ellen Bagley; boy in the white shirt is Frank Bagley. JCS Collection

expense.[15]

The location of this school in 1868-69 is strongly indicated by the tax records and the accompanying photographs of 1872 as being the lot on First and Church Streets, where the Veterans' Building now stands (formerly the Guerneville School).

Another form of county government recognition of the settlement arose when the Supervisors established the Miriam Road District. Road districts were established throughout the county under a road overseer. Miriam's was Crocket D. Yarborough.[16]

Roads were in a constant state of disrepair due to flooding and landslides in the winter and the constant traffic of heavy teaming cutting up and grinding them to fine dust in the summer. This was especially so in lumbering areas. Tan dust, three to six inches deep, was common all summer, likewise, mud, equally deep, was common all winter.

The possibility of a railroad and the movement for one for the usual reasons of transportation and freight would not be coming for another seven to eight years.

Heald & Guerne's Mill settlement was for all practical reasons isolated during the winter months. Only during the season for teaming did the outside world pay any attention to it.

With expansion of the lumber industry, it looked favorably upon any ways and means of getting its products out and supplies in. One gentleman thought he had discovered an answer to this problem and tried to apply it. Captain John M. King approached Heald & Guerne and a few others for support financially and materially in building a boat and a few barges. His "flotilla" was to ply Russian River from its mouth to Heald's Mill during the summer months and to Healdsburg during high water.[17]

He commenced to build the "Enterprise" in May of 1869. He succeeded in making a few round trips to Duncans' Mills at the ocean, but only one attempt was made to Healdsburg. He literally came to a rocky halt just below that town near the end of March 1870.

While the "Enterprise" was making an occasional shakedown cruise to Duncans' Mills, the people at Heald's Mill, in January 1870, were signing and passing a petition to be presented to the State Legislature for a stage mail route to Heald's Mill.[18]

At the same time, in Sacramento, the State

John Bagley's certificate of appointment as the Postmaster of "Guerneville." This is the first official U.S. document with the name Guerneville. Dominic Raitano Collection

Senate passed a "concurrent and joint resolution" with the State Assembly that the California U.S. senators and representatives be advised to procure an act that various public highways be declared mail routes.[19]

In order to achieve success, John Bagley sent a petition in February 1870 to Washington for the establishment of a post office "at Guerneville."[20] The petition was denied by letter March 25, 1870 because "...it [Guerneville] is not on any mail route now in operation, or under contract."[21]

The nearest post office was in Sebastopol, 14 miles away.[22] The existing mail routes circumvented the river settlements. The route went from Sebastopol to Fort Ross via Smith's Ranch (Bodega Rancho) and Duncans' Mill at the ocean. The route from Sebastopol to Healdsburg went through Santa Rosa.

This is not to say that these were the only trails and roads. The three main avenues in and out of Big Bottom were the trail to Duncans' Mill, the road through Pocket Canyon to Sebastopol, and the Healdsburg Road via Mill Creek.

The local public was trying anything and everything to establish a post office. Whether it was by design or chance, the people were risking the outcomes of both the State Legislature in Sacramento and Washington. If they had one source of government in their favor, they could use that as a form of pressure to move the other.

It appears that with a petition before the California legislature, Washington was shown a post office could be of service. The Post Office Department had John Washington Bagley appointed as "Guerneville's" first postmaster on July 28, 1870, and sworn in on August 13, 1870.[23] J.W. Bagley was commissioned October 1, 1870, at $26 per year.[24] With this done, how could the legislature in Sacramento deny a stage route?

A stage owned and operated by B.B. Berry of Sebastopol went into service September 1 and made two trips a week to Heald & Guerne's Mill.[25] This community finally had recognition by both state and federal governments, and not just by the County Board of Supervisors.

A correspondent described thusly:

the new town of Guerneville:

The mill of Messrs. Heald & Guerne is doing a large lumber business employing at this time 75 hands. Guerneville has 25 to 30 dwelling houses, one store, and boarding house, one blacksmith shop, one saloon.[26]

The store belonged to Bagley. The saloon was, as stated, Ruben Williams's. The blacksmith shop could belong to either or both John S. Marsh or A.S. Phillips, as they are the only ones known in 1870 or any prior date. The dwellings varied from family homes to, as one contemporary writer described, "shanties and little snuggeries for the lumbering population which consisted largely of bachelors."[27]

In the surrounding forest there were other families, settlers and mills. The people were making land patents or possessory claims on the standard 40-acre parcels. A few got larger parcels through a contemporary "G.I. Bill." The homes were scattered throughout the ridges and canyons. Besides Heald & Guerne's Mill in town, there were also one or two mills in Pocket Canyon and Hewlett's Mill about three miles upstream from Heald's. This site would be present-day Rio Nido.

Men of many vocations came to Guerneville, but in a few cases their jobs were not necessary at the time to fill a need. They would then naturally become employed in the woods and mills.

On the opposite side, some had a multitude of jobs, such as our friend, J.W. Bagley, who, besides being a merchant and postmaster, was the local sexton and a minor "country doctor." He, later in 1872, became district clerk for the school and a member of the same school's board of trustees, and a land surveyor.[28]

About 1869-70, the first Chinese arrived in the woods. The jobs commonly done by them were the most menial, such as digging and grading main logging skids or as water slingers. This second job entailed the throwing of water under logs to act as lubricant as they were dragged to the mills. Both jobs were the dirtiest in the logging industry, especially so during the summer.

The history of "Guerneville" has revealed up to this point in time many names of the locations. To the Indians, it was known as "ciyole." Earlier settlers called it "Big Bottom," and, with the lumber industry, was called "Heald & Guerne's," or, more commonly, "Heald's Mill." Politically, the Supervisors used the name "Miriam" for every kind of a district created in the area.

The name "Stumptown" was lightly used, if ever, until 1873, in print.[29] Stumptown did become popular with the townspeople and it was looked upon as a label of strong identification by the residents.

The population was finally counted for the first time. The census, taken every ten years, was not divided by areas smaller than townships. But the one taken for Guerneville was done by or for J. W. Bagley in assisting his application for the post office. The total population was 139 in 1870.[30]

With the established post office giving identification to the settlement, there were two movements left for the people in order to obtain some form of self rule and further identification. One was to create a township out of the existing townships in the area. This would give the townsfolk a judge and court and a constable and law enforcement. The other move left to them was incorporation. In surveying contemporary journals, papers and records, the latter was not remotely entertained by anyone.[31] But regarding the former, a petition was circulated by the citizens "praying for the formation and creation of a new township to be called Redwood Township."[32] It was presented to the supervisors on August 9, 1871, and they ordered the desired township created on November 10, 1871. The township boundaries put Guerneville almost in the geographical center.

With the township came appointments to the Justices of the Peace and constables. The first two judges were John Silas Pool, a homesteader on Pool Ridge, north of Gabe's Rock, and C. A. Brackett, of Murphy & Brackett Sawmill. The two constables were Ward S. Stevens and Ruben Williams, the latter the town's saloon keeper.

It should be noted here that with the township formed, the same name was applied to the road and election districts, and "Miriam" was dropped, except for the school district.

Official county records show no date of appointment for the Redwood Road District roadmaster, or overseer, but the first to appear was Crocket D. Yarborough in March of 1872.[33]

Two months following the formation of the township, on January 3, 1873, another petition was given the Supervisors from the local citizenry. This was unique — it was not for the creation of a new political division or area, but called for an end to the "political" career of Ruben Williams as Constable.[34] The people were dissatisfied because of his neglect of his appointed office. J.C. Pippin, a teamster, was appointed to the vacancy.

The first year as a township, Guerneville prospered, even during the winter of '71-'72. It must be remembered winter and roads did not mix well with travel and travelers. The only sure means left to adventurous merchants was the Russian River. Shipping by Russian River boats appeared for the second time. Yet apparently only mild success was achieved by this method. This was exactly the same thing Captain King and his "Enterprise" had tried to accomplish.[35]

The embarcation points were Healdsburg and Guerneville for "Captain" J.W. Bagley and his yacht, "Comet," and Joseph Livreau and his clipper, "Quickstep." The "Quickstep" made at least two round trips, and the "Comet," almost two, as it got snagged on a return trip to Guerneville.

The following is the total information found on this episode. "Arrived" and "Sailed" are in relation to Healdsburg.

Navigating Russian River

Some weeks ago J.W. Bagley built a boat in Healdsburg and set sail down the river, with about two tons of freight for Guerneville, twenty-five miles distant by river. We lately learned that he made port in four and a half hours running time. The boat returned yesterday.[36]

Russian River Flag, Feb. 22, 1872:

Arrived — February 20, 1872, the clipper boat "Quickstep," Livreau, master; two days from Guerneville, in ballast.

Sailed — February 19,1872, yacht "Comet," Bagley, master; to Guerneville; general merchandise . February 21, 1872, clipper boat "Quickstep," Livereau, master, machinery for Livreau & Ely's mill at Guerneville, and passengers.

Russian River Flag, February 29, 1872:

Arrived — February 25, 1872, the clipper boat "Quickstep," Peckinpah, master; 36 hours from Guerneville, ballast.

Russian River Flag, March 7, 1872:

"Letter from Guerneville:

'Dear Editor; I am informed by those who have seen Captain Bagley, that his loss by snagging the "Comet" was trifling. Everyone rejoices with him because of his fortunate escape from drowning. The clipper yacht "Quickstep," Dave Peckinpah, master, arrived from Healdsburg last Monday, Feb. 26, making the distance of 35 miles [?] in 3 hours and 17 minutes, the quickest time on record. She brought besides her own cargo, that portion of the "Comet's" cargo that was left on the bank of the river, near where the latter boat was snagged. Judging from Peckinpah's statement, Russian River is a hard road to travel besides being very dangerous.'

"February 29, 1872, Nixon."[37]

1. Bower's Map of Sonoma County, 1867.
2. Son. Co. Hist., 1889, p. 573; *Pacific Rural Press*, 30 October 1875.
3. *Russian River Advertiser*, Guerneville, 24 Feb. 1906, p. 1. Their ages were: Geo. E. Guerne, 28; J.W. Bagley, 37; T.T. Heald, 41; W.H. Willets, 47.
4. *Ibid.*
5. *Guerneville X-Rays*, 19 Nov. 1898, Vol. 1, No. 46.
6. *Democrat Standard,* Healdsburg, 24 October 1866.
7. *Son. Co. Hist.,* 1880, p.353
8. *Russian River Flag,* Healdsburg, 23 August 1869 (hereafter cited as R.R.F.). According to Scribner's Lumber & Log Book of 1882, the lower saw could run at 575 rpm, and the upper at 514 rpm.
9. Present-day Hacienda.
10. Sonoma County Assessor's Records, 1868.
11. *R.R.F.*, 7 Oct. 1878.
12. It must be remembered that women did not have the right to vote.
13. Bd. Supvrs. Mins., Vol. V, p. 255.
14. 1867-2; 1868-4, 1869-2
15. *Son. Co. Hist.*, 1889, p. 574.
16. Bd. Supvrs. Mins., Vol. V, p. 307, Jan. 7, 1868.
17. A detailed description of this venture may be found in Chapter VIII.
18. *S.D.*, Santa Rosa, 22 Jan. 1870, p. 5.
19. Statutes of California, 1870, Concurrent and Joint Resolutions, VIII Senate Concurrent Resolution, (Approved January 2, 1870)
20. Letter from Post Office Dept. to Bagley, dated Feb. 15, 1870, San Francisco. The reader should note that though the writer has used the name "Guerneville" up to this point, this is the first time the name "Guerneville" is used in a contemporary situation.
21. Letter from Post Office Dept. to Bagley, dated March 25, 1870.
22. Called the Bodega Post Office up to 1867.
23. Certificate of Appointment to John W. Bagley.
24. *S.D.*, 27 August and 3 September 1870, pp. 5, both issues.
25. *R.R.F.*, 18, July 1872, p. 3.
26. *R.R.F.*, 15 Sept. 1870, p.3.
27. See Appendix, "Pioneers & Early Settlers." Approximately 23 famllies were present.
28. See biographical sketches, "John W. Bagley."
29. *R.R.F.*, March 1874, p.5; and *S.D.*, 29 March 1873.
30. For populations for other years, see Appendix.
31. See other Chapters for attempts at incorporation.
32. Bd. Supvrs. Mins., Vol. 6, p. 98.
33. Yarborough was overseer of "Miriam" roads from 1868.
34. Bd. Supvrs. Mins., Vol. 6, p. 150.
35. See Chapter VIII.
36. *S.D.*, 1871 or 1872, newspaper article.
37. Map measurement comes to approximately 16 miles along river from Railroad Bridge in Healdsburg to 1922 Guerneville Bridge.

EXCURSION.

THE PEOPLE RESIDING IN THE neighborhood of Heald & Guerne's Mill on the bank of Russian River, having tendered a benefit to Capt. King, the
STEAMBOAT "ENTERPRISE,"
new building at that place will make her trial trip as an

EXCURSION!
TO DUNCAN'S MILL

AT THE MOUTH OF THE RIVER,

ON THIS DAY,

JUNE 4th 1869,

and back the following day.
A fine Quadrille Band has been engaged and there will be DANCING on one of the barges.

FREE LUNCH
on the trips down and up.

This is the heaviest timbered portion of the County of Sonoma, and the trip will afford one continuous panorama of the most beautiful and romantic scenery, and gives opportunity of seeing the broad Pacific and of visiting huge sawmills, lumbermen's camps and dense redwood forests.

TICKETS FOR THE EXCURSION may be had at Mulligan's Tin Shop, Meyer Brothers, and the Post Office in Healdsburg

N.B. -- The horses of those coming from a distance will be well provided for at a reasonable charge.

JOHN M. KING, Master.

Sonoma Democrat, courtesy Sonoma County Library

Chapter 8

STEAMSHIP ENTERPRISE

A pioneer movement in transportation was started in 1869 in "Stumptown." It created quite a bit of interest in the surrounding countryside and was regularly reported in the local newspapers, the *Healdsburg Russian River Flag* and the *Sonoma Democrat* of Santa Rosa.

Russian River Flag, May 13, 1869:

The Steamboat "Enterprise"; This boat, now being built at Heald's Mill by Captain John M. King, will be launched next Saturday the 15th. The machinery is all aboard now and the boat will be completed within two or three weeks, when she will make an excursion to Duncans' Mills on the coast, going down one day and returning the next. As many of our citizens will want to join the excursion, the Flag will give timely notice of the day set for it to come off. The livery stables will run stages down to the landing 12 miles from Healdsburg. Capt. King has been running a barge on the river drawing from 2 to 26 inches, according to load. He has made 6 round trips from Heald's Mill carrying in the aggregate, 200,000 shingles and 20,000 feet of lumber, besides considerable farm and dairy produce. He has built another barge drawing only 12 inches when loaded. He is now building the "Enterprise" to tow these barges. The boat is 50 feet long, 10 foot beam on the bottom, 14 and 1/2 on deck, engine 15 horsepower, draught 12 inches, depth of hull 44 inches, dip of paddles (stern wheel) 10 inches. She is built in a superior manner and filled up with a cabin and all necessary conveniences for carrying passengers. Capt. King, having a contract for carrying the lumber from Heald and Guerne's Mill, the regular trips of the boat will be between that point and the coast. In the season of high water, the Captain expects to run to Healdsburg. This would give us cheap freight between Healdsburg and San Francisco while the mud road to Petaluma was at its worst. We hope Capt. King's enterprise in building the "Enterprise" will be richly rewarded.

Russian River Flag, "Letter from Big Bottom," May 29, 1869:

Mr. Editor: The most important event of the day to the people of Lower Russian River, is the successful launching of the steamboat Enterprise built at Heald's Mill by Capt. J.M. King. The scene was witnessed by many of the citizens — ladies and gentlemen — who met there on the occasion. The little boat sat on the water beautifully and promises all that her sanguine friends could have anticipated of her.

The excursion trip is postponed for a few days owing to an unavoidable accident which will be soon remedied, when all will be right again. When remedied, due notice will be given. — Visitor

William Beaver penned what he witnessed on that day:

I was a small boy when the steam boat was built by a man by the name of King, and he named it the Enterprise. I remember the day when the small population of Stumptown turned out to see the boat start on its first trip down the river.[1]

Russian River Flag, June 3, 1869:

Excursion Tickets — 2.50. Is not everybody and his wife or girl going to Heald's Mill tomorrow to take a grand ride on the Russian River? Who would like to miss the opportunity of going on the first trip ever made by steam boat on this beautiful stream? You can leave here tomorrow and be down at the mill in ample time to join in the excursion. Young men, you are wanted. Trot out your horses and bring on the buggies and girls.

My friend, your wife has been cooped up in

the house long enough. Let her have some fresh air and a chance to see nature's panorama as it appears along the 'Banks of that deep rolling river.'

Read Capt. King's advertisement carefully once more and decide whether you can afford to lose the trip. (See previous page.)

Russian River Flag, August 12, 1869:

Heald & Guerne's Mill — Reverend J.H. Miller furnished the following Heald's Mill item:

The steamer "Enterprise," Capt. John King, has steam up again and is running. It will make a trial trip to the mouth of the river this week. The Capt. has constructed a dam and lock which gives the river a three foot rise above the dam. He will open the lock and let the boat ride through to the sea on the accumulated waters — Capt. King says that three locks would be sufficient to make Russian River navigable to Healdsburg the whole year; also that we may expect to see his boat up here after the first fall rains.

Russian River Flag, August 23, 1869:

We visited the steamer Enterprise, lying one mile below the mill. Captain King is quite confident that he will visit Healdsburg by steamer before Christmas. Says he intends next summer to make regular trips three times a week to Healdsburg.

Russian River Flag, September 2, 1869:

Capt. King of the steamer Enterprise was in town last week having some repairing done to the machinery of his boat, which will soon be skimming over the waters of Russian River.

Russian River Flag, December 23, 1869:

The Steamer Enterprise – We are pleased to learn from Mr. J.W. Bagley that Capt. King's boat, the Enterprise, is now successfully running on Russian River. She left Heald & Guerne's Mill on the 16th with several passengers for Duncan's Mill with barges in tow loaded with charcoal. On her next trip she will carry hoop poles and several thousand Christmas Trees for San Francisco. At last after several unsuccessful attempts Russian River is navigated by a live steamboat and we hope when the river rises to see the little vessel throw out her bow lines and her stern lines and spring lines to the Healdsburg wharf. Capt. King is entitled to great praise for his indomitable pluck and perseverance under difficulties and we hope his "Enterprise" may prove a great success.

Since the above was in type we are informed that the boat will leave Heald & Guerne's Mill today at 12 o'clock on a pleasure excursion to Duncan's Mill and return at noon tomorrow. Fare down and back $2.50. Two barges fitted up for dancing will be in tow.

In Healdsburg, Henry Hudson operated a public ferry attached to cables stretched from bank to bank across the river. Hudson was engaged in the mercantile business in Healdsburg and also created and sold a subdivision of the town.

Hudson, having the welfare of his hometown in mind, conceived the idea of placing Healdsburg on the maps as a city with a waterfront by having Russian River recognized by the government as a navigable stream.[2] The Hudson Bill was evidently proposed in the State Legislature by Thomas W. Hudson (a relative?), assemblyman from Sonoma in the 18th Session (1869-70). On February 18, the title of the bill, Assembly Bill No. 217, was "An act to provide for the improvement of the navigation of the Russian River and to declare said stream navigable." It did not pass the Legislature.[3]

However, the lack of a bill did not thwart the movement.

Sonoma Democrat, February 26, 1870:

The steamboat which was built for the purpose of navigating Russian River started from Heald's Mill on Thursday for Healdsburg loaded with lumber and shingles.

Russian River Flag, March 10, 1870:

The Enterprise — Some weeks since Captain King attempted to make a passage to Healdsburg with the Enterprise but a little above Heald and Guerne's Mill the pilot backed the boat upon a snag and sank her. This occasioned delay and considerable expense but the indomitable Captain has got her afloat again and with the experienced help of friend Capt. Parker of Mare Island Navy Yard he will make the first voyage to Healdsburg as soon as some obstruction can be removed from the river which he is now engaged doing with a force of fifteen men. The boat is now above the mouth of Mark West Creek about ten miles below Healdsburg. The

Captain has brought new sixty horsepower engines for her and he will keep her here when she comes up until they are put in.

From about three miles above Guerneville (to just above the mouth of Mark West Creek), passage was hindered a little but the obstacles were overcome by the use of the windlass on board. From Mark West Creek on through the use of a bull team was engaged to draw the beleaguered boat closer to its destination over an increasing number of gravel bars.

Russian River Flag, March 24, 1870:

Captain King's steamer Enterprise will probably reach Healdsburg today as she is now but a short distance below this town.

. . . and this was the farthest that she progressed upstream. At this point, writers differ as to her final demise. J.M. Alexander of Healdsburg wrote:

She moved slower and slower each day, until she became firmly grounded on the gravel bar on the ranch of pioneer Captain Calhoun about five miles south of Healdsburg . . . She was there to stay. — Captain King dismantled his ship and left her hull as the ghost of a wreck on the gravel bar.[4]

Another version, written by J.C. Hobson, who resided across the river from present-day Mirabel Park, stated:

. . . [The] process of navigation continued to within five miles of Healdsburg, where, overcome with disgust from dragging over bars, the owners ordered the Captain to return to Guerneville . . . Again the Captain and crew teamed and winched over the bars. At last the navigators reached a point below what is now Mirabel Park, near the Hobson ranch. Thoroughly disgusted, the owners there dismantled the worn and battered Enterprise, and the frame of the steamer still lays buried under the sand bar

Russian River Flag, May 5, 1870:

We have heard with considerable regret that Captain King's boat Enterprise is, for the present, a failure. The Captain has met with many serious difficulties in his undertaking, the chief of which lately seem to have been the summary manner in which some of his creditors have secured their claims whether rightfully or not we have no knowledge and of course have nothing to say upon that head, though we have hoped that the Captain's energy and perseverance would be rewarded. At his request we publish the following letter:

Eds. Flag: I take this opportunity of thanking you for many favors you have done me during the time that Russian River is navigable. Although I differ widely from you in politics, yet as long as I can use a hammer and cold chisel you may consider me one of your subscribers. Messers. Heald & Guerne have attached my boat but that will not prevent me from making a living as some friends have engaged me to run the Perseverance Sawmill, which is located 13 miles above Cloverdale. They also attached my dog "Gipsy" which I valued more than money. They sold the dog for $200.00. This seems like a large sum but I would not have taken twice that amount for it. They may break me but they cannot keep me broke. The first of August I will commence building another steamboat at the mouth of Russian River, to be called the "Perseverance."

Again thank you for past favors. I ask that you do me one more favor by publishing this letter.

Respectfully yours,

John M. King.

Russian River Flag, May 12, 1870

Eds. Flag: If I may be permitted the space in your paper to correct sum [sic] errors of John M. King in your issue of May 5th. I will be thankful for the favor as it seems to throw the blame of failure of his boat where it does not belong. I think, however, the fact of his trying some four weeks to get the boat to Healdsburg, over the shoals with the river falling every day without any probability of a rise till next December and only making 12 miles should convince anyone that the Enterprise for the present is a failure and Heald & Guerne not wholly answerable for it if they had lately attached the boat as represented by King, and as to his dog "Gipsie," I never as much as knew he had such a dog. Heald & Guerne do not wish to 'break' J.M. King nor to keep him broke but suppose we will have the pleasure of seeing the "Perseverance" when she comes along.

Thomas T. Heald.

As can be seen, river boating was not exactly the fastest means of transportation in the county. On March 10, as stated, the boat was about ten miles below Healdsburg, near Mark West Creek. On March 24th, some two weeks later, all accounts agree the Enterprise got no closer than five miles. At a rate of five miles for two weeks, this venture could hardly prove profitable.

Why the Captain waited after the high waters of winter to pass and therefore make the passage a difficult task is anybody's guess.

Be that as it may, Petaluma breathed a sigh of relief!

Thomas C. Pippin with George Guerne and others were part owners of the "S.S. Enterprise."[5]

1. William J. Beaver, letter to *Guerneville Times*, Guerneville, March 3, 1933.
2. J.C. Hobson, *Guerneville Times*, February 1933.
3. The bill passed the Assembly and was sent to the Senate, where it died in committee.
4. *Son. Co. Hist.*, 1926, p. 471.
5. *Press Democrat*, 13 July 1910

Chapter 9

TREES & STUMPS — THE GREEN LEGIONS

The Forest

It is generally known that the tallest tree recorded at that time was the product of Guerneville, and only to be later exceeded by the Founders Tree at 375 feet before the latter was struck by lightning. This tree grew upon the west bank of Fife Creek just opposite town, and was known to all the early settlers of Russian River as "the Monarch of the Forest." It was the tallest specimen of redwood, or any other tree, that had ever been seen by man. It measured 45 feet in circumference at the base and was 367 feet and 8 inches tall.

Another big tree grew on the land of John Torrance, across the river from Guerneville, that reached the height of 347 feet, and its diameter near the ground was 14 feet. One tree measured 67 feet in circumference two feet above the ground. It measured 200 feet tall to the first limb, at which point it was about ten or twelve feet through.[1]

As already seen, various trees were given names, something that is still done today in city and country alike. In this area there were quite a few such as the "Clar Tree." This tree is standing today (2015), with a dead snag top, about one and one half miles below town on the left bank. It has a diameter of 20 feet, 337 feet high, and is the tallest tree in Sonoma County. In Hulbert Camp Ground (Guernewood Park) stood the "Beanpole" with a height of 344 feet. Another monster tree in the campground was known as "The Stable." It was at least 22 feet in diameter and one contemporary writer stated it measured inside 27(?) feet across. T.J. Butts wrote:[2]

> ... [it] is hollow at the ground, inside of which a man can stand upright and walk fifteen feet. It is capable of stabling twelve horses with a hay mow to supply them for one winter.

The inside of this hollow was made into a house of two stories. The lower story was for several years used as a reception room by the ministers during their camp meetings which they held there, while the upper room was used by them as a bed chamber. The upper chamber was reached by way of a winding stair which ran spirally around the outside of the tree, and in front of the upper door was built a banistered porch where they often used to sit after evening service. The chambers thus formed in this tree were each upwards of 12 feet in diameter, and it was no uncommon thing to see six or seven men comfortably housed in the hollow rooms of this great tree.[3]

Butts described the "largest" tree:

> The largest tree that ever grew in Sonoma County, so far as it's known, formerly stood on the bank of Russian River about a mile above Russian River Station (Monte Rio). This tree was 23 feet in diameter at the base, and was over 300 feet high. It was felled by a man by the name of William English and was manufactured into shingles of which it made upwards of 600,000, and afforded him labor for more than two years. The shingles, when sold, brought their maker $1,800. This tree was so large that English was unable to saw the log in proper lengths and was compelled to saw out a cut at a distance of 200 feet from the base where the log was still over 12 feet in diameter, and with a maul and wedge, he split the huge log (over 200 feet in length) in half.
>
> Had this tree been carefully sawed into lumber, it would easily have made 150,000 feet which would have been worth $3,000. The product of this tree would have been sufficient to fence with a 5-board fence a quarter section of land; to have built a 2-story house of ten rooms upon it; and a barn large enough to hold 100 tons of hay and afford accommodations for ten horses, and there would have been firewood enough left to

last a family two years.

> The first four feet of the base of that tree, if sawed off and split into cordwood, would have made fifteen cords. This gives some idea of the immensity of its size.

The last of the big trees of Big Bottom are now located in Armstrong State Park, just north of Guerneville two miles, and in Bohemian Grove, one mile east of Monte Rio. The two biggest trees in Armstrong Park are "Col. Armstrong," with a height of 308 feet, 14.5 feet in diameter, and "Parson Jones," with a height of 310 feet, diameter of 13.9 feet. The ages of both trees are approximately 1,300 years.[4]

The largest tree that was near Russian River Station was proven to be over 3,300 years old. It took root while Moses was wandering in the wilderness, was a thousand years old at the birth of Alexander the Great, and had attained a diameter of 17 feet when Christ was born.

Butts, in his detailed description of the Big Bottom forest, wrote that about 1873, parties were boring a well in Guerneville. At a depth of 38 feet they struck a redwood log and bored through it a depth of six feet. The tree had reached maturity, fallen, and was covered layer by layer with earth. Then on top of this 38 feet of dirt started the present forest 3,000 years ago.[5]

The natural way for a redwood to die is by falling down. No redwood tree has ever been known to die of old age or of disease, nor has it ever been laid low by the ravages of insects.

There stood in Big Bottom the finest body of timber in the area. The Bottom is about four miles long and was covered by a dense growth of mammoth redwood trees which, in the best localities, would yield at least 800,000 feet of lumber to the acre.[6]

The engineer for the California State Board of Forestry said:

> J.W. Bagley of Guerneville states that the yield of one measured acre scaled in mill lumber 1,431,530 board feet measured.[7]

R.A. Thompson, in 1877, printed in his Sonoma County Atlas:[8]

> In Elliot Canyon, Korbel Bros. own land which will yield 22,000,000 board feet; John Beaver, 60 acres, which will cut about 5,000,000 feet.
>
> In the timber section opposite Guerneville, on Russian River, R.C. Lewis owns 220 acres of land, which will cut 60,000 feet to the acre; a total of 10,800,000 feet.
>
> S.H. Torrance has about 60 acres, which will cut 60,000 feet to the acre; total, 3,600,000 feet. Henry Beaver has 120 acres which will average 60,000 feet, total 7,200,000 feet; other parties on Pocket Canyon 15,000,000 feet. Total timber opposite Guerneville and in Pocket Canyon, 33,000,000 feet.
>
> On the North side of Russian River, from Dutch Bill Creek to Hurlbut Canyon and Mission Canyon, 700 acres averaged 60,000 feet, equal to a total of 42,000,000 feet. In Hurlbut Canyon 2,000 acres at 60,000 feet to the acre, 120,000,000 feet. In Big Bottom, near Guerneville, W.H. Willits has 160 acres which will cut 10,000,000 feet. R. B. Lundsford has 200 acres and total 12,000,000 feet. Heald & Guerne, besides their Hurlbut-Canyon timber, have 360 acres which will average 60,000 feet, a total of 21,600,000 feet; Murphy Bros., 15,000,000 feet; Ike and Tom Smith, 120 acres; 60,000 feet to the acre, 7,200,000 feet; J.B. Armstrong, 420 acres, 20,000,000; James Peugh 40 acres bottom land 60,000,000; H. Speckerman 40 acres, 4,000,000 feet; J.K. Wood, 160 acres, 6,400,000 feet; Henry Miller 200 acres, 60,000 feet to the acre 12,000,000; S.B. Torrance, 20 acres 150,000 feet to the acre, 3,000,000 feet.

Logging

Charles Nordhoff, during his trip through the redwoods of the North Coast of California in the early 1870s, provides us with one of the most complete contemporary descriptions of the logging operations there.[9]

> A tree four feet in diameter is called undersized in these woods; and so skillful are the woodchoppers that they can make the largest giant of the forest fall just where they want it, as they say, they 'drive a stake with a tree.'
>
> To chop down a redwood tree, the chopper does not stand on the ground, but upon a stage sometimes twelve feet above the ground. Like the sequoia, the redwood has a great bulk near the ground, but contracts somewhat a few feet above. The chopper wants only the fair round of the tree, and his stage is composed of two stout staves, shod with a pointed iron at one end,

In the Guerneville woods. Photo: E. Cherry, Santa Rosa Art Gallery. JCS Collection

which is driven into the tree.

The outer ends are securely supported; and on these staves he lays two narrow, tough boards on which he stands and which spring at every blow of his ax. In chopping down the larger ones, two men stand on the stage and chop simultaneously at the cut, facing each other. One would be left-handed and the other right-handed. [Sam Tomblinson was a left-hand chopper hired by Sonoma Land and Lumber Company — author.]

They first begin what is called the undercut. The undercut goes in about two thirds the diameter. When it is finished the stage is shifted to the opposite side. While the chopping is being done, other men are building a crib, sometimes taking three days to make. A crib cushions the shock of the falling tree so that it will not shatter.

When the choppers are working on the second cut, it is a remarkable sight to see the tall, straight mass begin to tremble as the ax goes in. It usually gives a heavy crack about fifteen minutes before it means to fall. The chopper thereupon gives a warning shout, so that all may stand clear — not of the tree, for he knows very well where that will go, and in a cleared space men will stand within ten feet of where the top of a tree is to strike, and watch its fall; his warning is against the branches of other trees which are sometimes torn off and flung to a distance by the falling giant, and which occasionally dash out men's brains.

At last the tree visibly totters, and slowly goes over; and as it goes the chopper gets off his stage and runs a few feet to one side. Then you hear and see one of the grandest and most majestic incidents of forest life. There is a sharp crack, a crash, which, when you hear it from a little distance, is startlingly like an actual and severe thunder peal. To see a tree thus go down is a very great sight, not soon forgotten.

A five-foot tree occupies a chopper from two and a half to three and a half hours, and to cut down a tree eight feet in diameter is counted a day's work for a man. Ray Clar wrote:

> . . . Pa told me he had one partner would sometimes spend an entire week dropping one large tree.[10]

So many of the trees and so many parts of trees are splintered or broken in the fall that a master of a logging camp thought they wasted at least as much as they saved. And as the mills also wasted a good amount, it is probable that for every foot of this lumber that went to market, two feet were lost

When the tree is down, the sawyers come. Each has a long saw. He removes the bark at each cut with an ax, and then saws the tree into lengths. It is odd enough to go past a tree and see a saw moving back and forward across its diameter without seeing the men who move it.[11] Clar again: "Buckers practically always worked in congenial pairs, i.e., natural length of stroke."[12]

The logs are then stripped of their thick bark by barkers with long iron bars to rip it off. This process of removal is sometimes accomplished by burning it off. Then the jack screw men apply their labor, three or four of whom move a log about, easily and rapidly, which a hundred men could hardly budge. They head it in the proper direction for the teamsters and chainmen. Before a log was to be hauled away, at the front end of each, a sniper with his double-bitted ax would make a 45° cut clean around the logs, the purpose being to prevent it from pulling the cross skids out of their beds.[13]

The chaintenders or suglers attached a bridle chain to the log. The chain is divided into two parts. Near the end, and on the end of each part, there is a nearly right-angled hook. These hooks or "dogs" are driven into each side of the log near the end.[14] The other logs that are ready to move are chained and coupled together. The first log is the largest and those that follow are smaller, in succeeding size. To the end is anchored the "boat." The boat was a hollow fir sawn about twelve feet in length, then split through. It carried a variety of things, but most of the time it held all necessary equipment. The main reason for the boat was for the return of all of the coupling chains and dogs. If the bull team had a long load of small logs (20 or more), the boat would be well-laden on the return trip. The number of logs to a load depended on the size of the logs.[15]

A team usually consists of four or up to seven yoke of oxen. Then with many a surge, a "gee" and a "haw," and an occasional (?) oath, the load is drawn out on the skid roads. Water is used on the skids ahead of the logs to act as a lubricant. Water tubs are placed at regular intervals and water packed on mules with canvas water bags with a large plug in the bottom and is emptied into the tubs. The water slinger carries two buckets on a shoulder plate of wood and uses a small can in each hand to throw water on the skids ahead of the logs. The Chinese waterboys with their long queues flying hurried to keep water on the skids. On an overcast day it was easy to keep water on the skids, but on a hot, sunny day, it was an almost impossible task.[16] Hot tallow was used during very hot weather. The skids were small logs or poles spaced about one foot apart and laid across the roadbed.[17]

If a team stopped it was a real job to start again. To keep the teams moving the bullwhacker would use his goad. The goad is a small pole, usually an inch in diameter at the large end and a half inch at the other. It was about six feet long, and the smaller end had a small nail that was filed to a point to extend about a quarter inch. It was used to prick the oxen's tough hide, particularly during training, and on well-broken teams in case of an emergency to make the animals move in a hurry to save their lives from a rolling log. The use of the goad depended on the individual bullwhacker. Some were able to control their animals without the goad, and some used it cruelly.[18]

On steep ground, the chaintender or sugler rode the lead log. The crowbar was stuck deep into the log and then a notch was cut in the center of it. A rope attached to the heavy bridle chain had knots in it to increase its size and holding power. This rope passed through the notch to the sugler who held it, his feet braced on the dogs that held the bridle chain. Holding on to the bar, he rode this log until the bullwhacker, fearing the load would run into his team, would tell the sugler to drop the bridle and jump.[19]

Some logging operations had tramways or railroads that went part way into the forests. The logs were drawn out to the main trail and down to the landing place. This was before the

Logging near Guerneville, probably on the Willet's claim in Big Bottom, circa 1875. Augustus L. Guerne Collection

coming of steam locomotives into the area as we know them. There were three on record as having been in the area. These were located at Korbel's, Heald & Guerne's, and Duncan's Mill. The roadbed was usually well graded, cuts made where necessary, fills made where practicable. On the ground are laid heavy cross ties, and on them a 6" x 6" square timber. On this, an iron bar about half an inch thick and two-and-a-half inches wide is spiked the entire length of the track. The two rails were five feet five inches apart.[20] The cars were made nearly square with concave wheels. The power for these cars was horses, either two or three braces, or oxen. The track of Heald & Guerne's Mill ran up the north bank of Russian River for a minimum distance of one mile in 1873. Another was on Willit's claim in Big Bottom, west of Lone Mountain in 1875.

At most times, the logs were too large to be sawed into lumber by the double circular saws and, therefore, were drawn into the mill to the mule saw. This was a long ripsaw that stood perpendicular; it cut the log in half so that the circular saws could reach through. Ripping a log was a rather slow process. One-half was then put on a carriage in front of the double saws. It passed through this in rapid rotation until it was sawed into broad slabs of the proper thickness to make the desired lumber. It was then passed along on rollers to the "pony" saw, when it was again cut in pieces of lumber of different sizes as required, such as 2 x 4, 4 x 4, 4 x 6, et cetera. It was then piled upon a truck and wheeled into the yard and piled up ready for the market. The other half of the log was sawed into boards, three-quarters of an inch thick. At the pony saw, part of it was ripped into boards ten inches wide, and part of it into planks four inches wide. The ten-inch-wide boards passed along to a planing machine and came out as rustic siding. The four-inch plank passed through another planing machine and came out tongued and grooved ceiling. The heavy slabs which came off the first and second time the saw passed through were cut into different lengths and sawed into the right size for pickets. They were then passed through a picket header, a machine with a series of revolving knives which cut out the design of the picket head the same as the different members of a molding were cut.

The timber from which shingles were and still are made is cut into triangular or wedge-shaped pieces, about four feet long and about sixteen inches square. These are called "bolts." The first process is to saw them off into proper lengths. The blocks are then fastened into a rack which passes by a saw, and as the rack passes back, a ratchet is brought into requisition, which moves the bottom of the block in toward the saw, just the thickness of the thick end and the top end of the shingle to correspond with the thickness of the thin end. The block is then shoved past the saw, and a shingle is made, except that the edges are rough, and the two ends probably are not at all of the same width. To remedy all this, the edge of the shingle is subjected to a trimmer and becomes a first-class shingle. They are packed in bunches and are then ready for market.[21]

Loggers, Tools and Wages

As can be seen, there were many different jobs in assisting a log from tree to board. The loggers were divided into crews. A crew was composed of 20 to 36 men who kept one team of eight or ten oxen busy. A crew consisted of teamsters, choppers, chaintenders, jackscrew men, swampers, snipers, suglers, sawyers and buckers.

Teamsters worked with oxen, hence at times were called "bovine directors." A teamster had to possess (in more ways than one) agility, courage, a strong voice, and a rather descriptive vocabulary.

Stewart Holbrook, a noted historian of lumber business and the Northwest, wrote the most important man of a woods crew was the bullwhacker:

> His profanity long ago became legendary in the Western woods. When he raised his voice in blasphemous obscenity, the very bark of the smaller fir trees was said to have smoked a minute, then curled up and fallen to the ground. No sailor, no truck driver, no logger who hadn't driven bulls could hope to touch its heights of purple fluidity. And when both goad stick and profanity failed to rouse the plodding oxen to their best, the bullwhacker might leap upon the animals' backs and walk the entire length of the team stepping heavily with his caulked boots and yelling like all the devils in hell.

People of later years would often mention the "rape of the redwoods," and, "How could the lumbermen cut down those beautiful trees?", and, "Why didn't the government stop them?" These and a thousand other questions have been asked time and time again by people of today with present-day knowledge of controls in lumbering. There were some laws in the early years of logging that had to be observed before obtaining timber rights, but after those were obeyed, anything to cut timber was employed.

Ray Clar, author of numerous forestry books and employed over 42 years in the State Division of Forestry, was a native and former resident of Guerneville. In a letter to a member of his family, dated July 5, 1969, he wrote:

> Your attitude on the 'rape of the redwoods' bothers me as a longtime government forester. Yes, there was a tremendous amount of timber stolen. The loggers were only half the thieves — the remainder — and most irresponsible were:
>
> 1. the legislators at federal and state level who refused to meet the issue squarely; and
>
> 2. the profit-makers who shaped the government.
>
> In the 1870s and 1880s business and gov't ethics was stinking. The S.P. Company (Southern Pacific) had three men actually quartered in the state capitol to tell both houses how to vote.
>
> Lumber was needed much for the development of California. After gold discovery, much came from Oregon & Washington. Most timber area in California was in the public domain. The only way to get at it legally was to homestead under the few laws or purchase school sections granted the State of California. Around Guerneville area a few pioneers just settled — then when Guerne wanted the timber he paid their pre-emption homestead fee to clear their claim — then he bought the land and timber —

perfectly legal and cheap. I think Henry Hulbert was such a pre-emption homesteader.

In 1885 not many people were alarmed over stolen Gov't timber except the Old Board of Forestry — and they were put out of business by the Legislature in 1893.

A contract or agreement between timber owner and mill owner was signed by Willits and Heald & Guerne on May 28, 1872.[22]

Willits agreed to deliver from his claim, being the N.E. one-quarter of section 30 in township 8 north, range 10 west (160 acres in the middle of Big Bottom!) into Heald & Guerne's Mill pond four million board feet of peeled logs at a rate of not more than one million feet a year.[23] The logs were to be marked and scaled according to Spaulding's measure of scaling[24] on the cars in the woods.[25]

Heald & Guerne agreed to saw all the railing for the road track in the woods gratis and pay an excess of two dollars per thousand square feet for the Douglas fir logs.

Other jobs have already been described, those being choppers, chaintenders or suglers, jackscrew men, sawyers and buckers. Swampers were those who built roads over which logs were hauled. A sniper cuts an angle around the front of a log to prevent snagging, and he also assisted the barkers in removing limbs from trees.[26]

The first falling axes were single bit or pole axes with 44-inch handles. Double bit axes came later and were an improvement. The sniper used a broad double-bitted ax called a sniping ax, usually at least eight inches wide. The choppers and other ax-handlers usually would grind their axes once a week.[27]

The use of a cross-cut saw for falling (or felling) timber, instead of axes and wedges alone, was introduced in the late 1870s. These saws were quite crude with no raking teeth. A "raker" might be described as a "crosswise chisel" tooth which pulled the sawdust out of the saw cut. Cutters were later tried by pointing every other cutting tooth in the opposite direction out to the flanks of the saw then one raker tooth. In time came the narrow-backed saws with detachable handles.[28]

Wages were dictated by the two elements of economy: supply and demand. In Mendocino County, loggers worked a 12-hour day, six days a week, with a half hour for lunch, all for $20-$35 per month, with room and board (or "found," the word used then).

Nordoff, on his trip through the redwoods, wrote:

> A teamster receives $70 per month, a chopper $50, chaintenders and jackscrew men the same, swampers $45, sawyers $40, and barkers one dollar a day, with board for all.[29]

State records reported wages somewhat differently:

> Following are the wages paid: Sawyers receive $100 per month; engineers, fifty dollars; ax men, from thirty to fifty dollars; teamsters, seventy-five; all with board, and are paid in coin.[30]

Apparently Sonoma County was not exactly a workingman's paradise. The men were paid by a sight draft. They received $40 a month and had to wait 30 days until they could cash the drafts. This was the married man's salary. A single man who received room and board along with his wages received $15 a month, also on a sight draft.[31]

1. Butts, T.J., Sonoma County Homes and Industries; article entitled "The Sequoia of Sonoma," Proctor & Reynolds, Santa Rosa, 1898. Reprinted in Press Democrat, Santa Rosa, January 7, 1951.
2. Ibid.
3. Ibid.
4. Ibid.
5. Ibid.
6. R.R.F., Healdsburg, August 23, 1869; and R.A. Thompson, 1877, Son. Co. Atlas, p. 24.
7. Son. Co. Hist., 1889, p. 196.
8. R.A. Thompson, op. cit., p. 17.
9. Nordhoff, Charles, Northern California, Oregon, and the Sandwich Islands, 1874, Harper Bros., New

York, pp. 170-176.

10. Letter to Clarence Clar, July 5, 1969, by his brother, Ray Clar. The Clars are a well-known family about Guerneville, the first ones arriving circa 1877.

11. Son. Co. Hist., 1889, p. 192.

12. Ray Clar (letter, July 5, 1969), op cit.

13. "Logging With Ox Teams," Oakland Tribune, June 5, 1966, p. 23-CM.

14. Son. Co. Hist., 1880, pp. 252-253.

15. "Logging With Ox Teams," op cit.

16. "Logging With Ox Teams," op cit.

17. Ukiah Daily Journal, December 11, 1958, p. 8.

18. "Logging With Ox Teams," op cit.

19. Ukiah Daily Journal, op. cit.

20. Son. Co. Hist., 1880, p. 292-295.

21. Son. Co. Hist., 1880, p. 252-255.

22. Son. Co. Archives, Superior Court Records, Exhibit "A," four-page document. Though Willits sold rights to 4,000,000 feet, there were approximately 15,000,000 feet on his claim.

23. Spaulding's Scale can be found in: Statutes of California, 1877-78, pp. 604-611. Log scales give estimated board feet to be obtained at the sawmill by measuring diameter and length of each log.

24. The cars were part of a horse-drawn railroad.

25. Ukiah Daily Journal, December 11, 1958, p. 8

26. Ibid.

27. Ibid.

28. Nordhoff, Northern California, 1874.

29. Appendix to Journals of Senate and Assembly, 21st session, Sec. 4, "Transactions of the State Agricultural Society" (1874), pp. 403-404.

30. Press Democrat, July 28, 1958.

Timbering scenes at Korbel, Harpers Weekly, Oct. 30, 1886. Above, driving wedges for felling; below, carrying water for skidding

LUMBER! LUMBER!

THE LARGEST AND BEST ASSORTMENT OF

SEASONED LUMBER

In the County now for sale at

HEALD & GUERNE'S SAW MILL,

GUERNEVILLE, SONOMA COUNTY.

Bills of Lumber Sawed to Order upon the shortest notice, at Lowest Market Rates.

Lumber Furnished at the Mill as low as any Mill in the County.

Facilities for doing general Mill Work superior to any Mill on the Coast, north of San Francisco.

Sawed and Shaved Shingles

Manufactured, also

MOULDINGS, BRACKETS, FANCY PICKETS,

And in fact every kind of Wood Material necessary for Building.
Lumber from this Mill can be purchased at

A. H. SMITH'S LUMBER YARD

Mendocino Street, Santa Rosa,

Where Building Material of all kinds can be had at Lowest Rates.

HEALD & GUERNE'S YARD,

Opposite Hassett's Mill, West Street, Healdsburg.

L. SHORE'S LUMBER YARD,

AT THE DEPOT, CLOVERDALE.

The Patronage of the Public is respectfully solicited.

HEALD & GUERNE, Prop'rs.

Paulson's Directory, 1874. JCS Collection

Chapter 10

Lumber Mills — 1870 to 1875

On previous pages, information has been given on the foundings of the earliest lumber mills and their development, specifically that of Heald & Guerne's, up to and including 1869. Another mill in the area was that of Hewlett. A date of establishment has not been found, but a location has, being roughly in the area of present-day Rio Nido and Drake's Estates. He sold out in December 1870 to Messrs. Murphy & Brackett, who apparently had some prior mill experience.[1] Hewlett then came into possession of Power's Sawmill between 1871 and 1873, the

> **LUMBER! LUMBER!**
> HAVING PURCHASED THE OLD
> HEWLETT MILL,
> on Russian River, the undersigned
> are now prepared to furnish
> LUMBER OF ALL KINDS
> AT THE LOWEST MARKET RATES.
> And on short notice.
> We warrant our lumber equal
> to the best in the market.
> — MURPHY & BRACKETT

approximate site southwest across Russian River from Korbel's Winery.[2] He remained on his homestead selling timber to the new owners and supplied his sawmill, also.

Between December 1870 and March 1872, nothing is known of Murphy & Brackett's Mill. In April of '72, it was put in thorough repair and expected to contribute a large quota of lumber to the general supply.[3] By the end of May, they had in excess of 800,000 feet of assorted lumber.[4] From the product of a single tree, a thousand dollars worth of lumber was sold. In September, they had to shut down for repairs, the nature of which is not known.[5]

The name of "Brackett" was dropped, giving the impression that Rufus Murphy bought out his partner, and subsequent articles and advertisements in county newspapers beginning in late November 1872 substantiate this. Murphy about this time sold the steam sawmill back to Hewlett for $2,540.[6]

Between April and July 1873, he moved the remainder of his operation two miles down river and three-quarters of a mile north of Guerneville.[7] This mill was capable of sawing 18,000 feet a day and was rated second only to Heald & Guerne's in size.[8]

An advertisement dated March 21, 1874, in the Sonoma Democrat states:

> **MILL REMOVAL!!**
> A NEW TIMBER SITE!
> ....AND....
> Reduction of Prices.
> MURPHY'S WELL-KNOWN MILLS, near Guerneville, have recently been moved to a new and splendid body of timber in Sonoma County. From and after this date, Wyman Murphy becomes a partner in the business, which will be conducted under the firm name of "Murphy Brothers." Our mill is the only one in the county that cuts timber across the grain.
> The following will be governing prices for lumber at the mills:
> Common lumber (board and scantling) per M............$7.00

An April 13, 1873 outing with the Bagleys; left to right: Bert Bagley; unknown; J.W. Bagley with ax; Ellen Bagley and baby Alice; unknown woman and man, girls are Mary Louise and Jocie Bagley; J.H.P. Downing photo, courtesy of Mabel Peter

Dressed lumber (rustic, tongue, groove and surface) $17.00

Delivered in Santa Rosa and Vicinity: Rough, $15 per M, Dressed $20 per M.

Guerneville, March 17, 1874

— MURPHY BROS.

It was on what was known as the Laughlin Claim.[9] There was sufficient timber in the immediate vicinity to keep the mill running during the summer without hauling. The trees "were so immediate they had to be carefully felled to prevent crushing the mill."[10] The claim was located along the east side of Armstrong Road from Watson Road, north just past the junction of the Mine Road.[11] From this date, March 17, 1874, Wyman Murphy became a partner in the business which was conducted under the name of Murphy Bros.

They commenced work in April and finished sawing in November. The daily capacity was 25,000 feet.

A writer in the Country Gentleman, who visited this mill, wrote that the timber had to be carefully felled to miss the buildings:

> There were thirteen logs in a tree, each sixteen feet long. Another tree measured two hundred and eighty-eight feet from the stump to the end of the last sawlog. It had cut fifty-three thousand feet of boards; the top was left at four feet diameter, and near one hundred feet in length. Still another, which they were working into shingles, had already made three hundred thousand, and enough lay there in the log to make one hundred thousand more. It was perfectly free from knots and windshakes for two hundred feet. They count, usually, on having first-class clear lumber from the first one hundred and fifty feet. We measured two large trees, standing within fifty feet of each other, which were forty-one feet six inches, and forty-one feet, respectively, in circumference, at five feet from the ground.[12]

"Windshake" refers to vertical splits along annual growth rings due to heavy wind whipping a tree, especially during the spring growing period. Windshake damage was not common in redwood forests.

The Murphys started up again in the Spring of '75. Business was brisk in May. Forty

Logging in Russian River area, from a lantern slide by author's great grand-father Alonzo McFarland. JCS Collection.

teams arrived in one day to haul lumber out.[13] They again shut down in November for the winter.

Far up in the canyons of today's Rio Nido, above the old site of Murphy & Brackett's mill, Henry Miller and John Bayler were producing split lumber products — rails, posts, pickets, shingles, board bolts and three-foot shakes — all hand made.[14] This was a common endeavor by those who did not have sufficient funds to purchase machinery for sawing lumber. Quite a few of these independents could be found in the "glens and vales" of the area.[15] At times, one tree would occupy a man from one to two and, in some cases, three years splitting shingles and shakes. Income from this work amounted to $2,000 at the most per large tree.

Livreau, whose mill was located northwest of Guerneville about 3/4 of a mile, on the west side of today's Laughlin's Field (not to be confused with Laughlin's Claim as already described), bought four acres from P.B. Hewlett adjoining his steam mill in January 1872 for $1,200.[16] A mix up might arise in regard to Hewlett's location. There is little confusion, as he occupied and owned more than one parcel of land. About a month later, Livreau sold a half interest in the mill to Julia Ely for $3,000. Another partner in the mill, Oliver Ely, sold half of his interest to Julia for another $3,000.[17]

Prior to sawing for the season of 1872, they put in two new boilers that were brought

---

SPLIT LUMBER !

WE WILL FURNISH ON SHORT NOTICE

RAILS, POSTS, PICKETS

SHINGLES, BOARD BOLTS

THREE-FOOT SHAKES

We will either deliver the lumber or furnish the same at our ranch, eighteen miles below Healdsburg, on

Russian River, two miles from Murphy & Brackett's mill.

Our Post Office address is at Guerneville.

— HENRY MILLER

— JOHN BAYLER

down by the clipper boat "Quickstep," and made several alterations and additions to produce more than in 1871. To facilitate further sales, they had a lumber yard in Healdsburg.[18]

In November of '72, Oliver and Julia Ely sold their interests to B.F. Pendleton for $6,000.[19] Livreau and Pendleton remained partners in 1873, as shown in tax records of that year.[20] Sometime in early March 1874, Livreau and Pendleton sold out to Messrs. Mead and Hassett of Healdsburg. They got a late start in sawing, but were in full operation by the end of May. The mill had a capacity of from 15,000 to 20,000 feet a day, and with about 160 acres of timber land. At the end of November, they disassembled the mill and moved it to a lot in the rear of Guerneville on Second Street.[21] In mid-December, the two-story frame was up and just about ready for the machinery,[22] but apparently the mill was not finished, and there was talk about town the machinery was sold. There was no mention of the mill operating after this, but the structure was still standing mid-1876.[23] The machinery was finally sold by Heald & Guerne to Robert Norton in September 1877 for use in a mill in Long Valley, Mendocino County.[24]

Henry Ludolph's Mill was a new operation in 1872. It was in the area opposite Murphy & Brackett, on the river, two miles from town.[25] It was described as "a very valuable body of timber."[26]

In early 1873, Ludolph was joined in partnership by F. Korbel. A new saw and planing mill was located at "McPeak's Woods"[27] by them (probably at or near present Korbel Winery) and was capable of cutting 16,000 feet of lumber a day.[28] In midsummer of that year, Korbel bought out Ludolph and purchased a Santa Rosa lumber yard from W.A. Arnold to promote further sales of his products.[29]

During the winter of '73 to '74, Korbel enlarged and rearranged the mill, and in May of '74, was joined in partnership by his brothers, Anton and Joseph Korbel.[30] It was stated they had purchased 1,383 acres from Hewlett for

Korbel Mill Tramway, Sept 12, 1875 Healdsburg Museum Collection

the round sum of $20,000.[31] State records noted:

> The mill cuts twenty thousand feet a day. The proprietors have a large manufacturing establishment in Santa Rosa for all kinds of building, ornamental and fancy work, to which they intend at an early day to add a wine cask factory, the casks to be made of selected timber from their mill. They have about twenty-five thousand acres of land.[32]

By June 1875, they had installed a double circular saw. Additional machinery to produce other makes and types of lumber was one mule saw for flooring material, rustic and surface, and across the grain; a 24-inch planer, one edger, one crosscut saw, one ripsaw, and a picket machine. It was all powered by two 60-HP engines with two boilers 12 by 24 feet. The mill had a capacity of 20,000 board feet per day.[33] The brothers employed 50 men in 1875, and it took 16 large teams to haul the lumber to their yard in Santa Rosa and points throughout the county.[34]

Looking north at Heald & Guerne logway and log pond on Fife Creek, July 21, 1875. House on left is George Guerne's, about where 2nd St. crosses Fife Creek. JCS Collection

Things remained pretty much uneventful between 1869 and 1872 at Heald & Guerne's Mill. In June 1871, the first reported fatal accident occurred when Gordon Weaver, 20, was drowned while floating logs down Fife Creek to the mill.[35] During this era, any industry operating for six years without a fatality was remarkable. The reader should not be misled into believing that no accidents occurred in Big Bottom mills. This will be brought forth in due course.

In August of '71, Heald & Guerne built a lumber yard in Healdsburg to expedite more sales.[36] During the winter of 1871-72, when the logging areas became bogs, they turned out shingles at the mill at a rate of 15,000 to 20,000 a day.[37]

By early April 1872, their mill was in full operation — as were the others — engaged in laying out a railway to haul logs and building a new dam across Fife Creek for a log pond.[38]

The railway was a crude affair powered by oxen and horses. A more detailed description of a logging railway is given in Chapter VIII.

In mid-August of '72, there was a breakage in machinery, as described by a correspondent:

> The arm or crank broke off which caused the pitman to pull out one of the eyeheads and break the coupling of the piston at the crossheads. The damage by breaking will amount to at least $100 while the loss of time will amount to more than $1,000.

The mill was completely furnished with all the modern machinery of the times requisite for the most elaborate ornamental work in moldings, brackets, et cetera. The mill was complete in all its appointments from the large circular saws to the delicate machinery necessary in cutting out the handsome cornices which adorned the best-furnished buildings.[39] The work when complete was all moved and stored in a large open warehouse at a safe distance from the mill in case of fire. It was capable of cutting 25,000 feet a day.[40]

The mill was put in order for the coming lumber season with a large addition constructed and new machinery put in.[41] Nothing out of the ordinary transpired in relation to the mill during 1873; it was kept running until the heavy rains commenced. They did construct the redwood railroad along the north side of the river towards Ludolph's Mill.[42]

The mill ran during the winter of '73 -'74, producing shingles until they had 1,500,000 sawed.[43] Then they went through the usual shutting down, repairing, cleaning, and the

---

SHINGLES ! SHINGLES !

R. B. LUNSFORD HEREBY NOTIFIES builders and others that he has on hand shingles in any quantity desired, at the following low rates—$2 12½ per M. at his mill, one mile north of Guerneville, and $2 25 per M. delivered on the cars ready for shipment.
apr26dwtf

Santa Rosa Democrat, April 26, 1871

Loggers' and millhands' shanties with Livreau and Ely's Sawmill on the right, located northwest of

firing of the boilers again for the season's cutting of 1874. The season saw Heald & Guerne close down the lumber yard in Healdsburg, but other than that, it passed uneventfully, as did the winter of shingle-making during which 1,000,000 were produced.[44] The capacity for rough lumber per day was 20,000 feet.

From the start of the lumbering season in '75, shipping was brisk, with an average of 30 teams arriving a day,[45] and in June, the mill was cutting a daily average of 25,000 feet.[46] The whole season was a relatively prosperous one in which was seen only one minor breakdown which occurred in October when an engine strap broke and necessitated a half-day shutdown for repairs.[47]

There were a few other mills in the area which were given a passing notice in contemporary writings at this time. More will be said regarding later years. In most cases no specific location was given, but at times, maps did. These mills were Norton's Mill across the river in May's Canyon, and R.B. Lundsford's bark and shingle mill on the north side of Big Bottom.[48]

As already hinted, there were accidents in the early days of the lumber industry. Accidents took place everywhere: out in the woods, in the log piles, the mills, and in the lumber yards. Man and animal alike were injured and maimed for life. And in some cases, life, itself, would receive the blow. Already related was the first fatality at Heald & Guerne's.[49] It was also the first accident to be noted in contemporary chronicles. Other accidents from passages in the papers tell the story:

... Orender, who runs the edging saw at Livreau's & Ely's Mill at Guerneville, had his thumb and tips of two fingers of his left hand cut off.

Samuel Moore, a workman at Ludolph's Mill, had his leg broken by a log which rolled over.

William Braden took it on the chin at Murphy's Mill. A log rolled off a car onto the platform while he was prying with a crow bar. The crow bar snapped up and broke the victim's jaw in two places.

A shinglemaker . . . had the misfortune to cut his foot badly across the instep while chopping

Guerneville at the base of Pool Ridge, April 12, 1873. JCS Collection

and hemorrhaged profusely.

. . . Ritchie had his left hand caught by a saw and had two fingers and the thumb badly lacerated (at Mead & Hassett's).

. . . George Mogland, employed by Murphy Bros., met with a serious and perhaps fatal accident being caught between two logs and badly crushed.

An ox belonging to R.G. Longly was killed by a falling tree.

John Hansen, a sawyer in Clar's shingle mill, had his left thumb cut off early Monday morning.

The cases and stories are legion. Some were injured slightly; others met slow and horrible deaths. They continued month after month, year after year.[50] The most grisly death to occur during these years was that of a young man named George Donaldson, who worked at Heald & Guerne's logging camp.

In blasting a log, the charge had failed to throw it open and he got upon it to drive a wedge. When the strain on the chain, by which the cattle were pulling on one half, caused it to separate suddenly, he fell forward between the halves. A piece of redwood slivered by the blast fell upon him, causing his death in a few moments.[51]

Mills, large and small, usually started sawing for the season when the roads were passable for heavy freighting after the winter and spring storms. The closing down was usually brought about with the first heavy rains of winter.

While each individual mill had its minor ups and downs financially, they remained pretty close together. The "Big Four" (Heald & Guerne, Murphy & Brackett, Livreau & Ely and Ludolph) united early in 1872 to form the Sonoma County Redwood Association and ran the following advertisement in the Russian River Flag and Sonoma Democrat for the season:[52]

Lumber Rates

The Sonoma County Redwood Association have this day agreed upon and established the following scale of prices for lumber at the mills.

To dealers having yards and who are conducting a legitimate business:

Common lumber per M	$10
Clear lumber (rough) per M	$20
Surfaced & timbering lumber per M	$20
Rustic per M	$22
Siding per M	$18
Retail Prices	
Common lumber per M	$12
Clear lumber (rough) per M	$24
Surfaced & timbering lumber per M	$24
Rustic per M	$27
Siding per M	$20
Half-inch siding per M	$24

Anyone purchasing 20,000 feet or more at retail prices will be entitled to five per cent discount. All bills of lumber sold will bear interest at the rate of 1% per month after 30 days.

— Livreau & Ely

— Murphy & Brackett

— H. Ludolph

— Heald & Guerne

I hereby certify that the above is a correct statement on the scale of prices agreed upon and established by the Sonoma County Redwood Association.

— Oliver C. Ely, Secretary.

In 1873, the association was still in existence although not by title. The "Big Four" plus a new associate, Korbel, again placed an advertisement of mutually agreed prices:[53]

We, the undersigned lumber manufacturers in Sonoma County, agree to sell our lumber at the following wholesale and retail rates, from date, until the same shall be changed by consent of all parties concerned. Wholesale dealers are only those who keep yards and pay license for the same.

	Retail	Wholesale
Rough board & scantling	$10	$9
Surface & flooring	$20	$18
Rustic	$22	$20
Rough Clear	$18	$16

Two dollars ($2) extra for sizing and surfacing. All bills of lumber sold to bear interest at the rate of one per cent after thirty days.

— Heald & Guerne, R. Murphy, Livreau & Pendleton, W. Korbel, B.F. Pendleton, Secretary.

1874 was a slow year and saw a slump in the lumber market. The mills quit running about the 1st of November, except Heald & Guerne, which ran on short time. Murphy was the only mill to advertise until September; and his prices, as stated in the advertisement, were $3 lower per thousand board feet than in 1873 of the "Big Four."

Common lumber (board scantling per M)	$7
Dressed lumber (rustic, tongue & groove & surfaced)	$17
Delivered in Santa Rosa and vicinity:	
Rough per M	$15
Dressed per M	$25

— Guerneville, March 17, 1874.[54]

The association was late in having their prices printed for the cutting season. Five months later, the advertisement announced:

September 5, 1874, Sonoma Democrat

The Sonoma County Lumber Manufactuers and Dealers have this day agreed upon and adopted the following Scale of Prices:

For Lumber at the Mills	
Rough wood and scantlings	$11
Surface and flooring	$20
Rustic	$22
Rough clear	$18
For Lumber at the Santa Rosa Yards	
Common	$20
Surface and flooring	$30
Rustic	$32
Shingles	$3
Fancy pickets	$35

$2 extra for sizing and surfacing. All bills of lumber sold will bear interest at the rate of one per cent per month after thirty days.

— Heald & Guerne, Murphy Brothers, F. Korbel & Brothers, Meeker Brothers, F.F. Gifford, Hassett & Mead, John K. Smith.

R.G. Longley's bullteam in front of Livreaux & Ely's Sawmill near Willet's timber claim, April 12, 1873. Amy Bagley Hatch Collection

I hereby certified that the above is a correct statement of the scale of prices agreed upon and established by the Sonoma County Lumber Association.

– A. Korbel

Secretary of the Association,

Santa Rosa, August 15, 1874.[55]

The Association may have been an experiment in monopolizing the lumber industry by uniting against the independents that were spread throughout the redwoods of Sonoma County. In later years such small and transient sawmills were called "peckerwood mills" or "gypos," for gypsy. No prices were given by the individuals, save that of Murphy, in '74 to compare and see if the association was high, low, or about normal.

1875 was rather prosperous. Teams were coming in to haul by the middle of March. As already stated, Murphy's Mill, in May, had 40 teams arriving in one day and Heald & Guerne averaged 30 per day. So brisk was business that there was quite a rivalry a among the teamsters as to the size of the wagonload taken on single trip.

...One team started with 8,000 feet of lumber, but failed to reach Santa Rosa with load intact. Today another eight-horse team left town with 7,356 feet placed upon two wagons, one in rear of the other.[56]

The county bought lumber from Heald & Guerne for the Redwood Road District at $18 per 1,000 feet of redwood and $20 per 1,000 feet of fir.[57]

By the end of June all mills were running to their greatest capacity. There was such a demand for shingles during the summer that the 1,800,000 sawed at Heald & Guerne's Mill as well as the split shingles made in the woods by independent parties were hauled out — all of them.

The men who achieve excellence in their respective professions, whether they be blacksmith, stage driver or doctor, earn recognition from their peers by producing the maximum from the resources available. So it was with the loggers: the ones who actually wielded the blade and reaped the forests. The most predominant name was Peckinpah, the surname of five brothers. These men, John, Dave, Charles W., Edgar and H.H., were loggers, mill operators, a boat captain, and, in the words of the townfolk, "were musicians of superior attainments" and were "not excelled by any this side of the bay."[58] John was a mill operator and harness maker, Dave the pilot of the "Quickstep" during its short life. Edgar, H.H. and Charles were loggers. All of them were employed at Livreau & Ely's Mill in one capacity or another. In 1878, they remodeled Lundsford's Shingle Mill, and in '79, took charge of it.

Others that received recognition for their expert and superlative work were Davis Brass, E.O. Carter, Lumbard, A.S. Hewlett, Whiting, H.S. Savage, and Alf and Allen Williams.

One anecdote has been around for over 100 years about the church located in Santa Rosa that was built from one tree. This tree has its own history recorded, something not done to all the other redwoods in this region. This particular tree was about a mile northeast of Guerneville. In 1873, John Woods felled the 275-foot redwood, and the top shattered upon landing, but the tree was not wasted. It was cut into saw logs by Ferdinand Secott. Then James Hindley's oxen dragged the logs to the landing where William Smith came in with his horse teams and hauled the logs to Murphy's Mill. Rufus Murphy was given an order for enough lumber to build a church, so for a little free advertisement, and secondly, to display the end product of one California redwood, he had specifically ordered all the lumber be kept separate. Alonzo Hewlett was foreman and manager of Murphy's Mill and thereby followed the directives. The lumber was edged by a man named Harrison and was planed by T.J. Butts. The final yield was 78,000 board feet of which, as the lumber people were wont to point out, 57,000 feet was free of knots. The top portion which broke off was converted into shakes for the building.[59]

1. R.R.F., December 29, 1870.
2. Power's Sawmill had many sites: Mirabel Park (date unknown); Summer Home Park, 1864-67; Pocket Canyon near Shortridge's, 1867; near Korbel's, 1868-71.
3. R.R.F., April 25, 1872.
4. R.R.F., July 18, 1872.
5. S.D., September 1872.
6. S.D., June 28, 1873.
7. S.D., November 15, 1873.
8. S.D., March 3, 1873.
9. R.R.F., March 16, 1874.
10. S.D., May 2, 1874.
11. Land Patents, Book A, p. 624, Sonoma County Recorder's Office.
12. Appendix to Journals of Senate and Assembly, 21st Session; State of California.
13. R.R.F., May 4, 1875.
14. R.R.F., June 29, 1871.
15. R.R.F., March 7, 1872.
16. R.R.F., April 11, 1872.
17. R.R.F., February 21, 1872.
18. R.R.F., April 25, 1872.
19. R.R.F., November 7, 1872, and S.D., July 5, 1873.
20. Sonoma County Tax Records, 1873. In possession of Sonoma County Library.
21. Today's Main Street. The frame remained standing until February 1881.
22. R.R.F., November 28 and December 26, 1874.
23. R.R.F., July 24, 1876.
24. R.R.F., September 24, 1877.
25. R.R.F., April 25, 1872. He was running a mill on Pine Creek, a branch of Atascadero or Green Valley Creek, in 1867.
26. See map of 1864.
27. S.D., September 6, 1872.
28. S.D., March 3, 1873.
29. S.D., August 2, 1873.
30. Promiscuous Records, Book B, p. 14. Sonoma

County Recorder's Office.

31. S.D., August 12, 1874.
32. Appendix to Journals of Senate and Assembly, 21st Session; State of California and Santa Rosa Times, March 4, 1875.
33. S.D., June 17, 1875.
34. Bancroft Scraps, Set W, Vol. 5, p. 277.
35. R.R.F., June 29, 1871.
36. R.R.F., August (?) 1871
37. R.R.F., March 7, 1872.
38. R.R.F., April 25, 1872.
39. R.R.F., August 22, 1872.
40. S.D., September 7, 1873.
41. S.D., April 5, 1873.
42. Sonoma County Archives and Tax Records
43. R.R.F., March 16, 1874.
44. R.R.F., January 15, 1875.
45. R.R.F., May 4, 1875.
46. R.R.F., June 5, 1875.
47. R.R.F., September 7, 1875; and Sonoma County Atlas of 1877, p. 35.
48. R.R.F., August 10 & November 23, 1875; and Sonoma County Atlas, op. cit.
49. See page 59.
50. R.R.F., July 20, 1872; and S.D., June 20(?), 1875.
51. R.R.F., May 4, 1875.
52. R.R.F., May 23, 1872; and S.D., July 6, 1872.
53. S.D., August 14, 1873.
54. S.D., March 21, 1874
55. S.D., September 5, 1874.
56. R.R.F., June 8, 1875.
57. Bd. Sup. Roads, Book 1 (April 7, 1873) p. 24.
58. R.R.F., March 7, 1872.
59. The Church Built From One Redwood Tree; reprinted by Ann M. Connor, Coronado, California, pp. 33, B, C, D.

Guerneville circa 1873, looking south at today's main intersection, before the railroad arrived. Building on left is RubenWilliams saloon. Large building on right is Guerneville Hotel. JCS Collection.

Guerneville on July 21, 1875, looking west toward Guernewood Park. Photo by J.H.P. Downing, Healdsburg. JCS Collection.

Chapter 11

GUERNEVILLE 1872 – 1875

The first few years after the creation of the Redwood Township were uneventful: most of the basics had been established to form a community, so there were not many "firsts" left for any person to do. The community developed further with what it had and expanded.

There were only two places for various governmental procedures in 1872 that periodically occurred in town. One location was the school, used for elections and tax collecting, and the other was Bagley's Store just down the block on the south side of First Street.

People of the area shopped at least at two groceries, one being Bagley's, but who the other was is confusing. All available information has a more favorable inclination towards Ruben Jones, rather than Frank Stewart. One newspaper states:

> . . .the two groceries . . . appear to be in a very flourishing condition. One of them lately changed hands and the new proprietors, Ruben Jones & Company, are erecting a fine new building on the site of the old one and intend to run a first class saloon.[1]

Three months later the paper printed:

> Guerneville now contains two stores: one kept by J.W. Bagley and one by Frank Stewart.[2]

It also stated there were two saloons, probably those of Ruben Jones and Ruben Williams. Jones kept a good line of ginger and water. Saloon-keeper Jones surely must have thought "there must be more than one way to skin a cat" and tap the loose change of the people of temperance.

Other buildings in town were the Temperance Hall, a social hall, the school, a hotel, and various residences.[3]

The town became large enough to have a scheduled stage running from Santa Rosa via Sebastopol, Forestville, Ludolph's Mill, and Murphy & Brackett's Mill. As the *Sonoma Democrat* reported:

> Regular communication with that part of the county has been for a long time an urgent necessity. There is a large population in and around Guerneville and the adjacent mills who heretofore had no means of communication with this place [Santa Rosa] except by private conveyance to Sebastopol, where they connect with the Bodega Stage. This stage will start from this place on Tuesday, Thursday, and Saturday at 7 A.M., returning the same day leaving Guerneville at 1 P.M.[4]

It was run by J.P. Clark of Santa Rosa. During the winter, the roads were washed out and so was the schedule. However, Clark, like the rest of the transportation in the county, ran again as soon as the roads were passable. In 1873, he had the contract to haul the mail between Sebastopol and Guerneville for the next five years.[5] His business was successful, and he purchased a new eight-passenger wagon made by H.M. Black & Company of San Francisco. On its first run, it made Guerneville in 3 1/2 hours with nine passengers.[6] The stage ran until the end of the year with "Raney" at the reins.[7]

The above quote about "regular communication" and a stage schedule leads to two questions: (1) what happened to the stage of 1870? and, (2) how was mail brought to and from Guerneville between 1870 and this date of 1872? No answers are found.

The roads were few and far between. Most were trails and not surveyed or proclaimed county roads save Pocket Mill and May's Canyon. A public road was applied for to run along the north side of Russian River to Chormicle's, about where the present-day forestry station near Korbel Winery is located. This proposed public road was surveyed, viewed and recommended in March 1873.[8] This road has become a vital artery to the lower Russian River from the Santa Rosa Valley via present-day Mirabel Park and Hacienda.

The roads opened in the middle of April, but in December 1873, were closed uniquely as well as abruptly. It had snowed to a depth of a foot and, due to the weight, the limbs would break. The end result was blocked roads, and to such an extent that while some literally hacked their way through, others used either the creek or river beds.[9] Raney, Clark's driver, took all day to cut his way to Guerneville from Forestville.[10]

Another road which was very much sought after was a thoroughfare to the newly worked Cinnabar Lode on the western slopes of Mt. Jackson.[11] There was a little trouble in trying to establish it. The road that was in existence and use was not a declared public road; it started at Ruben Williams' home in town and went north to Murphy's Mill, thence through Peugh's and Piggott's lands to the Cinnabar Ledge.[12] A petition was presented to the Board of Supervisors by the local populace to have it declared as a public road. Peugh and another party apparently did not want it as such. The Board had the road viewed, was dissatisfied with the report, and asked for another. The results were still not desirable, and the road petition, plus the viewers' report, were rejected.[13]

The description of the roads during these years was not flattering as the reader now knows from previous pages. A perceptive writer stated:

> Some cities and towns build their hopes of future success and greatness upon the fact that they are at the terminus of a railroad . . . as Healdsburg once did. Guerneville, however, cannot quite do that, but we can boast of being the terminus of all the wagon roads that come into the place; and even better than that, for they all terminate before they get here for about four months in the winter.[14]

An attempt was made to have a perma-

Paulson's Directory, 1874. JCS Collection

nent bridge constructed across the Russian River from Pocket Road to Guerneville in 1875. Petitions, five in number, were circulated throughout western Sonoma County, that part consisting of Salt Point, Ocean, Mendocino, Redwood Townships, and part of Santa Rosa Township. There were over 1,000 signatures for the erection of the structure.[15] The petitions were presented to the Board of Supervisors on May 3. The Supervisors visited Guerneville "for the purpose of selecting a suitable site for a bridge across said river."[16]

An engineer was appointed to draw up plans for erecting a bridge and a rough idea as to costs. The report stated it would have had two 180-foot spans at a cost of $18,500.[17]

Two days after the Board viewed the site, they reconvened at the county seat, and the matter was taken up for consideration. They considered it and rejected it.[18] The rejection was probably based upon the prohibitive cost and the small population such a bridge would

1872   1873   1874   1875

Guerneville School Teachers Left to Right: Ellis T. Crane, 1st Grade; C.H. Raney, 2nd Grade; E.R. Lillie, 3rd Grade, died August 1875 and buried in the first Guerneville Cemetery; J.N. Keran, 4th Grade; he married Sarah Torrance, daughter of S.H. Torrance. Photos by Joseph Downing, courtesy of Jesse Peter Collection.

serve. There was, of course, a low-elevation temporary bridge constructed across the Russian River each spring.

The road overseer from 1873 to 1874 was C.D. Yarborough when the roads were requested to the mines and to Korbel's. The overseer from January 1875 to 1877 during the agitation for a bridge was . . . John W. Bagley.

In 1873, John Taggart opened a new hotel on St. Patrick's Day.[19] It was located about where Buchanan's Cafe is now, facing South, on First in the block bordered by today's First, Church, and Second Streets and Armstrong Road. High compliments were paid to Taggart in conducting his establishment. He proved it with his grand opening,[20] supplying a dinner at a ball,[21] and serving the general public.[22]

Schoenfeld & Cassel's, a Santa Rosa firm, established a large branch store in town.[23] Even though they were doing a good business, a year later they sold their merchandising concern to Jacob Selling and his son, both of Sebastopol. It was then known as Selling & Company.[24] Selling (also spelled Schelling) sold all the supplies required of the school with the exception of textbooks.[25]

The Miriam School in Guerneville proceeded to grow in size and in number of students. From 1870 with 68 enrolled students, the juveniles increased to 159 enrolled in 1875. The number of schools in the district fluctuated from one to three. The Guerneville school was not of sufficient size to handle the daily attendance, so the menfolk had a vote in January 1875 to build a new school. The plan was negated by six votes, so the trustees put up an additional room. As a writer to the *Russian River Flag* said:

> It is to be regretted that those who ought to be interested did not think it a duty to provide better accommodations for the rising generation and at the same time a more ornamental structure than the present inferior building.[26]

The addition was constructed and finished at a cost of $1,000 by March 20, 1875.[27] The value of the property at this time was $1,730. This also included the other two schools in the district.[28] It appears lumber, labor and materials were easy to come by.

The Miriam School District was divided in November 1876, the new district called Ridenhour School District. The school building was east of Korbel's mill about 400 yards.[29]

John Taggart was appointed the third trustee for Miriam.

Julia Guerne, daughter of George and Eliza, wrote this anecdote about Guerneville's school in her notebook:

> Willets cut timber, selling to mill operators. One incident related was to the effect Mr. Wil-

lets was falling a big tree and it just missed the school house which was in session. The teacher, Mr. Clover, hurried his pupils to a place of safety.[30]

So much for recess!

The town really was jumping. Besides the school room being added onto the old building, the carpenters were busy in other parts of town. Abel Line, Daniel Giles and George Locke were among those pounding nails, square ones at that.

Another building was erected in early 1874 for the purpose of holding social gatherings, dances, et cetera. The "Independence Hall" was built and owned by 25 to 30 of the residents as a joint stock company. Its dimensions were 30 by 66 feet, about 40 feet high,[31] and was located just west of Bagley's store. The lower floor was used as a store. The Temperance Hall was located just east of Bagley; his own store had a social hall upstairs. If one hall was not in use, then another was.

Work was begun on the first church in Guerneville on February 15, 1875; it was completed and dedicated June 13 by the Rev. Charles J. Lovejoy of Santa Rosa.[32]

Other construction on a livery stable (Connell's or Ellison's) and saloon was brisk and was completed within three weeks during the same month of February. In early April, a restaurant was started along with two new saloons. This made a total of five saloons in town.[33] The restaurant was closed by legal attachment in June, and one saloon was closed due to a lack of profits in July. In May, a new hotel went up and was opened formally by John Folks.[34] The building activity slowed during the summer months with only a barber opening a tonsorial saloon in September.[35]

Another badly needed improvement was the bringing of potable water into town from springs on the neighboring hillsides. This came about in early July 1875. In September, the rumor was circulating the water cart was going to withdraw water delivery due to few customers. The people hoped it was only a ru-

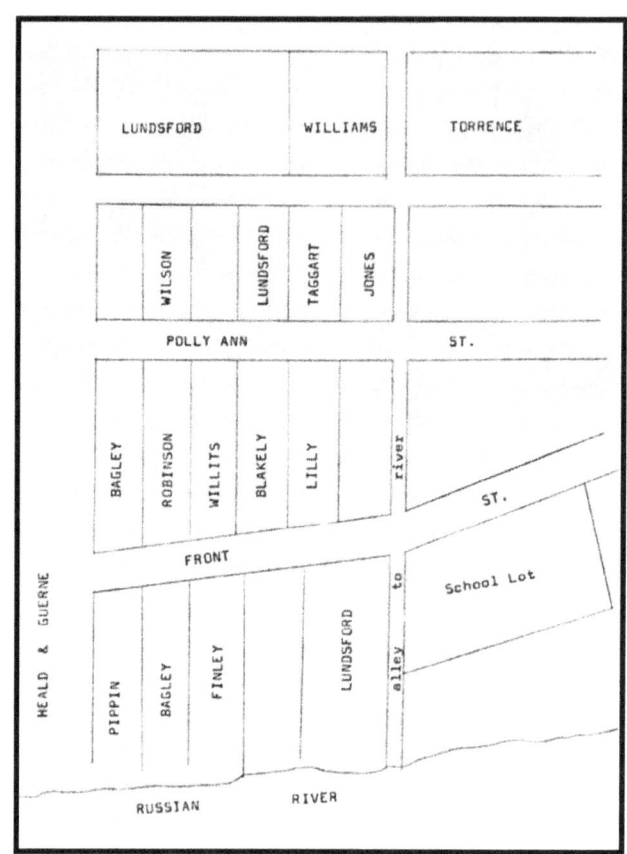

Guerneville in 1873, based on tax records

mor because as one citizen said, "Pure water is a luxury I should prefer to retain."[36] Ah, for the good old days!

Even with construction going up there was almost none coming down, whether by design or accident; there were one or two, though, by fire. One occurred when "a wooden chimney of the house of J. Poole ... caught fire."[37] The next was a year later, in 1874, when a fire was discovered under the board sidewalk in front of the Independence Hall.[38] Both were subdued with little effort.

Two weeks later, on June 6, 1874, the first serious fire occurred when T.J. Alley went to sleep with a lamp burning. He awoke to find the room ablaze. He tried to extinguish it, but only succeeded in burning his arm severely. The alarm was given, but too late. All was lost. Two neighboring houses caught fire, but by hard work of all present, the contents of one was saved and the other was confined to minor damage.[39]

T.C. Pippin's house on Front St. (now 1st St.) April 12, 1873. J.H.P. Downing Photo, Healdsburg Museum

Another fire took place a year and a half later in November 1875. The fire caught from a stove pipe in a connecting building to Schelling & Son. The stock was cleared from the shelves by the townsfolk while the bucket brigade, plus axes and crowbars, did their work in subduing a potential conflagration. The damage to the building was minimal, but injury to the goods by water and removal was considerable.[40]

Such were the beginnings of the Guerneville Volunteer Fire Department.

Though the era of the 1870's was of a lawless nature in the state, if not the country, segments of society tried to correct or help their fellow man. And so it was with the temperance movement that started in the mid-60's, trying to save people from alcohol and its sea of human misery.

As the reader now knows, Guerneville was not without a local chapter in support of abstinence.[41] Guerneville, with other chapters of the I.O.G.T., and other temperance people, probably brought pressure to bear on the California Legislature, for in March 1874, the solons passed "an act to permit the voters of every township or incorporated city in this state, to vote on the question of granting licenses to sell intoxicating liquors."[42]

The act stated that after one-fourth of the voters in the township petitioned the Board of Supervisors, the Supervisors had to proclaim a special election for a liquor license or against a license. If passed, no one could sell or dispose of any intoxicants in quantities less than five gallons. However, it would not affect druggists in selling liquor for medicinal purposes. A violation of the act was a misdemeanor with a fine of $25 or one day in jail for each dollar of the fine.[43]

A petition was circulated in Redwood Township and was signed by 86 men of both camps, abstinence and indulgence. The resulting election was a victory for temperance, there being a 15-vote majority for the cause. The *Russian River Flag* correspondent reported:

> The vote was the largest ever polled in this precinct, both parties bringing out their full strength. The bars were closed but the whiskey was outside, as I have been told it was placed by the well at the saloon, free for everybody. The feeling ran high, both sides working with a will. There were several wild battles fought and one man received five knife wounds, all caused by whiskey.[44]

The temperance advocates celebrated their victory by building a bonfire, Peckinpahs' New String Band played away, and the people fired anvils.

Then the State Supreme Court stepped onto the scene and felled a crushing blow to temperance.

The turn-about came when George Wall, a Contra Costa County resident, petitioned the California Supreme Court to be released from jail after conviction in violation of the liquor law. Arguments presented to the court both for and against were long. After deliberation, the court made the decision that, in summation, "the power to make laws conferred by the constitution on the legislature cannot be delegated by the legislature to the people of the state, or to any portion of the people. Let the petitioner be discharged."[45]

There was just as much a celebration at the revocation of the law as there was passing it, and Guerneville had its share of them:

John Taggart, Jr., Washington Finley, John Wilson, and another man, were firing anvils . . . on the reception of the news on the decision on the Local Option Law by the Supreme Court. The firing continued from 11 until around 1 o'clock Wednesday morning. The four were close around the anvil. From the best accounts, the young men were priming the anvil. Wash Finley stood near with a bottle of powder containing, it is thought, three pounds.

It is supposed that a particle of the card which covered the previous charge was on fire, either in the anvil or around it. As one of the party was preparing for the shot, the explosion came; simultaneously the bottle burst in the hands of Finley and the whole party was hurled through the air. The scene which followed was painful beyond description. Finley, who held the bottle, was fearfully burned. His face, hands, and neck are badly powder stained and cut by fragments of glass. He can hardly speak, and his eyesight is in great damage. A fragment of flying glass severed Taggart's jugular vein and the blood spurted to a distance of several feet from the wound. For a time his life was in jeopardy. A man named Hickey succeeded in tying the vein. Taggart's face is also badly cut and powder marked. John Wilson received a bad cut over the eye which lowered the upper lid over his cheek, he is otherwise cut and burned. The fourth man escaped with little injury. Mr. Twombly, one of our leading Good Templars of Guerneville, was on hand administering to the wounded.[46]

Though this was a setback for Temperance, it was not a major one. As we saw, some legislation could be passed. In this case it was arrived at through legally weak channels.

1. *R.R.F.*, April 25, 1872. Up to this time Ruben Williams had the only saloon.
2. *R.R.F.*, July 18, 1972.
3. *R.R.F.*, April 25, 1872.
4. *R.R.F.*, July 10 and 18, 1872. The social hall was above Bagley's store. See *S.D.*, November 1, 1873. The hotel was called a boarding house.
5. *S.D.*, September 7, 1872.
6. *S.D.*, April 12, 1873.

7. *Ibid.*
8. *S.D.*, December 13, 1873.
9. Bd. Sup. Records, "Roads," Bk. 1, pp. 6 and 14.
10. *S.D.*, December 6, 1873.
11. *S.D.*, December 13, 1873.
12. See Chapter XIV "Quicksilver."
13. Bd. Sup. Records, "Roads," Bk. 1, p. 112.
14. Op. Cit., pp. 141 and 157.
15. *R.R.F.*, March 16, 1874.
16. Son. Co. Archives, Original petitions to Board.
17. Bd. Sup. Records, "Roads," Bk. 1, p. 211.
18. Son. Co. Archives, original report to Board.
19. Bd. Sup. Records, "Roads," Bk. 1, p. 222.
20. *S.D.*, March 22, 1873.
21. Ibid.
22. *S.D.*, November 1, 1873.
23. *S.D.*, May 2, 1874.
24. *S.D.*, June 27, 1873.
25. *R.R.F.*, March 16, 1874.
26. Son. Co. Archives, County School Records.
27. *R.R.F.*, February 27, 1875. "The addition to the school is 24' x 18' and still the school isn't much." S.D., February 13, 1875.
28. *R.R.F.*, March 20, 1875 & S.D., February 13, 1875.
29. See appendix, "Miriam School."
30. *R.R.F.*, December 4, 1876.
31. From undated note written by Julia Guerne.
32. *R.R.F.*, March 15, 1874. See "Former Associations," Chapter 22.
33. *R.R.F.*, June 22, 1875.
34. *R.R.F.*, May 15, 1875.
35. *R.R.F.*, June 8, 1875.
36. *R.R.F.*, September 28, 1875.
37. *R.R.F.*, September 7, 1875.
38. *S.D.*, March 22, 1873.
39. *R.R.F.*, June 16, 1874.
40. *R.R.F.*, June 30, 1874.
41. *R.R.F.*, November 9, 1875.
42. See I.O.G.T, Chapter XXIX.
43. *Statutes of California*, 1873-74, Chapter XXX, p. 434.
44. R.R.F., June 2, 1874
45. *California Reports*, Vol. 48, 1874, pp. 279-322.
46. *S.D.*, October 1874.

SANTA ROSA
— AND —
GUERNEVILLE STAGE
To or from the City in One Day.

ON AND AFTER MONDAY, June 14th, the Guerneville Stage will leave Santa Rosa immediately on the **Arrival of the Morning Train from San Francisco.**

Leave SANTA ROSA Mondays, Wednesdays, and Fridays at 10:30 A. M.

Leave GUERNEVILLE Tuesdays, Thursdays and Saturdays at 8 A. M. connecting at Santa Rosa with evening train for San Francisco.

je12 tf   J. P. CLARK, Proprietor.

Santa Rosa Daily Democrat, 1875. JCS Collection

Felling trees at Korbel from Harper's Weekly, Oct. 30, 1886. JCS Collection

Chapter 12

LUMBER MILLS 1876 — 1880

In previous chapters, twelve mills were described covering as many years with their changes in partnership and locations. The large mills of Murphy, Heald & Guerne, and Korbel got larger these next five years, while a few small operations sporadically sprang up around the neighboring countryside.

Murphy's Mill, located on the Laughlin Claim,[1] started the sawing season of 1876 in February. The season for them remained short, though, due to the great amount of lumber that was on hand and the small amount of customers; the last cut of lumber was the end of July.[2]

By the first of April 1877, they built a new road down to Guerneville for the new season's hauling.[3] Lumber trade was better in '77 than '76, as it was still brisk in October, and they had only a grand total of 100,000 feet of lumber on hand.[4] They shut down after the first heavy rain in mid-November. By this year, the mill had an increased daily capacity of 30,000 board feet as compared to that of 18,000 feet in 1872. This made the annual product approximately 5,000,000 feet. Their reserves were about 15,000,000 feet.[5]

The season of 1878 started in April as usual with short hours for the mill hands who were getting ready to cut. The loggers were working full time building up a stock pile of logs at the mill,[6] but nothing out of the ordinary transpired during the summer. In November, the Murphy brothers purchased a town lot adjacent to the railroad for a lumber yard, and at the end of the month shut down for the winter.[7]

Save two exceptions, nothing was mentioned about the mill in 1879. In November, T.J. Ludwig of Santa Rosa bought all the lumber at the mill,[8] and the amount that Murphy's sawed during 1879 was perhaps something over 2,000,000 feet.[9]

In February 1880, the Murphys had some minor litigation in the courts in a dispute between themselves.[10] Wyman Murphy, in April 1874, bought a half interest in the mill for $10,000. It was to be paid in full by December 1878. One year later, in 1879, $1,943 was still due. He was forced to sell some property at public auction by court order in order to fulfill the contract.[11]

After litigation, the mill spent three weeks making repairs for the coming season and started up on March 8. Business was brisk up to July when a few minor repairs were made.[12] The most important event is deliberately omitted here, but will be given due notice later, that being the joining in partnership of Guerne, Ludwig and Murphy.

The winter of 1875-76 was not an idle one around Heald & Guerne's Mill. They were producing furniture, tables, brackets, picture frames, and a variety of ornaments from birds-eye and curly redwood.[13]

On February 5, they, being desirous of ascertaining the capacity of their machinery for shingles (and adding some excitement to a hibernating village) made an experiment. The results were 180,000 shingles made and one bunch ready for market.[14]

There were three on-the-spot "reporters, (actually local residents — Nate Manning, Ellen Bagley, and a third, unknown) who relayed this information to the *Russian River Flag* and the *Sonoma Democrat*. Manning wrote,

Messrs. Heald & Guerne had concluded to

see how many shingles they could cut at their mill (running two saws) in a day's run; therefore on Saturday, the 5 inst., operation started at an early hour and everybody was on the double quick to do their share of the work. The jointers in particular were doing their level best, vowing that when the day's work was done their special machine should be ahead. The machines in use are first, the Huntington which is in general use on this coast; the other an old Hall machine which has been knocking about in these woods for quite a while, and was considerably the worse for wear until improved to sum [sic] considerable extent by Mr. Geo. E. Guerne one of the proprietors. Formerly, when run by Mr. Willets, it did an average cutting of from 5 to 6,000 shingles a day, but enough of the history of the old machine.

The race was closely contested the Huntington being the general favorite in the morning but at noon they were about even and the Huntington backers began to weaken and go over to the old machine. When the run was finished and all the shingles bunched, the tally was as follows: Hall machine, 90 1/2 thousand, Huntington, 89 3/4 thousand, making a total day's run of 180 1/4 thousand, showing the old Hall machine 3/4's of a thousand ahead, being a very close race.

Messrs. Robinson and Klein jointed on the Hall machine — two of the best jointers in the mill — while Messrs. Seward, Guerne, and several others worked the Huntington. During the time and while the excitement was at its highest several parties took advantage thereof and trimmed up their fingers to suit them. Among these were Mr. Dave Plank who thought two of his were too long and therefore shaved the points off and Mr. [George?] Locke, who thought one of his too long and too large, so he clipped the end off one and trimmed the side of the other. They now express themselves well satisfied with the length and shape of their fingers.

I almost forgot to mention an improvement which Mr. Geo. Guerne has added to the Huntington machine which naturally facilitates putting in the block. It consists of a small carriage so arranged that when a block is put on, a very slight move will run the block into the machine and it is ready for cutting almost as quick as thought. A block can be put in and cut while the other machine cuts one shingle. The above sawing was done with an average quality of blocks and Mr. Guerne says that with choice blocks he can cut 250 thousand shingles in the same length of time.[15]

Another wrote that this number of shingles was,

> ... the largest number ever made by the same force on this coast. The usual run is 5 thousand shingles in two hours. The run was started with a number of blocks on hand, but stopped with an equal number. The force to run the machines was: one man to haul up the logs, 2 crosscut sawyers and 6 men exclusive of fireman, engineer, and saw filer. The shingles are bunched by boys at the rate of 12-1/2 cents a thousand. A boy at work for Mr. Guerne aged 17 named Henry Ayres bunched in 11 hours 50 thousand shingles.[16]

They shut down for a couple of days so that all the mill hands could clear the mill pond and creek of the winter's flotsam that had collected there during heavy rains and flooding. Shingle production continued to the

HUNTINGTON'S PATENT SHINGLE MACHINE

For simplicity, durability and rapidity of action, these machines have no equal, cutting from 3,500 to 4,000 per hour. They are now used by all the principal millmen on the Pacific Coast.

PRICE, complete, with One Saw, $450.00.

JCS Collection

Heald and Guerne's Mill, looking west. The office building at lower left stood until 1969; this area is now Safeway Market. Atlas of Sonoma County, 1877.

end of February.

In March, a foundation was laid for a new two-story building to be used as their office, part of which was to be used as a reading room by their employees. It was completed by the end of April.[17]

The season's milling began the first of April with the use of a new improved edger. It was an uneventful season with only one week's idleness due to needed repairs in mid-August. In early October, they went to running on short time to obviate lighting up the boiler. The mill shut down for over two weeks, though, because of a storm that lasted without cessation for four days the last of October.[18] The season then became good enough for hauling and the mill continued operations until the holidays.

A summation of lumber products from Heald & Guerne's Mill during 1876 was taken from the edger's book:

April	18 days cutting		460,950 feet
May	24	"	596,180 feet
June	20	"	456,200 feet
July	12	"	340,600 feet
August	18	"	500,700 feet
September	24	"	586,200 feet
October	13	"	358,000 feet
November	7	"	170,500 feet
December	14	"	200,060 feet
Totals	150	"	3,669,390 feet

...making a daily average of 24,463 feet, all sound, good lumber, 2/3 of it being clear. During this time 500,000 plain and fancy pickets were made.

From the 1st of January to the 1st of April they sawed shingles, making 1,500,000.[19]

The lumber season for 1877 saw a railroad siding in their lumber yard. They built tram ways leading from the mill along each side of the rail siding to convey the lumber for easy loading of the cars. The lumber trade was, for them, prosperous during the year. Only one breakdown occurred, this in July when the main shaft broke.[20] They switched to short

Heald & Guerne's Mill, at 1st and Mill Streets, looking west, circa 1875. Amy Bagley Hatch Collection

Murphy's Mill north of Guerneville, two miles north of town, 1875. Amy Bagley Hatch Collection

time in mid-September, though business remained brisk, and shut down in December for the winter's holidays.

The daily capacity during 1877 was 30,000 feet per day,[21] though some sources state that Heald & Guerne were cutting 25,000 to 35,000 feet.[22] The annual product was 3,000,000 to 4,000,000 board feet.[23]

Tax records for 1877 show that the firm had in its possession:

Land	1,180 acres
Lumber	350, 000 bd. ft.
Shingles	800,000
Cordwood	150 cords[24]

In 1878, rain storms were sufficient enough to deny the company time to cut from mid-January to mid-March (no mention was made of any mill producing shingles). Steam was up in the boilers for a couple of days the first of April and needed repairs were made for the coming season's run. At the same time, loggers were stockpiling logs in Fife Creek pond.[25] The crews remained shorthanded, as they were on short time until mid-May. By then they were just six hands less of a full crew and were cutting 20,000 to 25,000 feet a day.[26] By the middle of June, business was at full crew and capacity. On August 23, the cylinder head blew out, and the mill lay idle about two weeks while repairs were being made.[27]

The loggers filled the pond with logs while the mill was in its state of repair. One day's tally was over 50,000 feet, hauled from the Willets Claim by one four-mule team.[28]

Autumn saw the mill change to short hours in late September and shut down in early December.

On March 2, 1879, the greatest storm and flood known up to that time by anyone occurred. Lumber was scattered, a portion of the mill fell into Fife Creek, and buildings were moved.[29] The lumber was salvaged as were the buildings; the cleanup lasted two to three weeks.

Summer Bridge at Guerneville, July 22, 1875. This load of lumber is going to Santa Rosa via Pocket Canyon. Downing photo, courtesy Healdsburg Museum

The milling, which started in April, was interrupted with a few breakdowns. In June, a shaft snapped, in mid-August, a log, eight feet in diameter and twelve feet long, scaling over 4,000 board feet, was being drawn up into the mill when the ramp under the weight of the 16-plus-ton log gave way. The ramp was repaired and the sawyers continued the following day. In mid-October, the mill was idle while a pump was fixed.

The season's total sawing in "round numbers, three million feet of lumber" was reported by T.H. [Heald] to the *Flag*:

> The amount of labor employed was 5,218 days at a cost in a round number of $15,000. One million feet of the timbered sawed was furnished by W.H. Willets, on a contract and cost $6.25 per thousand feet, or $6,250 for the million feet delivered. The remaining two million feet at the same rate would amount to $12,500, total cost of timber, $18,750. The other incidental expenses amount to between $2,000 and $3,000.[30]

His report stated the number of carloads shipped by Heald & Guerne were 358 of lumber, 56 of cord wood, and seven of posts and pickets.

The joining of Guerne and Ludwig of Santa Rosa and the disposal of Heald's holdings, alluded to before, occurred in the month of November 1879. This was the first change in ownership since 1865. T.J. Ludwig bought all the lumber at Murphy's Mill the first of that November, and by the end of the third week, purchased Heald's share of the Guerneville Mill.[31]

The mill operated on and off from December through February because of the holidays and weather.

Then another change occurred in the ownership of the mill when the Murphys joined the firm on March 23, 1880.[32] At the same time, if the reader recalls, the Murphys had just finished litigation and started up their mill for the season, which operated apparently as a separate enterprise for the year.

Guerne and Company had a branch of the railroad extended to the "logging camp" with a switch and landing in April.[33] From past information as to where most of the timbering was occurring, indications are that this line ran up to the Willets Claim, described before as present-day Laughlin's Field.

The mill started cutting in May, which is late for the season. One cause, besides legal matters, was a late storm which lasted five days in late April and washed out the railroad.[34] However, once the mill was going, it ran 12 hours a day[35] and employed approximately 50 men.[36]

In July, financial trouble again struck the lumber firm. The mill shut down, but most of the mill hands found employment at the other mills.[37] The problem was between Guerne & Ludwig and their creditors.

The problem arose the first of the year when they stopped paying their bills and signing promissory notes. They then failed to pay the notes when due. The creditors got together and filed their civil suits on July 6, 1880.[38] They were:

Korbel Bros.	$400 note,
	$2,100 in lumber
S. Armstrong	$2,000 note
G.W. Thompson	$250

Santa Rosa Daily Democrat, March 15, 1877

A.S. Pierce	$600
Bloom & Cohn	$352 in goods
Mather & Co.	$752 in goods
G.A. Davis	$741 in goods
SF & Northern Pacific Railroad Co.	Unknown

All cases except the railroad and Armstrong were dismissed September 29, the parties having reached a mutual agreement. Armstrong got a default judgment November 8 for $2,197. The railroad's case lingered on and was finally dismissed in 1902.

The mill resumed shipping about the end of September[39] at a rate of four rail cars a day.[40] They fired up again mid-October and ran to the end of the year.

The firm had 700 acres in its possession in 1879-80 besides a lumber shed at Fulton and yards at Cloverdale and San Rafael.[41]

Another operation upstream was Ball & Cain's Shingle Mill. In the contemporary writings, confusion exists as to who were the partners and the mill's location. Some items state "Ball's Mill," another item "Cain's Mill," and another article "Ball & Cain's Mill." It could be possible, though highly improbable, after perusing the numerous accounts of the mill(s), that there were three separate mills. The mill will therefore be handled as a single enterprise rather than a multiple one.

Early in 1876, the mill was well stocked with shingles. Cain, in July, moved the mill and put in new machinery — exactly where is not known, but it was in proximity to Guerneville.[42] Similar to the lumber mills it ran through December, but with only a few men working during late fall.[43] The immediate area had "quite a settlement" surrounding it.[44]

Only one accident was reported, when H.D. Oliver kicked a line instead of using a board to guide it on to a "bull wheel." His heel caught and he was dragged around the wheel several times, his head striking the floor with each turn. Two months passed before he could "carry on in a reasonable way."[45]

The Peckinpah brothers, in October of 1876, put up a shingle mill down river near Dutch Bill Creek.[46] Later, C.L. Peckinpah leased Lundsford's shingle operation in May of '78.[47] After it was remodeled by the brothers, it was capable of turning out 30,000 shingles per day. A season's run would produce five million.[48]

1879 saw the same arrangement between Lundsford and the Peckinpahs. In September, the mill shut down for the season, which was extremely early, but it was due to a lack of business. The last day's run produced 50,000 shingles.[49] In mid-November, they ran for a short spell which made a year's total of five million shingles cut, the same amount as in 1878, but in less time.[50] They started running again in June 1880 with the shingle mill they built in 1876 (both operating at the same time).[51]

Norton & Penquite's Mill was located in May's Canyon. They started their 1877 season the first of July. The head sawyer was G.W. Wertz. They were operating in 1878.[52]

A new mill was erected by Messrs. French and McFadyen on the Torrance and Beaver claims in 1880.[53] These claims were located at and included the mouths of Pocket and May's Canyons. This land had not been touched, though roads run through it and mills were located in the upper segments of the canyon. By July, the mill was finished and sending carloads of lumber products by the end of the month.[54] In December, they purchased the machinery from Powell's Mill and installed it in theirs.[55]

The lumbering industry changed in the fashion as most industries do, producing more in less time with lower costs. To do this the mills installed better machinery that performed at lower costs and at a higher rate. Examples taken from previous pages show a higher production rate:

Murphy's Mill

| 1872 | 18,000 Board Feet/Day Capacity |
| 1875 | 25,000 Board Feet/Day Capacity |

1877	30,000 Board Feet/Day Capacity	

Heald & Guerne

1876	24,500 Board Feet/Day Average
1877	24-30,000 Board Feet/Day Capacity

Lundsford's Shingle Mill

1877	15-25, 000 Shingles/Day
1878	30,000 Shingles/Day
1879	50,000 For one day

Other Mills Between 1876 and 1880

Other mills that were given passing mention were Smith's Mill "across the river,"[56] Mead & Hassett's Mill, that was described in Chapter X on Polly Ann Street,[57] and Korbel's Mill. Korbel's (as big an operation as it was) was given little attention other than the attraction of tourists to the big trees in the area. In 1877, its capacity was 30,000 feet, and annual production was put at 5,000,000 feet.[58] In June 1879, they shut down for two weeks and possibly for the season.[59]

Torrance's Mill in 1875-76 was producing pickets. It is not known if this was his old mill by the river or the new one.[60]

Another mill was Kimball's "near Guerneville." The only fact known about it is a year's production. From December 1875 to December 1876, they cut 4,220,872 feet of lumber and 1,576,550 shingles.[61]

One man who appeared at this time was Col. James Boydston Armstrong. His mill cut just as much as the others, but what he did with his timber reserves is history and worthy of a separate chapter.

1. See Chapter X.
2. *R.R.F.*, July 24, 1876.
3. *R.R.F.*, April 2, 1877.
4. Son. Co. Tax Records, 1877.
5. *Son. Co. Atlas*, 1877, p. 17.
6. *R.R.F.*, April 8 and May 6, 1877.
7. *R.R.F.*, November 4, 1878.
8. *R.R.F.*, November 3, 1879.
9. *R.R.F.*, December 1879(?) article on lumber production.
10. Son. Co. District Court Records, Case #2876.
11. At this time, Rufus Murphy was going through divorce and needed money. Son. Co. District Court Records, Case #2717.
12. *S.R. Rep.*, July 21, 1880.
13. *R.R.F.*, December 7, 1875 and February 11, 1876.
14. *R.R.F.*, February 11, 1876.
15. *S.D.*, February 19, 1876.
16. Ibid.
17. *R.R.F.*, March 21, 1876 and April 10, 1876.
18. *R.R.F.*, October 30, 1876 and November 13, 1876.
19. *R.R.F.*, February 22, 1877.
20. *R.R.F.*, July 2, 1877.
21. *Son. Co. Atlas,* 1877, pp. 17 and 24.
22. Bancroft Scraps, Set W, Vol. 5, pp. 277 and 284.
23. *Son. Co. Atlas,* 1877, pp. 17 and 24.
24. Son. Co. Tax Records, 1877; McKinney's District Directory 1878-79, p. 245. In 1878, they had 1,260 acres.
25. *R.R.F.,* April 8 1878.
26. *R.R.F.,* May 20. 1878.
27. *R.R.F.,* August 25 and September 9, 1878.
28. Ibid.
29. *R.R.F.,* March 10 and March 24, 1878; letter dated March 5 1878, San Francisco Chronicle.
30. *R.R.F.,* December (?), 1879, article on lumber production.
31. *R.R.F.,* November 25, 1879.
32. *R.R.F.,* March 23, 1880.
33. *R.R.F.,* April 6 1880. In 1881, they ran the iron track to Hulburt Canyon.
34. *R.R.F.,* April 27, 1880.
35. *S.R. Rep.,* May 19, 1880.
36. *Son.Co. Hist.,* 1880, p 353
37. *R.R.F.,* July 20, 1880.
38. Son. Co. Superior Court Records, Case #164.
39. *R.R.F.,* September 20 and October 11. 1880.
40. *S.R. Rep.,* October 7, 1880.
41. *Son. Co. Hist.,* 1880, p. 353.
42. *R.R.F.,* July 31, 1876.
43. *R.R.F.,* December 18, 1876.

44. *Ibid*
45. *R.R.F.*, January 18, 1876.
46. *R.R.F.*, October 9, 1876
47. *R.R.F.*, May 6, 1878
48. *R.R.F.*, May 20, 1878.
49. *R.R.F.*, September 22, 1879.
50. *R.R.F.,* December (?), 1879
51. *R.R.F. Rep.*, December 2, 1880
52. *R.R.F.*, July 2, 1877
53. *R.R.F.*, May 25, 1880
54. *R.R.F.*, July 20, 1880
55. *S.R. Rep.*, December 2, 1880.
56. *R.R.F.*, June 26, 1876.
57. *R.R.F.*, July 24, 176
58. *Son. Co. Atlas,* 1877, p. 17
59. R.R.F., June 23, 1879
60. S.D., October 9, 1875
61. S.D., January 20, 1877

Russian River looking upstream towards Mt. Jackson from the summer bridge at Guerneville, July 22, 1875. The town is to the left, Pocket Canyon to the right.
Downing photo, courtesy Healdsburg Museum

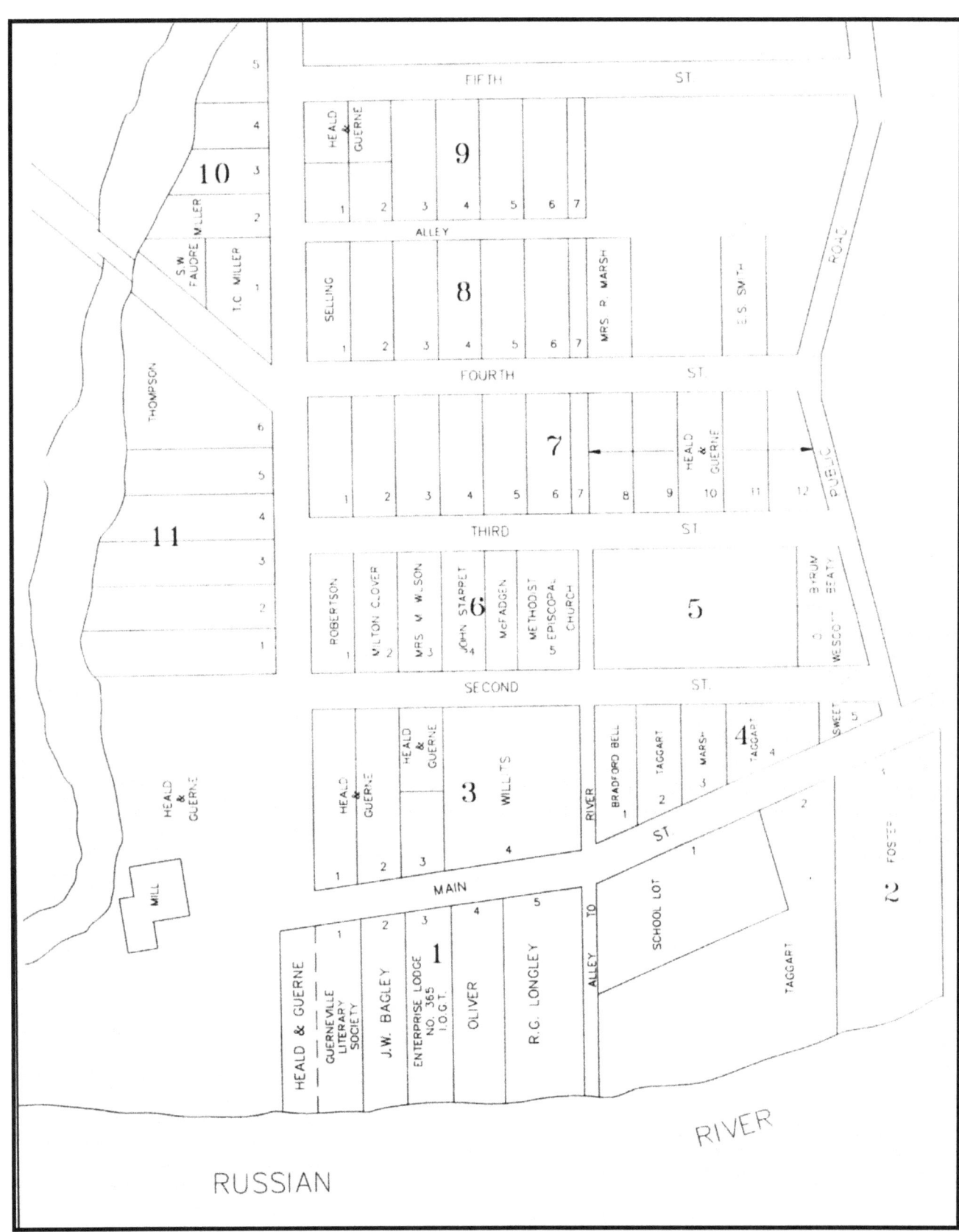

**Guerneville 1877, based on Sonoma County Tax Records. North is at top.
Map by Keith Schubert, 1995.**

Chapter 13

Guerneville 1876 — 1880

After the "building boom" of 1875 died down and the mercury mines were producing steadily, the townsfolk turned to other forms of industry to produce more varied products and more jobs, thereby increasing the wealth and importance of the community.

In February 1875, there was talk around town about starting a chair factory. The chair factory upstream at La Cross [Hacienda] had been producing since about 1868, and the factory at Forestville had a wide reputation for a like product.[1] In June a meeting of Guerneville citizens at Bagley's Store formed a joint stock company to start a chair factory. The capital stock of $4,000 was subscribed.

> The company will, after incorporating, commence the erection of buildings adjoining the mill of Heald & Guerne, who will furnish the steam power to carry on the factory. A responsible party agrees to take 2,000 chairs monthly at mutually satisfactory prices.[2]

This, with a proposed mill, would use and render marketable the oak timber scattered about the local ridges.[3]

The factory started producing in 1876 and, with the arrival of the railroad in 1877, its rate of production increased.[4]

It is known that there were three factories, although some writers believe there was only one, located in Forestville. S.W. Faudre, besides owning the factory and property at La Crosse, also owned property in Guerneville along Fife Creek.[5] The atlas of 1877 of Sonoma County states that, "Guerneville has one chair factory run by S.W. Faudre."[6] A news article by a regular Guerneville correspondent, dated September 24, 1877, says:

> S.W. Faudre has disposed of his chair factory to Messrs. Florence & Bonner, who will continue the business at the same place.[7]

In 1880, it was still owned by them.[8]

The Forestville factory was started by Faudre, also. Again, to quote the atlas of 1877:

> The Factory was started by S. Faudre on Russian River, three miles from Forestville. He continued the business for five or six years, selling chairs from two to three dollars a piece. He then moved the factory to Forestville where it has been for the past ten years. S.P. Nowlin ran it for six years then sold it to John Manlett.[9]

Using that information, it appears that Faudre started in 1861-62, then moved to Forestville in 1867, and, circa 1871, Nowlin took over. Faudre then left, apparently to his own factory at the river.[10]

The flood of 1879 damaged the Guerneville factory, all of which will be told later. Everything was corrected, as its capacity of production was 70 chairs per day in 1880. The machinery was being run by an eight-horsepower engine.[11]

It was also in 1876 that the first movement for incorporation of the village took place. It was first discussed and agitated by the "solid" and "the more enterprising class" of the town's citizens in February of that year. The boundaries of the valleys were surveyed and established by A.L. Cox of Santa Rosa, which was one of the steps toward incorporation.[12] However, that was as far as the endeavor got, and nothing more was accomplished.

What made them think they could qualify as a municipality?

By June 1875, there were 47 roofed buildings. There were 33 families, equaling 175 persons, not including mill hands.[13] Heald &

Guerne employed approximately 100 men.[14] Other businesses were the chair factory, a butcher store run by K.A. Kemper, a blacksmith, two stores (Bagley and Jacob Selling, proprietors), two hotels, four saloons, Clark Bros. Cabinet Shop and two shingle mills.

Building during the six-month period from November 1875 through April 1876 totaled 30 constructions, principally dwellings within the village limits.[15] However, these facts and figures were not the reasons for incorporating. The remains of the major industry, stumps, was the cause of it:

> Huge redwood stumps and logs encumber even the most public street which is narrow, crooked, and almost wholly destitute of side or crosswalks. Other streets are in a more lamentable plight even and to invest our thriving little village with municipal privileges is the only way of bringing order out of this utter chaos.[16]

Improvement of the town continued without incorporating. In January 1876, Brad Bell, town butcher, built a new market next to his house on First Street. His former place of business, next to the post office, became Clark's Cabinet Shop. On the rear streets, several homes were built. Between January and June, the whole town buzzed with activity. Stumps were being cleared from the streets, and Heald & Guerne's and Lundford's additions were re-surveyed for homes. Taggart put an addition onto his hotel, and Heald & Guerne built a new two-story office. Ruben Williams, not about to be left out, had a new residence built on the old site. James Watson had the second restaurant, the first to stay open (the first closed in a few months during 1875). Business in boring wells showed a parallel increase with the growing amount of homes.

Not all construction was fit, however. There are those in every occupation that do not quite make the grade or achieve even a semi-professional status. They remain bumblers:

> A carpenter lately came to town and agreed to put up a building according to the plan in two weeks' time. He built it with such a twist and wind that he couldn't put up a square foot, as was wanted, without tearing down and rebuilding. Every time he took a good look at his work, he would get drunk, and finally ran away, leaving the building for others to finish.[17]

Immigration to this part of the country continued. Houses were still in demand and real estate was constantly changing hands. This influx of population was possibly stimulated by the impending arrival of the railroad in Guerneville. The railhead was located at this time, 1876, at Korbel's Mill and was being pushed down river to town. It was commonly reported in local gossip that the Korbel Brothers made Guerne and partners pay dearly for the railroad extension because the former enjoyed a tremendous transportation advantage for a couple of years. With the railroad, an increase in trade with the outside world could be expected and more jobs to be had in the vicinity.[18]

The railroad, after much anticipation, finally arrived in town with its dignitaries, the town's hopes of prosperity, the Chinese, a cut into the profits of the teamsters, and much revelry; it was the bearer of tidings good and bad.

> On Saturday, Feb 24, 1877, the cars steamed into town for the first time. They were greeted with a salute from anvils, and blasts from the mill whistle, to which the engine responded. It was a general holiday in town, and nearly everyone was out to see the long and anxiously looked for train was no illusion. The track is laid nearly to the creek [Fife Creek], and Polly Ann Street is fast becoming a network of rails, side tracks, switches and the like.[19]

Just as quickly as the train came in, it went out. The rains came, and slides blocked the track. It did not return for three weeks. This was to be an oft-repeated episode.[20] With the railroad came tourism, not on a grand or profitable scale, but tourism just the same. Prior to the advent of the railroad, a few people would venture through glens and vales of the area to see the redwoods. So began the future way of a major enterprise of Guerneville and the Russian River resort area.

Besides rails, there was still that natural avenue for freighting and travel: the river. As has been stated before, several serious attempts had been made to use the river commercially by King, Bagley and Peckinpah.

During the winter of '76-'77, boats were used to haul passengers from the south side to the town side of the river. One belonged to S.H. Torrance. Beginning every winter when the first rise of the Russian River forced the removal of the foot and vehicle bridge, Torrance would render ferry service until the passing of the spring rains.

Until the completion of the railroad, passengers would ride to the railhead at Korbel's and then take Peckinpah's Russian River barge to town. As one passenger wrote, it was "rather a novel and romantic trip but lengthy and uncomfortable."[21] Even after the completion of the railroad, the barge was pressed into service during winter months. Slides, as already stated, would close the rails at Korbel's, so to bring the freight down the river, Peckinpah's boat was used.[22] The vessel was withdrawn upon the clearing of slides in spring.[23]

During the winter of '77, C.W. Ragan built a stern-wheeler which was a marked improvement over the barges. Passengers and freight were hauled during the times when all roads were closed.[24] At the end of March, it was chartered for a successful round-trip to the ocean.[25] Thereafter, it disappeared from history's pages.

The third means of transport, besides the rails and river, were the rutty roads. On May 1, 1876, J.W. Bagley submitted to the Board of Supervisors a report of county roads in Redwood Township. The total mileage came to 27. The bridges costing over $50 were:

> The bridge across Russian River at Guerneville [summer bridge].
>
> The bridge across Russian River at the old chair factory [Hacienda].

FIRST OF THE SEASON.

GRAND EXCURSION
TO
GUERNEVILLE

FOR THE BENEFIT OF

Santa Rosa Library,

SATURDAY, MARCH 24, 1877.

If the Railroad is open to Guerneville at that time and the weather is fair. If not, the following SATURDAY is designated.

HO! FOR KORBEL'S MILL,

Guerneville, the Quicksilver Mines,

AND

THE REDWOODS.

THERE WILL BE TIME ENOUGH FOR those who can get carriages at Guerneville to go out and visit the famous Mount Jackson and Great Eastern Quicksilver Mines, through Big Bottoms, the finest body of Redwood timber in the world.

The Excursionists will be conveyed on the elegant cars of the San Francisco and North Pacific Railroad Company, under the direction of COL. A. A. BEAN, the careful, attentive and obliging Superintendent of the road.

Tickets for sale by the Librarian.

Fare, Going and Coming, only $1.

☞ Every care will be taken by the management for the comfort and pleasure of excursionists.   mar9-dwtd

Santa Rosa Daily Democrat. JCS Collection

> The bridge across Russian River at Korbel's [Odd Fellows' Park].
>
> The bridge across Carmichael Creek.
>
> The bridge near John Cargile's [Hacienda].
>
> The bridge on Pocket near old Kemper Place.[26]

Undoubtedly all of these bridges were partially dismantled when heavy winter rains came.

During some storms, the roads were impassable. When the stage couldn't make it all the way to town, the drivers would carry the mail for the remainder of the journey on foot. It would take, at times, two days to arrive from Santa Rosa, a rate slightly better than one-half mile per hour.[27]

The Pocket Road was a constant problem for the teamsters. The worst part was the "dreaded" Pocket Hill grade. In February 1876, Roadmaster Bagley started constructing a new grade to avoid bridges and culverts that washed out with every heavy rain.[28] The grade was finished in May. The funds allotted by the Board of Supervisors for this construction amounted to $1,000. A release of $750 was made after the Murphy brothers and Heald & Guerne applied $500 in work in conjunction with Bagley on the grade.[29]

Another road went from Guerneville to the new mills on Dutch Bill Creek. This was opened by John Folks and L.M. Ellison in August of 1876. Ellison, in conjunction with J.E. Sweet, ran a stage three times a week from town to Dutch Bill, but two months later they ceased the regularly scheduled trips and ran only when passengers or freight were to be carried there.[30]

A third road was petitioned for in 1877. The road would shorten the distance from the coast to the county seat and greatly benefit any and all travelers. Viewers were appointed, surveys made, and estimates taken, but nothing came of it.[31] Be that as it may, the local populace applied to the Board of Supervisors again in January 1879. The Board made appropriations to prepare the opening of the road, provided it was supplemented by private subscriptions. Over $1,800 in labor and money were pledged upon completion.[32]

The possible reason for requiring matching funds was that county funds were small for such a large project. Of course, local property taxes supported practically all government services in those days. Most tax money went into roads and schools. Poor settlers could "work out" part of their poll tax by working themselves and teams on road repair and construction. An example of available monies for such construction was given by Roadmaster C.D. Yarbrough for 1878:

Redwood Road District Funds	
Cash from Road Fund	$583.00
No. of Poll Tax Returns	$264.00
Amt of Poll Tax Sold	$792.00
Total Receipts	$1,330.00
Expenditures for Road Work	$1,364.14
Overseer Paid Per Diem (Total)	$ 306.00
Total Expenditures	$1,670.14 [33]

The new road went from Guerneville to Ingram's (Cazadero) and on to the coast at Henry's Sea View.

A direct result of an increased population with its needs of transportation and shelter was the arrival of Wells, Fargo & Co. in 1877. A branch office was established in town at Selling & Co. with Jake Selling as agent.[34] Selling, a year later, retired from business, and Mr. S. Schloss took over his company. The express office was removed, and Messrs. Heald & Guerne became agents. In 1880, Postmaster Gerhardt Dietz, who maintained a jewelry store, was appointed as express agent.[35] His office was located at his establishment across the main street from the school.

Wells, Fargo & Co., being express and mail carriers, attracted larceny to its conveyors. Although crime has been with Man since Adam, there are those certain unlawful acts — usually those of violence by force or fear — that become infamous or near infamous. One man who became infamous by literally harassing Wells, Fargo was Charles E. Boles, alias "Black Bart." The third holdup of a stage in his career of 28 is the one of local interest and curiosity. It is believed after he robbed the Fort Ross-Russian River stage on August 3, 1877; he then proceeded to Guerneville. Many histories and articles have said the stage came to Guerneville, but, as stated before, the road to the coast was not constructed until 1879. The idea of the stage coming into Guerneville possibly originated from the fact it was believed

John Folks' Hotel on 1st Street between Church and Armstrong Road, July 22, 1875

Black Bart came to Guerneville the next morning.[36] This is the only connection Black Bart has ever had with Guerneville.

Being remotely located, any diversion from the daily routine was seized by the populace with enthusiasm, and such it was with the coming centennial of the United States. In May of 1876 a group of citizens came together to decide how to raise funds and lay out a program. In a few weeks the committee could report they had $250 on hand, a fairly good amount. For comparison, a mill hand earned approximately $30 per month.[37]

The various committees worked with a will. John Folks, proprietor of Folks Hotel on First Street, was retained for the birthday dinner since his "reputation for fine cuisine was well known throughout the county." The entertainment committee engaged Clark's Band. Advertisements were put in "local" newspapers, the weeklies such as the *Russian River Flag* of Healdsburg and the *Sonoma Democrat* of Santa Rosa.[38]

Then the long, anxiously looked for day arrived, the Fourth of July 1876. The mills were silent and the lumber teams penned. Flags were flown to the breeze and fire crackers were exploded by Young America.

At 10:30 a.m., the procession left for the

> **GRAND CENTENNIAL**
> **Celebration in Guerneville!**
> On the 4th of July, 1876.
>
> THERE WILL BE A GRAND CENTENNIAL CELEBRATION in Guerneville on the 4th of July, 1876. The necessary funds and a No. 1 brass band having been already secured, a good time is expected.   may27-dwtd

Sonoma Democrat. JCS Collection

Anna Taggart, who played the Goddess of Liberty, at the age of 14. At 18 she eloped with Omar Shoemake in Jan. 1880. She died in 1888. Mabel Peter Collection

picnic grounds in the tall redwoods one-half mile north of town.[39]

The parade was led by three young ladies, J. Steel, Julia Smith and A. Smith, on horseback, each dressed in a color, red, white and blue. Then came the carriages with 13 representatives, each bearing the name of one of the 13 states, and in their midst was Miss Annie Taggart, costumed as the Goddess of Liberty. Along behind Guerneville's beauties came the townspeople in carriages and on foot, some 500 of them, nearly the whole town.[40]

The entertainment "was given in a genteel manner. A select choir sung the soul-stirring national airs in a charming style assisted by Miss Etta Folks as organist." Officers of the Day were:

President	Mr. John Taggart
Marshall	George Guerne
Chaplin	"Father" Walker
Orator	S.F. Hadsell

The Declaration of Independence was read by Samuel Duncan, Jr. The oration by Hadsell 'was a most excellent one. It was delivered and received undivided attention from the listening multitude."[41]

Then a basket dinner was enjoyed, followed by dancing through the afternoon. In the evening the Independence Ball was attended by 100 couples where they "chased the hours with flying feet to the enlivening strains of Clark's Band."

The celebration wound up at Folks Hotel at daylight the morning of the 5th. There was no liquor drunk by the celebrants nor accidents to mar the day.

But others back in town were celebrating the Fourth of July with a glass of cheer. Samuel J. Finley, age 55, went into Hi Epperly's saloon and tried to get a drink on credit. The bartender, Lambert Reardon, refused him as per instructions from Epperly. Finley got indignant about it, drew his knife, and said he would twist it into Epperly.[42]

The next time Finley came to town was on July 15, and his first stop was at 30-year-old Hi Epperly's. George Lidell was there and offered him and the boys to take a drink. Epperly, behind the bar, said, "The first man to take a drink without paying for it, I'll hit with a glass. I've given away enough whiskey and I'm going to stop it." Finley left saying he did not want any more.

The next day Finley went back to Epperly's saloon and asked Hi if he meant him when he spoke that way.

Epperly responded, "I mean you as well as the others. The boys have quit giving me money and I'm going to shut down on giving away free whiskey."

Finley then went down First Street to Folks's Hotel. There he related the incidents to C.S. Coleman and said he was not prepared for any trouble right then, but was going to carry a pistol for Epperly as long as he stayed in town and would use it.

Hi Epperly killed Sam Finley in a showdown in front of Ruben's Saloon, the building with a front porch on the upper left. The white building above with a single window is Epperly's Saloon. July 21, 1875. JCS Collection

Left: Hi Epperly's saloon on Main Street at the east end of town, 1875 Downing photo, courtesy of Healdsburg Museum.

That night Coleman told Epperly what Sam Finley said and to look out for him because Finley would kill him if he did not keep out of his way.

A week later, on July 22, Lambert Reardon was tending again at Epperly's when Finley came in and wanted a drink. Since Epperly told Reardon not to trust Finley with any more liquor, he told Finley that he could not charge it — Epperly did not want him around the saloon any more. Finley left. A while later Finley returned and declared he expected trouble with Epperly and was fixed for him. He showed Reardon a sheath knife with a four-inch blade and left again. Reardon told Epperly what transpired.

About 5 p.m. that afternoon, Epperly was shaving John Folks in the barber shop portion of his saloon. Finley was on the street, abusing him verbally. Epperly, getting nervous, excused himself and went out on the sidewalk. Finley dared Epperly to come over to him and said he would get him yet. Epperly declined to stake his life and went back into his saloon. Finley went into Williams' saloon across the street.

Dr. J.S. Wooley had a conversation with Sam Finley. Finley told him he had some words with Epperly, tried to get a fight out of him, and told him he was too big a coward to fight. He called him everything he could lay his tongue to in front of the doctor. Dr. Wooley spoke to Epperly in his saloon and told him to stay in his own place.

Epperly told the doctor he was afraid Finley would come into the saloon and go after him with a knife or a pistol. He said he had no pistol but showed the doctor a loaded shotgun he kept in his establishment.

Upon hearing the third threat that day, Epperly asked H.C. Rainey for a pistol. Rainey had one he was keeping for W.H. Manning and gave it to Hi, not knowing there was anything brewing between Hi and Finley.

Finley visited Ruben Williams' saloon that day on three occasions. It was well known around town that Finley had a turbulent character, especially so when under the influence of alcohol.

Around 7:30, Epperly crossed over to Williams' saloon where Finley was in the back room playing "pedro." When he entered the back room, he said, "Wash Finley stole my horse and Sam Finley is accessory to it."

Finley never said a word.

Epperly walked right up behind him and said to him, "I want you to stop this game. I want to settle this right here."

Williams stepped up and told Epperly his horse was up on the range. Epperly insisted the game be stopped.

Finley finally responded, "Mr. Epperly, I will talk with you after awhile. I'll see you later."

Williams again told Epperly not to bother the game but to go home and fix himself up because there was going to be a little dance at his (Williams') place. Then Epperly left.

It was close to dusk at this time, and the lamps in the various businesses were lit.

About ten minutes after Epperly left, Finley and H.C. Rainey walked out onto the porch. Finley mentioned the trouble to Rainey and said that he was going over to Epperly's Saloon. He stood on the edge of Williams' porch and hollered angrily, "Where's Hi Epperly, the damn son of a bitch! I'm ready to settle the fuss." E.W. Clark, joining them, told Finley, "He's not over there."

"Where's Hi Epperly, the damn son of a bitch!" repeated Finley.

They waited a minute, then Epperly appeared from his bar. "Here I am, but I'm not a son of a bitch, you damn coward."

About a dozen people gathered about upon hearing the commotion. Finley dared (or "stumped" as one witness put it) Epperly halfway across the dirt street, to which Epperly did in answer to the dare. Finley "stumped" him to come the rest of the way. Epperly said he didn't see any use in coming any further.

"You dirty coward, you've got nothing to shoot with," said Epperly.

"Maybe I hain't, maybe I hain't. Come on over a little closer and see if I have or not."

Epperly walked up with pistol in hand to Finley, who was still on the wood porch with his hand in his hip pocket.

"You have no pistol, if you have, you're afraid to use it," he said, as he stuck his pistol to Finley's chest.

At the same time, Finley pulled his hand out, saying, "You see, I have nothing." Then he made a quick motion.

The people saw Finley strike down at the pistol twice, solidly.

Epperly backed away and fired.

Finley followed him for 15 feet, striking at him twice more, but in vain. He threw up his hands, turned around and fell on his face in the dirt street, dead. A foot from his body lay a pocket knife.

Epperly went back to his saloon and said, "Boys, I'm sick and badly hurt." Ben Simmons went over to where Epperly was sitting and removed his vest and shirt.

Dr. Wooley examined Finley's body and found a bullet wound just above the heart. He then went over to Epperly's saloon and took a look at him. The doctor found where a knife had struck right over his heart, a scratch. And then as the knife came further down, it cut clear through to the bone, just to the center of the breast, a cut of close to four inches long. There was another wound near the nipple, straight in.

Epperly was arrested and taken to Santa Rosa. On March 5, 1877, eight months later, he bailed out. His jury trial started in mid-October and ended two weeks later. The jury deliberated 26 hours and came back with a verdict of not guilty, and with that, Epperly left Guerneville. For a small town such an event was a source of gossip for months and years.

Mother Nature dealt the area a blow which began Monday night, March 3, 1879. It caused the greatest freshet ever known since Guerneville was first settled.

Above: flood in Guerneville, looking at Lone Mountain, March 6, 1879. Photo by A.F. Allhands, Healdsburg.
Below: looking towards cemetery northeast of town. JCS Collection

In mid-February, there was over a week of rain without cessation — not enough to flood, but enough to saturate the ground and let the river remain fordable. Then the March storm hit. Tuesday afternoon, the river began to rise at a foot an hour, then slackened, cresting Thursday morning, March 6. It was 42 feet above the low water mark.

The track of the San Francisco & Northern Pacific Railroad was submerged as far as Korbel's old mill. The trestle work at Korbel's Mill in Elliot Canyon was 40 feet above low water mark, and the water stood six inches above it.[43] Damage to the mill and lost material were not less than $6,000, and as great as $8,000. The engine and boilers were all submerged.[44]

Near Guerneville, the bed for over 100 feet slid into the river, leaving the tracks dangling. Three weeks passed before the train returned.

Havoc occurred in Guerneville. The river overflowed its banks and backed up through Fife Creek until the entire town was inundated, with the exception of a portion of First Street. A few houses in other places were surrounded, but escaped being flooded. Twenty-two families were driven from their homes Wednesday night, the 5th of March. The houses were mostly one story high and had water to the ceilings. Those families living in two-story houses were removed by boat from the upper floors and taken to the Good Templars' Hall and Taggart's Hotel. Other places used by refugees were the church, post office, and the few homes that escaped damage.[45] The town's inhabitants vied with each other in their exertions to render needed aid and food.

An eyewitness for the *Sonoma Democrat* counted 18 houses that were either afloat or off their foundations. Two homes were washed away by the caving of the river bank. Fortunately their contents were removed some hours before. Joseph Batchelder's house floated off and settled down on a side of a hill some distance from the original site. Fences were carried off and barns and sheds tumbled every which way. Jim Taggart's barn floated

Left: Della Willets Caylat, mother of Thomas Willets Caylat, who died of diphtheria. Right: Dr. Toundrow came to Guerneville in 1877. JCS Collection

up the canyon near Murphy's Mill, sailed all over that section, finally returned, and settled near its original location — about a two-mile trip. The workingmen's cabins in the neighborhood of Heald & Guerne's Mill floated up to Murphy's also.

Heald & Guerne's Mill was hard hit. A portion of it fell in Fife Creek due to soil erosion. The two-story moulding house nearly did the same, but was saved by being secured with ropes. The mouldings, brackets and other wood work which were stored there in large amounts were removed. The lumber yard was a massive mess. Lumber piles were lifted up and scattered in all directions, some of them lost to the river. By the end of the flood, all the piles were gone.

The chair factory was lifted up and carried out into Fife Creek, but floated back to its place in a wrecked condition. The warehouse, containing several hundred chairs, was broken up and its innards scattered.

The fuel woodchoppers were heavy losers; their cord wood was swept away.

The danger was great, but "some scenes were grand." The air Wednesday was filled with the crash of falling timber — forest giants, over 300 feet in length, continued falling from the banks of the river and, on striking the water, "they would splash the yellow flood one hundred feet high."[46] Even after the flood subsided, the runoff down hillsides worked to loosen timber. Falling trees could be heard for days and presented danger on all sides for anyone who ventured out into the canyons.

When storm and flood abated, cleaning up became the order of business. Fences were reset, barns and sheds were righted and set in their proper places. Driftwood, trash and mud were removed from lot and house alike. Heald & Guerne's entire force took pump and hose, washed and re-piled the lumber. Some plane bits, lost in the mud of the creek when the portion of the mill fell in, were recovered by sluicing. Upon completion of repairs, the loss was totaled at roughly $1,000. The moulding house was moved alongside the railroad and restocked.[47]

The railroad, as previously stated, took three weeks to repair before the first train arrived. It was welcomed with a salute of the mill whistle. The locomotive returned same.[48]

All damages were repaired, and the town returned to normal.

Our friend, John Bagley, was the closest thing to a doctor until December 7, 1875, when Dr. F.A. Wooley arrived. He temporarily set up his office in Taggart's Hotel and before the end of the year moved to a permanent residence and office just down Main Street.[49]

He took care of townsfolk and the grisly accidents that befell the woodsmen — being crushed by rolling logs, cutting themselves with axes, mill workers cutting off fingers and hands.

A year and a half later, Dr. N. N. Toundrow of Fresno came to town. Guerneville could now boast of two medical practitioners.

In 1879, both doctors were sorely needed. The epidemic first to be identified in the Guerneville area occurred in late 1879. The culprit, diphtheria, made its first appearance in February 1877 when Freddie Folks, son of the Guerneville Hotel owner, was stricken.[50] He died February 11, 1877 at 5 yrs, 2 months, 3 days (from grave stone.) In November, the disease was rampant in other neighboring areas. Three deaths occurred in one week in the Occidental-Freestone district, while in St. Helena, Napa County, six died.[51]

The sickness did not show again for two years. Then it hit the community, and an epidemic ensued. Its first reappearance was made about November 18, 1879, and the first toll from diphtheria took place five days later when Bessie, the baby of Charles Willets, died.[52] Then David Currant, another child, passed away.[53] The epidemic spread up and down the river. The number of non-fatal cases is not known. All that is known are several cases that were fatal.[54] Three weeks later after a few days' sickness, a daughter of C.D. Yarborough succumbed.[55]

The toll was now three at Guerneville.

By mid-December, other members of the Willets family — the youngsters "Widdie" Willets and Thomas Willets Caylat — died.[56]

The toll: five.

With the arrival of the year 1880, no new cases developed, but for the Yarborough family. Six children were afflicted, and three of them died, including the daughter already stated.

The toll: seven.

Although the epidemic slackened as far as the general population was concerned, children were still dropping at the same rate: one a week. On Sunday, January 4, Squire Craver's daughter died, and on January 10, a little son of Aleck Watson of Austin Creek.[57]

The toll: nine.

"Bertie Yarborough died of diphtheria."[58]

The toll: ten.

Then the scythe of death abated. Only one case of sickness was reported in the month of February, none in March and none in April.

The epidemic had ceased.[59]

One of the first graveyards used by Russian River residents was Shiloh Cemetery near Windsor. This was during the mid-1860s. A few years later the McPeak Cemetery was developed at Hacienda. The earliest date of death found there on a headstone is 1859. But most early graves were late 1860's.[60]

Many of Guerneville's pioneers are buried there because no other cemetery was in the area. The family names of Blakely, Cargile, McPeak, Guerne, Ridenhour and Yarborough can be found there.

The first cemetery in Guerneville was located on top of the hill behind the Catholic church and west of the "Big Tree." Milton Clover was the first buried there in October 1876. Only three or four people were interred at this locale. Later in the year a new graveyard of three acres was laid out and surveyed by our friend, John Bagley,[61] located where it is today.

1. *S.D.*, Jan. 17, 1870.
2. The Forestville factory was producing 100 chairs a day and had produced 8,000 in three months. *S.D.*, July 31, 1875.
3. *S.D.*, June 5, 1875.
4. *R.R.F.*, June 8, 1875. S.W. Faudre is, according to Alley & Bowen's *History of Sonoma County*, 1880, supposed to have been established in 1874.
5. *S.D.*, Feb. 26, 1876.
6. *Son. Co. Atlas*, 1877, p. 24, Son. Co. Tax Records, 1877, and S.D., Feb. 3, 1877; bounded on North by Ayers, East by Pippin, South by Heald, West by Creek.
7. *R.R.F.*, Sep. 24, 1877.
8. *Hist. Son. Co.*, 1880, p. 353. Bruner and Bonner could be one and the same.
9. *Son. Co. Atlas*, 1877, p.23.
10. *Ibid.* States that it was moved in 1867 and remained in Forestville. *S.D.*, Jan. 17, 1870, states, "Faudre's is situated at LaCrosse and employs quite a number of men." Maybe he split his operation and had two concerns.
11. *Son. Co. Hist.*, 1880, p. 353.
12. *R.R.F.*, Feb. 22, 1876, *S.D.* Feb. 19, & Feb. 26, 1876.
13. *S.D.*, May 29, 1875.
14. *S.D.*, Apr. 10, 1875.
15. *S.D.*, Apr. 8, 1876.
16. *S.D.*, Apr. 9, 1876.
17. *R.R.F.*, May 8, 1876.
18. During the latter part of the decade, a depression occurred, caused, or so the people thought, by the presence of cheap Oriental labor in the western states. See Ch. 15, "Whites vs. Chinese — Part 1."
19. *R.R.F.*, Mar. 5, 1877.
20. A most complete story of the San Francisco and North Pacific Railroad (later the Northwestern Pacific) and specifically the Guerneville branch has been written by Fred Stindt.
21. *R.R.F.*, Mar. 21, 1876.
22. *R.R.F.*, Feb. 11, 1878.
23. *R.R.F.*, May 6, 1878.
24. *R.R.F.*, Feb. 5 1877.
25. *R.R.F.*, Apr. 2, 1877.
26. Bd. Sup. Recs., Vol. 6, p. 455. Actual report in county archives.
27. *R.R.F.*, Feb. 11 & Oct. 30, 1876.
28. *R.R.F.*, Mar. 6 & May 22, 1876.
29. Bd. Sup. Recs., "Roads," Book 1.
30. *R.R.F.*, Oct. 9, 1876.
31. *R.R.F.*, Apr. 2, 1877.
32. *R.R.F.*, Jan. 27, 1879.
33. *S.D.*, Mar. 29, 1879.
34. *R.R.F.*, Apr. 16, 1877.
35. *R.R.F.*, Jul. 6, 1880.
36. Wells, Fargo & Co. "Wanted" poster, Wells Fargo Bank, San Francisco.
37. *R.R.F.*, May 5, 1876, *S.D.* May 14, 1876.
38. *S.D.*, May 27, 1876.
39. *R.R.F.*, July 10, 1876.
40. *Ibid.*
41. *Ibid.*
42. *S.D.*, Oct. 27, 1877. The facts of this incident are from the testimony given during trial.

43. *S.D.*, Mar. 15, 1879.
44. *Ibid.*
45. *R.R.F.*, Mar. 10, 1879; *S.D.* Mar. 15, 1879. All information regarding the flood was obtained from these sources.
46. *Ibid.*
47. *R.R.F.*, Mar. 24, 1879.
48. *R.R.F.*, Apr. 7, 1879.
49. *R.R.F.*, Dec. 1875.
50. *S.D.*, Feb. 17, 1877.
51. *S.D.*, Nov. 24, 1877.
52. *R.R.F.*, Nov. 25, 1877.
53. "Register of Burial, Guerneville Cemetery." Ledger at Redwood Chapel Mortuary.
54. *R.R.F.*, Dec. 9, 1879.
55. Ibid.
56. *R.R.F.*, Dec. 16, 1879, "Register of Burial."
57. *R.R.F.*, Jan. 13, 1880.
58. *S.D.*, Jan. 10, 1880.
59. *R.R.F.*, Apr. 6 & May 10, 1880. Two other deaths due to diphtheria occurred in Guerneville, but these cases, two children, were from Canada — William Torrance's boy and William H. Bartley's oldest boy.
60. *Cemetery Records from Sonoma County California, 1846 to 1921*, by Daughters of the American Revolution of California, 1950.
61. Map of 1876, by Bagley.

Left: North Pacific Coast advertisement from 1877 directory. Right: Railway timetable, Santa Rosa Times, July 6, 1876. JCS Collection

Articles of Incorporation
OF THE
Great Eastern Quicksilver Mining Co.

Know all Men by these Presents, that we, the undersigned, have this day associated ourselves together for the purpose of incorporating, under the laws of the STATE OF CALIFORNIA, a CORPORATION, to be known by the corporate name of *The Great Eastern Quicksilver Mining Company*

And we hereby Certify, that the objects for which this Corporation is formed, are: *To Extract Quicksilver, and other metals from all ores, in the County of Sonoma, in the State of California, and to acquire by purchase or otherwise such real and personal Estate as may be necessary to carry on the above undertaking*

That its **Principal Place of Business** shall be in *The City of Healdsburg, Sonoma County California*

That the **Time of its Existence** shall be *Fifty* years from and after the date of its Incorporation

That the **Number of its Directors** shall be *Five*; and that the names of those who shall be directors and serve as such officers until the Election of their successors and their qualification, are:

NAMES.	RESIDENCE.
Isaac Gum	Healdsburg Cal.
A. J. Kane	" "
Ransom Powell	" "
Richard Abbey	" "
Willis Gaul	" "

Articles of Incorporation for the Great Eastern Quicksilver Mine, March, 1875.
Sonoma County Clerk's Office.

Chapter 14

Quicksilver — Part 1

Some mining had been occurring for several years in Sonoma County before the discovery of cinnabar on the western slopes of Mt. Jackson. In the northeast section of the county around Pine Flat and the Geyser area, mining activity was great and had wide recognition throughout the state. When discovery was made of cinnabar north of Guerneville, many thought it was just a low-grade pocket of ore and that all attention would focus again on the northeast. The *Sonoma Democrat* reported, "There is quite an excitement in Guerneville about mines, silver and quicksilver. The boys think they have struck it."[1]

The ledge of cinnabar was first discovered by R.E. Lewis in 1872, but he did not file a claim or announce it.[2] Who discovered the quicksilver deposit and who spread the word is unknown, but the news of the 1874 strike spread rapidly. One Guerneville resident, Hi Epperly, wrote:

> **Guerneville, April 21, 1874:**
>
> Almost hourly new discoveries and new locations are being made on well defined ledges of cinnabar, some of which are considered by experts to be as rich as the richest. Excitement is general. It can be truly said that Guerneville has quicksilver on the brain. Business here has been almost entirely suspended. Sawmills have been shut down and whole mill crews, headed by the most prominent men of the place, armed to the teeth with picks, shovels, and hammers, can be seen rushing furiously over the mountains digging holes, breaking rock, and posting notices of new discoveries. On the 18th, we held a miners' meeting, formed a new district, and elected our old friend, N.E. Manning, recorder. He finds his hands full of business every evening recording the claims located during the day.[3]

Manning became more than a recorder. He also became a partner in the "Croesus" and the "Lone Star." His partners were from Guerneville — Guerne, Fowler, Watson and Rodgers.[4]

The mining fever in town grew. The *Sonoma Democrat* decided to send one of its own reporters to get first-hand information as to just exactly what was going on:

> On reaching Guerneville we found the town in a feverish state of excitement. On the north fork of Big Bottom Creek [Fife Creek], the remarkable outcrop now known as the Great Eastern and Great Western mines is situated. The creek seems to have cut a passage way through the ledge which crosses it at right angles. From the bed of the creek on each side the wall of the outcrop, an ochre-colored cinnabar rock, rises to the height of nearly 50 feet perpendicular. The Great Eastern Mine extends 1500 feet and the Great Western mine the same distance on the other side in an opposite direction. On both ledges the outcrop appears above the surface. Near the creek bed and at many places on the hill the rock broken from the ledge shows cinnabar of good quality. We think there is an excellent prospect for a mine which would fully justify the expenditure of a sum sufficient to determine its value. The owners are Jack Gumm, Al Zane, William Zane, J.S. Palmer, W.T. Palmer, W.S. Cannon, Ransom Powell, Sam McMiller, and M. V. Hooten. Just below the mine described a claim has been located and is owned by the following parties: Ruben Williams, James Hickey, Rueben Jones, Lewis Wilson, Oliver Wescott, L. Cassel, and Jacob Selling. This location is supposed to be on a parallel ledge. They are at work upon it and have taken out good specimens of cinnabar.
>
> To sum up we think that the people in this vicinity are somewhat stricken with the mining fever, and may be led further than they now intend. Hundreds of claims have been located out of which it's probable that not more than one or two at most will ever repay the work and labor expended upon them.[5]

Workers of the Great Eastern Quicksilver Mine, circa 1885. Top row, second from right, owner Richard E. Lewis; top row fourth from right, Perry Mothom (?). Courtesy Ed Langhart.

How prophetic he was!

Another group of men from town formed the Guerneville Mining Company comprised of our usual, more-than-average successful businessmen:

George Guerne   John Bagley
August Guerne   C. Brown
Daniel Guerne   Levi Sutton
Samuel Graham   John Starrett
Robert Graham   D. Brass
R. Rowan[6]

Bagley was elected secretary (of course) and George Guerne was made treasurer (it figures). The chairman of the board is unknown. The gentlemen joined together in June 1874, but two years later the company was in debt $60 and had no working claim, so the enterprise folded. Their claim was the "Tiger."[7]

With all the claims being located, a proper survey was a necessity for each of the claimants. Of course, the inevitable dispute arose. Whenever a mine is about to prove valuable, adverse claimants are sure to appear. In one incident the owners of the "Roaring Lion" declared the survey for the "Great Western" encroached on their ground.[8] The deputy county surveyor, J.P. Wade, completed his survey by the middle of July '74 and forwarded it to the Surveyor General's Office as required by law prior to application for a patent.[9] The "Roaring Lion's" claim became a suit entitled *Selling vs. Zane* in February 1875. The disposition of this case is unknown. Another dispute much more serious arose a month later in August 1874. Epperly reported:

> The Great Eastern which joins the Great Western can only be described as a mountain of metal all of which, in my opinion, can be put through the furnace with satisfactory results. It is at present superintended by Capt. Eastman and leased by the Whilton Brothers. An old company wearing the name of the Santa Rosa Company, composed of a number of our best old pioneers located and recorded this nine years ago and are trying to hold it under the lay over law of 1863.

Left: Nate Manning, Mining District Recorder. JCS Collection
Right: August L. Guerne, brother of George, on Nov. 25, 1877. Mabel Peter Collection

Wilburn Williams, Jeff Campbell, E.C. Bray, James Peugh, and Seth Keeley, a part of the old locators, went to work on the mine this week to comply with the requirements of the law, but were persuaded by a part of the new company, R. Powell, W.S. Cannon, Zane Brothers and others, who carried elegant shotguns and seemed inclined to use them, to pack their tools and seek more genial company in Guerneville. Sudden is the life in the land of cinnabar.[10]

This "new" company was composed of Healdsburg men. They, like the Guerneville people, filed just as many claims — Zane Ledge Claim, Lewis Claim, Black Claim. The odd thing is although all claims were in the same area, these three claims were filed with H.M. Wilson, district mining recorder of the Healdsburg Mining District. Wilson was a justice of the peace for Healdsburg and, just like Manning of Guerneville, was a justice and mine recorder. No further distinction can be made as to who had legal jurisdiction in district recordings or which title — Healdsburg or Guerneville — was valid.[11]

The four main operations in the Guerneville District were the Great Eastern, probably named after the ship of the same name at that time, the Tiger, the neighboring Great Western, and the Roaring Lion, west of the Great Western.[12]

New claims were being located weekly and by February 1875, there were at least 75 locations filed in recorder N.E. Manning's books.[13]

Between mid-August and mid-September 1874, the Great Western became the Mt. Jackson Mine. In October, the Great Eastern was leased to Tiburcio Parrot and others for six years. Their agreement was the owners would get one flask of metal out of every four. A "flask" of mercury was a heavy cast iron cylinder which would hold about 76 pounds of the fluid metal.[14]

It was during all this commotion that a furnace became a necessity to reduce the ore to a refined product. In mid-July '74, a site was selected on the Mt. Jackson claim, and by mid-August was well under way in construction, using bricks made specifically for this job by Parrot & Co. of Santa Rosa.[15] The job was superintended by J. Winterburn. The size of the furnace was 45 feet long by 9 1/2 feet wide by 18 feet high. This was in the class of the Almaden Quicksilver Mine.[16] Its capacity was 13 tons.[17]

Mt. Jackson Mine, by October, had an adit (tunnel) over 200 feet in where they struck the ledge and thereafter through 15 feet of pay rock.[18] The Roaring Lion went in only 12 feet and drove a cross-cut through a well-defined ledge 40 feet in width.[19] The Great Eastern was driving in four adits with the idea of thoroughly prospecting it before building, much in the way of surface works.

The early days of the mines were not without hazard. The portal of one of the tunnels caved in upon some miners engaged in sinking a shaft. Others rushed to the rescue and found them uninjured.[20]

The construction of a community at the mines was not only inevitable, but a necessity due to their remoteness in those days. The first buildings to be mentioned were boarding and lodging houses erected for the Great Eastern and a grocery store.[21] Even temperance had its advocates: the miners were forbidden to patronize the bar under penalty of receiving their walking papers. More boarding houses and other buildings were constructed later in 1875 along the ravine leading up from the furnace to the Great Eastern and other mines. In March, another hotel was built and a saloon was opened by Secott & Company.

In January 1875, the Mt. Jackson Mine became the first mine to incorporate.[22] The first board of directors was comprised of: Richard Abbey, W.S. Canan, J.B. Smith, J.H. Vaughan and Robert West, all residents of Healdsburg. The amount of capital stock of the company was $1,500,000, divided into 30,000 shares at $50 each.

Two months later the Great Eastern incorporated. The amount of capital stock for this company was $3,000,000 divided into 60,000 at $50 each.[23] The greater amount of capital was probably due to the greater richness of the claim, the need for monies to buy neighboring claims, and to expand. The officers were Isaac Gumm, A.J. Zane, Willis Zane, Ransom Powell, Richard Abbey and E.E. Whipple.[24]

On May 5, 1875, R.E. Lewis, discoverer of the cinnabar lode, refiled his claim for the Great Eastern, and it was granted. This was done in compliance with the revised U.S. statutes, and probably done to maintain his position as owner of the claim.[25]

After a year of claims, exploring, mining and smelting, surface works were rebuilt. In April 1875, the Mt. Jackson put in eight new condensors, and in September, rebuilt their furnace, adding a new ore chamber.[26] The Great Eastern's retort, with its capacity of two tons and five flasks of metal, was replaced by an experimental revolving retort of the Wallridge Patent at the same time. Its capacity was eight to ten tons of ore a day.

The Great Eastern, after a six-week run with its standard furnace, fired two tons of ore every 24 hours to produce 185 flasks.[27] The price of quicksilver during this time went from 70 cents a pound to 67 1/2 cents. They shipped 40 flasks between July 23 and August 3.[28] Their total production of flasks for 1875 amounted to 412.[29]

All the excitement of discovering a cinnabar lode led men to explore for other riches. In May 1874, an assay of ore taken 2 1/2 miles from Guerneville showed tin.[30] In the same section as the mercury mines, "a rich coppermine, the Olive, was being worked."[31] N.E. Manning, Guerneville Mining District Recorder, reported that by February 1875, eight locations were filed as gold and silver claims.[32] In 1878, chrome iron was discovered near the mines and was reported as having every indication of iron ore. Another mineral discovered was coal. According to the Sonoma County Delinquent Tax List, the Mt. Jackson Coal Mining Company had been formed with W.S. Cannon as president. He was also a member of the board of directors of the Mt. Jackson Quicksilver mine.[33] The coal mining claim was 1,500 feet in length in the same area as the quicksilver mines.[34] By the end of July, prospectors were looking everywhere for signs of iron and coal, but nothing showed as fruits of their toil.

After the first years of locating, sporadic mining, and prospecting throughout the neighboring countryside, events settled down to a steady pace at the two mines.

The Great Eastern, in 1876, continued to be productive with its Eames furnace, the results being two flasks a day.[35] Production in 1877 yielded an average of about 160 flasks per month. The richness of the mine averaged two per cent or 40 pounds of mercury per ton of ore.[36] At the end of one week, they shipped 125 flasks.[37] The mine was running day and night with a work force of 40 hands.[38] By this time over 10,000 feet of tunnels and five shafts had been excavated. The ore was brought to the furnace at a cost which did not exceed ten cents a ton. The monthly production with their Eames fine ore rotary furnace was about 200 flasks per month. The total amount produced to mid-1877 was 1,000 flasks.[39]

STATE OF CALIFORNIA, DEPARTMENT OF STATE.

Sacramento, January 29th 1875.

DRURY MELONE, Secretary of State of the State of California, do hereby certify that a copy of **ARTICLES OF INCORPORATION** was filed in this office, on the twenty-ninth day of January A.D. 1875, containing the following statement of facts:

1. That the Name of the Corporation is the _Mount Jackson Quicksilver Mining Company_
2. That the purpose for which it is formed is _to carry on and conduct a general mining business in Sonoma County, California_
3. That its principal place of business is _in Healdsburg, Sonoma County, Cala._
4. That the term for which it is to exist is _Fifty Years_
5. That the number of its Directors or Trustees is _Five (5)_

And the names and residences of those who are to act as Directors or Trustees during the first year and until the annual election of officers are		Residence
	Richard Abbey	Healdsburg, Sonoma Co
	H. S. Craven	do
	J. B. Smith	do
	J. H. Langhan	do
	Robt West	do

6. That the amount of its Capital Stock is _One Million Five Hundred Thousand Dollars_ and the Number of Shares into which it is divided is _Thirty Thousand (30,000)_

Witness my Hand and the Great Seal of State, at my Office in Sacramento, California, the 29th day of January A.D. 1875.

Drury Melone
Secretary of State.

By _____ Deputy.

Articles of Incorporation of the Mount Jackson Quicksivler Mine, 1875. JCS Collection

Check, left (JCS Collection) made out to Guy R. Skinner, right, Mabel Peter Collection

In July 1878, it was noted the Eastern was producing four flasks a day, and construction had begun on a new furnace and two new retorts. The furnace was a 30-ton Maxwell which was capable of producing eight flasks each 24 hours.[40] The president of the company, Isaac Gumm, supplied facts and figures up to and including 1879:

> Expense, $4,346.11; applied towards part payment on the furnaces, by the stockholders of the Great Eastern Company, $2,660.67; dividends paid, $14,051; cash on hand, $289.50. Total, $21,347.28. The terms of the lease are that Mr. Parrott puts on all improvements, pays expenses, etc., and received therefor seven-eighths of the production.
>
> The largest portion of the above expense item ($4,346.11) was incurred after Mr. Parrott took the mine, and includes cost of patent, lawsuit, etc. There have been $160,000 taken out of the mine in five years.
>
> The company has given Mr. Parrott a new lease for five years, although his present lease will not expire till a year hence. There is now due Mr. Parrott from the mine $38,000 (in other words he has put in $38,000 more than he has received from the mine), and according to the provisions of the lease the stockholders are to receive one-eighth of the product till that amount is paid, above working expenses; when, if quicksilver rises to fifty cents per pound, they get one-sixth; if it rises to fifty-five cents or over, they get one-fifth. At the expiration of Mr. Parrott's lease, providing the stockholders take the mine, they are to pay him a fair valuation for all the improvements he has made.
>
> An important improvement now being made at the mine is the addition of hoisting works, capable of working at six or seven hundred foot levels; there will be an ore cage and a double stroke pump, the latter being needed to free the lower levels of water. A kiln of 60,000 bricks has recently been burned at the mine, and the little Eames furnace is to be taken down; another one will be built upon its foundation, with Haskins & Halls patent ore chamber attached. There is now in use at the mine a twenty-ton Maxwell furnace, almost new, and in fine condition. The improvements in the way of buildings, roads, etc., are numerous and substantial. At present, the hoisting works are being adjusted, and it is expected that the mine will soon be in full operation.[41]

The Mt. Jackson Mine owners, upon seeing the efficiency of the Eames furnace at the Eastern's works in 1876, tore down their furnaces and erected three Eames furnaces.[42] After the construction was completed in May, the furnaces were fired and production was again under way. No statistics are available for comparison before and after the Eames were built, but production was pretty steady:

September 23, 1876 47 flasks shipped
October 28, 1876   22 flasks for the week
November 25, 1876   28 flasks for the week
December 23, 1876   21 flasks for the week

Other production figures were reported erratically from 1877 through 1879:

February 10, 1877   100 flasks
March 10, 1877   24 flasks shipped
May 4, 1878   22 flasks per day
August 10, 1878   8 flasks per day

Miners at the Great Eastern Quicksilver Mine. Photo courtesy Ethel Carrier.

1. S.D., April 8, 1874.
2. Son. Co. Hist., 1888, p. 381.
3. S.D., Apr. 25, 1874.
4. Son. Co. Recorder's office. Promiscuous Records, Book A, pp. 325 & 329. Dates of 3 Apr. and 9 Apr. 1874 given.
5. S.D., May 2, 1874.
6. J.W. Bagley, Survey Book #1, pp. 131-33, original field notes.
7. Ibid.
8. R.R.F., May 19, 1874.
9. S.D., Jul. 18, 1874.
10. S.D., Aug. 22, 1874.
11. Son. Co. Recorder's office. Promiscuous Records, Book A, p. 334.
12. "Roaring Lion," letter by Clarence Clar to author, July 9, 1969.
13. S.D., Feb. 20, 1875.
14. S.D., Oct. 10, 1874.
15. S.D., Jul. 22, 1875-
16. S.D., Aug. 22, 1874.
17. S.D., Oct. 10, 1874.
18. Ibid.
19. S.D., October 29, 1874.
20. R.R.F., Nov. 28, 1874.
21. R.R.F., Dec. 26, 1874; S.D., Oct. 29, 1874.
22. Articles of Incorporation, #105, Son. Co. Clerk's office; mlcrofilmed.
23. Op. Cit., #113.
24. Ibid. Richard Abbey cannot be accused of a conflict of interest as he, being an officer of both corporations, undoubtedly was looking after his own. As to a conflict between the two companies or because of his position, none was evident in the immediate future.
25. Mineral Certificate No. 44, General Land Office, San Francisco. The laws and statutes regarding the land of the United States were constantly changing between 1850 and 1900. This was due to the tremendous expansion of the country and to meet the needs of people, country and industry alike as they arose. Hence a refiling by R.E. Lewis on his own claim.
26. S.D., Sep. 11, 1875.
27. Ibid.
28. S.D., Aug. 7 and 21, 1875.
29. Mines and Mineral Resources of Colusa, Glenn, Lake, Marin, Napa, Solano, Sonoma, Yolo Counties; California State Mining Bureau, July 1915, p. 175.
30. S.D., May 23, 1874.
31. 0p. Cit., Jan. 2, 1875, and Appendix to Journals of Senate and Assembly, 21st Session, Sec. 4, p. 401 (1874). State Printing Office.
32. S.D., Feb. 20, 1875.
33. Op. Cit., Jun. 8, 1878.
34. S.D., Feb. 25, 1878. No further information is to be found in any mining bulletins.
35. S.D., Mar. 4, 1876.
36. S.D., Feb. 3, 1877.
37. S.D., Feb. 10, 1877.
38. Atlas of Sonoma County, 1877, p.
39. S.D., Feb. 3 and June 16, 1877.
40. S.D., Nov. 30, 1878.
41. Son. Co. Hist., 1880, p. 37.
42. S.D., Apr. 29, 1876.

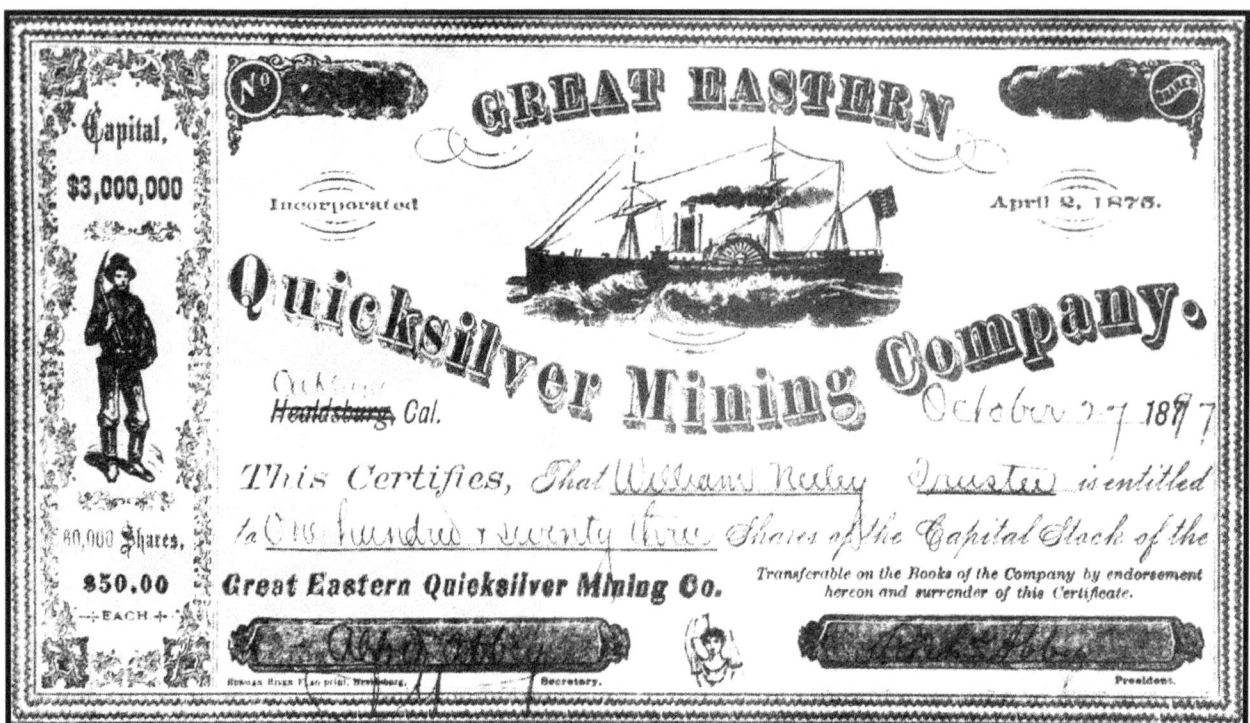

Jim and Edith Neely Collection

Chapter 15

WHITES VS CHINESE — PART 1

"Pacific Chivalry" by Thomas Nast, Harper's Weekly, Aug. 7, 1869

The first Chinese immigrants to California arrived from Hong Kong in February 1848. They were two men and a woman.¹ Thus began an immigration that would shake the foundations of local, state and federal governments.

At first the Chinese were more than just accepted by their host country: they were wined and dined. But when the impact of their willingness to work for wages less than their Caucasian counterparts was felt, racial lines were drawn. White government and unions worked to oppress and persecute the "heathen Chinee." In the 1850's, the Chinese were to be found in the Sierra gold towns and mines, but social and economic pressure by white miners towards the end of the decade made them flock to San Francisco and the Bay Area.

In the 1860's the Chinese were a small number in Sonoma County, only 51 in the 1860 census. In the logging camps and settlements, they were few. By 1869, however, they were working in the camps along the Russian River. Just who these pioneers were has not been discovered.²

There is then a break in time between this and 1873 when nothing is mentioned about the Oriental in Sonoma County, save the census of 1870. It reported 473 in the county, which was one per cent of the Chinese counted in the state.³ There were four in Duncan's Mill (at the mouth of the river).⁴

Laws were passed by the state legislature

in the early '70's prohibiting the employment of Chinese on public works, prohibiting them from owning real estate, and from obtaining licenses for certain kinds of businesses.[5] Apparently the Redwood Road District, which was in and had the same boundaries as the Redwood Township, chose to use Chinese labor anyway. C.D. Yarborough paid an undisclosed number of Chinese men $148.50 for road work during 1873.[6] The private enterprises of the area hired them or not, as they wished. The Murphy Brothers placed an advertisement in the Sonoma Democrat saying they cut lumber "without employing Chinamen."[7]

On the opposite side, the Great Eastern Quicksilver Mine at Mt. Jackson had 25 in their employ, but the Great Western Mine used none.[8] The Murphys at their mill reversed their hiring practices in '75 by employing at least one.[9]

In February 1876, an unusual event, as far as Guerneville is concerned, took place. "Mr. R. Murphy started sawing Tuesday. The Chinamen part of his crew 'struck' the first day because one of their countrymen was not detailed to cook, but the difficulty was compromised and they went to work again."[10]

This is most unusual when we consider first, times were hard for the white laborer as witnessed the agitation for exportation of Chinese in general: the whites wanted jobs. Secondly, Mr. Murphy advertised that he used no Chinese labor in 1874, and 18 months later hired them. They "struck," and he rehired them. Third, the information of a strike or pseudo-strike is the first to occur in the history of the area.

Although the Chinese filled a need throughout the state — that of cheap and reliable labor — they were undesirables in the white community. "They were industrious and economical; there were no Chinese tramps . . . their habits and morals were bad. Their quarters in the cities reeked with filth and immorality."[11] This is how the "heathen Chinee" appeared to the "white devil."

In April 1876, the outside ideas and prejudices became a stronger influence on the thoughts of the local populace in Guerneville. A letter in the Sonoma Democrat signed by "a laboring man" from Santa Rosa assailed Mr. John Bagley, roadmaster, for hiring Chinese ". . . to the exclusion of many white laborers that are idle at the time. . . Mr. Bagley need not plead inability to procure white laborers, for I know that enough men could be found in Santa Rosa and Guerneville to complete the Guerneville Road in less time than he will do it with his Chinese . . . people may have desired Chinese immigration some years ago. I don't believe they want the public money to go to them at present to the exclusion of the many needful white laborers."[12]

A week later in April, a more outright demonstration occurred in town. The pressure of undermining the Chinese economy by closing or withdrawing employment opportunities mounted. The bastions of Chinese labor were slowly succumbing to the pressures of the ruling society:

> The heathen chinee is doomed. Following the wake of many larger towns, the leading businessmen of our village have formed an organization pledging themselves, after the first of May, not to employ Chinamen or patronize parties who do. Prominent among its members are Messrs. Heald and Guerne, John Taggart, Murphy Brothers, and some 70 others. If every town would manifest the same spirit displayed here, in resisting the encroachment of this element, the last Mongoloid would soon disappear from the Pacific Coast.[13]

Whether towns or their industries would agree to such an idea or not, one industry would not be affected: the railroads. The Fulton & Guerneville Branch of the San Francisco and North Pacific employed Chinese, as did the North Shore narrow gauge railroad. The narrow gauge specifically reported: "Work has been commenced . . . in Dutch Bill Canyon. Thirty whites and sixty Chinese are manufacturing ties, posts, and pickets, and chop-

Chinese working the railway through the redwoods along the Russian River. Frank Leslie's Illustrated Newspaper, Nov. 23, 1878.

ping wood on the right-of-way."[14]

Be that as it may, the Mt. Jackson Quicksilver Mine followed the general desires of the population and ceased working Chinese.[15] April continued to be a month of anti-Oriental agitation. The subject of the Chinese was talked of in open discussion in "town hall" meetings.[16]

> April 10th. The Chinese question is being duly agitated here [Guerneville], but the result is not very perceptible as yet. The subject was debated in the Lyceum last Friday evening and continued until the next meeting.
>
> April 22nd. The Chinese question is raging high in our midst. Debate is with Messrs. Keran, R. Murphy, N.E. Manning, and Donahue.
>
> April 29th. The Literary Society discussed the Chinese question last week, Messrs. Keran and Donahue making it appear that the celestials are an injury to America. Messrs. Murphy and Manning — argument to the contrary, not withstanding.

And it continued on into May, but at a reduced tempo.

> May 22. A medicine wagon was in town overnight, and the vendor of drugs held forth in the evening on the vexatious Chinese question. His argument was good, and well supported by facts and figures.[17]

Just what was the "vexatious Chinese question"? It was, after all was said and discussed: "Should the Chinese be immediately ejected from California?" The complaints were based strictly on racial bigotry. This was done on one isolated occasion in Forestville. They did not totally escape the turmoil of the social problem, but they handled it promptly when the first Chinese arrived in town. One of their populace wrote: "We have one thing to brag about in our town. We have no Chinese here. Some did want a house here, but our people said no! Hurrah for the people of Forestville."[18]

In essence what they said was, you do not have a racial problem if you do not have a racial minority present.

It was during this time, the mid-1870's, that the federal government was passing acts related to immigration and rejection of Chinese and Japanese for purposes of, firstly, "coolie" trade, and, secondly, prostitution. The state passed a resolution supporting its laws that were, in effect, against "coolie" labor. Sonoma County, so far as research has been able to disclose, passed no ordinances against the Oriental. But the populace was definitely anti-Chinese — at least a goodly portion. One political party campaigned on the anti-Chinese platform in 1878-79.

In San Francisco where the Chinese population was the greatest, wholesale rioting and murder was directed against them by the criminal element of the Barbary Coast. This was too much even for the white population. The Vigilantes nearly came into existence but for the National Guard to suppress the hoodlums.

Although the Chinese were being harassed elsewhere, times, so far as it is recorded, were not violent for them in Sonoma County, but were uncomfortable.

After the month of May 1876, and for the year following, no agitation was reported in Guerneville by any newspaper. People *seemed* resigned to the idea that the Chinese were going to be present for awhile. There were no reports of any meetings for discussions, proclamations, or petitions. It appears that a quiet atmosphere, in general, prevailed around Guerneville, and the Celestial was left to his own devices.

Then a totally Oriental enterprise came to town:

> "A branch of the Santa Rosa China Store [was] opened in town for the benefit of the *hundreds* [author's italics] of Celestials employed on the railroads."[19]

Between 1873 and 1875 the first Chinese names in the town area to be uncovered were from county road records, those being Lo, Lee Sam and Hop Kee. Lo was just a name on the road report, but the other two worked one day and five days respectively in August 1873. Two years passed and Hop Kee appears again, this time on the tax rolls in 1875. He failed to pay his personal property tax. He left town this year.[20]

The following years, Yarborough, the local road overseer, hired more men, listing 17 Chinese by name, and in 1877, he named 63 working (including the absent Hop Kee!)[21]

In 1877 the Chinese store changed its name to Tong General Store, after its owners, Tong Chung and Tong Gin.[22]

Jim Taggart hired a cook for his hotel in town by the name of Ah Jim. He was among the chosen few of his people for he left town to visit his family in China, and was allowed to come back into the country and return to his job at Taggart's.[23]

Down at Dutch Bill Creek, the Chinese occupied themselves, besides working on the railroad, with doing "wash and selling whiskey."[24]

Where the Chinese lived while in the

French Brothers logging crew with a Chinese water slinger, near Guerneville, 1882. JCS Collection

Guerneville area is not known. There are no clues to give an idea or make a guess as to their abodes and store locations.

While the Chinese went about their business as best they could, the "white devils" were still, as far as can be ascertained, seeking legal means to oust the Chinese without resorting to violence. As a news item stated:

> Nearly all the men in the mills and Guerneville have discussed the Chinese question. They seem to think their only hope of relief in that direction is with the Democratic Party. They say the Republicans made many promises to amend the [Burlingame] treaty,[25] etc., but notwithstanding, they have continually had the power in Congress, nothing has been done, and now they intend to try the Democrats and when the latter get control of both branches of Congress, they believe the treaty will be abolished or at least amended as to prevent the large influx of Mongolians who are now coming to the country. They are satisfied nothing will be done so long as the Republicans control the Senate.[26]

Others involved in politics, those that represented this area in Washington, D.C., and Sacramento, were trying to pass legislation to the detriment of the Chinese. U.S. Senator Booth suggested a reservation similar to those created for the Indians. Sonoma's representative to Congress, J.K. Luttrell, presented a bill to the House of Representatives asking that no Chinese be naturalized.[27]

The wheels of government were still not turning fast enough so various political parties sprang up: the Communists, Citizens & Taxpayers' Party (a hybrid of Republicans and Democrats) and the Workingman's Party, to name a few.

Although no Communists have been discovered in Guerneville at this time, the Workingman's Party was present. It was formed in April 1878, in opposition to the Taxpayers' Party. The officers of this literally fascist organization were John Starrett, president, George E. Guerne, vice-president; Dr. Towndrow, treasurer, J.M. Keran, secretary. Dr. Wooley and John W. Bagley were additional members of the executive committee. Others were Rufus and A. Murphy, Jake Selling, Roscoe Longly, plus two others.[28] The presence of the Workingman's Party in Guerneville was obvious with their notices posted all over town that stated, "The Chinese Must Go."[29]

At some great stretch of the imagination it might be justified to say the common white laborer had reason to be irritated because the Chinese were hired at lower rates. And to read and discover the founding fathers were bigots is mildly astonishing: "mildly," because one should reflect upon the past environment and culture in which they were educated. It is not too surprising that their political positions would be where they were. If the reader noticed, there were two doctors on the committee. Educated as they were, their income came from their fellow whites, and since other doctors were available in neighboring Forestville, et cetera, they were probably "coerced" into joining the ranks of the party.

The talk in the streets, as a correspondent to the Sonoma Democrat put it, was "about like this" in Guerneville:

> In 1855 we began to agitate the slavery question and now the slaves are free. Now we propose to agitate the Chinese question and if the same expenditure of blood and money is required as was necessary to settle the slavery question, it must come. I have heard this statement from several, and when we consider that

Graphic of 1879 Sonoma County voting slate for the Regular Workingmen's Ticket. Courtesy Sonoma County Library

> some branches of the movement are under arms does it not present a portentous aspect?[30]

That is the last heard from that Guerneville reporter.[31] Although he disappeared from the newspaper, the Chinese did not. In Howard's (Occidental) they hung the Celestial in effigy. In Santa Rosa, it was printed: "The best way to kill off the Chinese is to teach them how to aid kitchen fires with kerosene oil cans."[32]

The anti-Chinese sentiments in Guerneville continued on the economic "front" in 1879 when a petition was presented to the Board of Supervisors. The petition was signed by 130 local men requesting to have no Chinese employed in the construction of the Guerneville and Coast Road.[33]

The 1880's were very much like the '70's. There were continual abuses, the hiring in some quarters, "No Chinese employed" in others. They were always employed by the railroads for building and repairing same. The one location on the Guerneville & Fulton Railroad (a branch line of the San Francisco & North Pacific) that was in constant need of repair, especially so during the winter, was the "big cut" between Korbel's Mill and Guerneville. The numerous news articles over the years placed this just east of today's Rio Nido. The Chinese would just keep shoveling the slides over the bank.

The winter and spring of 1880 were extremely wet. Chinese were taken from all the branch lines to keep the main trunk line open

Barber C.F. Sloan of Duncans Mills was one of the River area's few black residents in the nineteenth century Courtesy Duncans Mills Depot Museum.

even as late as May that year.[34] With the majority of the Chinese gone to repair the railroad in other parts, the remainder could be found mostly at the quicksilver mines, a few doing farm work, and as cooks.

The census taker made his appearance as he is scheduled to do every ten years. His list separated the white populace from the Chinese. With the railroad having taken most of them, there were 34 Chinese counted in the Redwood Township out of 904 for the county.[35] The enumerator listed the occupations of all enumerated, but not one Chinese was counted as having worked in any form in the lumber industry. This leads one to believe his list probably was not complete.

The Chinese were not the only ethnic minority in this area. Blacks did not appear on the Russian River until 1879-80. They were present in the county in few numbers outside of one or two families. A search of the census of 1870 shows none in Mendocino Township, of which Guerneville was then a part.

Trying to find Blacks in contemporary records, newspapers, et cetera, was more difficult than with Chinese. Few governmental records had people discerned as to race, so the search was complicated as the Black people had taken Anglo-Saxon names, while the Chinese retained their names indigenous to their culture.

One of the few black residents of the lower River area was "Professor" C.F. Sloan, a barber and news agent at Duncans Mills. Born in Philadelphia February 17, 1819, Sloan came 'round the horn in 1850 and ran a barbershop and bath house in Oakland before moving to Duncans Mills in 1876, where he lived for 22 years. He died January 10, 1899 at 80 years of age and is buried in Duncans Mills. His obituary in the Jan. 12, 1899 issue of the *Santa Rosa Republican* acknowledged his status as a legendary local character who could recite history "by the yard" and confirmed "all who knew him will be genuinely sorry to learn that the old man has laid aside razor and brush forever."36

A search of the 1880 census and the various annual school census up to then revealed no Blacks in Redwood Township. The newspapers give slight information, but information, nevertheless, of the first appearances by them. A second (and anonymous) Negro was present during a ball given by the town's ladies on February 20, 1890. He was there in the capacity of a "waiter, [who] between dances passed around glasses of water for the comfort of the gentlemen."

The second appearance on the Russian River, although not in Redwood Township, came a year and a half later: "Prof. Sloan (Colored barber) has returned to his old stand at Duncans' Mills."37

No other blacks are known to have lived or traveled through the river area up to 1900.

1. J.M. Guinn, *History of the State of California*, hereafter cited as Hist of State of Calif., Chapman Pub. Co., Chicago, 1904, p. 229.
2. Harry R. Coolidge, *Chinese Immigration*, Henry Holt & Co., New York, 1909, p. 503; R.R.F., Jun. 3, 1869.
3. *Chinese Immigration*, op. cit.
4. U.S. Census, 1870.
5. *Hist. of State of Calif.*, 1904, p. 231.
6. S.D., Jan. 17, 1874, "Redwood Township, C.D. Yarborough's report: 51 work days by chinamen at $1.20 = $76.50, 4 work days by Chinamen at $1.20 = $5.00; 40 work days by Chinamen at $1.25 = $62.50."
7. S.D., Sept. 12, 1874
8. S.D., Jul. 18, 1874. "Ten Chinamen are at work on the road from Secott's to the Great Western Mine." To these Chinese goes the honor of building the first road to the mines from the Big Bottom area, S.D. Oct. 10, 1874.
9. R.R.F., May 15, 1875.
10. S.D., Feb. 26, 1876.
11. *Hist. of State of Calif.,* op. cit.
12. S.D., Apr. 1, 1876.
13. S.D., Apr. 8, 1876.
14. Ibid. This is now Bohemian Highway between Monte Rio and Occidental.
15. S.D., Apr. 29, 1876. Formerly the Great Western Mine.
16. S.D., Apr. 10, 22, 29, 1876.
17. R.R.F., May 22, 1876.
18. S.D., June. 23, 1877.
19. R.R.F., Aug. 14, 1876.
20. So. Co. Recs., Road Report of August 1875, Redwood Township, and S.D., Jan. 30, 1875, "Delinquent Tax Rolls, Redwood Township."
21. So. Co. Tax Recs., 1877, Sonoma County Historical Society.
22. Ibid.
23. R.R.F., Nov. 18, 1879.
24. S.D., Jun. 2, 1877.
25. The Burlingame Treaty declared, by agreement with the U.S. and China, that Chinese and American citizens alike had freedom of religion and no fear of disturbed cemeteries, of travel and change of residence and allegiance, of a public education, and that any emigration or immigration was voluntary. The treaty did not establish a quota on immigrants.
26. S.D., Aug. 18, 1877.
27. S.D., Jan. 19, 1877.
28. S.D., Apr. 27 and May 4, 1878.
29. Ibid.
30. S.D.; May 11, 1878.
31. This correspondent used to work for the *Sonoma Democrat*. He moved to Guerneville and wrote to the paper for about four weeks.
32. S.D., Feb. 22, 1879.
33. Son. Co. Archives, Bd. of Sup's. document, original petition dated February 7, 1879. A survey of all known material discloses no further information or disposition.
34. R.R.F., May 25, 1880.
35. U.S. Census, 1880. See Appendix.
36. R.R.F., Feb. 24, 1880.
37. S.R. Rep., Nov. 19, 1881.

Middleton Box Factory, on Fife Creek, Guerneville, Sept. 17, 1884. Left to right: unknown boy; Fred Dagget, box maker; Sam Rhodes, engineer; George Pippin, son of T. C. Pippin, shingle packer; L.C. Wind, foreman; Charles Folks, shingle sawyer; Ivon Clar, shingle packer; Charles S. Middleton, owner; William Falone, cutter; M.C. White, watchman; W. Arthur Turner, shingle sawyer. C.R. Clar Collection.

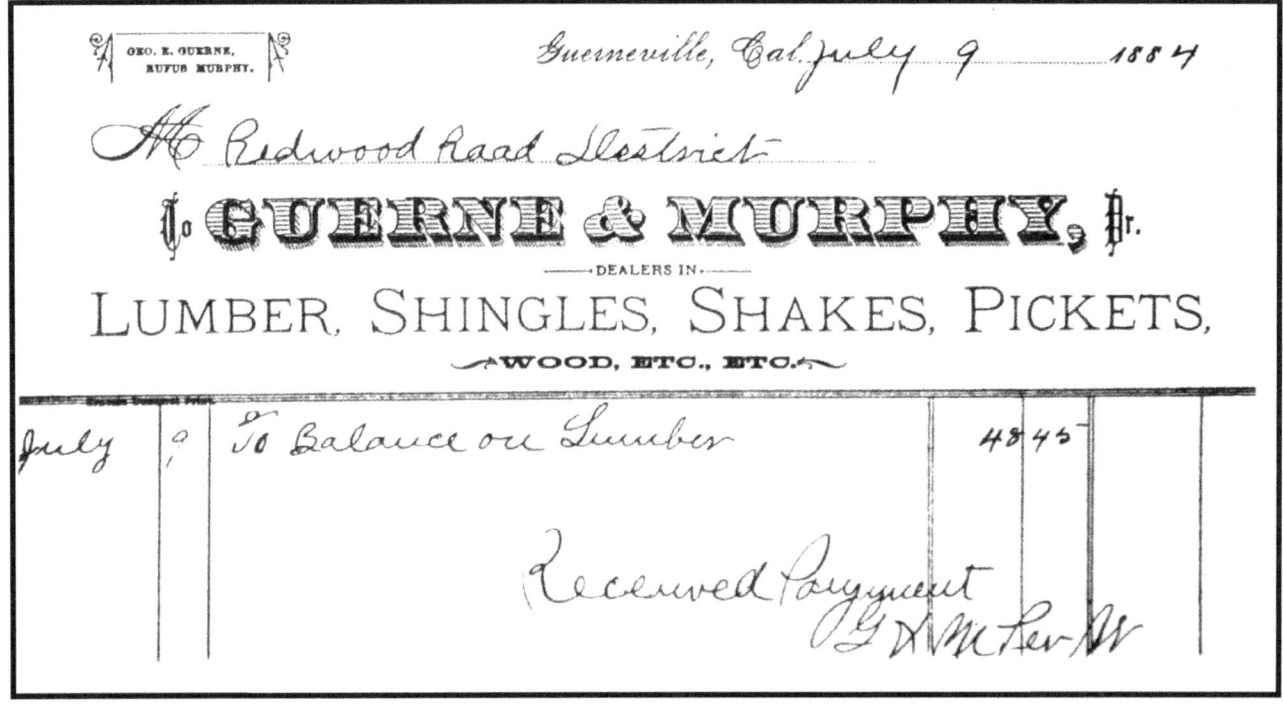

Bill to Redwood Road District from Guerne & Murphy Mill, 1884. JCS Collection

Chapter 16

Lumber Mills — 1881 to 1885

As the years progressed, fewer lumber mills remained, and those were the larger mills. The small timber concerns, excluding those that worked splitwood, became almost nonexistent in the Guerneville area.

After the New Year of 1881, T.J. Ludwig left the partnership of Guerne, Murphy & Ludwig. Upon his leaving, the firm launched upon expanding its operations by building a railroad downstream "to that magnificent body of timber in Hulbert Canyon."[1] Iron rail was purchased in January from San Francisco & Northern Pacific Railroad. A locomotive and several cars were bought elsewhere.[2]

The actual construction started in early March. Costs ran as high as $3,000 a mile for grading, ties and trestle work, not including the rails. By mid-May the railhead reached the canyon and continued on to Hulbert Creek, a distance of about 150 yards, while the other end of the road was connected to the SF & NP. A year later, Guerne & Murphy extended the line up the canyon about one-half mile.[3]

The railroad was damaged considerably by rain in March of '84. Repairs were made, but the following winter another storm hit, and the trestle work was carried away. In December 1885, an ill wind again struck the Hulbert Canyon operations when the switch engine fell through a trestle ten feet down with two cars loaded with logs. It was badly smashed, but luckily there were no injuries.[4]

During these five years, 1881 through 1885, logging and sawing remained pretty much the same at the mill. The mill started 1881 cutting only 17,000 board feet of lumber a day, weather permitting, and shipped orders daily.[5]

On January 30, a flood occurred, with minor damage. The dam on Fife Creek for the mill pond broke, washing away few logs, as most had been boomed for safety. It took approximately two to three weeks to make repairs.[6]

Guerne & Murphy started their cutting season in earnest the first of May, but the year remained basically uneventful. However, the dam in late June caved in, losing water from the pond. The summer run ended with the discharge of most of the hands in early October. The mill shipped an average of four cars of lumber a day. T.J. Ludwig, the former partner of Guerne & Murphy, bought all their lumber and had it shipped to Santa Rosa in November. This was the only mill running at the end of 1881.[7]

During the dead of winter in '82, the mill was idle. A logging contract was made with the French brothers, George and John, and in May, the mill fired up its boilers and ran at full capacity for the season.[8]

The year 1883 was just as uneventful as '81 and '82. Their lumber yard held 1,100,000 feet of lumber by the first of May and they were still sawing. One unusual board of clear redwood was cut 56 inches wide, 18 feet long and two inches thick. Later, the mill closed for the season for the usual holidays and rain.[9]

In mid-March 1884, Guerne & Murphy put the mill in order and started the season on May 8th. On June 20, severe rains and deep mud caused logging to become impossible, and the mill shut down. When things dried, the logging contractors, G.W. French and Torrance, kept the 40 mill hands busy. Production had increased from 17,000 feet a day to 25,000 feet by this year.[10]

The French Brothers logging crew near Guerneville, 1882. Note the 2-2-0 locomotive, the Polly Ann, on the lower right. It was purchased in 1881 by Guerne and Murphy. JCS Collection

The schedule for 1885 was the usual starting up in early May, with July 4th off for the hired hands, and shutting down the first of December. The Fourth was a traditional holiday for lumberjacks everywhere. Rufus Murphy stated their firm "ships from 3,500,000 to 4,000,000 feet of lumber each year, and at 6,500 feet to the railroad car, the number of cars we ship is easily estimated being 538 to 615 cars."[11]

Lunsford's shingle mill (still under Peckinpah contract) started cutting 45,000 shingles a day in January 1881. The contract ran out in September, so Lunsford hired Oliver West (Oliver Wescott?) to build a lumber mill to run in conjunction with his shingle operation. By the middle of the month, shingle cutting resumed and the new mill started cutting railroad ties. In charge of the new mill was Foreman Brantover. The Peckinpahs went down to the mouth of Howards Creek (today known as Dutch Bill Creek) and ran their own shingle mill.[12]

Nothing is known about the Lunsford concern during 1882. In January 1883, McFadyen and Thomas Heald, former partner of George Guerne, leased Lunsford's shingle mill.[13]

In 1884, a year later, John French bought the mill property, made various repairs, and then started manufacturing. He stopped at the end of January and skipped all of February because of inclement weather.[14] In early March, he started shingle making and was grinding bark. The reason for bark grinding is unknown and totally foreign to the times and place.

In 1885, this mill followed the annual schedule of starting and stopping. Reported production was about 40,000 shingles a day.[15]

In mid-February 1881, French & McFadyen's company gained another partner in the person of Thomas T. Heald. They built and operated a mill on the Beaver and Torrance claims across the river from Guerneville. This new mill is not to be confused with the shingle mill, although the owners are the same. The machinery in the mill came from Ransom Powell's mill on Mill Creek near Healdsburg and was re-erected here in 1880.[16]

Less than a year later, in May 1881, fire destroyed the mill. It was running at full capacity at the time with 20 men. A short distance away from the mill was the sawdust pile. A fire started, when is unknown. After smoldering underneath, it surfaced, ignited and raced across the top of the pile. It quickly engulfed the building. The workers just as quickly abandoned the mill, and in a few minutes, the structure was a total loss. The machinery was comparatively uninjured because the superstructure was lightly built and none of the heavy timbers fell on it. Damage was $3,000 to $5,000. There was no insurance coverage. They immediately began to rebuild and were running again by mid-June.[17]

The first of July brought another fire scare when flames got near the mill and burnt a large amount of cord wood. By September, the mill was cutting 22,000 feet a day. About the middle of October, the company went to short time and was the only company running in December.[18]

John French sold his interest in the mill to his partners, McFadyen & Heald, in January 1882. The remainder of the year was uneventful. Heald and McFadyen were producing lumber by April, but due to high water they were unable to transport it to the railroad across the river.[19]

In October, a large redwood was felled on the Torrance claim for them that measured 347 feet tall and 14 feet in diameter. The mill hummed along until it shut down in mid-December.[20]

During the winter of 1882-83, they leased Lunsford's Shingle Mill, as previously mentioned.

In Spring of '83, they made a purchase of timber in Hulbert Canyon and moved their mill to the new location. Besides a new location, a new partner joined the business which then became known as Heald, McFadyen & Brown. The foreman at the new mill site was William Burier, and under his guidance the mill was producing a moderate 18,000 board feet per day.[21]

Four months later the company bought up all of W.H. Willets' timber lands. Willets' Woods even at this time, after various operations had logged in parts of it, was said to contain 9 million board feet of stumpage and thousands of feet of fuel cordwood. At the first of January 1884, Heald withdrew from the partnership, making it McFadyen & Brown. A month later, the two remaining partners leased the Big Bottom Mill from James B. Armstrong to assist them in cutting the new timber purchase. (This new lease was probably caused by the sale of the shingle mill to French, thus causing their old lease to be terminated.)[22]

This mill went through the ritual of undergoing repairs and proclaimed it was "going to start up next week," a proclamation that was reissued continually from January to June.[23]

It appears that after the Big Bottom Mill got to operating, their old mill in Hulbert Canyon ceased production and remained idle for some time. Then in June of '85, a fire of unknown origin occurred from which the frame was destroyed and the machinery considerably damaged. After the conflagration, the firm with the leased mill was still selling products. In December they had over 3 million feet stocked in their lumber yard.[24]

Murphy's Mill, near the present elementary school (1980), owned by Wyman Murphy (brother Rufus was in partnership with Guerne), continued producing wood products with stoppages in accordance with holidays and local custom. In other words, 1881 was uneventful.

In 1882, his was the first mill to ship wood and lumber and the first to shut down by mid-October.[25]

Inside Livreau Mill, Sept. 12, 1875.
JCS Collection

The year 1883 progressed with some trouble when the "eccentric engine" broke and took five days to repair in July.²⁶ In August, J.B. Armstrong purchased the mill along with the Murphy timber claim. John H. French, a former partner with McFadyen and Heald, was made general superintendent of the whole Armstrong operation. Pursuant to the purchase, the mill was overhauled and a new machine was installed, probably taking the place of the old "eccentric engine." The daily production subsequently in September was an acceptable 20,000 feet. Operations then ceased for the holidays in mid-December.²⁷

In February 1884, Armstrong leased the Murphy/Big Bottom Mill to McFayden and Brown, as stated above.

Korbel's Mill has no record of lumbering from the end of 1880 to the middle of 1883. This is not to say they had ceased operating. Accounts state they worked the seasons, but that was all.

In 1883, the Korbel brothers followed the example of Guerne & Murphy by laying track for more timber along the river bed. A short time later an average storm washed out portions of it. Besides the new railroad, they also built a summer bridge across the river to their timber claims on the south side in 1884.²⁸

Another mill was constructed on a Mr. Crocket's timber claim by Turner and his partner, John French, in early 1884. This mill was probably the Lunsford property bought from him at the end of 1883. They employed some 35 men, not including a considerable number of people getting timber to the mill and working split stuff. The mill cut only an average of 15,000 feet a day by mid-year. Their timber resources elsewhere near Guerneville amounted to 400 acres.²⁹

In 1885, they were sawing timbers for the new Guerneville bridge. They shut down in October and removed their mill to a new site about three miles downstream, probably the 400 acres.³⁰

Other mills mentioned in passing were the Riley, and another Ludolph's Mill located in Oregon Canyon one-quarter to one-half mile from Pocket Road (Highway 116).³¹

Of course, current newspapers emphasized news about mills, but mention was given to the loggers and related industry. Two logging crews were Burk's (Burke's) in Hulbert Canyon and that of George W. French's brother, John. Though the mills would be shut down during the dead of winter, as many as 500 men would be employed by the various firms, cutting away all the small and knotty timber left by the loggers. This slash was cut into fuel wood. The prices commanded by cordwood ranged from $1.65 to $2.25, but it did not pay to sell at less than $2.00. This cordwood was shipped to Santa Rosa and other towns, along with hardwood charcoal. Other important products were pickets, posts, shakes, tan bark, et cetera. Such cargo would constitute 10 to 30 rail cars per train.³²

1. S.D., January 15, 1881.
2. Ibid.; S.D. February 16, 1884; R.R.F., January 24, 1881.
3. S.D., March 19, 1881; May 21, 1881, and March 4, 1882.

4. S.R. Rep., March 17, 1884; S.D., December 27, 1884, and December 12, 1885.

5. S.D., January 15, 1881; R.R.F., January 24, 1881.

6. R.R.F., February 3, 1881, February 17, 1881.

7. S.R. Rep., June 20, 1881, S.D., August 27, 1881; R.R.F., November 20, 1881.

8. S.R. Rep., May 1, 1882, June 19, 1882.

9. S.R. Rep., May 1, 1883.

10. S.D., June 21, 1884.

11. S.D., February 16, 1884.

12. R.R.F., March 28, 1881; S.R. Rep., September 12, 1881, September 26, 1881; S.D., February 5, 1881, September 3, 1881.

13. S.R.Rep., January 29, 1883

14. S.R. Rep., January 14, 1884; S.D., March 15, 1884.

15. S.R. Rep., April 12, 1885.

16. R.R.F., February 1881; S.D., February 12, 1881.

17. R.R.F., May 22, 1881.

18. R.R.F., September 5, 1881; S.D., July 2, 1881, December 3, 1881.

19. S.R. Rep., January 16, 1882, April 3, 1882, December 18, 1882.

20. Petaluma Argus, October (?) 1882; Son. Co. Hist., 1888, p. 190.

21. S.R. Rep., April 16, 1883; S.D., June 21, 1883, June 30, 1883, July 7, 1883. The same Burrier in November was "arrested" for insanity, released and re-arrested, then placed under $1,000 bond to keep the peace. S.R. Rep., November, 1883.

22. S.R. Rep., October 22, 1883, January 14, 1884.

23. S.D., February 2, 1884, May 31, 1884.

24. S.D., June 20, 1885.

25. R.R.F., April 1, 1882; S.R. Rep., October 16, 1882.

26. S.D., July 7, 1883.

27. S.D., August 4, 1883, August 11, 1883. The articles in newspapers named the Big Bottom Mill as Murphy's Mill, as well. S.D., September 8, 1883.

28. S.D., March 15, 1884, March 29, 1894, May 17, 1884; S.R. Rep., September 17, 1884; S.D., December 15, 1883, January 2, 1884.

29. S.R. Rep., January 14, 1884.

30. S.R. Rep., October 19, 1885; S.D., May 30, 1885.

31. S.R. Rep., September 4, 1882; S.D., September 13, 1884.

32. Echo, November (?) 1884; S.D., November 8, 1884, November 7, 1885, November 28, 1885, December 5, 1885.

TEN NIGHTS
IN A
Bar-Room

This popular Drama will be given by

THE GUERNEVILLE
DRAMATIC CLUB

—AT—

INDEPENDENCE HALL, GUERNEVILLE,
JUNE 3d, 1881.

CAST OF CHARACTERS.

SAMPLE SWICHEL	C. G. SULLIVAN.
SIMON SLADE	T. J. BUTTS.
JOE MORGAN	E. PECKINPAH.
FRANK SLADE	D. COBB.
HARVY GREEN	C. M. PECKINPAH.
Mr. ROMAINE	H. PECKINPAH.
WILLIE HAMMOND	W. MURPHY.
Mrs. SLADE	Miss EMMA BEESON.
Mrs. MORGAN	Mrs. SIMONTON.
MARY MORGAN	HATTIE FOLKS.
MEHITABLE CARTRIGHT	Mrs. C. G. SULLIVAN.

To conclude with the laughable farce

Courtship ✧ Under ✧ Difficulties.

ADMISSION - - - - - - - 25 CENTS.
Children under 10 - - - - - 10 "

SOCIAL DANCE AFTER PERFORMANCE
TICKETS, 50 CENTS.

Proceeds to go to the new School-house fund.   Come one, come all.

THE SONOMA DEMOCRAT PRINT.

Handbill for the Guerneville Dramatic Club, 1881. JCS Collection

Chapter 17

Guerneville — 1881 to 1885

As winters come and go, some are noted for being long or longer, wet or wetter than usual. After the flood of 1879, the river was not expected to rise up to the occasion again for at least a number of years. But nature has ways of making "experts" and old-timers look foolish.

At the end of January 1881, a large storm blew over the state and the rainfall set records in many locations. Guerneville measured a storm by how high the river rose. On January 30, the river crested at 41 feet eight inches above the summer level, three inches below the record flood of 1879. Some 20 families were forced to leave their residences and accept help from their good neighbors. Marshall's old store, the church and the Good Templars' Hall were used as refuges, also. When the river receded, it left a thick slime deposited on everything. Wood, lumber, fences and houses were "scattered about in picturesque confusion."[1]

The railroad was unable to make it to town. The company crews used two steam pumps to assist them in repairs; the train arrived three weeks later. The quicksilver mine was also flooded from the mountain runoff and had to shut down until early May.[2]

French & McFadyen's Mill was inundated with minor damage to equipment, but was lifted off its foundation. Being located at the junction of Pocket and May's Canyons, it would inevitably be flooded.

After repairs were made and cleanup done, the attention of the town folk centered on the school. The original building was erected in 1868, with an addition constructed in 1875. It was a dark, rough and rustic-looking edifice. Agitation for a new one began in April of '81. Dances, cake sales and the usual fundraising events were promoted by the womenfolk.[3]

An election was conducted by the men on May 14. Two hundred votes were cast and the majority were for a new school. It wasn't until October that school trustees advertised for proposals. B.F. Murphy was awarded the contract, and F.J. Rufus did the building. Even during December storms his construction proceeded at a fair pace. The outside was near completion by January and the bell installed. In February, the interior was completed with lath and plaster, and painted.[4]

There were three rooms, two for teaching and one for the principal. There was an anteroom with a wooden sink. A tin cup on a chain was located at each end of the sink — one for the boys and one for girls. Besides cups there were roller towels, again the boys' separate from the girls', and mostly dirty. There was also a single comb on a chain for everybody. Out in the playground there was a boys' side and a separate girls' side. When play period was over, the children would line up and march in on their respective sides to the beat of drums. One such drummer was Ernie Shulte.[5]

The new school was sufficient to cope with the student population for only a year. In March 1883, a third teacher was a necessity. A primary school room was made in the rear of the Congregational Church with Miss Allie Watson the teacher in charge. From August 1883 to 1884, a subscription was passed to help raise funds for an addition to the school.[6] No direct information about building the little annex has been found, but judging from vari-

The second Guerneville School, looking southwest, June 19, 1882. JCS Collection

ous photographs it was built around summer of 1884.

The youngsters were not the only ones being taught the "Three R's." W.S. Rutherford instituted an evening school in the spring of 1883 at Taggart's Hotel. Later in 1885, a Mrs. Mason opened a private school, which was well patronized.[7]

As to the public school, Gertrude Schulte recalled the boys would play baseball, mumbletypeg, ante-over, three-legged race, leap frog and tug-o-war. The girls played button-button, London Bridge, drop-the-handkerchief, one-foot-in-the-gutter, and go-forth-and-face-your-lover.[8]

The grown-ups also played baseball. The first recorded ballgame was on May 8, 1881, between Fulton and Guerneville, on the Guerneville diamond. The local boys took the game by 11 points (the score is unknown). The only player identified was the first baseman. A few weeks later they played Healdsburg on their opponents' diamond and beat them by four runs.[9]

On June 23 the following year, a formal ball club was organized. The officers were J.P. Strasburgh, president; Walter Murphy, secretary; A. Gramman, treasurer; D.L. Cobb, captain. Their first game was against another Guerneville team called the "Unknowns." The final score: Stars 5, Unknowns 0. Then the club's story is lost for several years. It will be continued later.[10]

There were other forms of relaxation and ways to spend free time. Back in 1872 there was a state law regulating the days merchants could be open. The "Sunday Law,"[11] as it was commonly called, was not enforced in Guerneville until the end of 1881 when the local judicial system decided to apply it to all violators and be strict about it:

> Messrs. Morrison, Schloss, Taggart, Joost, Folks, and Shoemake were taken in by Constable Mead, Tuesday, the first two for keeping stores open and the remainder four saloons. Messrs. Folks, Joost, and Schloss having been arraigned in Guerneville were compelled to pay a fine of $34 each, the constable's mileage and sundries coming out of the amount. Much complaint was made about this as it being their first

offense, they thought that the penalty should have been less severe. The fine was no more than is allowed by law and was considered by the justice a very lenient one.[12]

The law apparently worked to a great extent because the next Sunday, " . . . all businesses were closed except Omar Shoemake's saloon, who, no doubt wishes to contribute toward defraying the county debt."[13]

The story of temperance versus non-temperance is never finished quickly. This instance is no different. The same battle lines were drawn again, but the weapons were used differently. Omar Shoemake paid his fine, but that was only to satisfy the law. He kept his place open, threatening that if he was arrested again he would subpoena every temperance advocate within ten miles of Guerneville. His threat worked as he was not molested again.[14]

Another proprietor tried a different method to circumvent the law. On the complaint of Jake Akers, John Folks was arrested. The case showed that Folks had opened his saloon only as a sitting and reading room for his patrons. He sold no liquor. Justice of the Peace Miller, who tried the case with a jury, instructed the jury to find a verdict of "not guilty."[15]

The *Sonoma Democrat* commented,

" ...such arrests are made contrary to the intent of the law and are productive of no good effects. Considerable feeling in regard to the matter exists about Guerneville, as Mr. Folks has lately complied with the law as evidenced by the outcome of the indictments against him for violating it.[16]

This trial gave support to the idea of "ignoring the law." A week later three saloons were open on Christmas, a Sunday. "Who cares?" The following Sunday, New Year's Day, 1882, two saloons were open. The proprietors were arrested on Monday, but due to a lack of complaining witnesses, the cases were dropped. A week later, Sunday, January 7, all the saloons were closed except for that of John Taggart.[17]

For the next several months most estab-

Ulhorn's 1884 Sonoma County Directory, JCS Collection

lishments obeyed the law, but for Taggart and Shoemake. An attempt was made to convict Shoemake again, but after a change of venue, the case was dismissed: There was a strange disappearance of the case papers from Squire Hudson's desk.[18]

Nothing more occurred from then on. Temperance was slowly regulated back to a less dominant position in town. A year later the State Legislature repealed the "Sunday Law." Nobody celebrated or mourned its demise.

Occasionally families were split in their viewpoints of indulgence versus temperance. A fire razed two buildings in town, but the excitement did not end when it was put out. By great efforts two structures were saved, so free drinks were the order of the hour. As a result, firefighters and spectators were soon involved in a great celebration. This caused wives and sweethearts of several men to apply immediate civil service reform. The results were two luckless ones badly "pulverized" by their better halves and a third chased home.[19]

This fire could have been very serious, starting from unknown causes. It was discovered coming from the roof of S. Schloss's home about 8 a.m., and had a large headway by then. Nothing was saved from his upper story, but some goods and a piano were rescued from the ground floor. The building was a total loss.

Oscar Morrison's store, July 5, 1882. Note Fourth of July flags on porch supports. JCS Collection

John Taggart's neighboring barn caught fire and was torn down to prevent further spreading of flames. Other structures were smoking several times, but wet blankets saved them.

Schloss was insured for $1,000, but the loss amounted to $1,500. He had a new home built by July and a month later built an addition. Nathaniel Manning moved into the rebuilt old Schloss home. A Mrs. Pool moved into Manning's old home.[20]

Another go-around at the same time took place when George Deal moved to his timber claim, then John Hicks moved in to Deal's old residence, and Sam Graham took Hicks's. And another three homes were built for newcomers.

Commercial properties often changed hands and new businesses were built. John Folks moved his hotel to the corner of Church and First Streets, then later built a store next to it. Another store was constructed for a barber and shoe shop near Folks; Oscar Morrison put up a large warehouse.

New merchants continually moved to town: David Hetzel, cigar maker; J. Clark, blacksmith; Jacob Joost, saloon keep; A. Jacobs, tailor; Mrs. A. Cobb & Bell, ice cream parlor; Friedman, goods and lace shop; Smith, shooting gallery; Crealman, lunchroom; Lafferty, shoemaker; Hewitt, tin smith. And there were some who could not quite make it and left.

Since business appeared to be stable, if not brisk, construction was proceeding with homes and commercial properties. The lumber industry was well established. The financial environment of Guerneville was prosperous enough for the establishment of a money institution. Approximately April 1882, several men formed the Guerneville Loan Association and filed incorporation articles on May 8 with the County. The first directors were: J.A. Burns, S.H. Torrance, John Taggart, N.E. Man-

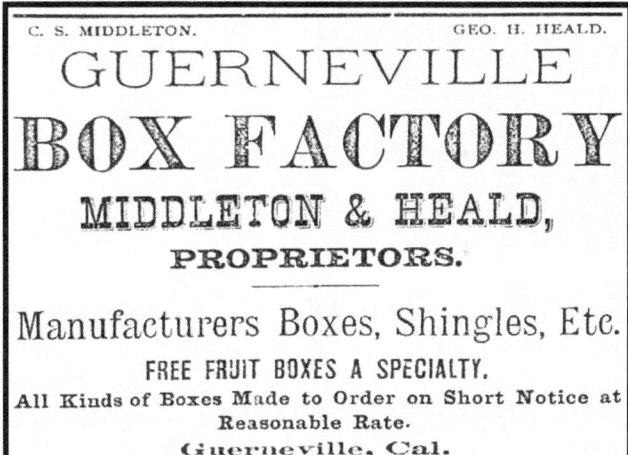

Uhlhorn's 1884 Sonoma County Directory.
JCS Collection

ning, W.H. Torrance. The other subscribers were: C.S. Middleton, R.G. Longley, Roscoe McKenney, Bradford Bell, Oscar Morrison, G. Deitz.

Their capital stock was $50,000, divided into 500 shares, with the value of each share being $100. Again, searches of county records, newspapers, et cetera, have been futile. Another dead end.[21]

On November 9, 1882, an attempt was made at torching the town, but the culprit was caught. Why he did it and his role in the history of Guerneville is covered in Chapter XVIII.

The people were interested in almost any major concern of the area: temperance, lumbering, roads, et cetera. On one occasion, two men, one temperant and the other imbiber, settled their differences by an altercation.

It was Saturday night, and a few of the boys were passing their time in Folks' Saloon. One Morris Hartnell had the reputation of being a drinker and, while liquored up, quarrelsome. The other, John Tomblinson, never touched the stuff. (This is according to contemporary news articles. If he was a prohibitionist, why was he in a saloon?) Others were in the saloon when a drunken Hartnell asked Tomblinson for work. Apparently Hartnell did not like Tomblinson's answer and began quarreling with him. He pressed Tomblinson for a fight, and they fell to blows. Hartnell was hit or kicked over the heart and died. No criminal charges were filed against Tomblinson.[22]

Another interest of prime importance to the people during 1882 was the "Chinese Problem." Because of the size of the supposed threat by another ethnic people to Guerneville's European ethnic majority another chapter about Chinese, number XVI, is given later.

Winter set in, mills shut down, social functions became popular again after the busy summer. Christmas 1882 came and went.

And so did people: Some were born and some died. Most were known, but occasionally a person comes and goes leaving no history or knowledge about himself except the fact of his mere existence.

> The remains of an unknown man were found last Saturday, near the Furgerson spring in Hurlburt canyon. They must have been there for several months, being in an advanced stage of decomposition, and nothing was discovered by which they could be identified. The man had collected some boughs, and laid a small mattress on them. Then partially disrobing, he had lain down, and carefully wrapped the covers about him, the quilt and blankets being still undisturbed. A handkerchief was pinned to some branches over his head, and two others were with his clothes under his head. He was of medium height, and apparently 50 or 60 years of age, his hair being quite gray. No whiskers were discernible. His teeth were nearly all gone. The few left being much decayed. His clothing was white knit underwear, coarse dark woolen suit, cotton socks, gaiter shoes, woolen over shirt, check jumper and two hats. All of which were whole and in good order. There was nothing in his pockets, but in a box he had a small mirror, a comb, shoemaker's awl and nails, ball of shoemaker's thread, spool of thread, a needle stuck into a piece of cloth, pair of scissors, pocket knife, buttons, matches and cigars. A coroner's inquest was held and a verdict found in accordance with the above facts, and the remains were decently interred near where they were found.[23]

The town passed winter quietly. Snow fell in January, leaving three inches to start 1883 in an untraditional fashion. School started again after the holiday. Minor improvements were

Gerhard Deitz standing in the doorway of his shop on First Street located next to Morrison's Store, June 7, 1882.

made on homes and stores.[24]

In February, Messrs. Charles Middleton, George Heald and John Starrett started building a two-story box factory near Guerne & Murphy's Mill and the railroad. The equipment and machinery were powered by a 35 hp engine. This engine came from the Mt. Jackson Quicksilver Mine — the mine had shut down. (See Chapter 27, "Quicksilver," Part II.) They were ready to do business the first of May. The company turned out boxes at a good rate, barely keeping up with the orders. Their specialty was "free" fruit boxes for cherries, apples and grapes. In November they switched to producing shingles, again the demand nearly overwhelming them.[25]

Not much else in the way or business or building occurred during the first part of 1883. Many social events occupied late winter: New officers were installed by the various clubs; birthdays and house warmings were the usual fare through spring.

In May a fire struck town. The entire business section was leveled. About midnight, May 21, a fire broke out in the rear of Oscar Morrison's store in a bunkhouse occupied by two Chinese employed by Taggart.[26] The flames spread quickly. Rufus Murphy was fire director, and it was only by superhuman effort that Brad Bell's meat market, Thompson's saloon, the school, Ellison's stable and the Methodist Church were saved.

The losses were: Schloss's general store and home; Taggart's Hotel, home, warehouse and other buildings; Folks' Hotel; Shoemake's saloon, home, and other structures; Glidden's variety shop; Savage's variety shop; Dr Burns' drugstore; the railroad depot; Mrs. McKenna's livery stable and home; Hewitt's tinsmith and hardware store; Coon's blacksmith; Deitz's jewelry store, which included the post office and Wells Fargo Express; Jacob's tailor shop; Wood's shoe store; Hetzel's cigars; two barber shops and a couple of other businesses.

Morrison's clerk, Wharton, nearly lost his life because he was asleep during most of the conflagration and woke just in time to escape the burning building.

Nearly everyone burned out moved to temporary locations, renting or making use of extended friendships. John French quickly rebuilt and, for about a month, was the only store open. He then sold out to Starret & Glidden and went into the lumber business. The area was completely rebuilt by the end of August.[27]

The I.O.O.F. rebuilding was started at the end of June by J.T. Ryus of Santa Rosa. The two-story building received its roof and laths for plaster the first week of August. One of Murphy's laborers fell from the top, but luck was with him, and he sustained only minor injuries. On August 18, Ryus announced the building was finished. It was dedicated four months later, on December 19.[28]

On the first floor were the businesses of Oscar Morrison, general store; Gerhardt Deitz, Post Office, Wells Fargo Express and jewelry; and Dr. J.A. Burns, drugstore.[29]

With the new hall available for meetings, three organizations started recruiting members to establish chapters in Guerneville. The first was the Council of Mutual Companions, a passing curiosity as far as the town was concerned. There was also a debating society formed, but nothing else is known. The third group was the Knights of Pythias.[30]

Another diversion from the rigors of life has occasionally found its way to Guerneville on three occasions up to the present (1980) — a circus. The first arrived in September 1883. Giant posters covered the blank walls of local buildings; the tent was erected on the river beach. Two performances were given, to which nearly everyone turned out. The tents were struck, and the troupe traveled on.[31]

The town snuggled down for the coming winter as the mills slowed down to cutting on short time. A few weddings took place in October to liven things up a bit. Minnie Schloss, local school teacher, married Charles Rothschild of Yountville. The other ceremony was between Miss Annie Willets and Charles Hill. After the marriage, the bride's father, W.H. Willets, one of the first people to reside in Big Bottom, sold his home and timber claim and, with the remainder of his family, moved to Santa Rosa.

Slipping back for just a moment to June 1881, we find a small article in the Santa Rosa Republican from Guerneville:

> R.B. Lundsford appeared on the street Saturday with his newly invented vehicle, a self-propelling carriage, something between a bicycle and preambulator. It needs a little remodeling, when he will try it again.

Discovered in Guerneville — an inventive mind! An inquisitive mind! Not one just concerned with mills, lumbering, mercantile or social life. But for the following two years, facts are void about this inventive sojourn.

In October 1883, Lundsford suddenly appeared in Santa Rosa.

> R.B. Lundsford attracted a great deal of attention by traveling about Santa Rosa in a four wheel vehicle driven by foot power.

And a week later:

> [It is] called a quadracycle. He made latest run along the road from Guerneville to Healdsburg.[32]

With that trip into history, he put it away from public comment. What a potential new form of transportation! Gottlieb Daimler and Karl Benz in Europe did not come forward with their petrol powered vehicles until 1885-1886! I often wonder just how close Lundsford did come to fame and fortune.

At 1 o'clock in the morning of Tuesday, November 2, 1883, the cry of "Fire!" was

J. B. PRESSLEY, M. D.,
Physician & Surgeon,
GUERNEVILLE,
SONOMA COUNTY.

Uhlhorn's 1884 Sonoma County Directory. JCS Collection

heard again in Guerneville. Bells rang, and in a few minutes the town turned out to do battle. The fire gained on the fighters. Within a minute, Taggart's saloon was engulfed. But with rapid work, the fire was contained to the one building. At times, Schloss' store adjoining it caught flame, but it was quickly extinguished. There was definite evidence of arson at the point of origin. The loss amounted to $2,000.[33]

About two weeks later, three men were arrested for the fire and for grand theft of $500 from Schloss's store. As far as existing court records are concerned, no charges were lodged against the three, and the case was dropped.

It was after these fires that Guerne & Murphy developed a water line. A reservoir was built 3/4 mile from town, 300 feet up a hill. The water mains from it were 2 1/2 inches in diameter. A test was made, and the water was thrown across Main Street from building to building, approximately 40 feet. The residents of the village felt relieved as it was a long-sought savior.[34]

Christmas 1883 came and went with a dance at French Hall and Kris Kringle distributing gifts about town. On New Year's eve, a social dance and luncheon was held at Folks' Hotel.[35]

The rains came in January and with it many social gatherings. It was during one of these parties that the home of William Van Voast, saloon keep and lumberman, was razed by fire. The belongings saved by man and wife were the clothes on their backs. It was suggested that a spark of coal from a heating stove dropped to the carpet below.[36]

Winter passed into March, and the outside world was again affecting Guerneville. New faces and businesses arrived. Since Dr. Pressly left in December there was only Dr. Burns to take care of the population. Occasionally a Dr. Shearer would assist him. Dr. Burns was always a good-natured fellow. Quite often when riding to a call, he would be asked, "Where you bound for, Doctor?" With a twinkle in his eye, the doctor would reply, "Got to catch a rabbit, got to catch a rabbit." It was his announcement a new citizen was about to be born. A new physician, Dr. S. McGuire, arrived for a permanent stay. Another family, the Hicks Brothers, opened a meat market. Sometimes special services would be provided on a temporary basis, an example being Ray & Wilburt, dentists of San Francisco, drilling and improving the town's dental hygiene.[37]

The rains continued and caused the usual damage to roads, low bridges and culverts. More social events were given: John French's birthday, school fundraising, weddings, anniversaries, club parties.

The highlight of the winter was the instituting of a new chapter of the Knights of Pythias. During this era of Guerneville's history,

The Guerneville Band in Armstrong Grove, 1885. Left to right: Jack Granley; Abe Colwell, baritone; Bill Glideen, solo alto; Henry Ungewitter; Charles Folks, B-flat coronet; Herbert Bagley, B-flat coronet; Ivon Clar, B-flat coronet; Adam Stuart, E-flat coronet; Arthur Turner, E-flat alto, O.O. Cobb; Bill Graham, E-flat alto; George Wescott, F-flat tenor; E.W. Smith, E-flat tuba; John Pool; John Ungewitter, base drum.

organizations played a vital role in the community by providing a sense of cohesiveness and identification. A Santa Rosa Republican reporter showed just how important the local populace considered societies:

> After 40 minutes' ride we were more than astonished to find from two to three hundred of the residents of Guerneville and vicinity in waiting at the depot; and all seemed surprised at seeing a delegation from Santa Rosa. Several exclaimed, 'Well, I guess they've come!' On the other side was heard the remark: 'This reminds me of Broadway, New York.'[38]

There were 64 people on the train. The two to three hundred Guernevillites represented approximately 20 percent of the town's population. The Knights of Pythias was formally chartered March 15, 1884.

Occasionally people would form a theatrical group for the town's entertainment, such as the "Bon-Ton Minstrels," The Fern Leaf Social Club, and last, but not least, the Guerneville Dramatic Club. There would be two months of study, practice and staging. And finally, the play was presented: "The Limerick Boy," "The Stage Struck Yankee," "The Persecuted Dutchman," "H.M.S. Pinafore," and, typical of the town and times, "Ten Nights in a Bar-Room."[39]

The town had various piecemeal musical groups, none formally organized until November 24, 1884, when the Guerneville Cornet Band was formed. By the end of six months the 15 musicians had full uniforms in red. The band had, besides cornets, a tuba, snare and bass drums. The first performance was given on Christmas night of 1884 at Wescott's & Thompson's Hall. The second band session was on Washington's Birthday 1885, again at Wescott's.[40]

The biggest event of 1884 was not the Fourth of July, but the possibility of a telegraph in town. The people started working for one to be brought in during February.

The First Guerneville Bridge, built in 1885, from 1907 photo. JCS Collection

They made an offer to Peter Donahue, president of the railroad, to supply poles for a line to run from Fulton, the nearest connection to town. In May, Oscar Morrison and a Mr. Phillips, owner of the telegraph company, secured $1,000 from Guerneville citizens to aid in the construction of the line. On July 15, Tuesday afternoon, the line was completed with an office in Morrison's store. It was " . . . considered a notable event and one of great interest to all."[41]

The rest of the year 1884 passed quietly: no births, marriages, deaths, no fires or building. The year 1885 started with a gloom cast over the village. The Methodist preacher, "Father" Walker, died at age 87. He preached his last sermon in November '84 with his old-time energy, but after a short time, had to be assisted to his seat. His strength failed him. His wife of 62 years survived him by three months. He was one of those in the community who "was always there," a fixture of the town. His was not a blazing career, nor was he a ne'er-do-well. But his absence left a big vacancy among the people. He was buried up on the hill and is one of two people in the cemetery born in the 18th century: 1798.[42]

Along with sorrow, there is mirth. Three weddings took place in January. Then John and Abe Happy were caught killing hogs on John Bachelder's Ranch. They pleaded guilty before Justice of the Peace, Marshall Florence. He fined them $30 or 30 days' county jail. They were broke.[43]

On April 3, in the night, an attempted arson was discovered under French's Hall. A coat saturated with coal oil was found smoldering, but no clues to the guilty party were found.[44]

Since the town came into existence some 20 years earlier, the populace here and in the surrounding countryside had tried every means at their disposal to have the Board of Supervisors in Santa Rosa construct a bridge. This, after the arrival of the railroad, was their greatest desire. After every storm bridges, culverts and roads were badly damaged, as the reader now knows. A writer to the Sonoma Democrat said:

> Not an ounce of freight, nor a single passenger can get west of Russian River at this point, as far north as Healdsburg, 18 miles and westwardly to the ocean, except by rail. Several thousand people out here are thus hemmed in for about three months every rainy season. The fact is Guerneville needs a bridge across the river so that people on the other side can come here for

lumber, and so we may get out with teams to Santa Rosa. It is a burning shame.[45]

Back in 1875, a bridge would have been built except no one among the Supervisors and engineers could agree where to place it. Now the population of Redwood, Ocean and Salt Point townships had increased four-fold. The people's choice in locating the bridge was at the fording from town to Torrance's on the left bank. The banks had remained stable, as well as the river bed. The danger of floating trees was about over as the timber upstream had been nearly all cut away.

Letters from the area to Santa Rosa newspapers in support of a bridge were about one a week (the papers were weekly) for a period of five to six months. There were none against.

In July of 1884, the Grand Hotel was the scene of a town meeting. A committee of 20 citizens was selected to present a petition to the Supervisors. The names are familiar:

Rufus Murphy	R.E. Lewis
John Taggart	S.H. Torrance
L.M. Ellison	H. Haas.
Granville Thompson	John Folks.
M.D. Haskins	L. Ridenhour
C.D. Yarborough	S.D. Ingram
Henry Beaver	Dr. J.A. Burns
O. Shoemake	J.H. Fowler
A. Wehrspon	A. McFadyen
J.H. French	D. Hetzel
Dr. S. McGuire, secretary	
J.B. Armstrong, chairman [46]	

The petition was drawn and presented to the Supervisors on July 8. Duly impressed and finally recognizing that the people at large were demanding construction, the Board granted the people's wish.

The county had two proposed sites surveyed: one at the usual town fording, the second downstream where banks are higher and a new road would have to be constructed. This second site would place the bridge at right angles to river flow and enter the center of town. It would have been selected by the Supervisors in April 1885 only if the right-of-way would be given to the county by Guerne & Murphy, plus a few other minor contingencies. An agreement was not reached, so the first or upper site was chosen.[47]

The California Bridge Company of Oakland received the contract on their bid of $11,970. The trestle work ran $3.20 per lineal foot. The two main spans were Iron Pratt combination truss, 150 feet long, and two 60-foot spans of strain beam truss. Approximately 500 feet of trestle work for bridge approaches would be built. The work was to be completed within 100 days from May 8, the day the county and company signed the contract! Deadline: August 17.[48]

The first two weeks were spent preparing the grounds and grade and setting up the 80-foot pile driver. On May 25, work on the structure started by driving piles for the three 60-foot high piers. Each pier consisted of 26 pilings, 16 inches of clear heart redwood 80 feet long and driven 20 feet down. The piers were completed June 7. Thirty days gone.

With a donkey engine and a work force of 18 men, construction proceeded rapidly. The main spans with their iron and wood chords fairly flew together. Lumber was hauled from John French's mill as fast as possible. Stringers were slammed into place; pins anchored lateral and portal rods. Iron sheets plated the upstream points of the piers.

All joints and connections were painted and soaked with paraffin paint.

The builders predicted the bridge would be finished by August 1, 16 days ahead of schedule. But they were wrong. They finished on July 31, 17 days before the deadline!

Now freight, passengers and travelers of the northwest section of the County were not dependent upon the railroad during winter months to move in free commerce. Gone was the danger of losing life, stock or property while crossing the ford to Pocket Canyon and the south bank.[49]

"$5 fine for driving or riding on this bridge faster than a walk." Photo circa 1906.
JCS Collection

In September, as a final touch, signs were erected over each end of the bridge:[50] "Fine $25 for riding or driving faster than a walk."

Besides bridge construction, little else happened during summer 1885. A mysterious fire started in Schloss' store and spread next door to Haarms' Saloon, he a newcomer to town.[51] The water in the reservoir was low due to summer use, so only by strenuous effort was the town saved. Three smaller buildings were torn down and removed. Buckets and wet blankets saved adjoining houses, the Odd Fellows building, and the eastern portion of town. Haarms rebuilt, but Schloss, though he was covered by insurance for his store and home, did not.[52]

Other newcomers arrived, some locating in the hills. A new doctor, J.H. Mathers, joined Dr. Burns. Another organization, Post 86, Grand Army of the Republic, was chartered in August with an enrollment of 25 members.

The rest of the year was uneventful, save one incident that occurred in October. That story is told in the next chapter.

1. *S.D.*, February 5, 1881, *R.R.F.*, February 3, 1881.
2. *S.D.*, February 26, 1881; April 30, 1881.
3. *R.R.F.*, April 25, 1881; May 23, 1881, S.D., July 2, 1881.
4. *S D.*, October 13, 1881, *R.R.F.*, November 20, 1881, *S.D.*, January 7, 1882, March 4, 1882.
5. Interview with Gertrude Shulte, January 14, 1967; interview with Ernest Shulte, January 14, 1967.
6. *S.R. Rep.*, March 19, 1883; August 20, 1883, August 27, 1883.
7. *S.R. Rep.*, April 9 (16?), 1883, April 5, 1885.
8. Gertrude Shulte, op. cit.
9. *S.R. Rep.*, May 9, 1881.
10. *S.D.*, July 8, 1882.
11. Calif. Penal Code, 1880, #299. Sec. 300.
12. *S.D.*, November 28, 1881.
13. *S.D.*, December 3, 1881.
14. *S.D.*, December 10, 1881.
15. *S.D.*, December 17, 1881.
16. Ibid.
17. *S.R. Rep.*, December 26, 1881; *S.D.*, December 31, 1881; January 7, 1882.
18. *S.R. Rep.*, April 17, 1882.
19. *S.D.*, January 28, 1882.
20. *S.R. Rep.*, July 10, 1882.
21. County Records, Articles of Incorporation, #249.
22. *S.R. Rep.*, October 30, 1882; November 13, 1882; S.D., November 4, 1882.
23. *S.R. Rep.*, January 15, 1883. The appended note was by Ellen Bagley.
24. *S.R. Rep.*, February 19, 1883.
25. *S.D.*, June 2, 1883; June 23, 1883.
26. *S.D.*, May 2, 1883.
27. *S.D.*, June 2, 1883; *S.R. Rep.*, June 11, 1883, August 6, 1883.
28. *S.D.*, August 11, 1883; December 29, 1883.
29. *S.D.*, December 15, 1883.
30. *S.D.*, November 17, 1883. See Chapter XXIX, "Former Societies."
31. *S.R. Rep.*, October 1, 1883.
32. *S.R. Rep.*, June 13, 1881; *S.D.*, October 20, 1883; October 27, 1883.

33. *S.R. Rep.*, November 2, 1883.
34. *S.D.*, December 8, 1883. See *S.R. Rep.*, September 14, 1882.
35. *S.R. Rep.*, January 7, 1884.
36. *S.D.*, February 16, 1884.
37. *P.D.*, October 11, 1962, p. 15; *S.D.*, February 4, 1884.
38. *S.R. Rep.*, March 17, 1884.
39. *S.R. Rep.*, March 19, 1883; January 9, 1884.
40. *S.R. Rep.*, December 28, 1884; *S.D.*, December 27, 1884; February 23, 1885.
41. *S.D.*, February 23, 1884; May 10, 1884; *S.R. Rep.*, July 23, 1884.
42. *S.R. Rep.*, January 12, 1885; April 19, 1885.
43. *S.R. Rep.*, January 26, 1885; February 2, 1885; J.P. Report to Board of Supervisors, County Records.
44. *S.R. Rep.*, April 5, 1885.
45. *S.D.*, March 15, 1884.
46. *S.R. Rep.*, July 2, 1884.
47. Bd. Sup. Minutes, Vol. 8, October 1884; *S.D.*, December 27, 1884.
48. Bd. Sup. Records, originl contract: *S.R. Rep.*, My 14, 1885; *S.D.*, June 6, 1885, July 18, 1885.
49. *S.D.*, August 8, 1885.
50. Bd. Sup. Road Book #3
51. *S.D.*, July 11, 1885; *S.R. Rep.*, August 31, 1885
52. Ibid.

Starrett's home on the north side of Third Street in Guerneville, June 10, 1882. Note the railroad tracks in the lower right corner. Ed Langhart Collection.

GRAND HOTEL,

S. G. THOMPSON,
PROPRIETOR,
GUERNEVILLE, SONOMA COUNTY, CAL.

The First-Class Accommodations **AT THIS HOUSE** MAKE IT A FAVORITE STOPPING PLACE.

McKENNEY'S STABLE.

LIVERY SALE & FEED,
OPP. GRAND HOTEL.

Horses Boarded by the Day, Week or Month.

MRS. R. McKENNEY, PROPRIETRESS.
GUERNEVILLE, SONOMA, CAL.

Uhlhorn's 1884 Sonoma County Directory. JCS Collection

Chapter 18

ARSON

It was cold and wet in Guerneville that Thursday afternoon of November 16, 1882. Mr. Hicks, clerk at Morrison's Store, was poking around outside the building and the neighboring Haas Store and Post Office on Main Street. He discovered under the post office floor, protected from the rainy weather, a can of coal oil, paper, and a small pile of kindling. Hicks returned to the store and told his employer, Morrison, Dr. Westfall, and hotel owner, John Taggart, about his find. Between them, they agreed to watch the location of an obvious preparation for arson.[1]

Morrison switched the can of oil with a similar one filled with water. On Sunday night, Hicks was standing armed watch. About 8 o'clock, a man slipped out a back window of the Haas Store and into the night. He went to the secreted materials, took the can, and splashed its contents on the kindling. He lit a match. It was Haas!

Hicks shot and missed.

Haas took off running.

Hicks fired, again missed, and chased Haas out into the dimly lit street. Haas ran into Taggart's Hotel, where he was captured.[2]

A week passed with Haas in jail. The preliminary examination was held in Guerneville, when he was charged with attempted arson. Deputy District Attorney Ware represented the State, "Judge" Rutledge for the defense. After all was said, defendant Haas was held to answer for the crime by Justice of the Peace Hudson, who set bail at $2,000. Haas secured it and was released.[3]

On December 4, in Santa Rosa, he was arraigned in Superior Court, and two weeks later entered a plea of not guilty.

His trial began in mid-January 1883. Testimony was taken for three days, then the case was given to the jury to decide. They deliberated 4 1/2 hours and declared themselves hung: 11 jurors said not guilty, one juror said guilty. Obviously there was more to this story than was related in the newspapers and, unfortunately, court records reflect no further facts.[4]

The case was continued from time to time through February, March and April. The retrial began on May 1 and proceeded through May 3. It created a lot of interest, so much so about 30 Guernevillites took the long train trip to Santa Rosa to witness the proceedings.[5]

The case was given to the jury at 5 p.m. In less than an hour, they returned with a verdict of not guilty.

The spectators rejoiced and rushed to congratulate Haas. Among them were some of the principal businessmen of town. When he arrived home, a serenade was given him on that balmy May evening.

Haas's character,

> ... has always borne a good reputation both for business integrity and as a citizen, and with but very few exceptions he is generally respected and is held in the highest estimation by all his neighbors and townsmen.[6]

As previously noted in Chapter XVII, fires continued to occur because of arson, accidents and carelessness. These happened on May 21 and November 2, 1882; February 16, 1884; April 3 and July 11, 1885.

Parmilly J. Etheridge was born in Michigan and was a member of a Michigan Regiment during the Civil War. He later went to Minnesota, and then came to San Francisco and Guerneville in 1874. Since his arrival, he worked at Guerne & Murphy's sawmill,

John Taggart's Hotel, south side of First Street, August 22, 1882. Ed Langhart Collection

receiving good wages. He was well known about town. Etheridge was addicted to gambling, but not to alcohol. In 1883 he went back to Minnesota, but returned two years later to Guerneville. He looked up his old employer, George Guerne, and told him a startling story.[7]

One morning back in 1883, Etheridge met Haas under a tree in front of the school. Haas, knowing that Etheridge was a little short of cash from playing cards, said there was a good job for him. After a little chitchat, Haas told Etheridge that if he would set fire to his (Haas') store, he would give Etheridge $500. If Haas got all the insurance, he would give Etheridge $1,000, since the store was heavily insured.

This offer was presented to Etheridge after Haas was caught for the attempted arson and was about to go to trial. The deal was accepted. Haas told Etheridge to do the deed some night during the trial, when he, Haas, would be locked up in jail. Haas wanted the fire to occur while he was not present.

The plans were carried out in earnest. Haas supplied several bottles of coal oil and kindling. Etheridge was ready.

The trial came to pass, as related, in May, and Haas was incarcerated. The trial finished, but no fire took place. When Haas returned to town, he was irritated with Etheridge and said:

> "I will go to San Francisco in a day or so and while I am gone, you set fire and telegraph me the results at the Russ House. Be sure and save the books."

At midnight, May 7, Etheridge prepared the fuel alongside the Haas building, saturated the wall with coal oil, and placed a short piece of candle in the tinder pile. He lit the candle as a time fuse and went to bed at Mrs. Longley's, where he roomed.

Soon the cry of "Fire!" was heard. Mrs. Longley rushed to his room and got him up. He ran to the scene and joined the townsfolk in saving goods. Instead of going for the store ledgers, Etheridge went for the till. There was nothing in it.

The fire resulted in almost the complete destruction of Guerneville, a loss of $75,000.

Haas was telegraphed, and a day or so later, he returned to town. Etheridge asked for his money, but Haas paid him only a few dollars.

The town rebuilt and new stock was put up in the stores.

Etheridge had daily conversations with Haas: He wanted his money. Haas told him if he would torch the store again, he would pay him what was due, plus $1,000 more as soon as the insurance money was collected. Etheridge agreed again.

The second fire was in Taggart's Hotel on November 2, 1883. Again, Haas welshed on paying Etheridge, the total amount now being $1,500. Etheridge constantly pressed Haas for the money, but Haas kept telling him the insurance companies had not paid off. In truth, they had, to the grand sum of $12,000. Haas trickled money to Etheridge, $5 to $20 at a time, probably amounting in all to no more than $700.

Haas, finally tiring of the situation, sent Etheridge to Humboldt County. That did not last long. Etheridge came back. Haas gave him $100 and sent him to Minnesota. While there Etheridge was stricken with consumption, the common term for pulmonary tuberculosis. The country and weather had undermined his health. The doctors told him his days were numbered. So in June 1885, in despair, he returned to California and Guerneville, where he looked up Haas.

Later, he told Guerne the story:

> "I told Haas that there was a room whitewashed for him in San Quentin. Haas laughed at me and said, 'Nobody will believe you, so you will simply land yourself in San Quentin. I'm safe myself.'"

A short time later, in July, the fourth fire was set. A few days passed. Etheridge met Haas and said, "Well, you've made another haul."

Haas protested, saying he was a big loser with this last fire. Etheridge again demanded money. Evidently Haas became alarmed, for he took Etheridge for a ride and gave him two dollars.

Etheridge told Guerne of this latest development. In the meantime, Haas disappeared from Guerneville. On August 1, 1885, Haas was formally accused of his felonious crimes. Etheridge was not, only because his health was failing fast.

The townsfolk put up a reward of $500 for the capture of Haas.[8] A year later, on September 7, 1886, his wife of ten years, Rosa, daughter of S. Schloss, filed for divorce on the grounds of desertion.[9] Haas fled the state and disappeared from the Russian River country forever.

Etheridge died shortly thereafter from the dreaded affliction he had contracted.

1. *S.D.*, November 25, 1882; *S.R. Rep.*, November 20, 1882.
2. Ibid.
3. *S.R, Rep.*, November 25, 1882.
4. Superior Court Records, Case No. 1734, 1882; *S.D.*, October 3, 1885.
5. Ibid.
6. *S.D.*, May 5, 1883.
7. *S.R. Rep.*, October 1, 1885, *S.D.*, October 3, 1885. The following story was extracted from these two dates.
8. *S.D.*, October 31, 1885.
9. Superior Court Case No. 1543, 1886.

In the Redwoods of Sonoma County near Tyrone. JCS Collection

Chapter 19

Lumber Mills — 1886 to 1890

Little was printed about Guerne & Murphy's mill during 1886. By now the mill was an established act, solvent, and would always be there at the west end of town. The company did lay another half mile of track from town down to the picnic grove. The rails were already going up Hulbert Creek, so this line headed straight across Hulbert Creek, heading west.[1] This was May of 1886.

Some six months later, in November, Colonel Armstrong, Judge Overton and Albert Brown made a survey for a railroad to run north from town three miles to Armstrong's timber, terminating at a 50-acre park that he had set aside for public gatherings, such as picnics and band concerts. The survey called for several trestles, one to cross a dam 200 feet long! The railroad was predicted to be completed by the end of winter, after the right-of-way was obtained by purchase and/or condemnation. In March 1887, Armstrong and Brown were busy building the railroad. The cost of the branch line was figured to be $25,000.[2]

In May, these lumber barons were having problems obtaining certain lands to complete their railroad. The owners of the parcel were Guerne & Murphy. As one writer put it:

> ... it is a very rare thing for one company to help build up a rival; hence the opposition to the right-of-way.[3]

A suit was filed by Guerne & Murphy against Armstrong and Brown in June 1887.[4] The suit in its complaint prayed for the removal of the dam by the defendants from Fife Creek. When high water would come in the future, the lands of Guerne & Murphy would be flooded. In answer to the complaint, Armstrong and Brown stated without the dam they would be flooded. Jury trial was demanded by defendants. Battle lines were drawn.[5]

The trial lasted ten days. The jury returned a verdict to plaintiffs for $5 (past damages) and ordered removal of the dam. The defendants' costs amounted to about $3,000. The final result was no train for anyone to move logs.[6]

But this trial did not end the problems between the two companies. A second civil suit was filed by Guerne & Murphy against their old adversaries. The former had an unpaid promissory note of $2,833 against the latter. Again the parties went to trial. Armstrong and Brown fought the suit off and on for ten days from August 1 to September 5. After the smoke cleared, the decision of the Court was made in favor of the plaintiffs.[7]

At the same time, the County of Sonoma was also agitated with Guerne & Murphy. County Supervisor Connolly of Redwood Township informed the Board of Supervisors the road in Hulbert Canyon was obstructed,

> ... said obstruction being placed there by the domineering autocrats of Guerneville, Messrs. Guerne & Murphy, who have at said point appropriated for there [sic] own uses and purposes nearly seven hundred feet of the public highway and with characteristic impudence, refuse to remove said obstruction.[8]

This obstruction was their railroad up Hulbert Creek to their logging camp. As Supervisor Connolly said:

> the public highway [was] appropriated by the road fiends of Guerneville for private purposes.[9]

Another county road was surveyed by Road Overseer William Garrison to be alongside the tracks, and was later constructed.[10]

The "big mill," while the owners were in court, was run by 70 men and averaged 20,000 board feet a day.

In 1888, mill production and logging statistics are lacking because most Santa Rosa newspapers are missing for that year. (Some issues are in Bancroft Library, Berkeley, and the State Library, Sacramento. Only Ellen Bagley's scrapbook has any articles, and they are from the Republican.) One publication from San Francisco stated the Guerne & Murphy mill daily capacity was 50,000 board feet.[11]

Contrary to the normal way of doing things, the mill usually was shut down during the winter, but in February of 1889, they made a short run to fill lumber orders from the townfolk. Guerneville had suffered its greatest conflagration up to that time. Read the following chapter, XX, for the full story.[12]

The "big mill" returned to winter shutdown until late in the cutting season of 1889. When it did start production, it was under new ownership. After 24 years of different partners coming and going, George Guerne, the last of the original four owners, and his current partner, Rufus Murphy, sold all holdings for $100,000 to "Messrs. Robert Dollar" (later owner of the well known shipping line), and "et al." Et al was (were) Westover. It is not known if more than one Westover joined Dollar at this time. With new owners, a new name: Sonoma Lumber Company.[13]

The lumber mill lay idle for a week in July for boiler fixing. The San Francisco & Northern Pacific Railroad bought the rail extension from the mill to Hulbert Creek. The company then had the barn for oxen and horses moved across Fife Creek to the west side.[14]

A new and larger engine was built in Michigan for the mill to increase its capacity to 40,000 board feet per day and to drive the electrical generator for lights.[15] Lights? Yes, lights. They were used for night work. Along with the new engine, a larger dynamo was purchased so more lights could be used out in the lumber yard. In mid-January 1890, the new engine arrived.

The mill shut down and the remodeling began. The stumps under the old mill, probably used as supports, were blasted out and room was made for the new engine. By mid-February the new bed timber was placed. It measured 3 feet x 4 feet x 30 feet, equal to 4,320 board feet.[16] Finally, after Easter, April 6, the new boiler was fired, the new engine turned, and another season was under way.

Changes were also made at the administrative side of the company. In November of '89, Robert Dollar sold out his interest to Westover's sons and another gentleman. In April 1890, the Sonoma Lumber Company incorporated, locating its home office in San Francisco. The directors were William Westover of Bay City, Michigan; Delbert L. Westover of San Francisco; William W. Westover of Guerneville, J. Wallace Westover of San Francisco, and Lincoln Chapman of Duluth, Michigan. The Big Time had come to Guerneville.[17]

You would think a new corporation with its new plant and equipment would learn from the past. But no, they started right off doing things wrong. The dynamite, used for stump removal and log splitting, was stored at the mill. It accidentally exploded and blew out one end of the new building. Luck was with the people present and there were no injuries. The mill proceeded through the remainder of the year without incident.

The mill of Armstrong and Brown, the Big Bottom, acquired additional timber amounting to 40 million board feet in January 1886. Their yearly cutting capacity was from four to five million board feet.[18]

Two points of interest about the mill were a telephone and an iron railway running from there into the woods, part way. Remember, they were thwarted in completing it by Guerne & Murphy's suit.

Like Guerne & Murphy, they were a big lumber concern. But unlike Guerne & Murphy, Armstrong and Brown ran their mill all winter of 1886 with a full work force of 50 men. The logging crews worked the usual 12-hour day all year. Sharing the workload were ten yoke of oxen and five four-horse teams.[19]

All the men boarded at the mill with the exception of a half dozen or so who lived with their families near work.

Mill production rate was a modest 30,000 board feet per day, though on occasion reached 37,000. To fill a special order, the mill cut a plank 14 feet long, 5 1/2 feet wide, and 3 inches thick. The mill also set a new record for a season's cutting in the Russian River area: 5 million board feet.[20]

Winter passed. Spring and the 1887 cutting season was begun. Big Bottom Mill received a special order from Santa Rosa for that city's Third Street Bridge. That finished order filled two railroad cars. The company shipped 250 carloads of redwood lumber in March and proceeded to run full time.[21]

The company's saws were cutting lumber five to eight thousand board feet more per day than the year previous; the crew was larger, with 70 men compared to 50 in 1886. It was just as well as orders were coming from the San Joaquin Valley and as far away as Los Angeles. The orders poured in. By December, the company had cut nearly six million feet. They felled and cut one tree into 180 feet of saw logs. The net result was 28,700 board feet.[22]

As already stated, the year 1888 as far as publications are concerned does not exist; however, no cutting was done at the mill during 1889. The orders received at Big Bottom Mill were filled with the stock on hand. Lumber production was resumed in April 1890, then again it faded from the newspapers.[23]

The French Mill in May's Canyon was probably rated third in importance in the Guerneville area. Traditionally, the mill started the cutting season on short time up to April. Owner John French had 30 or more men working at the mill when it switched to full time. In May they were put out of work for a short period when one of the circular saws flew into pieces, one fragment cutting off a 2 x 6-inch rafter in the top of the mill. By luck, no

Mary Etta Folks French and John Henry French, circa 1882; Mary was the daughter of hotel keeper John Folks. Married in Green Valley Sept. 14, 1880. JCS Collection

one was injured.[24]

French's Mill, sawing a moderate 16,000 board feet per day, had some problem getting its product to the railroad in town. To relieve the problem, the company had a bridge constructed over the river, 400 feet in length and 12 feet above the water. The balance of the season progressed with nothing out of the norm.[25]

The sawing rate at French's for 1887 was more than double that of 1886. By the first of June it was 30,000 board feet a day, and in July it was upped to 35,000 feet. The work force both at the mill and in the woods was 50 men. In 1888, the daily cutting rate went up to 40,000 board feet.[26]

John French in 1889 went down river four miles to what he called "Big Flat Station," near Duncan's. This was probably Moscow (today's Casini Ranch), or Villa Grande. He stayed but one year, then took the steamer "Pomona" north to Humboldt County in May of 1890.[27]

French's Mill on Big Bottom Flat along what is now Armstrong Road, 1886. Foreground, far left, Henry Klein. Foreground center, leaning against stump, mull owner John French. JCS Collection.

Though there were only three big mills in the area (excluding Korbel Mill upriver), John French revealed in his memoirs the relationship between the three — the feud between Guerne/Murphy and Armstrong/Brown, and the part he played in the power struggle.

Back in 1883, while French was running a grocery store in Guerneville, Armstrong asked him to buy Murphy's Mill since Armstrong was not on speaking terms with Murphy. When the Murphy brothers cut all the timber which they controlled, they shut down, but left everything as though they would start up the next day. French paid $10,000 in gold coin for 40 cut-over acres, the old mill, cattle, a span of horses, cookhouse, chickens, everything.

John went to Armstrong, and the colonel repaid him. French worked for him for two months before the colonel asked him how much he owed him. French answered, "Colonel, give me whatever you think is right." Armstrong gave him $2,000 for the two months. Armstrong wanted French to come in with him as a partner, but French declined, desiring to be his own boss.[28]

Other operations in and about the Guerneville area were given passing mention in contemporary printings. One was the Riley Mill operating in 1886 and 1890 at the Russian River Station (Monte Rio). This mill was in the vicinity as early as 1882.[29]

Charles Middleton's shingle mill in 1885 was located on the left bank of Fife Creek, just north of Guerne & Murphy's hay barn. On Monday night, October 18, 1886, about 9:30, that old familiar enemy of the town struck again. Fire! It originated in the shin-

Letterhead of Ludolff & Wehrspon. JCS Collection

gle mill and quickly spread to the hay barn. The two buildings were lost, along with one of Guerne & Murphy's locomotives, 30 feet of trestle, and their log pond dam. In addition, a couple of dwellings belonging to Twombley were lightly damaged. The loss amounted to over $3,000. Insurance covered but $500 of the loss.[30]

Our old friend, Thomas Heald, got back into the wood business (some three years after he left McFayden & Brown in 1884) by purchasing 160 acres from the Korbel brothers to supply his shingle mill, The mill was Middleton's, of which he was a partner. The mill was rebuilt between October 1886 and April 1887.[31]

A new name, at least in this area of the county, appeared during this time, between 1886 and 1890. It later became well known in the River area — the family Clar. Ivon had first arrived in 1887 at the age of 19. His elder brother, Lawrence Frank, soon followed. Frank built a mill near present-day Mill and Main Streets. Unfortunately, it burned completely down one noon hour.

The Ludolph Mill remained obscure in published news until 1890 when it was noted that Henry Ludolph sold out his share of the company to his partner, August Wehrspon. The mill was still in its old location one-half mile from town, in Pocket Canyon. At the end of the year, Wehrspon had some redwoods known as the "Five Brothers" felled, and converted them into 40,000 board feet of lumber.[32]

Besides the area mills, there were still enterprising individuals working up split-stuff: shakes, posts, pickets, et cetera. One contract was made by R.E. Lewis with the railroad for 30,000 ties. Mr. Van Voast shipped eight carloads of redwood split work in early 1887. During the season of 1890, shipments of tanbark, cordwood, shakes, et cetera, were heavy, averaging one and sometimes two trainloads a day.[33]

After some 20-odd years of cutting away at the forest, there were still trees to fell. The volume of potential lumber in the Guerneville area was substantial.[34]

1. Armstrong's Timber   60 million feet
2. Guerne & Murphy, with
   Hulbert Creek holdings   30 million feet
3. May's Canyon & tributaries 10 million feet
4. Pocket Canyon & hills   6 million feet
5. Odd lots by different parties
   around Guerneville   10 million feet

Total   **116 million feet**

But along with wealth, there are taxes — property taxes and assessments, The amount of tax was then, as now, unequal per same value. Big Bottom Mill was assessed on two parcels adjoining each other, $50 and $60 per acre. Guerne & Murphy, in the same location as Big Bottom, were levied $30 and $37.50 per acre.[35]

It was during the 1880's that the cries of "waste," "pollution" and "lack of fire control"

Logging with a donkey engine near Guerneville, probably French's logging operation, circa 1888. Photo: California Art Gallery, Santa Rosa. J.C. Schubert Collection.

were first raised. The waste of wood from tree to finished product was (stated many times) above 25 percent. Many mill owners denied it was that high, yet other owners thought that was a fair percentage.

The first report by the California State Board of Forestry in 1885-86 came right out and said:

> The amount of waste made in redwood manufacture ... as well as we have been able to approximate it, is a fraction OVER 77 PERCENT. If we are right ... there is equally good reason that in the infancy of the lumbering art the efficiency was hardly more than 20 percent.[36] [Emphasis added]

Loss/waste was caused when a tree was dropped and shattered on the ground even with cribbing to cushion the fall. The first "slab" cuts to square up a sawlog were discarded or used to fire the boilers. Another form of waste was through the use of large circular saws. To retain metal strength because of the four-, five- and six-foot diameters, the blades were 3/8-inch thick. In 1888, Alexander Duncan of Duncans' Mills, was quoted as saying, "We can save a great deal more if the band saw is a success."[37]

The amount of sawdust from cutting a log was large, and with the years of operation the results were giant mounds at the mills. Heald & Guerne, and later, Guerne & Murphy, dumped their sawdust over the river bank, deposited for years in defiance of the law, and typical of this company's attitude. The law was to stop water pollution. An anonymous writer, obviously a fisherman, stated there was not much fishing (in 1887), even though the river was stocked with black bass five years previously. There were only suckers and hardmouths remaining.[38]

Incidentally, the huge pile of sawdust on the river bank near the mouth of Fife Creek was ignited by a trash fire about 1918. Old timers predicted it would burn for 20 years. During the summers for five or six years, it produced a miserable smokey nuisance. Then a high winter flood extinguished the hidden fire.

But Guerne & Murphy were not the only violators. Small mill operators dumped sawdust into mounds in canyon bottoms. These washed downstrean in fall, winter and spring, which, in turn, choked big streams.

There were also the slash, bark and ripped-up vegetation left by the loggers that contributed to the rapid change in the environment.

The biggest waster of all was forest fire. Prior to the mid-1880s, very little concern was given to such fires, because fire was commonly used by most loggers in clearing the area of brush, slash and bark, an almost everyday thing.

The first mention of a "forest fire," as opposed to "brush-clearing fires," was on October 9, 1886:

> A fierce forest fire has been raging near Guerneville since Sunday night, October 3. The fire started near town and traversed to near Korbel Brothers sawmill a mile away. Several cords of tanbark and cordwood have been destroyed. The fire is supposed to have started from a campfire.[39]

A second fire getting out of control occurred June 1887. It was near Guerne & Murphy's logging camp, "with 40 men fighting it while temperatures during the day reached 110°."[40]

In October of the same year, a large fire, which by today's standards would be noticed throughout the state and points farther away, received only three inches of newsprint on page 3 of the Sonoma Democrat.[41]

A Big Redwood Fire

> D. A. Foster, of Forestville, reports a big fire in the redwoods in that vicinity. The fire started from Lautren's Ranch near Guerneville last Tuesday where some laborers were burning brush. The fire swept with great fury and rapidly through the dense woods toward Forestville cutting a swath two miles in width. All day Wednesday seventy-five or eighty men fought the fire without success and Thursday it was burning in the Green Valley Switch about three miles (west) of Forestville. It is reported that several houses were burned. The fire-fighters attempted to get to the buildings but were driven back by the flames. A huge tract of county is reported devastated and a great amount of wood, tanbark and fencing destroyed and livestock burned. Lewis Ridenhour has lost 100 cords of wood; Wehrspon 100 cords of wood and 10,000 pickets. James Murdock, John White, C. A. Ricket, R. McIntosh, Sam Black, Al Fletcher, E. S. Shortridge have lost property in the fire but it is not yet known to what extent. The fire is now reported checked, if not under control.

Several fires in late 1888 were charring the countryside. Some damage was done to standing timber, cordwood and split stuff, "but a great deal of needed cleaning up was accomplished."[42]

During a fire in August 1889, one of several near Korbel's, a man dropped dead from fighting the flames. Others fell from exhaustion. A month later a fire was burning west of Guernevllle in Hulbert Creek/Mission Canyon. Two logging operations belonging to L.W. Burris and L. Streining were the heaviest losers. Again in September, two weeks later, there were two or three logging camps on fire.[43]

The five years covered here were periods of high lumber production and record employment in the history of Big Bottom.

1. *S.D.*, May 22, 1886.
2. *S.D.*, November 27, 1886.
3. *S.D.*, May 7, 1887.
4. May 4, 1887, Bd. Supvrs.; Road Book 3, p. 276.
5. *S.D.*, May 7, 1887.
6. Bd. Supvrs.; Road Book 3, p. 403.
7. *Op. Cit.*, p. 411.
8. *S.R. Rep.*, June 2, 1887; June 16, 1887. Note Colonel J.B. Armstrong owned the *Republican*.
9. Ibid.
10. County of Sonoma Superior Court, cases #1658 and 1661.
11. Bell & Heyman's, *Sonoma County & Russian River Valley* (May 1888), San Francisco, CA, p. 14.
12. *Healdsburg Tribune*, February 26, 1889 (hereafter

Ox team near Monte Rio. JCS Collection

cited as *Trib.*)

13. *Trib.*, May 1, 1889; *S.D.*, September 21, 1889. This name is not to be confused with a prior use of the same name applied to a mill near Duncans' Mills in 1877.
14. Ibid.
15. *Trib.*, September 4, 1889, November (?), 1889; *S.D.*, September 21, 1889.
16. *Herald,* February 7, 1890; February 22, 1890.
17. *Herald,* November (30?), 1890; Sonoma County Official Records, Corporation papers #342.
18. *S.D.*, January 23, 1886.
19. *S.D.*, Febuary 27, 1886; August 14, 1886.
20. *S.D.*, May 22, 1886; August 14, 1886; December 18, 1886; *S.R. Rep.*, July 11, 1886.
21. *S.R. Rep.*, March 31, 1887; *S.D.*, April 9, 1887.
22. *S.D.*, June 4, 1887; December 17, 1887.
23. *S.D.*, June 4, 1887; June 25, 1887; December 17, 1887.
24. *S.D.*, March 27, 1886, June 5, 1886; May 8, 1886.
25. *S.D.*, June 12, 1886; July 1, 1886.
26. *S.R. Rep.*, June 2, 1881; June 30, 1887; July 28, 1887; Sonoma County and Russian River Valley, op. cit.
27. John H. French Memoirs, p. 14, date unknown, but after 1918; in possession of Viola E. French, Richardson Grove, CA.
28. *Ibid.*
29. *S.D.*, June 12, 1886; *Healdsburg Herald*, Feb. 17, 1890
30. *S.D*, October 23, 1886; *Trib.*, October (20?), 1886; Sanborn Map 1888 of Guerneville.
31. *S.D.*, April 9, 1887; *Sonoma County & Russian River Valley, op. cit.*
32. *S.D.*, August 30, 1890; December 27, 1890.
33. *S.D.*, June 25, 1887; March 19, 1887; August 9, 1890.
34. *S.D.*, February 26, 1887.
35. *S.D.*, October 30, 1886.
36. Appendix to Journal of State and Assembly, 27th Session, Vol. 4, Sec. IV, (Sacramento: State Printer, 1885-1886), p. 149.
37. *Sonoma County & Russian River Valley,* op. cit.
38. *S.D.*, July 30, 1887.
39. *S.D.*, October 9, 1886.
40. *S.D.*, June 11, 1887
41. *S.D.*, October 22, 1887.
42. *Trib.*, November 14, 1888.
43. *Trib.*, August 7, 1889; September 4, 1889, *S.D.*, September 7, 1889.

Chapter 20

Guerneville — 1886 to 1890

The populace of Guerneville was not wanting for something to occupy its time during the winter of 1885-86. Arsonist Herman Haas had left town in August of '85, so the worry of fire had diminished somewhat. Attention was directed towards the second anti-Chinese movement (see Chapter 21 for more on this). The various societies — Knights of Pythias, Good Templars, Native Sons of the Golden West, and others, elected officers for the new year, 1886. The usual dinners and dances helped while away the winter months. The mills were running on short time, so there was some remnant of industrial activity.

In spring, two new hotels were built, which made three in town, including S.G. Thompson's Grand Hotel on First Street. The first was the St. Charles Hotel and Dining Hall, owned by builder John French, and managed by C.R. Bentley. The second was H.F. Ebers's Guerneville Hotel, located on the northeast corner of today's (1980) Main Street and Armstrong Road, and north about 30 feet.[1]

The St. Charles was open for business in early June. A month later, the cry of "Fire!" summoned the people again. It started about midnight in the St. Charles kitchen; by the time it was discovered, the flames had become a roaring inferno.[2]

The water company could not supply enough water for the firefighters, so the shingle mill at Fife Creek started its pump. With this assistance, the fire was rapidly contained, but not until it had consumed a number of structures. Destroyed were the hotel, Keaton & Bell's butcher shop, Bradford Bell's residence, Dr. Burns's residence, St. Charles Hall, Starrett & Glidden's general store, and their 50 cords of wood. As usual, the insurance coverage — in this case, $9,000 — was much less than the damage of $15,000.[3]

With the rainy weather over, the roads opened for the heavy traffic of lumber and freight wagons, buckboards and stagecoaches. People and families moved to town or went away.

One long-residing family of good reputation left this year for Fresno, California — the Peckinpahs. Up until the year of 1886, they provided entertainment at the celebrations of the small town weddings, holidays, society balls, engaged in the lumber industry from felling to hauling, from sawing to shipping, even to the extent they were probably the most successful river freighters with their boat the Quickstep.[4] A segment of the town's history makers had departed.

Spring gave way to summer. The commercial life of town replaced the social life. Summer was uneventful. At the end of July, the "fall" school session started.

School was a world unto itself. It operated on its own schedule, daily and yearly. From a child's viewpoint, the adults about town were over the fence and in a different world. There were only four adults on their side. After a student graduated, the secondary school nearest to Guerneville was in Santa Rosa where he or she could gain further education. Few could afford this opportunity then. Most children were required to work, especially on farms.

The school's yearly schedule reflected the influence of town and county upon it, and vice versa. From 1886 to 1890, the basic calendar was, according to the ledger for Ridenhour District School:

March 1	Spring session starts
April 5-9	Sickness, closed
May 31	Memorial Day
June 24	Spring session ends
July 19	Fall session starts
August 30-Sept 3	Teachers' Institute, closed
September 9	Admission Day
September 10-20	Hop picking, closed
November 2	Election Day
November 25	Thanksgiving
November 26	Fall session ends

The rainy weather was the major reason school started in March and closed in November.

The second greatest influence on attendance by students was hop picking. It was one of the few opportunities for everybody in town to earn money.

As the years progressed, the hop picking season became longer — there were more hops being grown as more land was cleared.

Other reasons for closing school were mass sickness and, on occasion, the death of a classmate.

October arrived with pending 1886 elections. The polling booths were located in Thompson's Grand Hotel, specifically in the saloon. Because of this location, a number of citizens (all male) petitioned the Board of Supervisors to have the booths moved. The petitioners were members of the I.O.G.T., the local temperance group. The Supervisors granted their petition and relocated the polls to the school.[5]

The town's political bent was no more Republican than Democrat. The Prohibition and American parties were lightly represented.[6]

Candidates spoke before large crowds. Election results for the offices of importance were:

Sheriff:
E.P. Colgan	177
C.N. Burger	85

District Attorney:
C.S. Farquar	110
George Pearce	104

Redwood Township Constable
William Bartley	187
George French	163

Redwood Township Justice of the Peace:
L.S. Jewett	147
Marshall Florence	117

The town's activity slowed in autumn. Lumbering went on short time, politics were put away, school was let out for winter vacation. Christmas was ahead.

January 1887 came, with rains washing out the railway and some local roads. No more rain fell, but week after week, the roads remained muddy from runoff. February passed. Five weeks, six weeks — no rain. March passed with no rain. At the end of that month, temperatures reached 90° in the shade. On April 5, a heavy rain turned the ways into quagmires again. Conditions were back to normal.[7]

Springtime. Townfolk were stirring about. John Folks, after ten years of hotel business, many times having property go up in smoke, decided to move to Monterey. John Keaton opened a butcher shop in competition with Bradford Bell, his old partner. Mr. Scroggins bought the Raney Saloon, and S.G. Thompson was found guilty of selling booze without a license.[8]

This year of 1887 was a propsperous one. Marshall Florence could not keep up with the orders coming in for his locally manufactured chairs. The mills had about 400 men working. C.E. Hewitt developed a business making cans. The brickyard near Korbel's, under Ridenhour's management, was shipping bricks as fast as he was firing them.[9]

In town all buildings, homes and houses were occupied. No vacancies were to be found anywhere. The growing permanent population in the area demanded an increase in school space, so an annex was built by a Mr. Burkhalter, just east of the main school building.[10]

No events of importance occurred during winter 1887-88 or spring 1888. As the summers passed, more and more tourists were coming by train and stage for excursions and conventions. The areas most used for outings were Armstrong's Woods and the campgrounds at Hulbert Creek owned by Guerne & Murphy Lumber Company.

The Druids, some 800 strong, came in June 1888 to hold a convention under the redwoods for a week. The Fourth of July celebration brought many townfolk out and many folks to town. The parade was led by Guerneville's own Cornet Band in their red uniforms, followed by the Grand Army of the Republic, Odd Fellows, Knights of Pythias, Native Sons of the Golden West, and the Druids.[11]

Summer was prolonged by Indian Summer. Campers came and went through the heat and dust. The long-desired rain finally arrived in mid-November.

As the old adage states, "When it rains it pours." It happened to the River area. The rain was not heavy, but was steady, for a month. The results were predictable: short time in the mills, dust turning to mud, turning to quagmires in the roads, the beginning of the social season.[12]

Students at Guerneville's Miriam School finished their fall semester in early December. The students graduating performed the requisite exercises before a packed audience at Odd Fellows Hall.[13]

The Druids held a public installation of their officers the same month, The Native Sons had a Christmas Ball at the Odd Fellows Hall, with dinner supplied by the Grand Hotel.[14]

The town's Christmas Party was in the church. Gifts were loaded on the tree, and these were distributed on Christmas night by a passing-through Kris Kringle.[15]

For the New Year, 1889, two dances were held in town. The weather was wet and dark. One-half hour past midnight, a big event occurred. The Santa Rosa Republican reported:[16]

GIANT POWDER
Guerneville Vigorously Shaken Up By It

Editor Republican: Some unknown persons welcomed the incoming of the new year by placing giant powder under the tender of a dismantled locomotive in a vacant lot near Guerne & Murphy's office. The explosion was terrific and no doubt surprising to the perpetrators. The tender was lifted about thirty feet away and a hole about three feet in depth yawned where it had stood. Several pieces were torn from the tender and scattered around. One lodged in the wall of the building occupied by the F. Emuker's family. Another broke through the roof of George Locke's home. A third piece ten inches wide and two feet long was thrown a distance of perhaps 150 feet over intervening houses, lodging in the ground in the rear of J. W. Bagley's residence. Other pieces were also scattered around. Scarcely a whole piece of glass is left in the lower windows of the three nearest buildings, and the upper windows are also riddled. The [?] are also broken and the doors torn from hinges and frames. Dishes were thrown from shelves and pictures fell from walls. The office building of Guerne & Murphy also suffered from broken windows, lamps, etc. The residence of John Robinson was damaged on the end nearest the explosion, and the ceiling in rooms thrown down near beds occupied by sleeping children who fortunately escaped uninjured.

Windows were broken in other houses in the rear of town. A clock was lifted from a shelf and set upon the floor still running. Another clock that had not run for years was set in motion and whirred and buzzed for some time. It is impossible to estimate the damage at present, but it will probably be several hundred dollars.

The general impression at the upper end of town where a dance was proceeding was that an earthquake had taken place. It is the prevailing opinion that it was a thoughtless joke, done by someone unacquainted with the power of the article used, and was not intended for malicious mischief.

In mid-January, the Knights of Pythias installed their officers and laid out a banquet at the Guerneville Hotel.

To add to what little diversion there was in the slumbering, wintery town, people began to wonder what happened to one of their popular merchants, Jack Davis of Peal & Davis. He had told friends and relatives he was going to San Francisco. That was before New Year's Day.

He was only going to be gone a few days. Some three weeks passed, and no Jack. Foul play was suspected. Someone thought to check the accounting books of the business. Aha! More investigating of his creditors led to the conclusion that his departure was based on the motive to defraud.

The scoundrel left a young wife and two small children. His father-in-law, his business partner, Amos Deal, and a brother-in-law, had all their wealth invested in him.

A few days after the discovery, the pressure of Jack's disappearance and the business going into receivership was too great for 63-year-old Amos. He dropped dead in the doorway of his home. All that was left, other than debts, was a widow, three sons, and two married daughters.[17]

Guerneville was extremely agitated, but Jack Davis remained gone. Two months passed. Then his wife received a letter from British Columbia. It was from Jack, asking his wife and family to join him. End of story.[18]

The same crime was committed again in October when the clerk for Wehrspon & Ludolph's Mill, a Mr. Stackpole, left for parts unknown with all the cash and checks in the company safe. Business was good at the mill, so the amount stolen was a fair sum. But unlike Jack Davis, he did not send for his wife and two children to join him, wherever he was. It reminds one of Herman Haas.[19]

Fire! Fire! For the ninth time since January 1882, that damnable four-letter word was heard again. It had been 2 1/2 years since the St. Charles Hotel had burned. This was, however, the most disastrous fire to hit Guerneville and Sonoma County to this date.[20] It was 3 o'clock p.m. on February 20, 1889, a Wednesday.

The fire started in the Grand Hotel, the largest public house in town. The cook was done with the noon meals in the kitchen and let the wood fire go down. By 2:30 p.m., the coals were barely glowing in the cook stove. He finished his chores, and, checking, saw no fire visible. He left, going to a neighboring saloon.

A group of "drummers," as traveling salesmen were commonly called, was staying at the hotel and had its stock laid out in the barroom. One sitting in the parlor hollered "Fire!" at the same time flame and smoke gushed from the kitchen and storeroom area. The salesmen just had time to grab their satchels and flee to the street when the whole lower part of the hotel burst into flames. Some salesmen did not have time to save their wares.

As the alarm spread, people flocked to the blaze to fight it with a will, but with none to lead. Flames leaped to the next door dwelling of the Thompsons and their post office. There was plenty of hose, but little pressure, as all the hydrants were turned on to fill buckets. The hose was useless.

Mrs. Thompson, postmaster, had only time to grab a handful of mail. Packages, money orders and other postals were consumed by flame. What mail was saved was put on the bridge some 25 feet away, but the bridge caught fire and burned for some distance until one of the main spans was blown up.

After making a turn around the east end of First Street, the fire made a clean sweep down the south side to the schoolyard at Church Street. The first structure to burn was Connell's Livery, where several horses died. It was impossible to get them out. Next to go up in flames were Omer Shoemake's saloon, store, home, and a new building intended as a restaurant and lodging facility. These were followed by the razing of Connell's home and Ungewitter's home and store. The last structure destroyed was Noonan's Meat Market. Only the schoolyard checked the flames on this side of the street.

At the same time these buildings were burning, flames were spreading out in other directions. On the north side of First Street, fire traveled just as fast as on the south side. Here was the heart of Guerneville's business district. Framed in wood, the structures

> **G. DIETZ,**
> PRACTICAL
> **Watchmaker and Jeweler,**
> Stationery, Notions, Candy,
> Jewelry, Clocks, Watches,
> **GUERNEVILLE,   SONOMA CO., CAL.**
> Wells, Fargo & Co's Agent and Postmaster.
> Special Attention given to Fine Watch Repairing. All Work Guaranteed.

> **N. B. TURNER, Jr.**
> DEALER IN
> **General Merchandise,**
> ALSO DEALER IN
> WOOD, POSTS, PICKETS,
> TAN BARK, Etc.
> **GUERNEVILLE, CAL.**

Uhlhorn's 1889 Sonoma County Directory. JCS Collection

fairly exploded: Colburn's Saloon, Pfeister's Barber Shop, Hewitt's Hardware Store. Next came the Odd Fellows block with Dr. Burns' Drugstore, Deitz's Jewelry Store and his Wells Fargo Express office, Turner's General Store, then Hetzel's Tobacco and Cigar Store. Above these merchants was Odd Fellows Hall.

Next to this building on the west side was Harm's Saloon and home, then John Keaton's store, the last to burn in that direction.

Down the south side of Second Street (just west of Odd Fellows), the railroad depot and Smith's Shoestore and residence were turned to ashes.

To the north of the Grand Central, flames leaped the railroad tracks and swept away Coon and Smith's new, but vacant, building, on to Ellison's livery where more horses burned, and then followed the Guerneville Hotel and Brian's home.

Sparks and ashes floated around the neighboring countryside. Loud cracks and muffled explosions came from the town's pyre. Weakened buildings twisted and collapsed, sending up fountains of sparks and writhing flame.

The blasts of heat were so intense that paint bubbled on the buildings across the streets reaching kindling point. Sparks ignited the ready fuel. No one could reach the new fires — extreme temperatures in the narrow streets drove them back.

Ahrens & Joost's Saloon, along with Ahrens' home, burned, followed by Wehrspon's empty house and Essig's shoe shop.

To check this holocaust, the men blew up structures, but to no avail. The fire traveled so fast that the whole downtown section was burning before the point of origin, the Grand Hotel, was wholly consumed by flames.

Few things were saved. Most of the effects in the express office were removed. The organizations of the Druids, Masons, Odd Fellows, G.A.R., Native Sons and Knights of Pythias, saved most of their regalia, along with the furniture of the I.O.O.F. Hall.

A number of safes brought their contents through the fire with no damage. Private business, however, was not so fortunate. Quantities of goods were piled in the streets only to be burned minutes later.

Only a single chimney, twisted pipe, and a row of charred trees remained. The fire burned from start to finish, when checked by vacant lots, from 3 p.m. to 4:30 p.m.

Though no one was killed, the horror of horrors was every drop of liquor in town was destroyed!

The total losses placed by insurance agents was $300,000.

Guerneville during the last half of the 19th century was Phoenix incarnate. Time after time it rose from its warm bed of ashes. This

A rare view of Guerneville between fires, 1886. Note passenger cars in front of railroad station.
JCS Collection

time was no different.

Connell had lumber on his lots while the ground was still warm, and he started a temporary structure. He located during the meantime under the remaining part of the bridge. By Thursday night, 24 hours later, all five saloons were once more open for business and doing quite well.[21]

A surveyor tramped over the still warm ashes with his compass and chain relocating property lines and corners. "Tenfooters" were being thrown up. Shoemake's building had a barber shop, saloon and store. "Shed row" on Hewitt's lot contained the express office, Hetzel's cigar store, and Oliver Wescott's saloon. With one or two exceptions, everyone rebuilt. The organizations met in the Temperance Hall at the southwest corner of town.

Connell's Livery was built on the natural bench, a level ground lower than First Street and higher than the river, where today's Johnson's Resort is located. Connell thought, and reasonably so, that damage by flood would be less than fire. His new livery, 48 X 76 feet, was built by Kuykendall and Nelson.[22]

A few people called it quits. Harmes left for San Francisco and E.W. Smith, shoemaker, moved to Healdsburg.[23]

After this fire, the Odd Fellows and several parties thought of building with brick instead of the quick and cheap way of wood. A contract was put out for bid. The winner was T.J. Ludwig, former lumberman, now of Santa Rosa. His estimated cost was $17,000. The rest of the city block east of Odd Fellows was to be constructed of brick.[24]

Work was begun the first of April 1889 by subcontractors Duncan and Fahrion. The hall was to be two floors, the first for stores, and the second for two meeting halls. The walls reached the second floor level the first of May, and the walls for the rest of the block east were started. Iron fronts and window frames were installed as the work progressed.[25]

The one-story brick construction was finished by May 22, and the secondary woodwork was engaged. By mid-July, new tenants had moved in: Wescott's Saloon, Hewett's Tin Shop, and Raney. Raney rented three rooms, one of which the Cogburn brothers fixed up as

Guerneville, 1887. Let to right: IOOF Building; fifth building from left, S.G. Thomspon's Grand Hotel; flat roofed building at end of street, Post Office; Wells Fargo & Co. and M.W. Burn's drugstore. Ruth Reid Collection

a saloon. The remaining two rooms were sublet to a Santa Rosa firm as a dry goods store.[26]

In mid-August, jeweler and Wells Fargo agent Dietz, Hetzel's Cigars, and Dr. Burns, with his drugs, moved into the first floor of the I.O.O.F. Hall. The two halls upstairs had electric lights installed and were finished with hardwood floors for the dance hall on the north half and with carpeting for the lodge rooms in the south half.[27]

The electricity supplied to the hall came from the big mill's dynamo. It was installed at the mill the same time the hall was built. The electric generator lasted a week, then burned up. A new one was telegraphed for from Chicago.[28]

The Odd Fellows took possession of their new hall on August 10, 1889.

With the last of the building done in town, the people settled back into routine — school back in session, lodge officers elected, getting ready for winter.

Several prominent Guerneville families left town this fall of 1889. With the sale of the big mill, Rufus Murphy and family moved to Santa Rosa, following George Guerne's example. Charles Middleton's family left for San Francisco. Nathaniel E. Manning, with wife and child, after living in town 19 years, moved to Monterey.[29]

Slowly the town took on the image of the larger, more cosmopolitan areas of the county, with such trappings as telegraph, electric lights, brick buildings, et cetera. Starting the first of the new year 1890, a new enterprise began: Guerneville's first and very own newspaper.

The history of journalism's beginnings in Guerneville was short lived. H.M. Calkins, managing editor, named the paper The

Guerneville Blade, a rather appropriate title. The press, type and other equipment came from San Francisco. Calkins published the first edition of this weekly paper on January 11, 1890. Shortly thereafter, Editor Calkins became sick with the grippe (influenza). Still, the paper made its deadline, but the quality must have suffered through February.[30]

The Healdsburg Tribune printed in its March 17 edition:

> The *Guerneville Blade* has been forced to suspend publication, and the entire outfit has returned to San Francisco. The whilom editor, H.M. Calkins, will enter other lines of employment.[31]

No copies of the *Blade* are known to exist today.

From about December 1878, for a period of three years, Guerneville was without a medical doctor. Doctors Wooley and Toundrow had since left. No doctor was present during the diphtheria epidemic of 1879. During the absence of doctors, death occurred from other diseases — cancer, for example. Four people died of typhoid during 1880 to 1882. Tuberculosis claimed five persons between 1880 and 1883. This was a dreaded contagious disease.[32]

In March 1882, Dr. J.A. Burns arrived in town and hung out his shingle. He repaired the mangled members of the woodman and millworker. He tried to keep disease to a minimum, but was not always successful.

The Wilson family lost three children to scarlet fever. Two others died of the same disease. All five deaths occurred ln 1883.

But the doctor struggled on. How many patients he snatched from the grasp of the "Grim Reaper" is unknown. Only the burial book of Sexton John W. Bagley records the causes of failure to a person's health.

1. The Dagget family lost four children in May 1886 to cholera.
2. Typhoid claimed for 1885 - 5; 1886 - 1; 1887 - 3; 1888 - 3; 1890 - 1; 1891 - 1.
3. Cancer took a greater toll than any other disease.[33]

Dentists were not the permanent fixtures in town that they were in other areas in the county. They would visit the surrounding countryside to bring their professional help to the rural citizen. One man did attempt to establish a permanent office, but Fred Allison stayed only from June 1880 to August 1881.[34]

There were other reasons to call a doctor. It was midnight. January cold and winter dampness hung out in the air. Few lights were burning in Guerneville at the hour.

Little Carrie Stewart ran out of her house, into the black street. Fear and panic were embedded on the child's face. She ran to a neighbor's house, with her aunt chasing her. As they both reached the front door, the woman knocked the child down.

The commotion roused the neighbor, who opened the door and grabbed Carrie before more blows rained down.

This was the first the community knew of Carrie as a victim of child abuse. The 9-year-old received the beatings at the hands of her aunt, Mrs. Carrie Pfister. Without going into details, the child exhibited the scars and some disfigurement of the battered-child syndrome.[35]

Mrs. Pfister's problem, in part, was alcohol. Most of the town knew it. The child's father had left Carrie with Pfister to be cared for while he was away working. He could not be found by telegraphing other parts of the country.

Carrie Pfister was arrested that night, January 10, 1890. Justice of the Peace Jewitt, after a preliminary examination, held her to answer the charges of assault with a deadly weapon, and fixed bail at $2,000. She was taken to County Jail by train and incarcerated only an hour when Rufus Murphy and Omer Shoemake put up her bond.[36]

Little Carrie was taken to Constable Bartley's home and cared for by Dr. Burns.

The news spread through Guerneville like a town fire. People visited her and left in shock. At the end of the month she was taken to San Francisco and delivered to Mr. M.J. Hunter, secretary of the Society for the Prevention of Cruelty to Children.

Mrs. Pfister's case was called in Superior Court #1. Testimony was given by Dr. Burns, Constable Bartley, and Omer Shoemake on February 2. On February 3, Pfister changed her plea to guilty. T.J. Butts, her attorney, asked the Judge for leniency in sentencing. He considered it and sentenced her to pay of fine of "$400 and in default of payment, be imprisoned in the County Jail until fine is paid at the rate of one day's imprisonment for every $2 thereof, not to exceed 200 days." Men usually served one day per one-dollar fine.[37] It is not known whether or not she paid the fine, or when she moved from Guerneville.

1. *S.D.*, May 1, May 22, June 5, 1886, *R.R.F.*, March 22, 1886.
2. *S.D.*, July 7, 1886.
3. *S.D.*, July 17, 1886.
4. *S.D.*, June 5, 1886. See Chapter VI.
5. Bd. Supvrs. Records: Petition filed October 8, 1886; *S.D.*, October 16, 1886.
6. Bd. Supvrs. Records: Books 6, 7 and 8.
7.
8. *S.D.*, February 17, March 26, April 9, 1887.
9. *S.D.*, April 9, May 7, June 4, 1887.
10. *Rep.*, June 30, 1887.
11. *S.D.*, August 13, 1887.
12. *Trib.*, June 11, July 11, 1888.
13. *Trib.*, November 14, December 12, 1888.
14. Ibid.
15. *Trib.*, December 26, 1888.
16. *Ibid.*
17. *Rep.*, January 7, 1889.
18. *Trib.*, January 16, 1889; *S.D.*, January 19, 1889.
19. *Trib.*, February 26, 1889.
20. *Trib.*, October 10, 1889.
21. The Fire of 1889: *Trib.*, February 21, 1889; *S.D.*, February 23, 1889; San Francisco Chronicle, February 21, February 22, 1889.
22. *Trib.*, February 26, 1889.
23. Ibid.; *S.D.* March 7, 1889.
24. *Trib.*, March 13, 1889.
25. *S.D.*, March 23, 1889.
26. *S.D.*, April 6, 1889; *H.T.*, March 27, April 27, 1889.
27. *Trib.*, May 22, July 24, 1889.
28. *Trib.*, August 14, September 11, 1889.
29. *Trib.*, August 14, September 21, 1889.
30. *Trib.*, November 13, December 18, 1889.
31. *S.D.*, January 18, February 8, February 22, 1890.
32. *Trib.*, March 17, 1890.
33. Bagley, John W. *Register of Burial*; Guernevllle Funeral Parlor, Guerneville.
34. Ibid.
35. *R.R.F.*, May 25, 1880; August 22, 1881.
36. *S.D.*, January 18, 1890.
37. *Healdsburg Herald*, January 15, 1890; *S.D.*, January 25, 1890.
38. Superior Court Records, Case #2335

Guerneville, 1886, looking east on First Street. Office of Dr. McGuire on left; I.O.O.F Hall on right; the French house on the hill behind is still standing. JCS Collection

Logging on Austin Creek, from "In a Redwood Logging Camp," Harper's New Monthly Magazine, May 1883

Chapter 21

WHITES VS CHINESE — PART 2

The racial tensions subsided from 1879 to 1882 between whites and Chinese to such a degree that nothing has been found to inform us regarding Guerneville.

In Washington, D.C., an anti-Chinese bill, Senate Bill 71, SP 1882, was vetoed by President Chester Arthur in April. One month later another was presented, and he signed it into law.[1]

This year was also an election year and anti-Chinese meetings were conducted by the Democratic party throughout the county. One of their advertisements declared:

**THE CAMPAIGN
DEMOCRATIC MEETINGS
EQUAL RIGHTS - EQUAL TAXATION
ANTI-COOLIE - ANTI MONOPOLY
GUERNEVILLE, SATURDAY EVENING
OCTOBER 28**[2]

This meeting was held in Taggart's Hall. The crowd was overflowing and called "one of the best Democratic meetings in Guerneville." The town fell right in step with County and State in all issues. Even ladies attended.[3]

The other political parties held meetings: Republicans, Prohibitionists, Greenbackers.

Then all the hoopla subsided. The town reported only occasional events by the Chinese for the next few years:

"Chinese New Year was scarcely observed."

"A Chinaman while chopping wood across the river, was caught by a falling tree and had both legs fearfully mangled."

"Chinese New Year is being celebrated today with all due ceremony and noise."[4]

So it went from 1882 to 1886. It was noted there were at least two wash houses and two shops owned by Chinese, and two others were employed by John Taggart and boarded at his hotel.[5]

In 1886 a new device was used to force the Chinese to vacate the town and local environs. This time nearly everyone in town responded and got involved. Some 200 people had a meeting and elected a committee of 15 businessmen to make sure "that the Chinese left at the expiration of two weeks, the time allowed them."[6] There was also the implementation of boycotting anybody employing Chinese.

"Plans" were carried out the first of February. After two weeks, all Chinese had vacated Guerneville for other parts. Some went to Duncan's Mills to join those Chinese residents. There they all received notice to leave in 30 days.[7]

One white man reported that on his trip from Guerneville to Santa Rosa he saw only two heading the same direction, carrying their blankets.[8]

What was implemented to enforce such a mass exodus after some 12 years of harassment and threat? Did they have fear for their lives? True fear? Pause and think. After 12 years, they leave in two weeks! An extremely thorough search has revealed nothing but for one incident on January 24, 1886.

Two Italians, Antonio Leonardo and Antonio _____ unmercifully beat a Chinese man locally nicknamed "Jim Mahoney." The attack was unprovoked and brutal. Two days later a jury trial took place before Justice Marshall

Guerne & Murphy's Logging Camp on Hulbert Creek, circa 1890. Note the three Chinese in the back row at left, one sitting on the fence and two standing. Ray Clar Collection

Florence. The charges were misdemeanor battery. The jury returned a verdict of guilty. Justice Florence sentenced them $100 each or 100 days, a very heavy sentence for a misdemeanor of those times, and I think reflective of the seriousness of the crime. The fine was paid.[9]

"Jim Mahoney"

Every town has a character who stands out in the community because of his or her personality — bizarre, or otherwise. "Jim Mahoney" was one of Guerneville's firsts.

This man from the Orient was well known as one of Guerneville's landmarks. His true name is unknown. In the Anglo-American culture, a nickname is a title given in jest, derision, friendship, or identification by the local population. It was probably because he was so named and well known that he was exempt from some of the social and economic pressures brought to bear on his fellow countrymen and also why his assailants were brought so quickly to trial.

Jim Mahoney was granted three weeks more than the two weeks the other Chinese received to leave town, so he could settle his business affairs about the village. That was all he needed.

He used the time to transform himself in the minds of the white population into adopting their ways, habits, customs and mannerisms. He was fond of playing poker and a "two finger glass of whiskey." He spent his money (where he worked is unknown) on the usual necessities and pleasures as the general population. To further remove any hostilities he made it known he would cut his queue, buy a silk hat, and go to an American school.[10]

The men about town all liked him: spending, drinking, gambling. Obviously, along with the name, he was the butt of jokes, protected from undue harassment, and treated as a mascot. He became the only Chinese in town.

He pursued the role of changing from one

culture to another:

> Our solitary Chinaman, Jim Mahoney, is learning to write English. He is a born adept at gambling, and irrigates fluently.[11]

Some four months passed since the mass exodus of February. In early July, Jim found another Chinese for a companion. And with that, these few paragraphs of his biography close; another deadend in history.[12]

In the summer of this year, 1886, a correspondent to the Sonoma Democrat gave passing mention that a Chinese wash house had started up in Guerneville.[13]

How did this happen? Six months prior the whole countryside was in an uproar over anything to do with the Orient. Now this? The mind fills with questions: Who were they? How many of them? What was the demeanor of the town? The social environment at this time? What were the individual feelings of the population when they saw the first Chinese come back? Did Jim Mahoney set the stage?

Whatever happened had little effect between the two peoples. The wash house remained located on the south side of Railroad Avenue (Main Street) where today's (2015) West America Bank's private drive is located.[14] The years passed. In June 1890, the wash house was raided and an opium outfit was found, with a white man and a Chinese sleeping nearby. They were arrested, but "because of some legal technicality," the case was dropped. The first "drug bust" in Guerneville was a failure.[15]

The census report for 1890 shows 1,338 whites and only 35 Chinese in Redwood Township, an increase of one, compared to 1880. But as stated before, this seems not to be a true report. There were no other ethnic groups present.[16]

The racial/ethnic breakdown countywide was:[17]

Whites	31,138
Chinese	1,173
Indians	284
Negroes	42

Japanese

The histories of minorities in Redwood Township are sketchy, at most, during the 1890's. The closest statement about the presence of Chinese and others was the declaration by industry that preference was given to white labor.[18]

In 1892, T.J. Geary, congressman from Santa Rosa, sponsored a Chinese Exclusion Act, which passed both Houses of Congress, the fifth such act since the first passed in 1869.[19]

Late 1893 was a period of serious consequences for one Ah Fong. Fong, also known as Pan, worked as the cook at Great Eastern Quicksilver Mine. A miner went to Fong's shanty to find out when dinner would be. He found Fong assaulting a white boy. The miner was incensed and, with other miners, tarred and feathered the cook. He escaped, but was arrested later in the day. He was charged with felony assault when he was arraigned. The judge set bail at $1,000 and set the trial date for December 27, 1893, in Santa Rosa.[20]

The trial started as scheduled with a jury. The case was tried and submitted to the 12-man panel, but on January 6, 1894, they declared themselves hung. There was no re-trial.[21]

No repercussions were reported taking place in Guerneville or at the mines toward other Orientals; nor were there any outcries towards the jury or judicial system (at least in print).

For nearly three years there was an absence of information about Chinese in Guerneville until late 1896. This year, 1896, was an election year. Voting polls were placed in each precinct. Redwood Township had two. West Redwood precinct had polls at the Odd Fellows building, and East Redwood precinct had polls at Yip Ching's.[22]

Who was Yip Ching? is another unanswered question. It was a name not mentioned or found before or since. The appearance of Yip Ching reflects a tolerant (?) attitude by the local Euro-American society as the years passed.

Another three years slipped by before the newspapers made mention of another Oriental man. He fell 18 feet from a trestle in Guerneville and was severely hurt. Promptly taken to the Santa Rosa hospital, he lingered one week before dying.[23]

The Chinese were relegated pretty much to occupations of laundry and agriculture in the area these later years.

To be sure, there were more Chinese, Japanese, Pomos and Blacks in town, the woods, and the mines than are recorded on these pages.

No thoughts or feelings of the Chinese people (or any other minority) are available as far as the River area is concerned. But no doubt their conversations in private or in public in their native tongues were filled with emotion against the "fahn kwei," or foreign devil, and the white feelings against them.

When whites confronted, harassed and committed crimes upon the Chinese, the recipients cursed their attackers and their ancestors.[24] Assaults did occur against a few. The offenders were fined or jailed, but not as harshly compared to a Chinese offender.

A few Chinese — native, naturalized or immigrant — have stayed permanently in the River area up to the present time (1980).

The early part of the 20th century regarding the Chinese was remembered by the old timers. A Chinese laundry located just at the east end of town, not to be confused with the Chinese laundry previously mentioned, was always busy. Two men worked there up to about 1917. They wore black pajama-type clothing and had the tradition-dictated long single queue of hair down their backs. On warm evenings they would come out and sit on the front porch of the wash house, smoking their pipes.

The tobacco most Chinese used was bought from Dave Hetzel's shop.

The sources of information about various peoples were sparse. The facts suffered from ethno-centricity (to use an academic phrase) of the dominant Euro-American culture; there may be more sources to be found.

This ends two short chapters of ethnic minorities during Guerneville's first 50 years.

1. *S.D.*, April 8, May 13, 1882.
2. *S.D.*, October 28, 1882.
3. *S.D.*, November 4, 1882.
4. *R.R.F.*, February 20, 1882, S.R. Rep., February 19, March 19, 1883, January 28, 1884.
5. *S. R. Rep.*, May 23, 1882.
6. *S D.*, February 20, 1886.
7. Ibid.
8. *S.D.*, March 27, 1886.
9. Justice of the Peace report to the Board of Supervisors, January 30, 1886.
10. *S.D.*, February 13, and February 20, 1886.
11. *S.D.*, May 22, 1886.
12. *S.D.*, July 17, 1886.
13. Ibid.
14. Sanborn Map, "Guerneville," 1885 and 1888, Sanborn Map & Publishing Co., Limited, 117 Broadway, New York; from the Library of Congress.
15. *Healdsburg Herald,* June 4, 1890.
16. *S.D.*, January 10, 1891.
17. Ibid.
18. *S.D.*, February 4, February 18, 1893.
19. *S.D.*, October 21, November 18, 1893.
20. *S.D.*, October 21, November 18, 1893.
21. *S.D.*, December 30, 1893, January 6, 1894, Superior Court Case #3395.
22. *S.D.*, October 24, 1896.
23. *S.D.*, May 6, 1899.
24. *Press Democrat,* September 12, 1896.

Chapter 22

BRICKS

Some ten years after the development of the quicksilver deposits at Mt. Jackson, another geological resource — potter's clay — was discovered up river. Thomas B. Brown and one of the McPeaks developed this extensive clay deposit at Hilton in 1884. They produced pressed and common bricks, drain tile, and flower pots. As a result, a railroad siding was built to handle their large shipments.[1]

The plant consisted of a Kells & Sons tile machine, run by a 16-h.p. (steam) engine, and a kiln of Pike & Castle design. Combined, the two operations could manufacture about 4,000 feet of tile per day.[2]

At the same time and location there was another clay operation: the Santa Rosa Planing Mill and Brick Company. It supposedly produced one million bricks a year with a work force varying from 16 to 60 men.

The bricks for Korbel's first winery, built in 1886, came from S.W. Ridenhour, whose "claim" was also at Hilton.[3]

The clay deposit was the only one in the area, and was developed by the first two companies. Later, in 1887, all companies were joined under one owner, T.J. Ludwig, former mill owner in Guerneville. He developed a market in Santa Rosa at his lumber yard and another yard in San Francisco. In July he had a contract for 500,000 bricks and, before the end of the month, had filled it.[4]

Two years passed, and the kilns lay cold. Then in March 1889, Ridenhour and Brown in partnership were producing drain tile. Their products were sold by agents in Santa Rosa, Petaluma, Windsor and Healdsburg.[5]

In September 1894, A.C. Mills, a contractor from San Francisco, bought the clay deposit and brickyard, He built the first brick-constructed kiln and used wood fuel for firing the clay. Ridenhour, in his employ, fired during the night, sometimes staying up all night. Someone had to; it took nearly a week to fire brick.[6]

The following year, Tom Brown was proprietor again. The July production was 50,000 bricks fired and 15,000 in the kilns. Approximately 300,000 were on hand.[7]

Besides the old kilns, the new one could fire up to a half million at one time.

Everybody made bricks the same way:

1. Wet down the molds.
2. Sprinkle sand on them.
3. Make a mixture out of six parts clay and one part sand.
4. Press mixture in molds.
5. Dry "green brick" in sun or on top of kiln.[8]

However, drying in the open had some drawbacks. In September of 1895, the season's first rain dissolved 75,000 bricks ready for the kiln.

They were then gathered and wheeled to the kilns by hand. The bricks to be fired were spaced 1 1/2 inches apart so the hot air could get between them.[9]

Few hired hands appeared to be needed

Russian River Advertiser, May 6, 1905

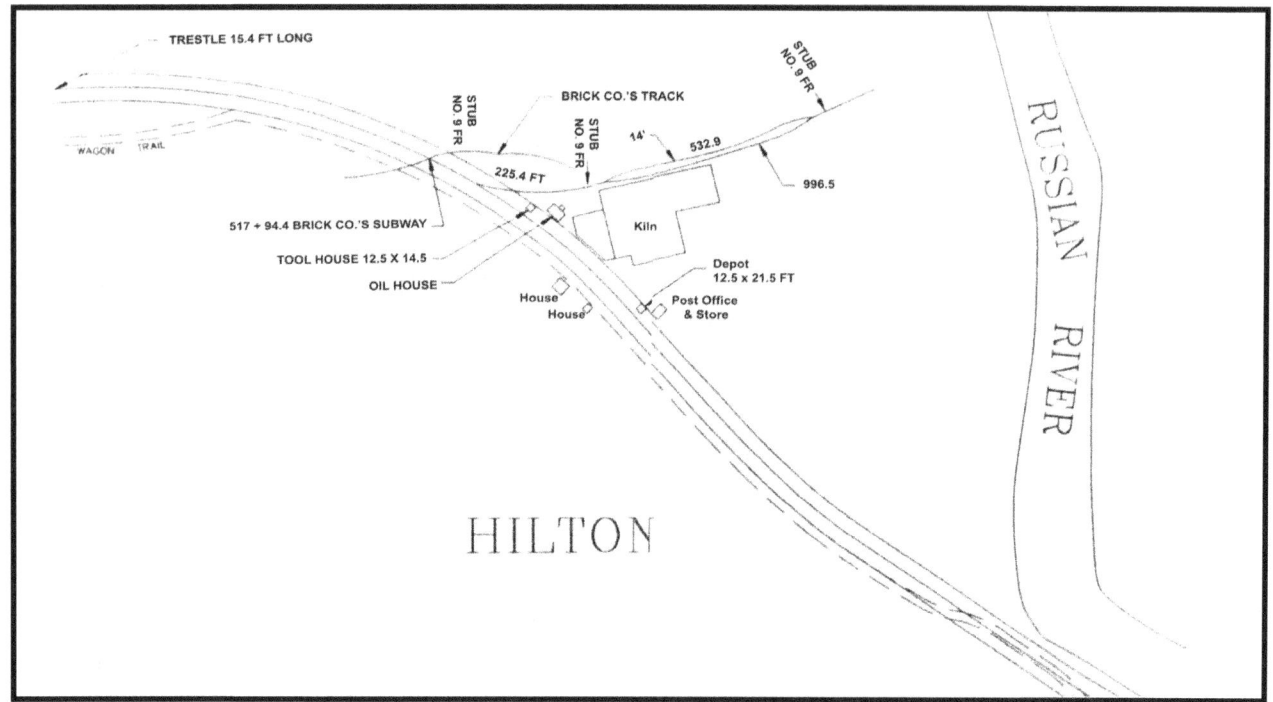

Hilton Brick Company circa 1915, drawn by Keith Schubert from Southern Pacific Railroad map.

at the kilns. At this time, with the exceptions of Brown and Ridenhour, all were from Santa Rosa: W.E. Parsons, George Parsons, Lambert Ducharm, J. King, and Bert Redenbaugh.[10]

After A.C. Mills left in late '94 or early '95, an English family — Souse — built a smoke stack 125 feet tall to draw off the heat and smoke from the kilns.[11]

Souse remained only a short time. Brown and Ridenhour took over again, making drain tile four, six, eight and ten inches in diameter, and made one-half turns (45°) and full turns (90°).

In April 1905, the partnership sold out to a group from the San Francisco Bay Area.[12] They promptly incorporated on April 27 of that year. The new possessors were Henry Mitchell of San Francisco, secretary; J.W. Wayne of Concord; E.A. Davis of Stockton; and George F. Bender and L.L. Bender of Fruitvale. The shares of the company amounted to $50,000.

They completely revamped the operation. Instead of the old brick forms, they installed a clay mill that issued a clay ribbon the standard height and width. The ribbon, as it passed under a large wheel, was sliced into proper lengths by wires spaced on the wheel like a cheese slicer. The brick production was increased from 25,000 to 60,000 bricks per day. They produced anything that could be made from clay, mechanically.[13]

The kilns were laid out in two rows of four. They would load up four kilns and fire them. Then the second four kilns would be loaded. After the first batch was done, workers fired the second, and the first was then unloaded and stacked onto railroad cars. The finished bricks were of three grades:

    1. Dark red next to the fire
    2. Light red
    3. Light orange furthest from the fire[14]

The railroad laid a spur alongside the kilns to facilitate shipping, and the company installed its own track from the clay pits to the factory.[15] At one time they had a stack of over two million bricks to be loaded on rail cars.[16] Fred Ogburn and Robert Ridenhour were hired to load the stack. After filling ten box cars with 30,000 bricks per car, the two young men quit.[17] The company then hired men from San Francisco. Another worker, Chester Arm-

Building the brick kiln at Hilton; store and post office are at right of railroad station, where people are standing. Writing at top says "Hilton, August 8, 1907 — Come up & help pick hops, Lizzie." JCS Collection

strong, was a brick burner.

Just down the railroad tracks about 150 yards, were some Chinese. They had a brick operation going, and resided there. Their resources were not clay, but dirt and sand. Both were dug from that immediate area. This sediment brick was acceptable, but it would not split correctly like a clay brick in a mason's hands.[18]

The Chinese had a "pug" mill for mining sediment and, at times, clay. It was a round hole in the ground where a horse walked around and around, much like a Spanish grain arrastra. This was in 1904-05.[19]

Nothing else is known about the operation.

In August of 1906, the larger brick company was sued by its foreman, George Funamoto.[20] By agreement, Funamoto was to pay some 40 laborers out of his own pocket at a rate of $1.40 per day per man. After a month he was not reimbursed and could not pay the men. The total owed was $341. Tom Brown also filed suit for $299 owed him for boarding and for team hire. The board of directors was in disagreement as to what to do, so they shut down the plant. The company defaulted. The courts levied an attachment on the company's holdings.

In 1914 the Division of Mines noted that the Hilton Brick Company, now Pure Clay Brick and Tile Company, had not fired any bricks since 1912.[21]

The last remnant of the industry, the brick smokestack, was razed circa 1930 and entered history.[22]

A traveler along the river highway can still discern the site of the Hilton clay pit, made evident by willows and other water-loving vegetation across from Hilton.

1. S.D., January 3, 1885; February 21, 1885
2. State Mineralogists Report, 1885, VIII, p. 635.
3. S.D., May 29, 1886.
4. S.R. Rep., June 30, 1887; S.D., July 9 1887.

5. S.D., March 2, 1889.
6. S.D., September 15, 1894; Robert Ridenhour interview, August 31, 1976.
7. S.D., July 25, 1895; Ridenhour interview, op. cit.
8. Ibid.
9. S.D., September 21, 1895.
10. S.D., July 27, 1895.
11. Ridenhour interview, op. cit.
12. Incorporation papers; Sonoma County Clerk's office, #750.
13. Ridenhour interview Ibid.; Sol Bonelli interview, July 5, 1976; Russian River Advertiser, Guerneville, May 6, 1905 (hereafter cited as R.R. Ad.)
14. Ridenhour and Bonelli interviews.
15. Southern Pacific Map, 1912.
16. Ridenhour interview, op. cit.
17. Sonoma County Voters Registration, 1906.
18. Ridenhour interview, op. cit.
19. Ridenhour interview, op. cit.
20. R.R. Ad., (?) August, 1906
21. See report of that year.
22. Letter of Ray Clar, October 28, 1975, to author.

Hilton, circa 1905. JCS Collection

Chapter 23

Lumber Mills — 1891 to 1895

Gurneville's nickname, "Stumptown," was more appropriate now than ever before. As the years passed, the loggers pushed the forest line further and further back into the canyons.

With fewer redwoods and pines to be cut, there were fewer lumber mills. At the height of the industry, there were no less than eleven mills, but during the "Gay '90's," the mills totalled six. With fewer mills, there were fewer jobs.

In May of 1891 all mills were working in full force with 100 to 150 men.[1]

The Sonoma Lumber Company of the Westover Brothers and Chapman was putting out 40,000 board feet a day during the '91 season, with a daily capacity of 55,000 feet. To reach new log sources, they extended the railroad up Hulbert Creek another two miles, and in 1892, they extended a railroad spur into Meeker Woods (to be later called Bohemian Grove).[2]

Though the company was the biggest lumbering concern throughout the area, little in actual facts is known about it during this half decade. It had all the modern machinery, but men could not saw when it rained. The loggers were still battling the elements.

Some loggers (at least one) came up with a quicker way to make a dollar. Jerry Hunt had a logging contract with the company and had it deposit $1,500 into a Santa Rosa bank. This was done so he could pay his men on the coming Saturday. On Friday, July 21, 1893, Hunt went to Santa Rosa and withdrew the money from the bank, but did not return. He went to San Francisco and from there telephoned his bookkeeper to tell his men he was away on important business and that D.L. Westover would be up on Monday to pay the men off. There were 45 men in camp.

When the men were told of the "hold up" in their wages, their verbiage was laced with emotion, describing what kind of forebears Hunt had, reflections upon his manhood, and

Sonoma Lumber Company invoice. JCS Collection

hobbies he might have pursued. However, Westover was more the man than any. He paid off every man on Tuesday, in full.[3]

The grand statistics of mass production, 20-plus ton logs, large, straight-grain planks were now becoming things of history. Occasionally, a flicker of the past would shine when a large tree or plank was cut, such as one that measured 16 feet by 6 1/2 feet.[4]

The year 1894 was like any other, until September. Some 75,000 feet of lumber burned in the biggest fire of the town's history (see next chapter). It was only the hard work of the employees that saved the mill from destruction.[5]

After a couple of months of cutting lumber for the rebuilding of Guerneville, the daily routine returned. Autumn brought shorter work days, and it finally closed down for the winter holidays.

The new year of 1895 swept in with rainstorms. A large barn was washed away that belonged to Westover & Chapman, along with some $5,000 worth of lumber, but this was not the only financial setback. Though the large mills did supply some of the local environs, the main market was the San Francisco area. Because of the demand for lumber being small, the mill did not start cutting until early July! Though the season was short, they employed about 100 men.[6]

Up the Mines Road, Armstrong's (ex-Murphy's) Mill had seen that services were no longer required, so in the fall of 1891, Armstrong had it torn down and shipped the machinery to Fresno. Armstrong had timber reserves at the headwaters of Fife Creek that totalled 640 acres, and their future disposal belongs more with the story of the formation of Armstrong Park than here.[7]

Frank and Ivon Clar's shingle mill on the north side of Russian River down on Clar Flat was fairly active through the first half of the decade, but no specifics are known. The brothers paid $1,400 for 120 acres in the area. A third brother, Leo Henry, was also working at the mill, probably as a bookkeeper. Many other employees (mill hands, loggers) resided in the area and near the cookhouse near the mill. The Korbels later paid $40,000 for Clar Flat.[8]

Log-hauling to Pocket Canyon and the Korbel Mill, at the intersection of Armstrong Road and Main Street, circa 1900. JCS Collection

The other big mill in the immediate area was that of August "Gus" Wehrspon, in May's Canyon. It ran later in the year than did the other mills, sometimes past Christmas and on into the dead of winter.

The fire of '94 was not used as a quick profit-making venture. Wehrspon lost his own home in that conflagration. He experienced what the townfolk experienced, so he lowered his prices as an inducement for others to rebuild.[9]

Another mill in the River Area was Ansell, Hunt and Company at Russian River Station. It was constructed during the summer of 1891. They shut down for a couple of weeks for repairs and to install a band saw, replacing the now-becoming-old-style circular saws.[10]

Just as the automobile replaced the horse and buggy, so did the band saw replace, in one mill after another, the circle saw. The lumber industry was entering a new era. As far back as 1888, four years earlier, people were experimenting with this saw. Alexander Duncan said then, "We can save a great deal more from logs if the band saw is a success."[11] The band saw has a thinner blade than the round saw of equal strength, therefore, there was less loss to sawdust and more lumber per log.

Out in the woods, the company made other modifications. A few months after the repairs were completed at the mill, they built a rail spur two miles up Smith Canyon to their timber reserves.[12]

Two years passed with the loggers cutting in the canyon until they had to extend the oxen skid road. In August of 1895, Ansel "emancipated the oxen of the logging teams in the camp on Smith Creek." He had purchased a new donkey engine with 1 1/2 miles of large cable and three miles of smaller size. With this machinery drawing logs to the railroad, he figured he would lower the cost of milling by one dollar per thousand feet of boards.[13] Yes, the lumber industry was entering a new era.

A fourth mill mentioned in passing, apparently a small operation, was the De Camp Mill.[14]

Other producers of wood products and by-products were still hacking and cursing away at the forest.

Dave Dollar, possibly connected to Robert Dollar of Sonoma Lumber Company from Hulburt Canyon, was getting out piles with a crew of 25 men for the Southern Pacific Railroad. This was in 1892.[15]

Tanbark peelers infiltrated the woods. 1895 was the biggest year of bark production up to that time.[16]

The cordwood fuel industry was big business, second only to lumber. In 1895, thousands of cords were stacked along the main branch of the railroad for shipment to Santa Rosa and the San Francisco Bay Area.[17]

The fewer number of timbered acres went together with the fewer number of mills. The "old days" of the 1870's and of the founding men were gone.

W.H. Willits had moved to Seventh and B Streets in Santa Rosa in 1885, after 18 million feet of lumber was cut from 160 acres. Tom Kerns and Branthaver had long since left Pocket Canyon and their small Pocket Mill.

Tom Heald now lived in Healdsburg; George Guerne was in Santa Rosa; Rufus Murphy was keeping a fine hotel in Ukiah; and S.H. Torrance was dead. John Bagley had long since quit the heavy woods and mill work.[18]

The local citizenry would think back to when the jingling of bells from the four- and six-horse teams would echo, muted by wooded canyons, canyons now stubbed by charred stumps. They recalled hearing the rattle of empty wagons coming from Santa Rosa, and the creak and groan of loaded ones from Guerneville. The festive, restless ox-driver no longer camped in the streets and made night more foreboding with his drunken howl. Harry Cooper and Joe Savage had gone.[19]

The country was becoming pastoral.

1. *S.D.*, May 16, 1891.
2. *S.D.*, September 18, 1891; February 4, 1892; Healdsburg Enterprise, September 5, 1891.
3. *S.D.*, July 22, 1893.
4. *S.D.*, February 24, 1893.
5. *S.D.*, September 1, 1894; December 8, 1894.
6. *S.D.*, January 26, 1895; June 8, 1895; June 22, 1895.
7. *S.D.*, October 24, 1891; November 22, 1891.
8. *S.D.*, August 15, 1891; November 22, 1891; C. Ray Clar letter to author, July 5, 1976.
9. *S.D.*, October 8, 1892; December 8, 1894; October 6, 1894.
10. *Healdsburg Enterprise*, September 8, 1891; S.D., October 15, 1892.
11. *Sonoma County & Russian River Valley*, Bell & Heymans, San Francisco, California, May 1888, p. 41.
12. *S.D.*, February 4, 1893.
13. *S.D.*, July 27, 1895; August 10, 1895.
14. *S.D.*, July 29, 1893.
15. *S.D.*, July 2, 1892.
16. *S.D.*, July 8, 1893; September 7, 1895.
17. *S.D.*, September 7, 1895.
18. *S.D.*, January 1, 1892; February 4, 1893; May 27, 1893.
19. *S.D.*, February 4, 1893; May 27, 1893.

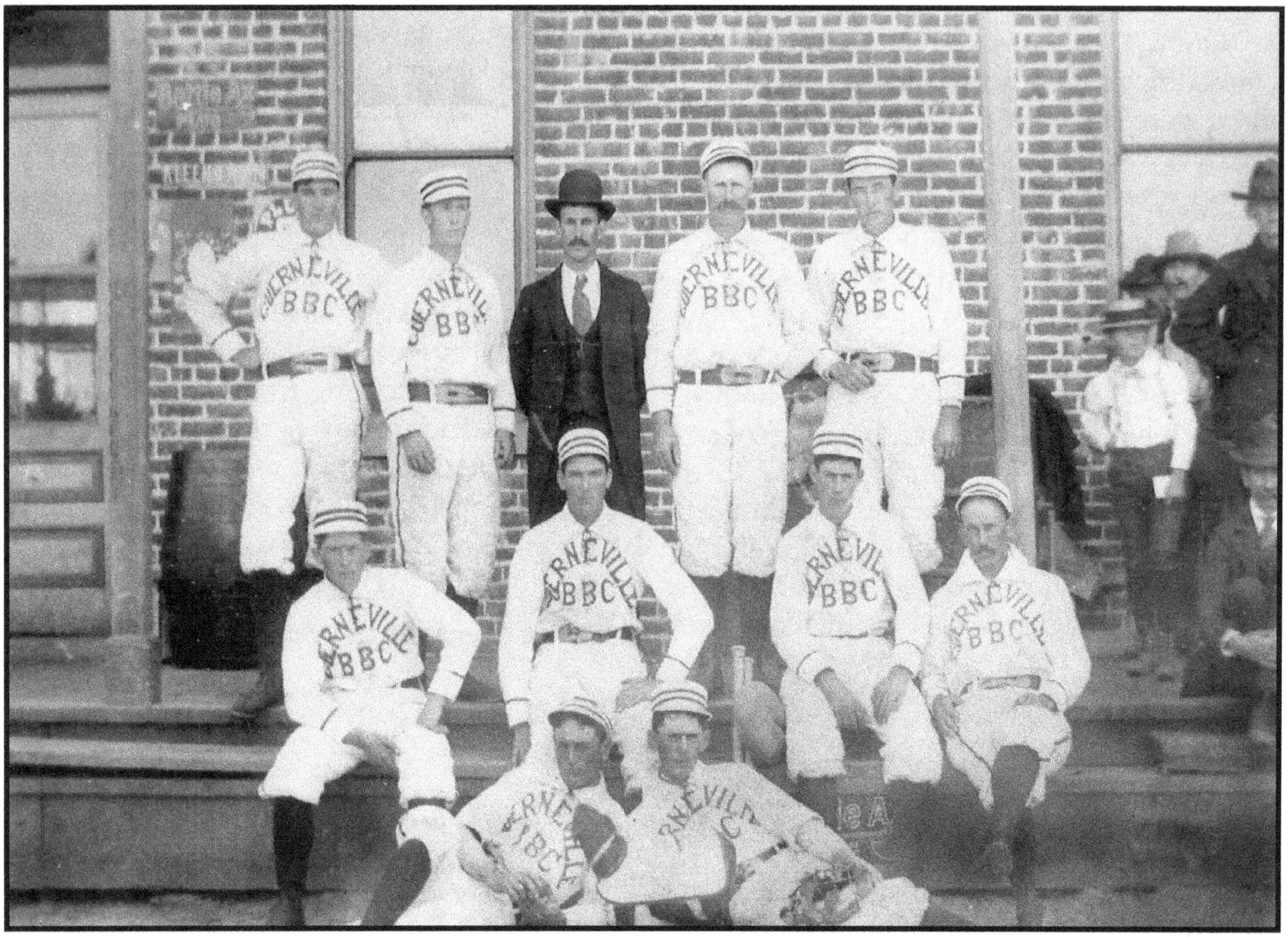

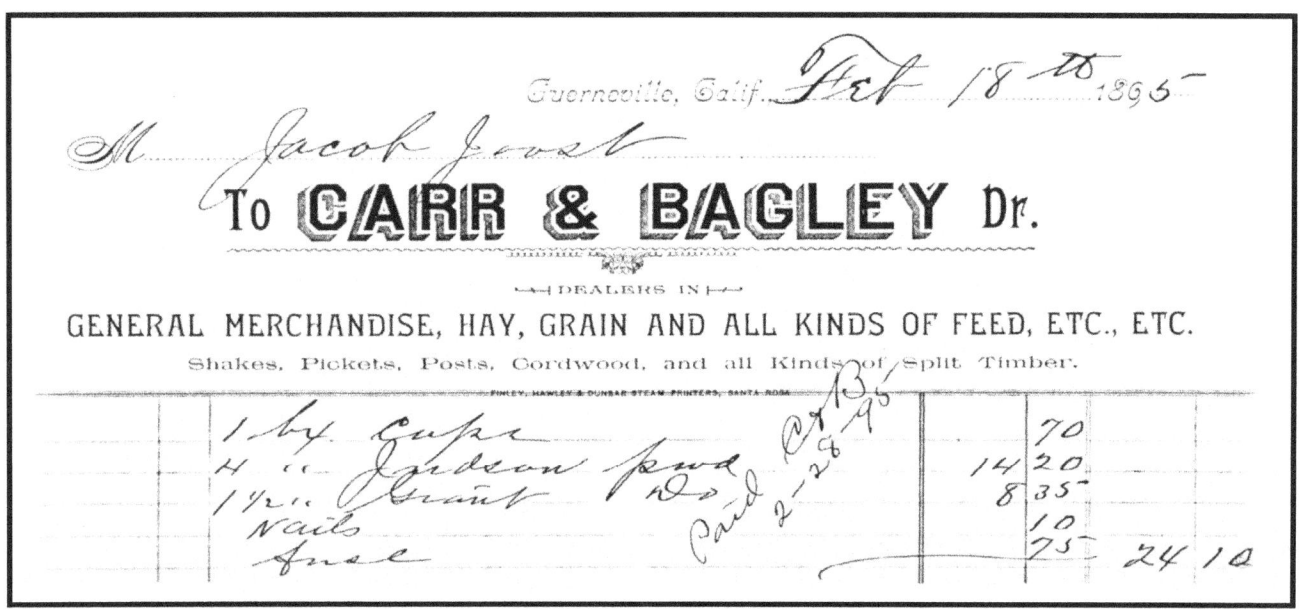

Guerneville Base Ball Club (note BBC on uniforms), 1893. Back row, left to right: Willard Cole, Jim Pells, Charles Pool (manager), Jeff Smith, Bob Garner. Front row, left to right: Ben Klink, Will Cole (Wilard's twin), Jack Brown, Willard Bagley; lying down: Frank Wescott, Steve Klink, and Ripley the mascot. Amy Bagley Hatch Collection

Guerneville, Calif. Feb 18th 1895

M Jacob Joost

To CARR & BAGLEY Dr.

DEALERS IN

GENERAL MERCHANDISE, HAY, GRAIN AND ALL KINDS OF FEED, ETC., ETC.

Shakes, Pickets, Posts, Cordwood, and all Kinds of Split Timber.

FINLEY, HAWLEY & DUNBAR STEAM PRINTERS, SANTA ROSA

1 bx. Caps	70	
4 " Judson Pwd	14 20	
1½ " Grant Do	8 35	
Nails	10	
Fuse	75	24 10

Paid C&B 2-28-95

JCS Collection

Chapter 24

Guerneville — 1891 to 1895

The excitement of Mrs. Pfister beating her niece, Carrie, had waned by the end of 1890.

The new brick buildings were the pride of Guerneville, giving the town the appearance of permanency. No longer was it a clapboard village. The population was counted in 1890 for Redwood Township by the U.S. Census takers: the district had 1,338 whites, 35 Chinese, and zero other ethnic minorities.[1]

The winter of 1890-91 was not out of the ordinary. The townfolk went about daily routines, not bothered by the familiar inconvenience of wet weather. So the months passed quietly into April and spring.

Fire!!! The quiet was rudely punctuated on April 11, at midnight. Flames broke out in Connell's Livery on the lower level, alongside First Street. Everything on the south side of the street from the bridge to the brick walls of the Raney Building was in ruins. If it were not for this building, the damage would possibly have doubled. Those burned out were Connell, Omer Shoemake's saloon, hotel and dwelling, Connell's home, Yerger's tailor shop, rented from Connell, and Scobie's store and home. Scobie's store was occupied by H. Barrow with a stock of gentlemen's dry goods. The total loss was roughly $15,000.[2]

Almost as quickly as the two-year-old structures burned down, the owners built new ones of wood. But not Dave Connell. He had a brick livery constructed on a new site. He first tried the south side of First Street, then the lower level, off First, then the location selected was bordered on the north by the railroad (Second Street), west by Armstrong Road, south by First Street. The 50 X 150 foot building was finished by mid-August 1891.[3]

Fires in Guerneville were a way of life. Structures were not complicated in those days by modern conveniences and laws. Therefore, fires were of relatively moderate consequence, and nobody was killed or severely injured. It was a seemingly endless repetition of a familiar event. Yet, a fire protection organization was not coming for decades.

In May, news arrived of the death of John Taggart, former hotel and saloon keeper, in San Francisco. The Irishman was 63 years of age.[4] His death brought back memories of parties in his hotel.

With the arrival of spring came a new cutting season. By mid-May, the mills employed 100-150 men. However, during the summer-like months, all was not work for the men. There was time for recreation after a 12-hour workday and on Sundays. One common sport during these leisure hours was baseball. It was back in '81 that the first team was formed. They played three games, winning all, and then faded from sight.

Ten years have now passed since 1881.

Professional and amateur baseball from the "outside world" exerted enough influence on Guerneville to have it form a team again, "The Gravel Scratchers." Their first game was against the Forestville Coyotes. The River boys won, 9 to 4.[5]

The team stayed together at least three years, long enough to finally get uniforms. The teams played on; however, their win/loss record is non-existent. Baseball again dropped from historical sight.[6]

The town passed through Summer 1891 pleasantly enough. Summer campers were becoming numerous, but were not a significant influence on the area yet. No serious accidents occurred at home, at work, or on the road.

The town, besides the usual shops and stores, supported about ten locations that dispensed liquor. The population of the township, about 1,000, was openly critical of the town's drinking water, and no wonder, considering the deaths in the area from typhoid and cholera. Who would question the reason for so many saloons, especially so during summer heat?[7]

The days grew short, and harvest time arrived. The vineyards, hops, prunes and apples were the major crops of the area. Agriculture was beginning to progress enough to become an important occupation.

December 1891. Christmas season arrived. Again, the cry of Fire! was heard. The people reacted quickly, and the blaze was contained to a single structure. Connell's building, rented to Yerger, the tailor, burned for the second time that year. Yerger's loss was $900, but insurance covered only $500 worth. The loss on the building was $300, insurance coverage, $100. The cause of the fire was Yerger's carelessness. He left a can of benzine near a gas stove.[8]

Because of this fire the populace was speaking loudly for a water system in town to control this all-too-frequent destroyer. However, no one was motivated enough to create a fire department or similar organization.

Winter of 1891-92 was uneventful — a fire burned the home of William Garrison in mid-February.[9]

A big event historically speaking, and not necessarily felt by the people, happened with an announcement in the Santa Rosa papers. On March 26, 1892, Col. J.B. Armstrong set aside 640 acres of the "finest" redwoods in Sonoma County for a botanical park. The complete story is given in Chapter 34, "Armstrong Grove."[10]

The first half of 1892 was dull: no fires, no floods. Crime was generally of a misdemean-

Oakland Nell, one of the "girls" of Guerneville.
JCS Collection

or nature during the years 1891 and 1892. Out of 16 cases during that time in the Redwood Judicial District, only one was a felony, People v. Martin E. Bowles. The case was tried in Superior Court in Santa Rosa. Bowles came into town and spent a night at the Guerneville Hotel. He stole a watch, valued at $75, belonging to a waitress, Emma Hentley. He was tried, found guilty, and sent to Folsom Prison for five years.[11]

There is one subject in history about which it is difficult to find facts, namely, sex, or anything related to it. By perseverence, bits and scraps of information were slowly uncovered. The case of Guerneville is no different from any other small town where everybody knew what was going on, but nobody talked about it. The Victorian Age still rules strong.

A faint picture of Guerneville's "ladies of the night," "painted ladies," "fallen women," "soiled doves" emerged after conversations with many "oldtimers " — men and women born around the turn of the century who lived most of their formative years in and about town.

The first "lady"/madam definitely identified was Alice "Henny" Bee, known as "Old Lady Bee." In 1892 her occupation, or lack of any, was alluded to in the following message to Mr. J.W. Juilliard, member of the Board of Supervisors. It also questions her qualifications to receive welfare.[12]

POST-OFFICE.
GUERNEVILLE,
Sonoma Co.,   Cal.

May 11, 1892
H: J.W. Juilliard
  I think Mrs. Bee allowings of $8.50 per month should be stopd for few months, she wont work and runs around town and get fellows in trouble. She wont take any mine washing say she has no tiem. please inquier.
      yours truly,
      G. DIETZ, P.M.

If you have not figured out the spelling, it is because Gerhardt Dietz, the town's postmaster, was born and raised in Germany. In so many words of the oldtimers, Old Lady Bee was short and heavy, known as the town gossip, but she never swore. She had one daughter, described as a beautiful redhead, who later left town. Since she was "kind of destitute," the menfolk would "donate" firewood, boxes of produce, et cetera, to "help her out."[13]

The summer of 1892 brought campers again to the redwoods and Russian River. A new steam launch with a capacity of 16 passengers was put into service between Guerneville and Duncans' Mills.[14] By early July, there were all of 10,000 people camping in the redwoods from the inland canyons to the coast. The schools let out for the usual one-month break, adding more footloose people.[15] The local school kids generally worked — farm kids on the farm, town kids in stores. August came, and the children returned to school. September came, and the campers returned home.

During the fall, men were nominated for various public offices. The election campaign of 1892 became vigorous as election day approached. Redwood Township had sufficient population this year to create two voting precincts. The polls were at Ellison's Hotel for East Redwood precinct and Hewitt's carpenter shop for West Redwood precinct.

The race for Supervisorial District No. 5 was one of great local interest. Two of Guerneville's residents, Jacob Joost and John W. Bagley, were in competition with J.C. Fisk of Stewart's Point, Tom Gould of Duncans' Mills, and F. Smith of Occidental, as well as with each other. The campaign was waged under the banners of political parties, even though supervisor is now a non-partisan position. Bagley was supported by the Prohibitioners (true to his temperance standing), and by the People's Party. The incumbent, Jacob Joost, was a Democrat, and received the support of the county's largest newspaper, the Sonoma Democrat. Tom Gould was a Republican. Smith and Fisk were independents.[16]

The Supervisorial District covered the whole coast of Sonoma County from Bodega Bay to the Mendocino County line, and inland to Cazadero, Guerneville and Freestone. The vote was cast.

The election results were: [17]

Joost	377
Gould	273
Bagley	121
Smith	77
Fisk	69

The winner was the incumbent, Joost.

The local offices of Justice of the Peace and Constable of Redwood Township were up for election, also. Those desiring public office and power were put on the ballot. The people's choices were:

Guerneville Cornet Band, looking east in front of the Guerneville railroad depot, July 1887. Amy Bagley Hatch Collection.

Justice of the Peace:[18]

N. B. Turner	138
Marshall Florence	138
Omer Cobb	113
William H. Barkly	112

Constable: [19]

George Brown	166
B.G. Pippin	139
William F. Graham	105
John S. Pool	87

The two with the largest vote count for Justice of the Peace and Constable were the victors.

The political gale died away during November. At the end of the month, a large storm blew in the winter season. Some 70 trees were downed across the Guerneville-Duncans' Mills road (this narrow, twisting road did not go along the river to Monte Rio, but over Duncan Road from Guernewood Park over the saddle to Monte Cristo, west of Monte Rio). Many redwoods were down in the forest, and damage was great to houses from fallen limbs and trees.[20]

Christmas and New Year 1893 were celebrated in ordinary fashion.

If a year had to be picked to separate eras of Guerneville's history, it would be 1893. This year marks the change in appearance of the river community from lumbering to agriculture. Granted, it was not a sudden event, rather, it was a gradual transition. Logging was still present, but only far up the reaches of canyons and distant ridges. The cut-over hillsides and flats were converted to agriculture. Apple and prune orchards, hop fields, tobacco, olive groves and vineyards were planted.

Various letter writers noted to the county's newspapers that the noise and commotion of the teamsters had quieted; loggers were not prevalent:

> Presto, chango! The region of Big Bottom, on Russian River, once a roaring lumber camp dotted with steam saw mills and alive with the industry of a thousand men, begins to take on the arts of the husbandman.[21]

Guerneville had some agriculture on a small scale dating back to 1875, with David

Hetzel and his tobacco plantations. In addition, Dr. Prosek was experimenting with olives in 1885. Hops were planted by various men, including George Guerne, as early as 1883. Col. J.B. Armstrong planted prunes north of town in the 1880s.

The changes to the countryside and town were not the only and obvious modifications. Most of the area's pioneers and town's founders were gone. The personality of Guerneville was changing. Thomas Heald moved to Healdsburg, Rufus Murphy was keeping a hotel in Ukiah, S.H. Torrance was dead, and George Guerne and Henry Willits were in Santa Rosa.

There were some "oldtimers" still in town: the Bradford Bells, Pippins, the Strode family, the Pools, Coons, Sarah and Henry Klein, and, of course, the Bagleys.

Besides a change in personality and horticulture, the town was also becoming a tourist and vacationing center. As previously noted, tourists came to visit the big trees and rusticate in the pleasing climate, but not yet in significant numbers. As the years progressed, so did the numbers of visitors. To help make things more pleasant for them, the town's Cornet Band presented an open air concert every Sunday.

The Fourth of July celebration of '94 took place at Guerne and Murphy's Park (Guernewood) with its sapling redwoods and laurel around massive redwood stumps, remainders of cutting 12 to 13 years earlier. The Cornet Band in full uniform ceremoniously serenaded the crowd.[22]

Two weeks later, in the relaxed atmosphere of the Gay '90's, Guerneville's citizens brought forth the idea of incorporating the town. A committee was selected, consisting of:

    David Hetzel, Chairman
    W.P. Ferguson, Secretary
    Dr. Cole
    John Bagley
    Henry Ungewitter

    Mrs. Ellen Bagley
    Mrs. Antoinette Lauteren[23]

This committee is unique in that two women were actively involved and on the record in a civic matter (not just a purely social organization) to help decide a matter that in the past normally involved only men.

This group became formally organized at Odd Fellows Hall on August 2, 1894 as the Guerneville Improvement Society. Following the patterns established by public and private associations, the officers were elected quarterly, rather than annually. The first elected officials were:

    James R. Watson, President
    W. Cole, Vice-President
    W.P. Ferguson, Secretary
    Antoinette Lauteren, Treasurer[24]

The society's goal was changed from town incorporation to raising funds to help promote the welfare and growth of the town. Their first public function was a picnic package at Guerne's Park. On August 17 in the afternoon there would be dancing to Guerneville's famed Cornet Band, with barbecue, boating, bonfires, a railroad excursion to the campgrounds, and, at night, fireworks — all for 35 cents![25]

Some 600 people — 60 from Santa Rosa — attended. The barbecue was roasted ox, green corn, baked beans, and coffee. The trees were strung with Chinese lanterns.

Because the railroad did not have a night train back to Santa Rosa, the travelers stayed overnight in Guerneville, adding more revenue to the town's coffers.

Though the charge was only 35 cents per person, the receipts amounted to $210. It was so successful another picnic was demanded by the communmity.[26]

With money in the treasury, definite plans were made:

    plant shade trees along the streets;

Guerneville circa 1892; in the foreground is the three-story hotel built and owned by August Wehrspon. In the backgound is the Russian River. JCS Collection.

houses and fences to be improved;

improve the Park [Guernewood];

induce settlers;

provide a first class summer resort;

raise the moral standards of the town.[27]

The society was flush with success. The future looked extremely good; but Fate can be cruel.

At the end of August there was a heat wave, with temperatures in the 100's. The cry of Fire! was heard again, but this time, the consequences of a town being slipshod in its municipal responsibilities — such as poor fire protection — were to be horrendous. The greatest holocaust ever to befall Guerneville occurred on Saturday, August 25, 1894. The whole town, with the exception of two blocks bordering the river, was razed — literally flattened. Only a few half walls of the Odd Fellows building stood feebly.

The fire completed its destruction in two hours. Half of the population was homeless, foodless, clothesless — 300 people. The biggest shock was the death of two people and the near trapping of a third. It was the first time a human life was lost to fire in Guerneville. A complete and detailed account of this fire is given in the following chapter.

Since the society's August barbecue was such a success, another was planned for the 20th of September. However, no one had time or money to work at it.[28]

The autumn of '94 and early winter were spent trying to rebuild the town — not haphazardly, but with some thought of intelligent community development. Arrangements were made with the Sonoma Lumber Company to have a four-inch water main laid from their mill up First Street to Armstrong Road. The pressure came from a 60-foot fall from the mill's water tank to better assist in firefighting.[29]

The new wooden residences went up fairly quickly. The brick buildings took several months to complete.

Being an even-numbered year, 1894 was one for elections of a Justice of the Peace and Constable. Besides putting up new buildings, the men found time to campaign and note their wishes in November. The election final

Miriam School, Guerneville, 1893. Far Left: Pet Ungewitter Belden and her dog; Gertrude Lautren Schulte. Girl on far right in white: Gertrude Joost Moore. Boy in white shirt lying down: Arthur Coon. Three teachers, left to right: Miss Talmadge, Principal Mr. Brairity, Missy May Burke. Photo from Gertrude Moore. JCS Collection

tally was:[30]

Justice of the Peace:
W V. Cole	142
W.T. Graham	134
R.B. Brown	123
C.E. Ellison	65

Constable:
B.G. Pippin	143
O.O. Cobb	113
G. Brown	112
F.J. Wendt	106

In January 1895, the river community was dealt another severe blow by nature. The third big flood in historic times inundated the town. The rains started on January 8th and continued for three days — at one time depositing six inches in 24 hours. On Friday, the 11th, the river rose nine inches an hour, cresting three inches higher than the highest in many a year.[31]

The rains slackened, the river dropped, Approximately a week later, another storm hit. The damage to the California North Coast was staggering. For just one example,

> A tremendous landslide occurred on the south fork of the Gualala River. Five acres of land well timbered ... slid into the river which entirely changed the water course and destroyed about the same amount of cultivated land.[32]

Numerous small bridges throughout the county were washed away. Railroads were cut in many places. The trestle crossing Laguna de Santa Rosa at Sebastopol was under eight feet of water.

Though the residents of Guerneville knew how to cope with floods, they were hard hit. All forms of communication were severed with the outside world — telegraph, telephone, wagon and railroad. For three days not a word was heard from Guerneville. Only later foot traffic by a few hardy souls carried news and information out of town.

The railroad between Forestville station (Mirabel) and Guerneville was seriously damaged. Tracks were swept off grades and displaced tens of yards. A big slide, claimed to be two miles long (!), shifted the road bed.

In town the water rose until it was within ten inches of the floor of the Grand Central Hotel on First Street (across from today's 1980 Lark Drug Store). The river height was about 44 feet.

Four large homes were raised, then tipped over and swept off their lots. Another had water up to the second floor windows. Four small homes were washed away. Eight others were inundated, among them those of Robert Starrett, Oliver Westcott, and John Connelly.

Sam Varner and family in Mays Canyon had a narrow escape from death. They saw a landslide coming, rushed from their home to their barn nearby, and turned to see the home carried away by the slide. It was swept into their swollen creek and washed downstream.

It was nearly three weeks before the railroad line reopened for any traffic. The first to traverse the hazardous roadbed were a locomotive and tender.[33]

A record of rainfall statistics for Guerneville does not exist. However, Healdsburg and Santa Rosa — the two cities nearest this town maintaining records — show that January 1895 was the high record until January 1909. Even then these two months were the two highest until 1930. The flood of 1895 subsided, and the people resumed building their new town.

The last few burned-out shops to be rebuilt were finished by the end of April 1895. Oliver Wescott fronted his saloon with a cement sidewalk, another new attribute to the town. Joost & Starrett's saloon was rebuilt on their old site at Second and Armstrong, with a concrete cellar. The new postmaster, Mary Ungewitter, moved into the new post office.[34]

The problem of too few residences still lingered on into March. Besides the losses to the flood, there were still people who were burned out by the Great Fire living on high ground and who had not rebuilt.

On June 14, Guerneville gave itself a celebration, proving to the world and itself that the phoenix had risen again. Guerneville's populace could obviously recover from any tragedy dealt it.

Redwood Lodge No. 281 of the Odd Fellows formally dedicated their new hall. The former brick building had been valued at $14,000. To reconstruct another structure, the lodges statewide donated $2,000 to the local chapter.[35]

Back in October 1894, debris had been cleared off the lot and the bricks salvaged and cleaned. The actual building of the hall (designed by DeSheil of Santa Rosa) started on December 1. The flood of '95 stopped work for several weeks, but it was resumed shortly thereafter. The structure was completed by June 1.[36]

The ground floor was used solely by businesses. Starting from the west end of the building facing First Street, there was David Hetzel & Son (Carl), the tobacconist, then Gerhardt Dietz jewelry and notion shop. Next was Carr & Bagley's General Store; and, last was Dr. Burns' Pharmacy, owned and operated by his widow.

Other stores in the brick block, next to, but not part of the Odd Fellows' building, were a barber shop, hardware store, saloon called the Capitol, (operated by O. Wescott), butcher shop, and general store with the post office.

On the second floor of Odd Fellows' was the large auditorium, 60 feet by 60 feet. Its seating capacity was in excess of 500. The stage was 18 feet by 14 feet, with dressing rooms to each side. Next to this large hall was a small banquet room.[37] The unusual thing about the construction was the Odd Fellows did the work themselves. They celebrated the completion of their building on June 14.

The town was decorated with flags and bunting flying. "All the pretty maids [were] in holiday attire." The show windows were decked out around town. The people came from all around. Nearly every hitching post had a rig tied to it.

At 2:30, the auditorium was packed, and the procession of Odd Fellows entered. The Methodist choir provided the music for the dedication ritual. Addresses from visiting Grand Masters were given. The audience joined in the Doxology, and the chaplain closed the ceremonies with a benediction. The dinner was donated by Carr & Bagley, and was held in their decorated warehouse.

At 9 o'clock that night, a grand ball was begun. The final decision of the townspeople: The ball was the largest and best social function Guerneville had ever witnessed. Close to 50 couples occupied the floor for every dance. The last strains of music ended in the early dawn.[38]

The religious were not to be forgotten amidst all the folderol over the Odd Fellows. The Methodist Church down on Church and Fourth Streets, southeast corner, received a new coat of paint.[39] The new Congregational Church, on present First Street, west of Church, was first used on June 9. New chairs arrived from San Francisco in September, helping to fill the church's capacity to over 200 people.[40]

Other civic improvements continued. The Grand Central Hotel was overhauled, minor repairs made, walls washed and repainted. The dining room was re-ceilinged and papered.

The school fence along First Street was repaired because of shortcuts made during the travels of the younger folk. Why use the gate?[41]

John Coon on Armstrong Road, between Third and Fourth Streets, expanded his blacksmith shop to twice its size. Slowly but surely, the citizens were filling up the vacant lots.[42]

The Guerneville Improvement Club was activated "from its suspended animation of nearly a year."[43]

The last commercial enterprise to rebuild after waiting 15 months (probably waiting for another fire) was the railroad depot. Ten men worked for one week on the structure. The town was now basically complete, again.[44]

1. *S.D.*, January 10, 1891.
2. *S.D.*, April 11, 1891.
3. *S.D.*, August 15, 1891.
4. *S.D.*, May 2, 1891.
5. *S.D.*, May 16, 1891.
6. *Russian River News*, "The Guerneville Nine," October 21, 1976, p.4; and *S.D.*, June 20, 1891.
7. *S.D.*, August 15, 1891.
8. *S.D.*, December 26, 1891.
9. *S.D.*, February 13, 1892.
10. *S.D.*, March 26, 1892.
11. County Records, Report of H.L. Bagley, 1892, Redwood Township Justice of the Peace.
12. Letter to Bd. Supvrs. Records.
13. Interviews and letters of C.R. Clar, J. Hetzel and A. Strode.
14. *S.D.*, May 21, 1892.
15. *S.D.*, July 9, 1892.
16. Bd. Supvrs. Records, Book 10, p. 610; S.D., Oct. 29, 1892.
17. Ibid.
18. Bd. Supvrs. Records, Book 10, p. 611.
19. Op. Cit., p. 613.
20. *S.D.*, July 14, 1894.
21. *S.D.*, February 4, 1893; May 27, 1893.
22. *S.D.*, July 14, 1894.
23. *S.D.*, July 21, 1894.
24. *S.D.*, August 4, 1894.
25. *Ibid.*
26. *S.D.*, September 1, 1894.

27. *S.D.*, August 29, 1894.
28. *S.D.*, September 15, 1897.
29. *S.D.*, September 15, 1894; October 6, 1894.
30. Bd. Supvrs. Records, Book 11, pp. 382-3.
31. *S.D.*, January 12, 1895.
32. *S.D.*, January 19, 1895.
33. *S.D.*, January 29, 1895.
34. *S.D.*, March 2, 1895.
35. *S.D.*, June 22, 1895.
36. *S.D.*, September 15, 1894; September 14, 1894; June 22, 1895.
37. *S.D.*, June 22, 1895; Sanborn Map of Guerneville, February 1897.
38. *Ibid.*
39. S.D., June 15, 1895.
40. *Ibid.*; and September 21, 1895.
41. *S.D.*, August 10, 1895.
42. *S.D.*, September 21, 1895.
43. *Ibid.*
44. *S.D.*, December 7, 1895.

Grand Central Hotel on the south side of First Street, a couple of doors west of the 1923 bridge. Photo circa 1898. JCS Collection

Chapter 25

PHOENIX

Of all the towns in Sonoma County and possibly the North Bay, Guerneville was, and probably still is, the town most battered and abused by Man and Nature. A quick check of dates from 1867 to 1894 of large floods and big fires tends to prove it:

1867	Flood
1879	Flood
1881	Flood
1883	Fire
1885	Fire
1886	Fire
1889	Fire

It should be remembered that intervening years had less devastating occurrences of flood and fire. During the '80's, fire was an annual event. Because of Herman Haas, every incident was considered arson until determined otherwise.

Guerneville's ability to recover rapidly from ashes could justly earn it the name of "Phoenix." The people would rebuild while the ashes were still warm. The fire of 1889 was the most destructive up to that time, but Guerneville was to be put to the test again.

August 24, 1894 was a summer Saturday, the hottest day of the year, registering 104° in the afternoon. A Mr. Twombley was living in Dr. Joshua Burns's rental near the corner of Mill and First Streets. He built an early dinner fire in the kitchen stove, then went across the street to the Good Templars reading room. The fire was doing well when a defective flue let the roof catch flame. By the time it was discovered, it was too late to save the building.[1]

The alarm was sounded. A four-inch hose was run from the sawmill to Mill Street and the burning building. It was not long enough! The firefighters had to stand in front of Bert Bagley's home, just to the west, and play a weak stream on the increasing fire.[2]

The heat was intense. Men could not approach close enough to tear down Burns's rental and prevent the spread of flames. The people were paralyzed. Instead of forming a bucket brigade, they stood around watching the feeble effect of the hose.

Finally realizing the fire had obtained a headway, they quickly tore down a neighboring house to check the spreading inferno. But the flames leapt over this new woodpile. A second cottage, which was rented to the Bixby family by Dr. Burns, quickly disappeared in flames.[3]

On the hills were large water tanks of the lumber company to supply the town with water for household purposes. This supply was sufficient under normal circumstances.[4] The mill had enough steam power to pressurize the pipe lines in all parts of town, but the strain of the newly formed bucket brigades and the continuous loss from broken pipes where homes had been was too much. Quickly the water supply and the pressure were nil.

From then on, nothing stopped the fire. The wood frame structures fairly exploded. D.C. Connell's home, a butcher shop of Mrs. Whited, Bert Bagley's residence, the last structure to the west — all were lost. They were followed by Finley's home to the east, La Gori Hotel, N.B. Turner's barn, filled with four carloads of wood, Benning's Saloon, J.R. Watson's, Walker's, Allison, and so on.

Every means was implemented to suppress the flames. Mrs. Lautren stood in a puddle on First Street, dipping buckets for the firemen.[5]

A horseman was sent to Wehrspon's Mill

Late summer, right after the fire of 1894, looking east on First Street. Grand Central Hotel in background on right. To the left the town was completely burned out. Note the collapsed brick walls of the Odd Fellows Building in center. Gertrude Joost Moore Collection

for assistance a mile away in May's Canyon. Eighty men responded, including many from Clar's Mill. More structures caught fire.

Attempts were made to save possessions. Household belongings and store merchandise were piled in the streets, but the intensity of the heat ignited the goods. People barely escaped from their homes.

"All I have in the wide world," said Gerhardt Dietz, "is a pair of trousers, shirt, and two shoes badly scorched."[6]

At the west end of town the battle for the big mill was being fought. The mill manager called in his loggers from the woods to help fend off the flames.[7]

To the east, a wall of flames crossed Church Street and rapidly consumed building after building. Most of the contents of the railroad depot were saved.[8] The employees at first alarm carried books, papers, and the most valuable merchandise into boxcars alongside the depot, and pushed them along the track until out of town and danger.

J.H. Ansell sent his logging train at full steam to his camp down river and brought up 75 men.[9] About 30 men were also sent from the quicksilver mine. However, for all the manpower available, there was no organization — no leadership. Every man did what he thought best to do, and as well as he could. It could hardly have been otherwise.

A wind this hot afternoon was blowing from the west and fanning the blaze bigger. This bigger blaze created its own wind, turning almost into a firestorm. A correspondent to the *San Francisco Chronicle* reported:

> "Forced onward by the wind the fire ran along Main Street as if the various buildings it encountered were only so many sections of a fuse. Fitful gusts from the canyon caused the blaze to pursue a devious course. Suddenly a heavier gust

San Francisco Chronicle engraving of damage, August 29, 1894, looking east along Main Street.

than usual burst out of the canyon and the fire ran across town to the northeast. Then again it bore down due east.

At Fourth Street it turned to the west. Then a great arm of fire razed the Methodist Church."[10]

The holocaust was moving mostly east, but the two-story brick Odd Fellows Building would stop it. There was an alley ten feet wide on the building's west side. With the brick wall, the alley, and their hard work, the townfolk had the fire arrested.[11]

However, it was soon evident that heat and flames were too great. The bricks and mortar began to crumble. Strenuous efforts were made to save the building. The Odd Fellows Hall was doomed. It was in flame.

Still the people continued to carry out goods. The regalia of the Odd Fellows, Masons, Grand Army of the Republic, and other societies were saved.[12] Oscar McKean, with Dr. Burns, was vacating the latter's drug store on the ground floor.

The porch roof of the Odd Fellows building extended out into First Street, directly across from the Grand Central Hotel porch.[13] This second porch also extended over a board sidewalk into the street. The porch awning caught fire, and in order to prevent the fire jumping First Street to the Grand Central Hotel's porch, the people cut the posts supporting it.[14] Just as Burns and McKean were coming out, the awning fell, burying both men, as well as the telephone messenger boy, Clyde Hewitt.

Though the heat was almost unbearable and danger of the walls collapsing great, everyone tore away the hot bricks and rubble. Five minutes later, they found the bodies of Burns and McKean. Hewitt was found a short time later, breathing, but unconscious. He had internal injuries and was almost asphyxiated by the smoke.

Two other men were thought burned since they were missing while carrying stock from the stores on the ground floor. Luckily, this rumor was in error.

Many other persons were hurt by falling timbers and were burned by the flames.

Two of the hardest fights of the day were made at the Grand Central Hotel and Connell's home, both on the south side of First Street. The hotel's balcony/porch extended, as mentioned, into the street. It was badly scorched, but saved.[15]

Next door, to the east of the hotel, was Connell's home. It could not escape destruction. Connell, the livery stable owner, had suffered losses in every major fire, and was determined not to go through the trauma once again. He called out wildly for volunteers, first offering $25, then $50, and, finally, $100 to the men who would save his house. A number of men responded, and with dippers, buckets, and anything else that came to hand, wet down the building.[16] They saved it.

Though postmaster and jeweler Gerhardt Dietz lost everything, his daughter was more resourceful in saving her piano. Rushing up town, looking for any kind of a wagon, she met a drunken fruit peddler who was inviting the panic-stricken people to help themselves to his fruit.[17] It took her a minute to have the fruit dumped into the street. She then jumped up on the seat, seized the reins, and galloped down the street to her threatened home. By crying out to the men scurrying in every direction, she collected five of them. They grabbed the piano and hustled it out into the wagon. Triumphantly, lashing the horse with the reins, she rushed to safety.

Animals suffered, too. Dogs, cats, pigs, chickens and turkeys were cremated. As the San Francisco Chronicle reported:

> "One man whose home was destroyed, gazed sadly at the charred remains the next morning. When asked if anything had been saved, he said, 'Yes, there it is,' and pointed to a black object in the embers. It was a roasted rooster."[18]

At the Corner of Fourth and Church Streets, the fire took a crazy turn. Two buildings on one side were quickly destroyed. Across the street, Mr. Jewett's home had half the roof burned off as the flames rushed to the northeast. A house next door to Jewett's was not even scorched.

At the end of Fourth, the flames ascended the hill that is topped by the French house, then home of Ansell.[19] The fire encountered Ansell's fence part way up. It burned along the pickets, then jumped to the grass. The house was sure to follow the town's demise. Halfway up the slope the fire sank quietly in the grass, and died out. (Incidentally, this house still stands; the second oldest in the town. It was millman Westover's home until 1913, when purchased by the Guy Laws family.)

By 4 o'clock p.m., two hours after the fire started, it was out. Only along the south side of First Street did any buildings remain. The area north of it was a grey, smoldering flat but for a large mound of brick and a few soot-covered, bent pipes. Over one-half the population was burned out.[20]

The people of Guerneville were confused, dazed and numbed by the suddenness of the inferno. Many were literally penniless and had only the clothes on their backs. Fire insurance costs were prohibitive.

With the death of Dr. Burns, there was now only one doctor in town — Dr. Cole. He was away tending to a patient when the fire started. All his books, instruments and medicines were burned in his office. The only thing to survive was his pocket case that he had with him.

Dr. Cole tended Clyde Hewitt for concussion and a broken upper jaw, as best he could, besides caring for others who had been injured. Hewitt's father summoned Dr. Thompson of Santa Rosa for further medical help, but that doctor, after examining Clyde, said he could do no more than what Dr. Cole had done. For several days it was thought Clyde would not survive his injuries, but Dr. Cole made good his recovery.

The funeral for the 72-year-old Dr. J.A. Burns took place at 2 p.m. the next day, Sunday. Most of the population from the surrounding countryside gathered at the schoolhouse for the services.[21] Pallbearers were M.A. McPeak, J.T. Keaton, A.P. Moseley, and Anthony McPeak. Dr. Burns' widow and daughter were in Willits at the time. Oscar McKean, a 35-year-old laborer, left a family of a wife

William Carr, Gertrude Lautren, and J.H. Ansell. JCS Collection

Dr. Cole, the doctor who survived the fire (no relation to the Cole twins of the baseball team). JCS Collection

and four small children destitute.

The first priority for the people was finding shelter.[22] The school declared a three-week vacation so the structure could be used as temporary housing. The Grand Central Hotel and the few surviving homes were thrown open to the victims. But the number of people accommodated was small. Most of the 300 homeless had to "camp out" in the open air. Along the tree-lined river, in the canyons and hop vines, one could see an assortment of blankets and quilts, scorched and discolored, hanging from low limbs. In some cases, families literally slept in the streets. There were no tents. There was no material to make them.

The biggest need was food. Local supplies from home larders, log camp cookhouses and quicksilver mine kitchens at most could last only a few days.[23] J.H. Ansell fed about 100 people the following day at his mill. At that rate, his provisions would be depleted in two days.

James R. Watson wrote:

"That night after the fire some 15 people were guests at the Watson's north of town. The women and girls cooperated in the kitchen while the men and boys set up lodgings. Nobody went hungry. Everybody had a bed; men and boys in the barn, women and girls in the house."[24]

Still, Guerneville was looking starvation in the eye. A relief committee comprised of J.H. Ansell, J.A. Jasper and William Carr issued a plea for assistance from any and all people.[25] Their funds consisted of $180 in the bank from the Guerneville Improvement Club. Ironically, their money was raised to install firefighting equipment; now it was being used for the burned-out homeless.

An emergency meeting of the County Supervisors was called by Supervisor Joost of Guerneville, one of the victims, to make an appropriation of $5,000 for the town. However, the law prevented them from doing so at that date in the state's history.[26]

This was the only setback for the town with respect to charitable aid.

Donations came from all over: Alfred Abbey of the quicksilver mine, $25; the miners,

Sufferers Combination, September 1894. Shops, left to right: O. Wescott's saloon, Hetzel's cigar store, Williams' candy store Dietz' newsstand and post office, and the Widow Burns' drug store. People: fifth from left, Jim Morrow with white beard; little boy in doorway, Dave Hetzel, Jr.; on his left, brother Carl Hetzel; third man to Dave Jr.'s left, Charles Tibbots (elected constable in 1930). Note pile of bricks from the Odd Fellows Building. JCS Collection

$25; J.C. Halloway of the Bank of Cloverdale, $20; A.W. Oates of Santa Rosa, $25; San Francisco Northern Pacific Railroad, $100; Kate and Lizzy Armstrong, $50.[27]

Santa Rosa responded quickly. The first day after the fire, the city formed its own relief committee and promptly sent $200 to Guerneville, with clothes and foodstuffs of some value.[28] This was only the beginning. On Sunday evening, the committee held a meeting at the Fifth Street Methodist Church. They passed the collection plate and received $150. Other collections about Santa Rosa netted $850.[29] More donations included about one ton of flour, 400 pounds of potatoes, furniture sets, sewing machines, beds and bedding, tables, chairs, et cetera.

Donations arrived from Petaluma, Duncan's Mills, Sebastopol, Cloverdale, Healdsburg and San Francisco. A few Santa Rosans donated $45 specifically to the McKean family, a considerable sum in those days.[30]

The following day, the National Guard, 5th Infantry Regiment, Companies "C" and "E" stationed at Santa Rosa and Petaluma,[31] sent 20 tents to the committee. Sperry Company shipped 50 bags of flour, and the Golden Eagle Milling Company of Petaluma did likewise.

The total loss to the citizens of Guerneville in dollars amounted to $112,500, with very little insurance covering the damages.[32]

However, the town did not wait around for handouts.[33] Dietz, who nearly lost all the post office property, handled business in Connell's Livery, alongside the telephone company and the temporary railroad depot. The merchants built temporary establishments by placing boards across barrels for counters and displaying signs reading, "Open for Business," or "Moved on Account of Heat" over their small stock.

It took about two days for sensible organization to rise out of chaos. The townfolk took their time planning and building a new town, but they worked with a will.

It was not until Monday, the 26th of August, when the people had their world back in some

Guerneville, California, after the Fire of 1894. The view is looking southeast toward the Grand Central Hotel. The railroad is the Guerneville branch of the San Francisco & North Pacific Railroad. Russian River Historical Society Photo

order, that inquiry was made of Twombly, the unfortunate soul who started the fire. He considered Dr. Burns his benefactor, and when he learned the doctor had been killed, he became grief stricken.[34] The man headed for the river to end his life, but was stopped. That night (on the day of the fire) Twombley stayed at John Bagley's home. Twombley left early Sunday morning, making a passing mention that he would possibly repeat an attempt at suicide again. It was believed he had, because he was not seen again.

The consumption of Guerneville by fire is only half of its metamorphic story. Just as the phoenix rose from its ashes, so did Guerneville — again. The difference between fable and life was in the future planning. Though the firebird is reborn with no change, it was different with the town.

The rebuilding started in the usual fashion with lumber being hauled to the ash-covered lots. Ansell and Kimball were burned out of the Frick Block building. Ansell said:

"I sent lumber up from the mill and we at once began the erection of a temporary structure for a store. While the carpenters were at work the owner of the lot, Mr. Berry, came along and requested us not to proceed with our temporary building. He thought that the erection of a cheap place would have a bad effect upon the town. He said he intended to put up a fine residence, and as proof of this intention he at once bought the lumber we had on the ground."[35]

The Odd Fellows planned to rebuild, and Miss Kate Armstrong informed them she would help by guaranteeing the necessary funds.

Besides the "shops" consisting of planks on barrels, there were other temporary structures erected.[36] In less than two weeks there were nine such dwellings. At the same time, three permanent ones commenced: those of N.B. Turner, August Wehrspon, and Hewitt. John Coon had his building completed in three weeks. His blacksmith shop was on Armstrong Woods Road, near Fourth Street.

Residences were under varying stages of construction by mid-September. W.C. Cole's home was nearly finished, while Alex Jensen had just laid the foundation for his house.[37]

There were still people tenting on the school grounds at First and Church Streets, however.

Mrs. Burns, now widowed, sold her business in Willits and contracted a carpenter to build a six-room cottage at Church and Second Streets.[38] The Methodist Church relocated by buying a lot on the southeast corner of Church and Fourth Streets.

One unique building came into being as a result of several merchants uniting their small assets.[39] This one structure, called "Sufferers' Combination," housed five businesses. There were Oliver Wescott, Dave Hetzel Cigars, Mrs. Burns' Drugs, Williams Candy Store, and Ger-

San Francisco Chronicle engraving of the fire damage, August 29, 1894. Top, Main Street after the fire, with an "X" marking the site of the building where the blaze began. Below, railroad tracks warped by the heat.

hardt Dietz's Post Office. The post office had moved from the livery.

Hotels were reconstructed by Montecelli, Ellison and Wehrspon. Rentals were desperately needed. Sonoma Lumber Company and Col. J.B. Armstrong each had two built.[40]

The brick block dominated in the past by the Odd Fellows Building was not started until December.[41]

January 1895 arrived, and with it, another flood. Some families had not recovered from the fire when stricken by rising water. Four "good-sized houses" were tipped over and pushed off their lots.[42] A two-story home had water up to the second floor windows. The Sonoma Lumber Company lost five thousand dollars' worth of lumber, besides losing a barn that was washed away.[43] The Sam Varner family, seeing a slide coming, beat a hasty retreat to their barn. Their home was carried away and swept downstream. Six other homes were inundated, and water entered the Guidotti boarding house (later called the Garibaldi Hotel, then Buck's Ranch).

The water rose nine inches an hour, and finally crested when it reached the railroad depot site located on the west side of the Odd Fellows Building,

Though the brick walls of the building were finished, the rains delayed the placing of joists in the Odd Fellows.[44] Construction resumed after the storm passed, and by mid-March the tinners were working on the roof.

Oliver Wescott added a new facet of urban renewal to Guerneville — a concrete sidewalk in front of his new saloon.[45] Another saloon was reconstructed on an old corner of town — Joost & Starret's. This bar later became a historical landmark of sorts, long known as "The Louvre."

The railroad company procrastinated about rebuilding the depot.

March passed, as did April, May and June. On July 14, 1895, the pillar of society and civilization, as far as Guerneville was concerned, was finally completed.[46] The Redwood Lodge No. 281, Independent Order of Odd Fellows, was dedicated with all the ceremonious proceedings and speeches that could be summoned.

Again, the phoenix of Guerneville had fully risen. For a few years, the empty lot formerly occupied by the depot was the only scar that remained of the Great Fire of '94.

1. *S.D.*, September 1, 1894.
2. *S.F. Chronicle*, August 28, 1894 (hereafter cited as *S.F. Chron.*).
3. *S.F. Chron.*, August 28, 1894.
4. *S.F. Chron.*, August 29, 1894.
5. Interview with Gertrude Schulte, May 7, 1961.
6. *S.F. Chron.*, August 27, 1894.
7. *Ibid.*
8. *S.F. Chron.*, August 26, 1894.
9. *S.F. Chron.*, August 29, 1894.
10. *Ibid.*
11. *S.F. Chron.*, August 26 & 28, 1894.
12. *Ibid.*
13. *Guerneville Times*, 1955-56 (?) article titled, "Looking Backwards," by J.R. Watson.
14. Interview with Charlie Bean, November 11, 1966, at Guerneville, California.
15. *S.F. Chron.*, August 29, 1894.
16-19. *Ibid.*
20. *S.D.*, September 1, 1894.
21. *S.F. Chron.*, August 29, 1894.
22. *S.F. Chron.*, August 28 and September 1, 1894.
23. *Ibid.*
24. *Guerneville Times*, J.R. Watson, 1955(?)
25. *S.D.*, September 1, 1894.
26. *S.F. Chron.*, August 27, 1894.
27. *S.D.*, September 1, 1894.
28. *S.F. Chron.*, August 28, 1894.
29. *S.D.*, September 1, 1894.
30. *Ibid.*
31. *S.F. Chron.*, August 28, 1894.
32. *S.D.*, September 1, 1894.

33. Ibid.
34. *S.F. Chron.*, August 28, 1894.
35. *S.F. Chron.*, August 29, 1894.
36. *S.D.*, September 15, 1894.
37-38. Ibid.
39. *S.D.*, October 1, 1894.
40. Ibid.
41. *S.D.*, December 18, 1894.
42. *S.D.*, January 26, 1895.
43. *S.D.*, January 12, 1895.
44. *S.D.*, March 23, 1895.
45. *S.D.*, March 2, 1895.
46. *S.D.*, June 22, 1895.

Engine 99, "the Coffee Grinder," San Francisco and North Pacific Railroad, 1904; man on far right is William P. Turner, conductor. This is an 0-4-0 locomotive. JCS collection

The Guerne & Murphy Lumber Company's "Bully Boy" in Mission Canyon (Hulbert Creek), 1896; this is an 0-4-0 locomotive. California State Library.

Chapter 26

Lumber Mills — 1895 to end

As the years passed, the lumbering industry became smaller. Bottomlands and flats had been cleared of redwoods, and only small, isolated stands of redwoods pinched by canyons and gullies remained. Few stands of virgin forest were left. The industry was playing a smaller role in the community. Rufus Murphy had once said he never touched a redwood that did not turn to 20-dollar gold pieces in his hand. Those were Guerneville's early days.[1]

As can be seen, the statistics and the lumber history of each five years have become less and less, the chapters smaller.

The logging and lumber story for 1896 is nil.

At the end of January 1897, August Wehrspon, having exhausted his timber sources in May's Canyon, had his mill moved to Hopland in Mendocino County.[2] This left the Sonoma Lumber Company in Guerneville, Korbel's Mill in Pocket Canyon, and Ansell's operation in Smith Creek, next to Bohemian Grove, the only going concerns. These mills were still working because various timber owners either built their own mills or had sold stumpage (standing timber) to those who had mills. An example of the former was Clar's Mill, located due south of Guerneville, on the left bank. Frank Clar owned 120 acres from which he cut enough shingle bolts to keep producing through 1908. In 1899 Clar had a ferry to haul his products from Clar's Flat (today's upstream end of Vacation Beach) to Guernewood Park, near the mouth of Hulbert Creek. It worked well, and "large quantities of wood [were] shipped on it."[3]

George Clar remembered on one occasion being at the mill:

"Pa took me to visit the mill when I was only three or four years old. I remember the steam-noise-saws. I was running around and one of the men told Pa, 'That boy of yours is going to get into trouble.' So Pa picked me up and stuck me in a barrel — it was like a cracker barrel. The only thing I saw was the roof. The mill was an open thing, a roof with no sides."[4]

Ivon Clar, George's father, was in the business up to 1908. Ivon told his other son, Ray, "If I could have made 25 cents on a bundle of shingles, I would have become a rich man."[5]

Another lumber mill contemplated in 1897 was Graham & Carr, of which little is known. Carr owned "a good body of timber on the Bohemian branch." It appears, though, the mill was not built. Did the Bohemian Club buy out Carr? No answer has been found. However, Carr and Graham are reported in separate articles two years later (1899) as running a lumber camp or camps. In April, Charles Carr had 22 men making 30,000 ties to fill a contract he had with the California Railroad. Graham, in June, had 20 men cutting wood.[6]

The third operation in the area was Korbel Brothers. Their mill was not at the winery, but on their property in Pocket Canyon. When the mill moved here is unknown. The mill ran at this location past 1907.[7]

Bacon & Son Mill & Lumber Company was one mile west of Sutherlands' in Hulbert Creek in 1905. In 1909, they had exhausted the timber supply at the Bronsert Ranch on the saddle between Finley Gulch and Kohute Gulch and moved to the Jones Ranch at the end of today's Siri Road, above Guernewood Park.[8]

In 1900, Ben Peugh built a small mill on the Henry Miller lands to cut stumpage there. The timber was located in a canyon which opens to the Big Bottom, north of Guerneville. The cutting lasted beyond 1906. Peugh cut out all the trees, with the exception of a small grove at the eastern edge of Miller's property line in the canyon.[9] Outside of Armstrong Park and Bohemian Grove, this is the only remnant grove of the old forest in the River area today. The trees are on Rio Nido Road, about one-half mile from its junction with Armstrong Road.

The Westover Brothers' Sonoma Lumber Company had their logging camps open in mid-April of 1897. The "big mill" at Guerneville was sawing at full capacity a month later. The company had acquired a good stand of timber up Smith Creek, across the river from today's Northwood. It ran a rail spur up the canyon three-quarters of a mile. The rail spur was connected to the line running down into Meeker's Grove/Bohemian Grove, some 4,800 feet. This line connected to the main track via the bridge at Northwood, built in 1892.[10] The first wood product taken from the Smith Creek watershed was 900 poles for a telephone line between Guerneville and Sebastopol. With this stumpage and other timber, the mill was cutting 40,000 board feet a day.[11]

Besides using a railroad to haul logs, there was still the old proven method of using draft animals. Sam Tomblinson and Sykes Meredith had four big horse teams hauling from the reaches of Pocket Canyon, while other teams were trucking logs over Cinnabar Avenue (Armstrong Road today) and dumping them into the Fife Creek pond.[12]

The last logs were hauled out of the woods in November for the season, but the floating stockpile gave the mill enough supply to keep sawing until mid-December 1897.

The woods in Smith Creek supplied fodder for the saws of Westovers in 1898. Because of the closeness of loggers to Bohemian Grove and the possibility of the Sonoma Lumber Company purchasing the stumpage on their retreat, the Bohemian Club bought Meeker's Grove.

David Benjamin "Ben" Peugh and Mary E. Yarbrough, daughter of C.D. Yarbrough, 1883. Georgia Guerne Peugh Collection

The only incident reported in the mill was a mechanical breakdown in mid-July. From then to August 1899, nothing of any significance was recorded. During that August, the mill was forced to shut down when an "edgerman" let the log car down the incline. He let it get out of control, heading into the log pond and breaking some gears. He put 40 men off work for a couple of days.

In the meantime, cutting and hauling logs from Mission Canyon (Hulbert Creek) continued with the "Bully Boy" tugging the flat cars. The crew was engineer, Mortimer Deal; fireman, Edward Teadman; and conductor, Thomas Lane. At least once, and sometimes twice a day, a trip was made to the mill in

Korbel & Brothers and A.W. Bacon & Son invoices to local blacksmith John T. Coon. Note Korbel Mill location in Pocket Canyon. JCS Collection

town.

One evening a string of empty flat cars in Guerneville, the higher end of the railroad, worked loose and coasted down towards Hulbert Creek. They came to a stop on a sharp curve below town. It was dark when the "Bully Boy" was making its last run of the day for home. Engineer Deal pushed the throttle wide open to make the grade with the six loaded log cars. They were rolling along at full speed. No one saw the empty cars.

The collision was terrific. The first empty car was shattered. "Bully Boy" was swung across the tracks by the cars behind and finally was pushed over on its side, totally wrecked. Deal and Conductor Lane were thrown high in the air and to one side. Fireman Teadman was thrown the opposite way. They were unconscious, badly cut and bruised when found.

Preliminary examinations of Deal and Lane by the town's doctors, V.B. Watson and W.G. Cole, gave little hope for survival. Deal's back and head were a mass of bruises; he had internal injuries as well. Lane had an injured back and shoulders, along with a fractured skull and internal injuries. A cut three inches deep ran down his thigh. Fireman Teadman had the fewest injuries. Although badly bruised and suffering a broken shoulder, he was up and hobbling about two days later. It was close for quite awhile whether or not Deal and Lane would live, but the doctors passed the word a week later that they were in the clear.

The "Bully Boy" was also put in for repairs and to have its wounds fixed.[13]

Besides shutdowns, train wrecks and injuries, there was always the inevitable end of the lumbering industry as Guerneville knew it. D.L. Westover told the Santa Rosa Press Democrat in October 1899:

> "The season was a good one. A great quantity of lumber was handled and many men were employed. Next year will probably be the last year for the location of the mill at Guerneville and it will be moved somewhere else owing to the fact that the timber will have been cleared out."

The market for lumber was the best since 1890. The mill was running at near capacity of 40,000 board feet per day. Forty men worked the mill, and about 60 were working the woods. Sales kept its lumber stock constantly moving through October and into November.[14]

The prediction by Westover about the mill closing in 1900 proved wrong. At the end of November 1899, Westover said:

> "We shall be there for some time yet. There is a large quantity of timber to handle. It seems as if the timber either grows while we are sawing it

or else we discover fresh timber somewhere."[15]

The company purchased a new logging engine, "99," to work along with "Bully Boy." However, "99" broke down and was sent to the Tiburon rail yards in Marin County for repairs, so "Bully Boy" took over "99's" schedule until it returned.[16] The two engines worked by separate schedules (heckuva way to run a railroad) that did not coincide. "Bully Boy" went down the line and found "99" disabled again. It hauled "99" back to Guerneville for another lay up of three months.[17]

The mill was working near full capacity in April and May of 1900. In July, there was a near repetition of the severe train wreck of a year before. An engine and six cars, three with tanbark, three with cordwood, were coming down the grade in Smith Creek when the brakes failed. The engine made one of the curves, but some cars did not. Luckily, there were no injuries.[18]

The summer passed uneventfully. Indian summer was on the wane when a fire broke out along Hulbert Creek. Apparently sparks from a logging engine ignited the dry brush. Two trains with firefighters arrived, and after hard work all through the night, they had it under control. The following day they had it out.

The damage was to young trees and Guerne's and McLain's land. Two railroad bridges in Mission Canyon were destroyed, but within two weeks, the crossings were repaired.[19]

In January 1901, Superintendent G.W. Heason took a tally of the logs in the mill pond for sawing. There were enought to last until February. The Press Democrat headlined an article, "THE MILL MUST GO."

The pioneers of Stumptown thought the redwoods were an unlimited resource. It took some 35 years to prove otherwise. The company slowly realized the supply was finite.

The "Day of Reckoning" was here: February 7, 1901. It was Saturday, 3 o'clock p.m.,
when the last log was sawn by the man who cut the first log back on that distant August day in 1865, John W. Bagley. Two others who were present at the first cutting appeared with him this last day: John's wife, Ellen, and Henry G. Klein. Klein was the only employee who worked for the mill from its start to its end.[20]

A large crowd gathered at the mill. In fact, nearly the whole town turned out. People came from around the countryside to witness this milestone in local history. On April 26, the last lumber was hauled out on flat car No. 71.[21] The last advertisement for the Sonoma Lumber Company appeared in the Russian River Advertiser on December 28, 1901.

Although other mills were still operating and would be for a few years to come, the closing of the Guerneville mill ended an era. One industry was dying, and another was starting — tourism.

The pioneer age was dead.

1. *Press Democrat* (hereafter cited as *P.D.*), October 10, 1896.
2. *P.D.*, January 30, 1897.
3. *P.D.*, May 17, 1899; Ray Clar letter to author, July 5, 1976, Sacramento, CA
4. Interview with George Clar, July 11, 1976, Guerneville.
5. Ray Clar letter, July 5, 1976
6. *Pacific Coast Wood & Iron*, March 1897; P.D., April 8; June 17, 1899.
7. *R.R.Ad.*, July 13, 1907.
8. *R.R.Ad.*, 1905; Pacific Coast Wood & Iron, May 1909, p. 9.
9. *P.D.*, December 27, 1899.
10. David Myrick, *Rails Around Bohemian Grove,* San Francisco; Lawton and Alfred Kennedy, 1973, pp. 14, 19; *Pacific Coast Wood & Iron*, July 1896, p. 17.
11. Ibid.
12. *P.D.*, April 17, 1897; May 15, 1897.
13. *P.D.*, September 2, 1899; San Francisco Examiner,

September 2, 1899; *P.D.*, September 6, 1899.

14. *P.D.*, October 14, 1899.
15. *P.D.*, November 25, 1899.
16. *P.D.*, April 28, 1900.
17. Ibid.
18. *P.D.*, July 11, 190°.
19. *P.D.*, September 20, 1900; October 10, 1900.
20. *P.D.*, February 8, 1901.
21. *P.D.*, April 26, 1901.

THE LAST LOG SAWED AT GUERNEVILLE'S MILL

Crowds Gather to Witness an Interesting Spectacle Saturday Afternoon in The City of the Redwoods

Three o'clock on Saturday afternoon was a memorable occasion in the town of Guerneville. With the hour passed away the active history connected with the Sonoma Lumber Company's big lumber mill there.

At 3 o'clock the last log was sawed and the buzz of the big saw was heard for the last time. The labor of over thirty-five years, as far as the mill was concerned ended when the log had been sawed through. When the workmen finished the turning of the boards at half past 5 o'clock the last day's work in the mill was done.

The last log was sawed by Pioneer J. W. Bagley, who over thirty-five years previously had performed a similar task with the first log. The idea was a neat one and a large crowd of spectators gathered to witness the performance of the work. In fact all Guerneville turned out and folk came from all the country round. Cameras were requisitioned to preserve for memory's sake a picture of the scene.

In the crowd witnessing the sawing of the last log were men who, while they had not the distinction belonging to Mr. Bagley of having run the saw through the first log, were present when he performed the task. These pioneers told a story of the day of long ago anew on Saturday afternoon and it was heard with deep interest. Down in their hearts these old-timers hated to see the saw make that last cut. It recalled the time when the mill was first built. Little by little, as the saw ran its way through the log the recollections of thirty-five years came home to them. Once in a while one of the old men would point with his finger to the open stretch of country or to the hillsides for miles around which had been robbed of the mighty redwood giants during the tenure of activity in the milling days that ended with Mr. Bagley's sawing of the last log. Others recounted the millions upon millions of feet of lumber that had been turned out by the mill and as to its value. It was a time of reflection all round.

The mill building will now be torn down and the machinery will be shipped to Shasta county where the company has big lumber lands. Without the mill Guerneville will not be the same place quite. It will be some time before all the lumber on hand will be cleared up and Superintendent George W. Heason will remain at Guerneville until everything is moved off.

The lighting plant which illuminates the City of the Redwoods by night and which is owned and operated by the lumber company will continue to furnish light for the present and possibly for an indefinite time. The location of the lumber mill at Guerneville has made times prosperous there in the years that have been numbered. Prosperous times are yet in store for Guerneville. New enterprises have been steadily advancing while the lumber business has been declining. Around Guerneville are many prosperous fruit and olive orchards and vineyards, and each year now the shipments greatly increase.

Santa Rosa Press Democrat, Feb. 8, 1901.

Great Eastern Quicksilver Mine, 1890. Perry Beeson Collection

Chapter 27

Quicksilver — Part 2

Six years have now passed since the "Rush of '74." Only two mining companies existed in 1880.

I. The Great Eastern Quicksilver Mine.

This mine maintained a production rate of 60 flasks of mercury a month during 1880. In 1881 the mine flooded due to the big rain storm that hit Northern California. (See Chapter 17.) By the end of April, the mine was back to full operation, with 30 people working. During the summer, Eastern's production was up 70-80 flasks a month.[1]

The year 1882 was a rich one for this company. For two months it filled 95 flasks per week, at 38 cents a pound; this equalled $27,616.50. The ore was rich enough to warrant the hiring of an additional ten men.[2]

In order to expedite the mine further, a request for bids was made in January 1883 to sink a shaft 300 feet. Its dimensions were to be 12 1/2 X 6 1/2 feet. The unknown successful bidder had a two-compartment shaft down 400 feet by November. This shaft and adit at the 480-foot level proved itself. The ore was assayed at 45 percent (!) or 900 pounds of mercury per ton of ore.[3]

Another shaft was sunk an additional 270 feet in March 1884. The furnaces were shut down until this new shaft was completed.[4]

Tiburcio Parrott at this time disposed of his interest in the mine, and M.D. Haskins leased/bought into the mine a year later. The owners now consisted of Richard Lewis, Alfred Abbey, and Haskins. Abbey was secretary of the concern, and Haskins was superintendent.[5]

In mid-1885, the mine was working with only half a crew. The mill capacity was 100 flasks a week, but it was producing only 15 per seven days.[6]

The mine's main shaft now went down 480 feet and connected at this level with a tunnel to another shaft. The top of this second shaft had a 250-foot adit, with its entrance at the surface, 20 feet from the main entrance. This circle of tunneling made for good air cirulation and provided a means of escape in case of accidents.[7]

By the end of 1885 the company had almost a full crew working, which consisted of ten men in the mine, four in the reduction works, and ten outside.

The State mineralogist in '85 reported the Great Eastern as the only quicksilver mine working in Sonoma County:

> It is kept clear of water by a No. 5 steam pump; a Burleigh drill with a compressor is used in assaulting the rock. The surface works or plant has two McDonald furnaces for coarse ore and a single furnace for fine ore. The production rate is 15 tons processed per 24 hours.[8]

He also reported wages differed according to ethnic group. Whites received $1.50 to $2.50 per day, with board; Chinese received $1.50 per day, with no board.

In 1886, the company had a new large ore cart made by Colgan & Hervey in Santa Rosa.[9]

Later this same year the two mines, Mt. Jackson and Great Eastern, formed a corporation and immediately started working at full force. The price of quicksilver at the time of merger was 36 cents a pound, the highest price since 1882, equal to $32.40 a flask.[10]

II. Mt. Jackson Mine.

Backing up to 1880, we pick up the story of the Mt. Jackson/ Great Western Mine.

An accident occurred that year when a Chinese and a white man went down into the mine with burning candles. These caused an accumulation of gas to explode, severely burning the two men. The Chinese did not survive his injuries.[11]

About 1882, Mt. Jackson shut down. A large part of the machinery was removed. The engine was used in Guerneville's box factory, and the remainder of the equipment — furnaces, retorts, et cetera — were covered by sheds.[12]

A fire broke out in these sheds on January 12, 1883, during the day, but it was quickly extinguished by men of the Great Eastern. Another fire started about midnight a year later to the day. These flames were discovered in a high roof, but because of darkness, it was difficult for the people to venture in and about the building safely. The fire spread to the other structures. After the flames were finished, it was discovered coal oil had been used to start the fire. The culprit was never caught. The loss was put at $3,000.[13] After this, the mine was abandoned — at least the surface works. The mine proper was leased to the Great Eastern about mid-1884.

III. A Single Operation

In 1886, Mt. Jackson joined the Great Eastern in the corporation, as already stated.[14]

The year 1887 started out with about 25 men working at the mine, whose efforts were producing 100 flasks a month. As the year progressed, more men were hired. Refining increased so by June there were 60 men producing 15 flasks a day. The price for quicksilver increased from 32 cents a pound in 1882 to 50 to 52 cents a pound, or from $27.46 to $42.90 to $44.67 per flask in 1887. (A full flask weighed 85.8 pounds.)[15]

From 1887 to 1891, little information is available about the mine area. It was recorded by the California Bureau of Mines that from 1882 to 1894 it was the only producing mine in Sonoma County. The federal government reported the Great Eastern had produced by 1888 over 11,000 flasks since its start in 1874.[16]

The number of men employed during this time (1887-1891) must have remained pretty steady. In 1887 there were 60 men, in 1891 there were 60 men, and in January 1892, there were 50 men.[17] Production was steady until 1893. During 1892 the company averaged 150 flasks per month, with July being the biggest month at 600 flasks. However, in February 1893, manager John Patton was preparing to close down, no pay dirt. He let about 50 men go and maintained only a skeleton crew.[18]

Up to 1893 the Great Eastern and Mt. Jackson operated jointly — supposedly. Now history has changed its facts again. As stated, the Jackson joined the Eastern in 1885-86, thereby making one operation. Now, in 1893, manager Patton is reported to have said he hoped the Mt. Jackson would not start as it had plenty of ore. The Sonoma Democrat reported:

> The Great Eastern Quicksilver Mine, near Guerneville, was opened a number of years ago and has since been regularly worked, giving steady employment to one hundred men the year round. The output has been over $1,000,000. It is now thought the mine is worked out. The plant cost $75,000 and the company is trying to dispose of it to the Mount Jackson mine, to which it is convenient, and it is to be hoped that they will sell it, and so keep up the work in that vicinity. It would be a paying investment for the Mount Jackson, as they have a good mine but no reduction works.[19]

What's the correct date? Did they join in 1885-86, or in 1893? The answer is not forthcoming.

Anyway, the Great Eastern made an agreement with the Mt. Jackson stockholders to work their mine.[20] The State reported in 1894, reflecting on 1893:

> The best ore shoot is apparently near the dividing line of the two. The work is carried on through the Great Eastern shaft, extending into the Jackson ground to a depth of 220 ft. At the 420 ft. level of the Great Eastern shaft a drift 400 ft. long was driven to the ore body in the Jackson. The stopes, 40 to 50 ft. long, were worked

10 to 12 ft. wide, requiring only small timbers. A tunnel 1,700 ft. in length, driven into the Jackson, cut the ground 150 ft. below the bottom of the shaft. The mine has been allowed to fill with water to the 150 ft. level, where it discharges through the Great Eastern tunnel, 1,000 ft. long. A compressor with two Burleigh drills is used. Last year's output was 1,400 flasks; the output at present is reported to be 120 flasks per month from fine-ore and coarse-ore furnace, with a capacity of 18 and 12 tons of ore, respectively, consuming 2 1/2 cords of wood per day, costing $2.25 per cord.[21]

Furnaceman D.B. Armstrong stated in the last report 1893 that 147 flasks were smelted during October.[22]

In '94 new machinery, an engine and a drier were installed. Everything was now in good shape.[23] Because of the amount of activity at the mine, the Mine Bureau did a follow-up report in 1896:

> Work is carried on through the Great Eastern shaft, 360' deep, which levels are run at 140', 220', and 360' depth, into the Mount Jackson property. They are now stoping between the 220' and 360' levels. The hoisting plant consists of an 18" drum, driven by a double engine with 8" x 14" cylinders. The steel rope is 1" in diameter. A 25 H.P. Phoenix air-compressor furnishes power for three Phoenix drills. The coarse ore is piled in sheds to dry and the line is spread on an inclined drier, composed of planks, over which, and about 2" above, is placed in a serpentine manner, 4" pipe heated by exhaust steam. When the ore is sufficiently dry, the movable foot-board is taken out and the ore falls upon the floor. There is a fine and a coarse ore furnace, each of 15 tons capacity. About 2,000 cords of wood is used annually, at a cost of $2.25 per cord. Round timber for the mine costs 5 cents per lineal foot. Great Eastern Quicksilver Mining Co., owner, Alfred Abby, 44 Nevada Block, San Francisco, secretary and superintendent.[24]

More statistics: In 1898 there were 40 men employed. The production rate was fairly level.

August	140 flasks
September	160 flasks
December	175 flasks
January 1899	165 flasks[25]

Mining cinnabar did (still does) have its hazards. On May 18, 1898, Fred Sicotte and Estis Prestwood, workmates, were down on the lowest level drilling when an explosion ripped through the adit. Both men were severely burned and were taken to the Guerneville Hotel. There, Drs. Cole and Watson tended their wounds. Prestwood died.[26]

The mine area after nearly a quarter of a century of existence had a fair-size population. Mt. Jackson school district was created in 1878. There were rentals, as well as permanent homes, the mine's boarding house, and a hotel. There was also a small Chinese "colony" of about 15 to 20 people. The U.S. Government was represented by a post office, established in January 1899, with Mrs. John Austin as Postmaster of this settlement called Mercury.[27]

The mine was improved with the installing of a 50-h.p. engine for the hoist and an 8-h.p. engine for sinking the main shaft. This shaft by 1899 was 500 feet down and serviced the 435-foot drift there.[28]

The surface works had changed little. There were still two furnaces with capacities of 14 and 18 tons. These were cleaned out once a month to reclaim mercury accumulations. Regular production results for July, August and September 1899 showed 230, 235 and 228 flasks recovered, respectively.[29]

There is a dearth of facts for the following years, up to 1903. Five years had passed since the last known accident occurred in 1898. In August 1903, Frank Thomas and Frank Perry were setting off charges in the mine, but miscalculated the time. They were caught by the blast. Their injuries were severe, but they apparently recovered. No further details are available.[30]

Another year passed. It was November 1904.[31] The swing shift (4 p.m. to midnight) was working on a Sunday evening. Four miners — Jim Leslie, Rollo Hooten, Peter von der Stratten and Fred Sicotte — were working at the 600-foot level, blowing out accumulated explosive gases, usually methane. These gases usually pool at the roof. Air is blown in to mix with this gas and to dilute and move it about the mine so it would not be a danger. In these days of mining the lamps worn by miners were not electric, but were either candles or carbide gas.

The reader probably now has put the problem together — methane gas and open flame.

The miners rigged up their gear and air hoses. Leslie told Hooten to hold his light higher. Sicotte thought this was dangerous and turned to see them when an explosion roared along the level.

Sicotte dropped to the floor, calling to the others to lie down and cover their faces. He lay there for awhile, then discovered his coat and hat were on fire. Sicotte labored for breath and realized the explosion had burned up the oxygen. He was suffocating.

Quickly the miner uncovered his face and stood up in the dark adit. Hearing the moans and cries of his coworkers, he stumbled and groped through the black world to the main shaft. He found the ladder to the next level, up 115 feet. It was at the 500-foot level where the signal station was located for the winze operator. (A "winze" is a small shaft, especially one connecting one level with another, as for ventilation, et cetera.) Sicotte climbed the ladder with burning and bleeding hands, on the verge of losing consciousness. He reached his goal, signaling the top level. It was promptly answered, and the four men were brought to the surface.

It was then found out the three miners did not heed Sicotte's warning, but tried to run through the fire. Leslie was not wearing a shirt, and was the most severely injured. He died in a San Francisco hospital two days later. The other two miners, Rollo Hooten and Pete van der Stratten, were also taken to San Francisco and were admitted to St. Luke's. After several weeks of burn treatments and convalescing, they were released.

Statistics, names, et cetera, are lacking from October 1904 to April 1906. The Mining and Scientific Press in its December 1904 issue printed the mine's current equipment was, in part, a 12-ton coarse-ore furnace and a 16-ton fine-ore furnace. October production was 190 flasks.[32] The mine was worked, though, between the two above dates. A state report on the amount of mercury from the Great Eastern claim shows 1904, 1,965 flasks; 1905, 1,785 flasks; 1906, 1,000 flasks. The same report for the Mt, Jackson states for the same respective years, 1,765, 1,065 and 1,052 flasks.[33] Again the question: Was it a single mine, or was it two operations?

In the morning of April 18, 1906, the San Francisco earthquake wrenched the coast of California from its morning slumber. Just as San Jose to the south and Santa Rosa to the north had rude awakenings, so did Guerneville and Mercury. Three miners were coming up in the cage when a big rock shook loose from an outcropping and rolled down the shaft, killing George Hanson, Robert Gorsky and Fred Miller. The shaft was partially wrecked, but was repaired. The levels lower than the wreck were not worked further.[34] It was not fully reopened until the pressure of World War I in 1915 created a new demand for mercury.

1. *S.D.*, November 23, 1880; February 12; April 30; September 17, 1881.
2. *S.D.*, June 24; September 16, 1882.
3. *S.D.*, January 13; November 3; December 8, 1883.
4. *S.D.*, April 5, 1884; *S.R. Rep.*, September 17, 1884.
5. *S.D.*, April 25, 1885.
6. Ibid.
7. *R.R.F.*, April 25, 1885.
8. Report of State Mineralogist, Sacramento: State Printing Office, 1885, Sec. II, p. 633.
9. *S.D.*, May 1, 1886.
10. *S.D.*, August 7, 1886.
11. *S.D.*, November 23, 1880.
12. *S.D.*, January 19, 1884.
13. Ibid.

Great Eastern Quicksilver Mine, looking north, 1904. JCS Collection

14. *R.R.F.*, April 25, 1885; Report of State Mineralogist, 1885, op. cit.; *S.D.*, August 7, 1886.

15. *S.R. Rep.*, January 6; June 30, 1887; *S.D.*, June 11, 1887.

16. California Bureau of Mines Report, 1913-14, p. 175; U.S. Geological Survey, *Geology of the Quicksilver Deposits of the Pacific Slope*, by George F. Becker, (Washington, D.C., 1888), p. 362.

17. *S.D.*, August 1, 1891; January 30, 1892.

18. *S.D.*, January 30; August 13, 1892; February 4, 1893.

19. *S.D.*, February 11, 1893.

20. *S.D.*, February 18, 1893.

21. California State Bureau of Mines 12th Annual Report, 1897, p. 371.

22. *S.D.*, November 25, 1893.

23. *S.D.*, November 25, 1893; June 2, 1894.

24. California State Bureau of Mines, 13th Report, 1896, pp. 602-03.

25. *Guerneville X-ray*, February 11, 1899; *P.D.*, September 24, 1898.

26. *P.D.*, May 21, 1898; *R.R. Ad.*, November 12, 1904.

27. *P.D.*, February 4, 1899.

28. *P.D.*, October 21, 1899.

29. Ibid.

30. *R R. Ad.*, August 15, 1903.

31. *R.R. Ad.*, November 12, 1904.

32. *Mining and Scientific Press*, December 10, 1904, p. 391.

33. California Journal of Mines and Geology, Vol. 35, No. 4, October 1939, p. 466, Tables I & II, "California Quicksilver."

34. California State Mining Bulletin 1913-14 Report, pp. 347-48.

"Salvation for All," a camp meeting in the redwoods in Guernewood Park, July 4, 1879. This grove was cut down in 1881 (see Chapter XVI); in the 1980's this area became Dubava Condominium Development on Highway 116. Photo by A.J. Perkins. Courtesy Glen Burch, Historian, California State Parks

Chapter 28

RELIGION

The Guerneville area was serviced by different faiths, some more so than others. The forest environment served a useful purpose in inspiring religious gatherings.

I. Methodist Episcopal Church

The earliest recorded religious event in the River area was when "the children performed for the benefit of Sunday School" in June 1874, probably conducted under the auspices of Methodist Episcopal (M.E.) circuit preacher Rev. E.A. Winning.[1]

The reverend performed marriages and other religious functions at the Good Templars Hall on First Street, since no church was present.

In early 1875 work began on a church, the first religious edifice in Redwood Township. It was located on the northwest corner of Church and Second Streets. The street acquired its name from the structure.[2]

The church was finished by mid-May. The pews and pulpit were installed shortly thereafter, and on June 13, the church was dedicated by Rev. Charles J. Lovejoy of Santa Rosa.[3]

The first funeral held in the church was conducted by Lovejoy. The earthly remains of E.R. Lillie, the town's schoolteacher, were buried in the old cemetery on the hill east of town.[4]

A little over a year passed, and then the ladies about town started raising funds to buy an organ. By various means they had $90 on hand in October. A church social in November netted $13. December lectures by Rev. R.L. Harford helped garner another $21, and so it went, a few dollars here, some more dollars there, until May 1877 when the women pur-

The Methodist Episcopal Church on the southeast corner of Church and 4th Streets, 1899. Ethel Carrier Collection

chased a Budett organ for $115.[5] Now that music was in the church, a choir was formed with Mrs. Kate Manning director and organist.[6]

The Rev. R.L. Harford replaced Rev. Lovejoy on the Methodist circuit and continued in this position for a year before his transfer moved him to San Jose in September 1877.[7] This was typical. Preachers of the M.E. Church would travel a circuit one year, then be transferred to another circuit or city. After Harford came Rev. John Appleton, who provided religious guidance to September 1878. However, everything is subject to change.

Rev. J.L. Burchard, either by choice or direction, served the area, travelling from church to church, for three years. Following him came Rev. Jesse Smith for two years' service.[8] After Smith left, no pastor is mentioned serving Guerneville for a year.

Various public functions were held in the church besides religious services. Near the end of 1882 the congregation saw fit to add a belfry. They had a bell for it, and on December 31, it rang in the New Year of 1883.[9]

Another year passed. Pastor J. Tallman was assigned to the M.E. Circuit from February 1884 to April 1885.[10] The next five years have no indication who were the M.E. pastors serving in Guerneville and the River area.

In October 1889, Rev. J.A. Van Auker was appointed permanent pastor to Guerneville, the town's first resident "man of the cloth." He reported that year, in the first statement about the congregation, there were "21 communicants, 150 scholars in Sunday School, and a church, valued at $500."[11]

The Methodist Church, at large, supplied preachers to the different areas and paid their salaries before Rev. Van Auker moved to town. But now the town had to support its own, at least a greater part of his income. Besides the usual tithings and offerings to the church, members of the congregation held cake sales and the like to generate funds. A concert conducted by local businessman Napoleon Bonaparte Turner was given in early February 1890 to supplement the pastor's salary. Other incomes were derived from conducting weddings, funerals, and baptisms. Baptisms for the church, as well as the conversions after revivals, were held in Russian River.[12]

There was one wedding ceremony Rev. Van Auken performed willingly, and instead of being paid, his cash flow was reversed — he paid for it. The wedding was his own. He married Ida Alexander (residence unknown) in May 1890 and brought her to Guerneville.[13]

He continued his services with lectures, revival meetings, and baptisms. In 1891 he and his wife left town because of church transfer.

The roster for the next seven years shows as many ministers:

1891	Rev. H. B. Sheldon
1892	Rev. J.E. Bailey
1893	Rev. J.E. Bailey
1894	Rev. Owen E. Hotle
1895	Rev. J.C. Bolster
1896	Rev. L.W. Simmons
1897	Rev. W.S. Trowbridge

And so it went: minister followed minister.[14]

Various church groups were formed by different churches. Facts pertaining to any M.E. organization during the 19th century are skimpy at best. But like clubs and societies, the M.E. church did have an auxiliary so people could enjoy fellowship with their peers. In this case, the Guerneville church had a Sunday School as early as 1874 for youngsters. Prior to 1903 church members formed the Ladies Aid Society, but no mention has been discovered regarding a men's church group.[15]

The M.E. pastor of Guerneville, being a resident, now rode a rapid circuit on Sunday. He conducted services in Mercury (the community at the quicksilver mines), Duncans' Mills and Cazadero. It was a busy day for the preacher. Sunday School was taught by the local elders so the pastor could conduct regular services and get on down the track to the next service. The Sunday railroad schedule dictated the times of the services.[16]

His itinerary on the Sabbath was:
Cazadero 11:00 a.m. service
Duncans' Mills 2:30 p.m. service
Guerneville 7:30 p.m. service

On Tuesdays he conducted a 7:30 p.m. service at Mercury.

There were three different M.E. church structures built over the decades because of fires that were all too frequent in Guerneville. But the building location was always the same: the northwest corner of Main and Church Streets, today (1980) the site of Pedroia's Chevron gas station. Every time the church was razed, it was rebuilt on that lot.

It appears the elders and congregation became tired of this constant destruction and, accordingly, purchased a different lot after the fire of 1894. This new parcel, purchased from Charles Middleton, is on the southeast corner of Fourth and Church Streets, currently (1980) occupied by Noonan's Garage.[17]

II. Camp Meetings

There was a redwood grove about a mile downstream from Guerneville and east of Hulbert Creek. Redwoods were large there, some 300 feet or more tall, and 20 feet in diameter. This area and the neighboring hills were not yet touched by Guerne and Murphy's loggers.[18] This grove, today's Guernewood Park, was the site of many camp meetings, both religious and temperance, which were held throughout July and August, usually two weeks long.

The assembly was 90 X 130 feet with a seating capacity of 2,000. The dining area could seat 150 to 300 people. There were several cottages and numerous tents for the participants. The pulpit was placed between two mammoth trees. Alongside the pulpit was a two-story house built in a redwood tree which served as a parsonage during the meetings. The various buildings were whitewashed, and stood out in contrast to the dark trees.[19]

The first camp meeting was held by the Methodist Episcopalians between August 16 and August 27, 1877. These were convened annually during the summer for the next five years.

Intermingled were the Temperance Union meetings, also held during the summer. The first Temperance convention, 1879, was the first in the county, if not the state. Close to 2,000 people were present to hear about the evils of "demon rum."[20]

In order to have camp meetings perpetuated, there was a movement to purchase the grove in 1881. But the idea never came to fruition. The year 1882 was the last of the meetings, for the grove was logged out starting that October.[21]

The Congregational Church on 1st and Church Streets, 1905. Alta Lutrell Collection

III. Adventists

There were other Christians in the River Area, besides Methodist Episcopalians, who organized or were provided services by their denomination, such as the First Day Adventists. As far as known, the elders made one visit for about a week in April 1875. The result of their labor was four baptisms.[22]

There were also the Seventh Day Adventists in Guerneville. They made their first notice in the newspapers in February 1881. Elders Granger and Morrison preached in Independence Hall. As their name states, their worship day is Saturday. They held their religious school every Saturday afternoon in Temperance Hall, under the supervision of S.A. Nystrom. Helen Bean was the secretary.[23]

IV. Christians

The Christian church came to Guerneville in 1879. Elder Barnes of the church came down to town right after the First Day Adventists left. He preached a few evenings, then left. He planned on returning in a few weeks to organize a congregation, but did not materialize.[24]

Four years later, elder W.H. Briggs of

Interior of the new 1904 Congregational Church on 1st Street. JCS Collection

Santa Rosa and James Martz of Guerneville got together and had several meetings. They formed the Christian Church in July 1879 with 17 charter members. Since they had no building in which to meet, they used Independence Hall.[25]

The church group was active during their first year. There were the usual benefit dinners, dances, and the like to support the church and Sunday School. One such event in September 1879 netted the congregation $60 and more. To really serve the Lord by action and not just talk, Elder Martz baptized five converts in June, three in August, and seven in September.[26]

Like the M.E. church not all preaching was on Sunday, but also at midweek, performed most of the time by elders of this congregation or by neighboring M.E. elders.

In October 1880, the Christian Church started meeting in the M.E. church, the only church structure in town. Elder Martz was still conducting services.[27]

For the next 15 years the newspapers printed little about a "Christian" church, except as noted above.

V. Congregational

This church was started in 1894 by Guerneville families who had been members of the Methodist Episcopal church. Through the years the M.E. church served those seeking spiritual help. But there were those who were looking for something they could not find with the M.E. church.[28] Inner turmoil caused a split, with some families leaving to form another church. These were the Lawsons, Ansells, Watsons, Coons, Garrisons and Connells.

Gertrude Joost Moore said,

> They [the defectors] first met in the old Templars Hall. It had been moved up Main Street [First Street, today] to the alley [parking lot in the middle of town] and they met upstairs over a bar. The division of the church was in 1893.[29]

The first organized meetings were Sunday School.

The new church group wanted to be associated with a wide fellowship. To help them

Catholic Church at Mines Road (Armstrong Road) and 4th Street, circa 1910. JCS Collection

with their plans, they contacted the Episcopal Church in Santa Rosa. The Episcopalians responded they would like to have a mission church on the River, but the Guernevillians did not want to be a mission. They desired to be their own church.[30]

The elders then turned to the Congregational Conference, and were welcomed. The River group submitted to the conference a plan for a church designed as a Greek cross. Everything regarding the plans was agreeable, except the Greek cross. It was not acceptable as a type of architecture of free churches.[31]

As Inza Lambert remembers, the plans accepted by the local congregation were drawn by local school teacher James R. Watson.[32] Changes were made so worshippers entered to the right, under the belfry, instead of the middle. The pulpit stood to the side of the altar, under the sloped portion of the wall, which acted as a sounding board.[33]

The first minister, Rev. Francis Lawson, who was also one of the organizers, came originally from Nebraska. He applied for the church to join the Sonoma Association of Congregational Churches on April 9, 1895. Two weeks later, the church incorporated. The articles were signed by Katherine Ansell, James R. Watson, Irvine McG. Coon, Lizzie Lawson, and Sam Garrison, as members of the Board of Directors.[34]

Construction of the church began immediately. Men of the church donated their labor. One of the hardest workers was George Heason, laborer at Sonoma Lumber Mill.[35] The church was finished and dedicated by the end of August 1895. Upon completion, 200 chairs were purchased for the congregation. Rev. Lawson served in the pulpit for the church's first five years.[36]

A complete history of the Congregational Church up to 1955, its 60th year, is kept by Rev. Robert Jones of the Church, written by Rev. E.E. Brown, former pastor.

VI. Roman Catholic

Because this book ends essentially just after 1900, the story of Catholicism on the River is skimpy, at best.

First mention of a Catholic service was on Thursday, May 23, 1878 when mass was held in Taggart's Hotel parlor. The next report was on Thursday, September 19, when mass was conducted by a Father Conway.[37] After these two events, the historical record jumps three years.

However, because of immigrating Italians and a few Irish during the late 1870's and thereafter, it seems logical to assume more Catholic services were held in Guerneville.

Three years after the first service, it was reported:

> There were services at the Catholic church last Monday. – Scribbler,
>
> Guerneville, Nov. 28, 1881[38]

This is confusing in that the first Catholic Church was built in town in 1905.

A history of an organized Catholic group until this time is not known to exist. In 1904 movement for a church building fund was started. A Saturday night dance was given in July to raise more money for the coffers.[39]

The building site of the proposed church was owned by Ivon and Elizabeth Clar and was located on Highland Drive one door up from Armstrong Road. This family donated the land.

The carpentry and all basic work was finished by the end of December 1905. The altar, railing and pews came from St. Sebastian's, the Sebastopol Catholic Church.[40]

Fr. Michael Mackey, rector of Sebastopol, was in charge of the Guerneville church. It was named St. Elizabeth's after the patron saint of Elizabeth Clar.[41] A short and concise story of St. Elizabeth's during the next 65 years can be found in the Russian River News, June 11, 1970.

VII. Judaism

The followers of the Jewish faith were few in and around Guerneville during the 19th century. If a Hebrew ceremony was to take place, a rabbi would come in from the "outside." An example was when Amelia Schloss and Antone Schumann were married in May 1882. The rabbi, a Mr. Brown, was brought from San Francisco. This is the earliest note of Judaism on the River.[42]

A year and a half later, in October 1883, another daughter of Schloss, Minnie, joined Charles Rothschild of Yountville in marriage. Again, Rabbi Brown came from San Francisco to perform the ceremony.[43]

There was not a sufficient number of Jews in all Sonoma County to support a rabbi until 1965.

VIII. Asiatic Beliefs

On prior pages we have covered all the reported Occidental religions in and about Guerneville. But we suspect not all religions extant in Guerneville and the neighborhood were described.

This comment is admittedly speculative, but the reader must remember there were Asian cultures present, also.[44] These people – Chinese, Japanese, and even possibly some Koreans – could have brought Buddhism, Taoism, Confucianism, or Shintoism.

Most Chinese during the 19th century came from Canton Province almost exclusively by way of San Francisco. To the dominant Anglo citizen of the time, all Orientals were strange, "different," and there was not likely to have been any general interest in their forms of worship.

1. *R.R.F.*, June 30, December 26, 1874.
2. *R.R.F.*, February 6, 1875.
3. *R.R.F.*, May 15, June 13, 1875.
4. *R.R.F.*, September 10, 1875.
5. *R.R.F.*, May 7, 1877.
6. Ibid.
7. *R.R.F.*, September 24, 1877.
8. *R.R.F.*, September 23, 1878; August 22, 1881; September 18, October 9, 1882.
9. *S.R. Rep.*, January 1, 1883.
10. *S.R. Rep.*, February 11, 1884.
11. C.V. Anthony, 50 *Years of Methodism*. San Francisco,

12. *Healdsburg Herald,* February 7, 1890, S.D., February 4, 1899.
13. *Healdsburg Herald,* May 12, 1890.
14. *50 Years of Methodism, op. cit.*
15. Sunday School Certificate of H.L. Bagley, circa 1877; *R.R. Ad.,* 1904
16. *R.R. Ad.,* January 11, 1902.
17. *S.D.,* December 1, 1894.
18. *R.R.F.,* August 20, 1877.
19. Ibid.
20. *R.R.F.,* July 7, 1879.
21. *R.R.F.,* July 11, 1881.
22. *R.R.F.,* April 6, 1875.
23. *S.R. Rep.,* March 12, 1881; *Healdsburg Herald,* February 19, 1890.
24. *R.R.F.,* April 6, 1875.
25. *R.R.F.,* July 21, 1879.
26. *R.R.F.,* September 22, 1879.
27. *R.R.F.,* May 10, 1880, *S.R. Rep.,* October 18, 1880.
28. Rev. Ernest E. Brown, *The Congregational-Community Church, of Guerneville* 1895-1955 (mimeograph), Guerneville, 1955, p.l.
29. Interview with Gertrude J. Moore, July 1966, Guerneville.
30. Brown, *Community Church,* p. 2.
31. Ibid.
32. Interview with Inza Lambert, July 1966, Guerneville.
33. Brown, *Community Church,* p. 2.
34. Op. cit., p. 3; Articles of Incorporation, Sonoma County Clerk's office.
35-36. Ibid.
37. *R.R.F.,* May 27, September 23, 1878.
38. *S.R. Rep.,* November 28, 1881. ("Scribbler" was Ellen Bagley.)
39. Dance ticket of that date.
40. *R.R. Ad.,* November 25, 1905.
41. *R.R. Ad.,* November 30, 1905.
42. *S.R. Rep.,* May 14, 1882.
43. *S.R. Rep.,* October 1, 1883.
44. See Chs XV and XXI regarding Oriental peoples.

1901, p. 424; Trib., October 16, 1889.

GRAND MUSICAL ENTERTAINMENT
To be Given in Aid of the
NEW CATHOLIC CHURCH
At Union Hall, Guerneville
SATURDAY EVENING, JULY 2nd, 1904
Child's Ticket - - - - 15 Cents

ADMIT ONE TO LECTURE OF
REV. E. R. DILLE, D. D.
OF OAKLAND
SUBJECT:
A TENDERFOOT ABROAD
At the M. E. CHURCH, GUERNEVILLE
FRIDAY EVENING, JULY 17, 1903
—FOR THE—
BENEFIT OF THE PARSONAGE FUND
ADMISSION - - - - - 25 CENTS

ENTERTAINMENT AND DANCE
TO BE GIVEN AT
UNION HALL IN GUERNEVILLE
MONDAY EVENING, JULY 13, 1914
For Benefit of the Catholic Church
EXCELLENT PROGRAM AND MUSIC
Admission, ... 25 Cents

Promotional cards, JCS Collection

I.O.O.F. Delegate Ribbon, Redwood Lodge No. 281.
Mike Capitani Collection

Chapter 29

Past Organizations

Organizations, societies (secret and civic), and religious groups have always been a part of man's communities. After the Civil War, all sorts of groups sprang up across the country. Some survived the years and the changes of society, and others lived out their span of interest. Some literally died with time, for example, G.A.R. This chapter will concern itself strictly with those organizations that are now defunct.

I. I.O.G.T.

The first organization of any sort to be established in Guerneville was the Independent Order of Good Templars, No. 365, Enterprise Lodge. It was chartered June 13, 1869.[1] One charter member was John Silas Pool.[2] The lodge name probably came from the steamboat that was gliding over the Russian River at that time.[3] The Good Templars was an early temperance movement and was a popular organization throughout the state.

The earliest members to be identified were those named in an obituary of a fellow member. Their "sleeping brother" was William Sandline, and the members who signed the obituary were William Berry, John Robinson, and Thomas T. Heald.[4]

Starting in mid-1874 there was a regular correspondent to the Russian River Flag who signed herself "E." This was Ellen A. Bagley, wife of John W. Bagley. She was a member of the Enterprise Lodge and gave the newspaper an up-to-date account of the Lodge, temperance in general, and the whole town. All the information related to this lodge and others came from her by way of the newspaper.

In 1874 the Templars had their own hall erected, called "Independence Hall." That winter a wedding was celebrated there, with the full observation of temperance. The reception was with "rich fruit" and a toast to the bride's health "in pure cold water."[5]

With the passing of a local liquor law in June 1874 stating no liquor would be served on Sundays, the membership increased and initiations were made at every Saturday night meeting.[6]

The first officer to be identified was Miss Maggie Pool, Worthy Vice Templar for the third quarter of 1875.[7] Officers were elected every three months. The first complete roster of officers installed was for November 1875 and read as follows:[8]

> Worthy Chief Templar - James F. Oliver;
>
> Worthy Right Hand Supporter - Mrs. Sarah Klein;
>
> Worthy Left Hand Supporter - Mrs. Lucinda Starrett;
>
> Worthy Matron, Mrs. L. Bearden;
>
> Worthy D.M. [?] - John McNeilage;
>
> Worthy Inside Guard - J.T. Stapp;
>
> Worthy Outside Guard - Henry Ayers;
>
> Worthy Chaplain - J.G.L. Twombly.

As one can see, there were only eight officers, due possibly to the moderate membership. Membership had its ups and downs with 102 members in November 1876, 96 in November 1879, 77 in February 1880, 115 in February 1881, 90 in August 1881, 88 in November 1883, and 89 in February 1889. The number of officers increased to 15 by August 1877 and to 18 by 1879. The positions added to the quarterly roster were: Worthy Vice Templar, Worthy R. Secretary, Worthy A.R.S. Secretary, Worthy Assistant Secretary, Worthy Treasurer, Worthy Financial Secretary, Past Worthy Chief Templar, Lodge Deputy and Past Lodge Deputy.

The Lodge Deputy went to all district and state Lodge functions. N.E. Manning held this position from January 1877 to November 1882, and was succeeded by John Robinson.

In January 1877 the members laid the foundation of a new building, measuring 28 feet by 48 feet. The upper story was used as a hall by the Lodge, and the ground floor was used as a store. The upper story was 26 feet by 38 feet, and 13 feet in height. George Locke, contractor for the building, took two months to complete it.[9]

The Lodge during the winter months sponsored various social events and conducted public meetings in behalf of temperance. The public meetings were quite popular with the local populace and, therefore, were held once a month.

In June 1879 the Good Templars had a camp meeting that lasted three days. There were approximately 2,000 in attendance from all over the San Francisco Bay Area. Meetings were conducted during each of the next three years. The last reported meeting of the Guerneville I.O.G.T. was in May 1885.[10]

II. Juvenile Temple

The Juvenile Temple was a branch of the I.O.G.T., and its membership was restricted to minors. It was Lodge No. 40, and the officers were:

> Superintendent - Thomas T. Heald;
> Chief Templar - Annie Willits;
> Supporters - Johnny & Jimmy Oliver;
> Vice Templar - Maggie Brown;
> R. Secretary - George Brown;
> A.R.S. - Nellie Folks;
> Financial Secretary - Bert Bagley;
> Treasurer - Charles Oliver;
> Matron - Belle Bronston;
> D.M. - Allie Hitchcock;
> Guard - Sarah Alley;
> Sen. - Leonard Wilson;
> P.T. - Eddie Longley;
> Chaplain - Emma Gould.

The Juvenile Temple was started on or about January 22, 1879. The officers were elected every three months, in the same manner as the senior Templars. The junior citizens copied the seniors in almost every detail, even to the extent of tending to the burial of their members, and participated in the temperance camp meeting. The organization was apparently short-lived. The last mention in the Russian River Flag was the announcement of the newly elected officers for the end of 1881.[11]

III. Sons of Temperance

Another organization formed for the abstinence of alcohol and tobacco was the Sons of Temperance. The Guerneville local chapter was called the "Enterprise Division." The Sons of Temperance was mentioned only once in the Healdsburg Tribune on January 20, 1889. The names of the organization and local chapter are similar to the I.O.G.T., and could be a carryover from that earlier organization. The Lodge was still active in February 1890 recruiting new members.

IV. Women's Christian Temperance Union

This organization, famous for its often firm and direct action, was in town by early 1890. Its members conducted an occasional program and sent delegates to the various county conventions.[12] It opened lunch rooms near the railroad depot in July 1890. The only officers' names of the local group that the author could determine were:

> President - Mrs. J.E. Yarbrough;
> Convention Delegate - Mrs. Nora Adams;
> and Mrs. Lydia Pool.[13]

V. Blue Ribbon Society

This society became permanent in September 1879. The first officers were:

> President - H.H. Peckinpah;
> Vice President - T.T. Heald; and
> Secretary - Rosa Beaver [14]

They held "open" temperance meetings once a month on Sunday at 4 p.m. The society was still meeting in March 1883.[15]

VI. Band of Hope

The Band of Hope was in existence by August 1872, and elected its officers every six months. They held open public meetings each alternate Sunday afternoon. The first directors to be mentioned were those of January 18, 1875

> President - Miss Jennie Bearden;
> Vice President - Miss Mary Ragan;
> Secretary - Miss Rosa Beaver;
> Treasurer - Miss Rosa Goode;
> Usher - Newton Helm;
> Deputy Usher - Miss Frances Faudre;
> Sentinel - Charley Oliver.[16]

This organization was similar to the Juvenile Temple of the I.O.G.T. It was created to help the young people of the community abstain from drink and tobacco when they reached their majorities. There were 81 members, past and present, by August 1875.[17] Nothing other than new officers every six months was recorded in the newspapers up to January 1879. It appears that it fell apart for a lack of incentive or enthusiasm.[18]

VII. The Lyceum

This organization, as its name proclaims, provided lectures, readings, debates, et cetera for the entertainment of the town. These were held every Friday during 1876.[19]

In a similar vein, a debating society was organized in November 1883, but nothing else is known about it.[20]

VIII. The Liberal Club

Another debating group was the Liberal Club. It appears that they really jumped into the middle of things. To quote the *Healdsburg Herald*,

> The Liberal Club, having been scorned in a sermon by Rev. H.J. Van Auken on "Christianity versus Infidelity," replied to him through F.J. Murphy on Tuesday evening in the public hall. There was a very large audience present to listen to the able address of the young man.[21]

About a month later another debate was programmed, "Resolved, that marriage is a failure. T.J. Butts and L.F. Clar affirmative, and Anson Hilton and F.J. Murphy, negative."[22]

So end the Great Debates.

IX. Druids

The Druids first appeared passively in an article in the Healdsburg Tribune. They were in the Fourth of July parade of 1888, along with other civic societies. This chapter was the Guerneville Grove, No. 69, the United Ancient Order of Druids.[23]

On the evening of November 16, 1888 they held an installation in "Druids' Hall."[24] They elected new officers and installed them every six months, in May and November. The only list of officers and members that this author has located was in the *Herald*:

> Nobe Arch - Charles Prosek;
> Vice Arch - Milton Bigsby;
> Secretary - J. Gibson;
> Treasurer - C.E. Hewitt[25]

Between 1910 and 1919 another chapter was in existence, Grove Ottavio, No. 103, in Guerneville.[26]

X. The Fern Leaf Social Club

This was organized by several young men of the town in November 1882. One of the first functions sponsored by this group was a ball held on November 24, 1882.[27] It was apparently a complete success. In April 1883 they put on another ball, which was just as successful.[28] After that, they were never heard from again.

XI. Athletic Club

This was probably one of the shortest-lived groups on record:

> July 30, 1881 - "The Athletic Club has been organized by a select few of our young men, and a room rented and fitted up for their use."

> October 17, 1881 - "The Athletic Club has disbanded."[29]

XII. Knights of Pythias

This lodge was instituted on March 15, 1884 and was called Guerneville Lodge, No. 98, K. of P. The charter names were: J.A. Presswood, N. Christensen, M. Florence, William Torrence, L.L. Jewett, J.R. Simmons, C.S. Hill, C.S. Middleton, Omar Cobb, John Starrett,

Phil Stoffal, Martin Ahrens, J.A. Griffin, John Keaton, Daniel Mahoney, P. Phister, Daniel Bailey, Oliver Wescott, George Robinson, G.A. Soff, E.D. McKee, N.E. Manning, George McKee, L.C. Wilson, J.O. Hicks, G.W. French, George Bearden, J.H. Campbell. W.C. Smith, Dr. J.A. Burns, John Novak, A.H. Stuart, Robert Starrett, W.B. Bareley, B.A. Houder and E.S. Hicks.[30]

The Knights remained fairly active through the years, up to 1890. They sent their delegates to the state conventions and sponsored an occasional party for townsfolk, as did most civic groups. Information given through the years was of a general nature, and did not contain anything specific.

XIII. N.S.G.W.

The Native Sons of the Golden West instituted a "parlor" (their name for chapter or local) on March 22, 1886 at Guerneville, and called it the Redwood Parlor No. 79. The officers for the charter and first year were: William Sowlett, W.W. Ungewitter, C.G. Sullivan, George Wescott, John Coon, Charles Folks, William McPeak, N. Bell, J.C. Smith, E. Laton, C.G. Sullivan. H.L. Bagley and R.L. Yarbrough.[31]

Their first Grand Ball was a social success, held on the evening of July 2 at St. Charles Hall. The reveling lasted until 5 o'clock the next morning, much to the pleasure of the community.[32] This is a typical example of the socials they sponsored for the public in general, occurring about once a year. They were still active in 1890.

XIV. Grand Army of the Republic

A post of the Grand Army of the Republic was semi-organized on the evening of August 29, 1885.[33] Several months passed before there was a formal, organized post. The new post was given the name of Joseph N. Morey Post No. 86, G.A.R., a tribute to the Commander of the Ellsworth (Santa Rosa) Post No. 20.[34]

The charter members and officers were:
Commander - Samuel Varner;
Sr. Vice Commander - David Hetzel;
Jr. Vice Commander - G.L. Cobb;
Adjutant - G. Dietz;
Quartermaster - J.J. Keaton;
Surgeon - M.J. Anthony;
Chaplain - Joseph Smith;
Office of the Day - Phil Stoffer;
Officer of the Guard - E.G.C. Thompson;
Sergeant Major - W.A. Cole;
Quartermaster Sergeant - W.M. Carr.

Comrades (members) were: Samuel Varner, Phil Stoffel, M.J. Anthony, Gerhardt Dietz, Joseph Smith, E.G.C. Thompson, Dave Hetzel, Guy L. Cobb, John Keaton, Samual Squibb, W.A. Cole, David Springer, William Carr and J.A. Crosby.

The Post had a few social gatherings during the years and always made an appearance at town meetings and all holidays. They formed up in parade fashion, usually lead position, with the veterans in their Civil War uniforms. J.W. Bagley wore his sergeant's uniform from the Mexican-American War.

XV. G.L. & S. Co.

As has been seen, if a few people had a common interest, they would join together, formally or otherwise, to promote or further their cause. And, of course, the commercial entertainments which almost overwhelm us today were not available in this isolated village.

Among the earliest of the groups that became established in Guerneville was the Guerneville Literary and Social Company. This was one of the relatively few organizations that was not a country-wide association. It was born, lived, and died in Guerneville. It was apparently short-lived. Only two sources of information were found on this group, and both were county records.[35]

On April 8, 1874 seven men drew up Articles of Incorporation of the "Social Company," having stock at $10 per share. It was the 95th company to file incorporation papers in the county since California had become a state 24 years earlier. The seven men who joined together — all sound men of the community — were George E. Guerne, John Starrett, George Crichton, John Robinson, John Pool, Charles M. Peckinpah and G.H. Klein.

One of the purposes of the "company," as set forth in a paragraph of the incorporation papers was,

Second: That the purpose for which said corporation is formed is the cultivation of the social virtues and the improvement of the mind in study of literature, art and sciences.

Although this paragraph has a slight touch of the hand of a woman in the background, not one clue has been found that any women were associated with this group. It appears to have been solely a man's organization.

The duration of the company that can be substantiated was at least four years, and it was located in its own establishment on First Street, next to the Heald & Guerne lumber office in 1877.

The Russian River Flag had several articles from as many correspondents at the time of incorporation of the company. While this was a joint stock company according to incorporation papers, the newspaper stated during the same time that a stock company was erecting a large dance hall that was "built, paid for, owned and named" by its members — being 25 or 30 residents of Guerneville and vicinity.[36] The lower part of the building was to be rented out, and the upper floor was to be used for balls, concerts, et cetera. This hall was being built next to Heald & Guerne's Mill and was to be called "Independence Hall."[37] This writer contends that the Social Club and Independence Hall party are one and the same.

XVI. Impovement Associations

There were several associations formed by and for homeowners up and down the Russian River. Some of these were:

1. Rionido Improvement Association - incorporated July 27, 1910.[38]

2. Russian River Heights, Montesano and Graystone Improvement Association, formed sometime after 1910.[39] Its members and officers were:

    President - S.C. Symon;
    Vice President - W.E. Schwerin;
    Secretary/Treasurer - R.H. McMannis;
    Director - J.M. Senkel;
    Director - L.C. Cnopius;
    Director - T.W. Larrabee;
    Director - Mrs. E.F. Clarke;
    Director - T.J. McMannis;
    Director - C.L. Ingler;
    Director - L.B. Harin;
    Director - Mrs. R. Townsend;
    Director - S.C. Symon; and
    Director - W.E. Schwerin.

Its committees and committee heads were:

    Finance - T.J. McMannis, L.C. Cnopius, Mrs. R. Townsend;
    Improvement - J.M. Sunkel, L.B. Hardin, Dr. D.B. Channell, J. Armstrong, T.J. McMannis;
    Membership - Dr. D.B. Channell, Mrs. J.M. Sunkel, Mrs. O.O. Cobb, Mrs. I.A. Coady, Mrs. E. Crowe;
    Publicity & Printing - Mrs. O.O. Cobb, Mrs. I.A. Coady, Mrs. E.F. Clarke.

3. Guerneville Improvement Club.[40] This association was in existence between 1900 and 1909. Its officers were:

    President - Mrs. A.M. Cobb;
    First Vice President - Mrs. Margaret Shoemake;
    Second Vice President - Mrs. Margaret Ayers;
    Secretary - Mrs. Ivon M. Clar;
    Treasurer - Mrs. Annie Starrett.

This chapter is limited only by the facts accessible. There may also have been some other societies in the Chinese community, along the River in other communities.

1.   *R.R.F.*, June 18, 1877.
2.   Op. Cit., December 7, 1875.
3.   See Chapter VIII.

4. *R.R.F.*, April 25, 1872.
5. Op. Cit., December 30, 1875.
6. See Chapter XI for information on local liquor laws.
7. *R.R.F.*, October 18, 1875.
8. Op. Cit., November 9, 1875.
9. For a more detailed description of the hall, see *R.R.F.*, June 18, 1877, "Guerneville Letter."
10. *S.R. Republican*, May 1885.
11. Op. Cit., November 19, 1881.
12. *Trib.*, May 5, 1890.
13. Op. Cit., May 12, 1890.
14. *R.R.F.*, September 1, 1879.
15. *S.R. Republican*, March 19, 1883.
16. *R.R.F.*, January 18, 1875.
17. Op. Cit., August 3, 1875.
18. It was at this time that the Juvenile Temple, I.O.G.T., was organized.
19. *R.R.F.*, April 24, 1876.
20. *S.R. Republican*, November 17, 1883.
21. *Trib.*, February (26?)1890.
22. *Trib.*, March (7?)1890.
23. Op. Cit., November 24, 1888.
24. Op. Cit., November 14, 1889.
25. *Healdsburg Herald*, May 12, 1890.
26. Letterhead of the organization.
27. *S.R. Republican*, November 13, 1882.
28. Op. Cit., April 30, 1883.
29. Op. Cit.., see both dates.
30. Op. Cit.., March 14, 1884.
31. *R.R.F.*, March 26(?), 1886.
32. *S.R.Rep.*, July 8, 1886.
33. *Healdsburg Republican*, August 31, 1885.
34. Op. Cit., November, 1885.
35. Sonoma County Clerk's Office, "Articles of Incorporation," #95; Sonoma County Tax Records, 1877, Sonoma County, California.
36. *Russian River Flag*, Mar. 15, 1874.
37. *S.D.*, March 7, 1874.
38. Letterhead of association
39. Letterhead of association. All officers, etc., are from the same sources. These three areas are located between present day Guernewood Park and Northwood, downstream two miles.
40. Letterhead of association. (See also Chapter XXV, "Phoenix.")

Chapter 30

Tobacco

David and Ovina (née Lund) Hetzel, 1897. Jack Hetzel Collection

California is not known as a state where tobacco is grown for commercial purposes, but occasionally an enterprising person would attempt to do so and meet with some minor success. During the Great Depression of the 1930's a cigarette company was formed in Stockton which managed to produce a maximum of 500,000 cigarettes a day (2,500 cartons) from California-grown tobacco. In Napa and Sonoma Counties there were areas the California Department of Agriculture thought might produce some average-grade tobacco on a small scale, such as upper Napa Valley and Alexander Valley.[1] In 1903 the Hermitage Tobacco Company of Cloverdale had some extensive acreage under tobacco.[2]

The start of Guerneville's tobacco story began about two miles above the quicksilver mines. In 1877 David Hetzel arrived and started planting on the western slopes of Mt. Jackson. About a year later, he was joined by Charles Schuler, and together they produced an acceptable leaf resulting in a salable cigar.[3] The first public mention of this was copy in a Santa Rosa newspaper:

> They plant and cultivate their own tobacco, of a good quality, cure it and manufacture it into cigars.[4]

Six months later, about the end of March 1880, they moved from the hills to Main Street (today's First Street) in Guerneville. They rented a piece of land along the river and cultivated ten acres of tobacco. Two years passed and the two men dissolved their partnership. Supposedly each was to continue manufacturing cigars, but, in truth, only Hetzel continued the trade. Sometime between 1882 and 1884 Schuler left Guerneville for Petaluma.[5]

In 1883, after one of Haas' fires, Hetzel moved into the new Odd Fellows Building on the second floor. He was burned out of that building, along with everybody else, in the

Left to right: 10-year-old Jack Hetzel, Ovina, Hilda Svender (girl in front), Fred Ewing in back, and Dave Hetzel, among the tobacco seed beds, looking east from Mill Street, 1912. Jack Hetzel Collection

fire of 1889. David constructed a temporary shed, then in July moved to his new permanent quarters at the southwest corner of the Odd Fellows' new brick building. The three rooms he rented were used for storage, factory and sale.[6]

He continued growing tobacco, experimenting with varieties, and eventually obtained the best results with the Havana type. Dave concluded that his end product, if raised throughout California, would be second only to that raised in Havana, Cuba. The season for 1895 was unfavorable in many respects. Hetzel planted 10 to 15 acres at a production cost of $100 per acre, yet he netted $150 per acre.[7]

This man was recognized for his efforts in the San Francisco Call newspaper. He was publicized as curing the Havana leaf under scientific controls during winter. He sweated the leaf in an underground chamber by regulating temperature and humidity. The resulting color — dark amber — flexibility and toughness were "second to none," the achievement of three years' effort and experimenting.[8]

Experimenting came about only after a futile attempt to converse with Luther Burbank. Around 1890 Hetzel drove by horse and buggy to Santa Rosa, some 20 miles over the old dirt roads. He stopped at a local pub to wash down the dust and water his horse, then went down to Burbank's home on Main Street. Burbank was working in his garden when Dave arrived and introduced himself. Burbank went over to the fence and, as they walked to the gate, Hetzel asked him about tobacco, specifically, how he could get better flavor from the Havana leaf. Dave entered the gate and Burbank answered he wouldn't have anything to do with tobacco or with anybody that drinks.

Hetzel said, "Thank you, sir," gave a military salute, did an about-face, and drove back to Guerneville.[9]

After 20 years or more, Dave was at last given recognition by his community and peers for quality and acreage of his tobacco. In an issue of the Russian River Advertiser, an article was published about a tobacco company:

Hetzel's tobacco field east of the wooden Guerneville Bridge, 1912. Left to right: Louie Montecelli, David Hetzel, Bert Klein, Fred Ewing. Shown here is Connecticutt Broadleaf tobacco 2 1/2 months old. JCS Collection

Five acres of tobacco are being transplanted by the Hermitage Tobacco Company in their fields near Cloverdale. The planting is being done under canvass which covers the entire five acres

— *Press Democrat*

If one hundred of our citizens would contribute from two to four dollars apiece per month, next year at this time the Russian River Tobacco Company of Guerneville — or any other name — could be transplanting twenty or more acres of tobacco, and a new industry could thus be started here.

We have it from a gentleman who recently visited the Hermitage Company's land that it is inferior for tobacco raising to the hundred or more acres in this vicinity suitable for that purpose. Moreover the land could be flooded every year thereby enriching the soil.

Now then, who will start the ball arolling and help establish what may turn out to be a grand and prosperous industry?[10]

A year passed. Adam Wolfrom, a cigar maker of San Francisco, was going to revisit his old home in St. Louis. He procured a few samples of Hetzel's tobacco to show his friends the degree of perfection our townsman had attained in growing and curing the weed.

Arriving in St. Louis and its World's Fair, Wolfrom went to the Agriculture Building looking for the Sonoma County display — but there was not one to be found! He was sent by Judge J.H. Wills of the Sacramento Valley Association to Solano County's booth, the county nearest Sonoma having an exhibit. There, C.W. Becker of Solano took the migrant leaves, by now losing some of their quality, and displayed them with a sign reading, "From Sonoma County." The intention was for them to be ornamental only, but Becker entered them for a medal, anyway. It was just in time. For the awards were soon made, and David Hetzel had one of them.

Hetzel heard nothing more from Wolfrom until the following letter reached him and he discovered his friend had entered his tobacco

Stringing tobacco at Hetzel's tobacco field east of the wooden Guerneville Bridge; left to right: Nellie Justis, Dave Hetzel, Nell Morrow. Women were hired only during cutting and curing time. The structure behind them was used only to shade tobacco, not to cure it. JCS Collection

for competition at the Exhibition.

The letter, in full, was printed in the *Russian River Advertiser*:[11]

DAVID HETZEL, SR.
AWARDED SILVER MEDAL
LOUISIANA PURCHASE EXPOSITION

California County Commissioners Assoc.
St. Louis, Oct. 17, 1904
Mr. D. Hetzel.
Guerneville, California
Dear Sir:
Yours of Oct. 8th received; also a box of cigars. I have passed them around to people who ar [sic] interested and they all pronounce them fine.

You were awarded a silver medal on your tobacco and I have no doubt you might have received a gold medal had it been exhibited on time and in the proper manner.

Yours truly,
C.W. Becker.

In March 1905, the U.S. Department of Agriculture queried Hetzel if there was a practical and profitable way to grow tobacco in California. His answer, paraphrased, was:

> . . . use the Havana variety in a rich sandy loam. The advantage of this soil is that it retains moisture and is easy to cultivate. Alkilia [sic] soil would be fatal in my estimation as the plants seem to absorb this chemical and destroy the flavor and injure the burning qualities of cured leaf. If carefully worked with and cultivated thorougly, an acre can produce 9,000 plants.[12]

As Jack Hetzel, his son, said,

> The seed-pod blossom of the numerous tobacco fields gave an aurora [sic] of beauty against the green garden of mighty wavering redwoods.

The following year David made a concerted effort and entered competition with his tobacco in the Lewis and Clark Exposition at Portland, Oregon. Again he was awarded a diploma and silver medal.[13] The Russian River Advertiser announced on its front page:

David Hetzel at the curing shed, circa 1910; leaves are being cured on the stem, not on wire rods.
JCS Collection

David Hetzel's Tobacco
To the Front Again
— Saturday, January 27, 1906

David Hetzel's tobacco has again received well merited recognition for its superior qualities. Mr. Hetzel was awarded a diploma for silver medal at the Portland Exposition for his leaf tobacco and manufactured products.

The diploma was forwarded to Mr. Hetzel through the California Commission, which also addressed him the following complimentary letter:

D. Hetzel.
Guerneville, Sonoma Co.
Dear Sir:
We take pleasure in handing you herewith the Diploma awarded to you on your exhibit at Lewis & Clark Exposition, and kindly ask you to acknowledge receipt of same.

We congratulate you on this testimonial of the merit of your display, and again thank you for your part in helping us maintain the prestige of California at that Exposition.

With best wishes for your success during the New Year, we remain,
 Very respectfully,
 THE CALIFORNIA COMMISSION,
 By J.A. Filcher,
 Frank Wiggins,
 Deputy Commissioners

Hurrah! for our Guerneville tobacco and cigars.

In 1907, Dave's 67th year, he was awarded his third medal — this time, GOLD! — and Guerneville was as proud of its "son" as a struttin' duck. The Advertiser printed:

FIRST PRIZES AND GOLD MEDAL

Again does old Dave Hetzel with his tobacco — grown and cured in Guerneville — come to the front by winning one of the four First Prizes awarded Sonoma county at the Sacramento State Fair, which closed last Saturday. If we had a few more go-ahead men like Mr. Hetzel here, this section would be far better known than it is. In speaking of the award the Santa Rosa Press Democrat says: 'The principal exhibitor was David Hetzel of Guerneville, the man who has made tobacco growing of commercial value in

Hetzel's 1904 award; Regina Hetzel Collection

this state and is the pioneer in its culture.[14]

This was Dave's last award. He had been growing tobacco for 30 years and had a proven product now via official recognition. He had paid his dues.

Dave shelled his own seeds from pods, sowed them in his nursery beds, then transplanted them in his fields. This was done as late as mid-July when the plants were six to eight inches tall. The crop was harvested sometime early in October. For the most part Dave did not irrigate his fields before or after transplanting. Two crops may have been grown; the second, known as a "sucker crop," grew from the stalk after the first crop had been cut.[15]

Until 1904 Hetzel used Sumatra leaf wrappers. But rains for that season were the right amount, so one-half of his crop of Havana was first class for wrappers. He did not import any for the coming year. It was probably this leaf that won David the silver medals.

His curing shed for all his tobaccos was George Guerne's hop house located just up from today's Brookside Resort (1980). His fields were located variously on the Mines Road (now Armstrong Woods Road), El Bonita (halfway between Rio Nido and Guerneville), Northwood, Forestville, and on Guerne's land near the hop house (today a vineyard north of Surrey Inn).[16]

Dave had various people assist him in growing his crops and products. Fred Ewing was generally his right-hand man. Besides his sons — David, Jr. and Jack — there were Ben Drake and Rudolph Brown working the fields. At the curing sheds were Nell Morrow and Nellie Justis. Others were hired to help the tobacconist make cigars. Usually there was only one, but on occasions, two were in his shop: George Gibson, Rudolph Brown, Edward Nee, Michael Dunn and Harry Schloke.[17] Brown worked for him several years.

One of the earliest labels of Hetzel's cigars was the "La Dulzura de Albuerney Menendez." This brand was probably made before the turn of the century. Later cigars were sold under some five different labels. The "Cabella Flora" sold for five cents, and the "Henry Clay" cost ten cents, but they were the same quality. The "Henry Clay" was a cheap saloon cigar. "El Resorto" was a ten-center that Hetzel sold only at his store, and "Hetzel's Best" went for twenty-five cents.[18]

His cigar boxes came from only one supplier — Joseph Korbel, one of the Korbels of champagne fame.[19]

The earliest-known assigned tax number by the U.S. Government was Factory #14, California District 4. This was prior to 1912. Then in typical government fashion it changed numbers and modified districts, resulting in Hetzel's operation becoming Factory 139, California District 1.[20]

The Korbels tried various enterprises with cleared land. For some years, heavy tobacco crops were grown on the ranch. However, they gave this up when the climate became cooler. This reason for abandonment is very questionable in light of Hetzel's success.[21]

Hetzel continued off and on after 1915 growing tobacco and making cigars. He finally ceased due to his age and passed away at age 95 in 1935.

1. Miller, Milton D., Tobacco Culture in California; U.C. Dept. of Agriculture
2. R.R.Ad., May 16 and May 23, 1903.
3. Hetzel, Jack. "History of David Hetzel," Mss., 1975., pp 10-11.
4. S.D., September ___, 1880.
5. R.R.F., March 23, 1880; S.R. Repub., January 30, 1882.
6. H. Rep., November 17, 1883; S.R. Trib., September 11, 1889; Son. Demo., November 24, 1883.
7. P.D., February 6, 1895, p. 5.
8. P.D., January 21, 1899.
9. Hetzel, "History of David Hetzel," op.cit., pp. 15-16; interview January 18, 1976.
10. R.R. Ad., May 23, 1903.
11. R.R. Ad., September 14, 1904; November 19, 1904.
12. R.R. Ad., August 5, 1905.
13. R.R. Ad., January 27, 1906.
14. R.R. Ad., September 21, 1907.
15. "History of David Hetzel," op.cit.
16. Ibid.
17. Interview of Jack Hetzel, January 18, 1976; Registrar of Voters for the years 1903, 1908, 1910, and 1914-1918.
18. Cigar boxes with labels.
19. Interview of Jack Hetzel, op.cit.
20. Cigar box numbers
21. *P.D.*, April 21, 1968.

Hetzel's 1905 award for tobacco. Regina Hetzel Collection

GUERNEVILLE, CAL., _____ 191 ___

M _____

TO D. HETZEL, DR.

MANUFACTURER OF

CHOICE CIGARS ᴀɴᴅ ᴅᴇᴀʟᴇʀ ɪɴ TOBACCOS AND SMOKERS' ARTICLES

David Hetzel's invoice heading, circa 1911, JCS Collection

D. HETZEL

MANUFACTURER OF CIGARS

——— AND DEALER IN ———

Tobacco and Smokers' Articles

GUERNEVILLE, CAL.

Hetzel's business card, circa 1911. JCS Collection

Chapter 31

AGRICULTURE

Agriculture and animal husbandry were practiced on a family level in rural Russian River country during the developing years. Front yards and back yards were used for growing some produce to supplement the family's larder. In bottom lands the first crop for cash and trade to be noted was corn. Corn was/is used by farmers as feed for livestock and poultry, besides being a vegetable on the dinner table.

The logged-over lands were converted to several uses. Some people let their land lie fallow and let nature run its course. In most instances the redwood stumps would rejuvenate themselves with sucker growth, eventually maturing into a second-growth redwood forest. Other people cleared their lands for an alternative use — agricultural crops as a business.

I. Olives

The first specific crop to be grown as a commercial enterprise was olives. Around 1885 Joseph Prosek, a doctor from San Francisco, arrived in Guerneville. He was a close friend of the Korbel brothers, and they allowed him to use some of their acreage for olives near the Humming Bird Saloon, today's Santa Nella in Pocket Canyon.[1]

By 1891-1892 he had cleared 100 acres of old forest land (at a cost of $96 per acre) and placed an "immense" water tank on a high hill, which was filled by a pump located on Pocket Creek. Eight miles of irrigation pipe were laid throughout the prepared plot, with a hydrant every 150 feet for a garden hose. This completed the water system.[2]

He planted the trees — Picolines variety — twenty feet apart. The fruit of these was almost worthless, but they are rapid growers. In two years the trees were six feet high. Prosek used this stock to be grafted onto with Cenudulina, Columella and Rubra varieties.[3]

The doctor's trees numbered 8,000 by mid-1894. The 20-foot-high trees included 26 varieties, some five to six years old.

This was the first year (1894) the trees produced a worthwhile crop. The branches were heavily laden with fruit in December. Because of this crop, Prosek built an olive mill this year, after experimentally producing 75 gallons of oil.

The mill contained all the latest developments in the olive industry. The building was 40 feet by 60 feet, two stories high, and had a concrete foundation. The crushers worked on the same principle as a flour mill: The basin was granite, as well as the two rollers, each of which weighed 1,500 pounds. The basin was round, and the rollers went in a circle in the basin. The crusher was patented in October 1894 in San Francisco at a cost of $1,000.[4]

There were other small presses, agate ironware tanks, boilers, separators, draining cans, et cetera. Power came from a 12-horsepower steam engine.

Prosek's business became known as the Sonoma County Pioneer Olive Mill. The location was a common landmark in the area, known for years as "the olive mill."

> "It makes me sigh," said Prosek during an interview,"when I start in to figure up the cost. But I have every confidence in the outcome, and think we shall surely be repaid in the end by our outlay."[5]

The tonnage for 1894 amounted to 30 tons. To supplement this, Prosek sent his brother/manager, Charles, to other growers in the county to purchase all the olives they could acquire. Captain Guy E. Grosse of Santa Rosa had 15 to 20 tons available, which they bought for $60 per ton.[6]

The olives produced one gallon of oil out of 50 pounds crushed, depending on the variety. Oil production started in mid-December and continued into March 1895 as each variety ripened.[7]

The oil was probably shipped throughout the San Francisco Bay Area. In July of 1895 six cases were sent east by rail, along with a carload of Korbel wine. Seven gallons were sent to Sebastopol.[8]

In August, brother Charles left the industry to run his own business in town. Consequently, the manager's position was given to a Baron Von Nollendorp.[9]

The crop of 1895 was very light because of serious frost damage at the end of November. Accordingly, the wages of the pickers were small. Some earned 50 cents a day, but most received about 30 cents for a day's work! They struck for higher earnings, either 2 cents a pound or $1.25 a day. It is not known what the outcome was.[10]

Still Prosek persevered.

Nothing out of the ordinary occurred in 1896. In July 1897 a black scale infested his crop, which resulted in a harvest smaller than that of 1896.[11]

The doctor continued buying olives to supply his mill, and his main supplier continued to be Grosse. In January 1899 Grosse sold Prosek all of his olives except for one ton which he picked and marketed in Santa Rosa.[12] Prosek's oil was considered to be of the highest quality.

Information becomes slight from this year on. Only passing mention of the olive crop being picked is found, the last information having been given in February 1905.[13]

Several lean and soul-searching years passed. Then a killing frost destroyed almost the entire orchard. Prosek finally gave up, and every tree was pulled.[14] Undaunted, the doctor planted his acreage with grapes. This new venture became the start of Santa Nella Winery in Pocket Canyon.

Dr. Joseph Prosek passed away in 1920.[15]

Olive trees can still be found in the River area at the Korbel Winery, Santa Nella, and along Buttner Road in Guerneville.

II. Hops

A second and later very important commercial crop in the River area was hops. This agricultural product was not raised by just one person, as in the cases of tobacco by David Hetzel and olives by Joseph Prosek. The first hop growers were R.S. Drake, whose property was located at today's Drake's Estates, and Mathew McPeak, with land upstream from Drake at Cosmo, today's Hacienda. Their acreages were twelve and nine acres, respectively.[16]

Their first crops were started prior to 1883. The 1884 harvest had Drake getting 40 bales and McPeak getting 73 bales of hops. Although 1883 is the first year hops are mentioned in print as a crop on the River, the Santa Rosa Republican stated in its Guerneville column that school was closed for two weeks to allow students to pick hops.[17] This indicates that hop picking was a strong enough influence to cause children to leave school for the "fortune" to be earned. There was nothing else to do but close school — an annual occurrence from 1883 through 1910.

Obviously this crop had to be established at least several years before 1883 in order for it to be a reliable as well as an annual event. The hop growers had to get their harvests in at certain times and so hired adults of all ethnic origins. These included Caucasian, Chinese, Japanese, Indians, Canadians, Italians, Negroes, and Californios. If the number of pickers was not sufficient, children were hired. As the years passed more children would leave school in greater numbers until it was useless to convene school. Some families made it mandatory for their youngsters to join them in the field and help supplement the family's in-

Weighing hops in Laughlin's field, west of Lone Mountain, circa 1900. Ray Clar Collection

come.[18] The hard-working people of the River community were far from affluent, especially after the lumber mills had ceased to operate. At the height of the harvest, Guerneville was nearly deserted during the day.

By 1891 McPeak had increased his hop field by one and one-half acres, but his crop had been reduced from the 73 bales of 1884 to 42 bales. Drake still grew on the same acreage, yet his hops increased from 40 bales to 80 bales.[19]

The hop industry had become big and important enough in Sonoma County to have the weekly Sonoma Democrat print a regular column entitled "Hop Affairs." There were quotes of prices for hops from San Francisco, Milwaukee and London, as well as advertisements of agents representing hop brokers. An indication of the importance hops had along the River area is an advertisement placed in the county newspapers by E.F. Manchester of Guerneville. He wanted 200,000 hop poles (which were used to suspend hop vines).[20]

In 1894 a new 30-acre hop field was developed near Guerneville. This was probably George Guerne's field, located on old Willits timber claim in Big Bottom, which is located west of Lone Mountain.[21] Guerne built a hop kiln at the south end of Lone Mountain, which stood until after World War I.

To hold and dry the ever-increasing crop, the Burk Brothers of Guerneville and King & Starrett of Montrio (today's Monte Rio) built hop driers.[22]

McPeak increase his hop field by 1895 to 20 acres.[23]

Harvest time 1895 arrived, and most of the population abandoned town again to profit from picking. Drake had his crop in from the fields by mid-September. The last four tons were in his hop house being dried when a fire broke out in a faulty flue. The hop kiln and part of his harvest were destroyed. The loss was estimated at $1,200.[24]

The increase of the hop harvest over the years was incentive for the Cuthill brothers — James and John — and John Bean to build hop kilns this year to aid those growers who had none.[25]

At the end of the harvest the pickers were treated to dances by their employers, usually in the hop barns.

Korbel Vineyard looking south, circa 1905. JCS Collection

Because the harvest was heavy this season at the Burk ranch, Mr. Haynes, lessee of the property, had about 30 women and children working into early October.[26]

The late George Clar, Guerneville's postmaster from 1923 to 1964, was a top hop picker in his younger days. He often made $12 a day — astounding wages for "piece work" — because his hops were clean; there were no leaves or vines with his blossoms. At the end of the day's weigh-in, the boss would inspect and deduct for "dirty" hops. Ray Clar, George's brother, wrote:[27]

> "Personally, I hated hop picking — I was slow, plus hops scratched a lot. Some people put mechanic's tape (friction tape) on thumb and finger — others wore gloves. Scratches had a poison effect on some people."

Though the crop was not all that good for 1896, the word spread around the countryside that hop pickers were in great demand. But no Chinese and few Indians would be employed.[28]

III. Fruits and Vegetables

Though there are sections in this chapter given to specific crops, some history has to be given about early agriculture in general about the River area. The earliest plantings of record, circa 1863, were apple trees belonging to Richard E. Lewis.[29] Vegetables were reported on the early U.S. Government land maps in the form of corn. Cornfields were scattered along the river bench where silt and sandy loam are found. These fields belonged to Lewis, Ridenhour, Anthony McPeak, Korbel's, J. Mahan, along the east side of McPeak's land, and Greenwood at today's Drake's Estates.

Other vegetables were potatoes, tomatoes, beans, radishes, and other root vegetables in yards next to homes.[30]

Other fruit trees planted were French plums also known as prunes. Col. J.B. Armstrong had such an orchard planted in the 1880's on his property north of Guerneville.[31]

Just as hops provided seasonal employment for local citizens, grape and prune picking became important up until the 1920's. Apples and cherries were lesser crops of the area, but required some seasonal pickers.

During the 1890's local agriculture had developed enough to occasionally be mentioned in the newspapers:

> [In Pocket canyon] Mr. Ruhlman has put out several hundred nut trees of different kinds.[32]

> Citrus culture is being considered around the highlands of Guerneville along with figs and other fruits.[33]

> In the vicinity of Guerneville the fruit crop has been imense [sic], and large quantities of prunes are now being dried.[34]

Vineyards were first planted about 1880 by the Korbel brothers (after experimenting with other ventures) and by pioneer S.H. Torrence. Like hops and apples, wine grapes proved to be successful. Soon vineyards were scattered on the hillsides.

Since the Korbel Winery is so well known and is compiling its own history, only the very beginnings of their other business — wine — is given.

As timber was being cut the Korbel brothers sought advice from the University of California about what to raise on their newly cleared land. They first tried their hands at a dairy-and-cheese factory, and bought about 50 cows. But with competition coming from the midwest, they quit in 1880. They also attempted to raise tobacco, but had discouraging results.[35]

Somehow — whether it was by intuition or the neighboring influence of Santa Rosa valley or by further inquiry of the University — the brothers set out a tract of hillside acreage for vineyards in 1881. The varieties of grape cuttings they planted under the management of a Mr. Bower were:[36]

Zinfandel	10,000
Filher Zagus	3,000
Frantinac	2,000
Traminer	1,000
Muskate (Muscat?)	3,000
Sultana	100
Berger	500
Gutedel (Charles)	7,000
Reisling	16,600
Black Pinot (Malnaze)	6,500

The first year for their grape crops brought troubles. Prices were so low the brothers refused to sell and crushed the fruit themselves, thus their initiation into the wine business.

As the land was being cleared it was put under cultivation with more vines and a few orchards. By August 1883, 40 acres were converted to grapes by twelve Bavarians brought to the River and Korbel's, specifically, for wine production. By the end of the year there were four large tanks shipped to the brothers for wine storage.[37]

In 1884 the brothers were so pleased with their viticulture experiment they planned to put their entire land into vineyard.

By the end of 1885, 100 acres were vineyard (other cleared acreage was planted with alfalfa and hops).[38]

In May 1886 the Korbels had their own winery built. Some 22 men, and possibly more, were involved in its construction over a period of five months. They included J.O. Burkhailer of Santa Rosa and three other carpenters under his direction, and John Abraham, who was boss of seven brick masons.

The building was 123 feet by 53 feet, and three stories high. The walls were built hollow to keep the interior cool.[39]

The main structure was built with lumber from their own mills, as were their fermentation tanks.

The supply of bricks has two different stories. The first is that L.M. Ridenhour, just one mile upstream from Korbel's, fired bricks in his kilns at Hilton on their special order.[40]

The second story is that Korbel's would not pay Ridenhour's price plus freight charges, so they had their own bricks made and fired on their property.[41]

At any rate, the brick work was finished in late June and the woodwork by the first of August. A year later, 22 large tanks were installed.[42]

In 1889 a fire started in the winery, but was put out with wine because there was insufficient water available.[43]

In 1890 another large winery was erected of brick, and a brick tower was placed at the east corner. This tower was for the brandy distillery.

In 1894 the brothers began producing champagne by the French method of fermenting in bottles.

A few vineyards still exist today around Guerneville (1980). They are Korbel's, Ginessi at the head of May's Canyon, and Ruffino on the ridge between East Austin and Finley Creeks. Old and abandoned vines can still be seen dotting the countryside. A good history of local viticulture can be found at the Korbel Winery.

1. *Press Democrat,* April 9, 1892; November 28, 1891.
2. Ibid.
3. Op.Cit., June 23, 1894.
4. Ibid., December 8 and December 15, 1894.
5. Ibid.
6. Ibid.
7. Ibid.
8. Op.Cit, July 6 and July 27, 1895.
9. Op.Cit, August 31, 1895.
10. Op.Cit, December 7, 1895.
11. Op.Cit, July 31, 1897.
12. *Pacific Rural Press,* January 14, 1899, p. 23.
13. *R.R. Ad.,* February 1905.
14. *Guerneville Times,* August 3, 1951.
15. *Ibid.*
16. *P.D.,* August 9, 1891; *Healdsburg Enterprise,* November 20, 1890.
17. *S.R. Rep.,* September 1883.
18. Ridenhour School District Records, 1881-1900, now in possession of Guerneville School District; Son. Demo., November 19, 1887.
19. *Son. Demo.,* August 1, 1891; January 1, 1892.
20. Op.Cit, October 28, 1893.
21. Op.Cit, March 10, 1893.
22. Op.Cit, September 15 and 22, 1894.
23. Op.Cit, July 27, 1895.
24. Op.Cit, September 21, 1895.
25. Op.Cit, October 5, 1895.
26. Ibid.
27. C. Raymond Clar, letter to author, November 26, 1976.
28. *P.D.,* September 5, 1896.
29. Bd. of Supvrs. Records, Petition for Road, dated June 8, 1863.
30. *R.R.F.*
31. *S.D.,* April 30, 1881; March 22, 1884; *S.R. Rep.,* September 1, 1886.
32. *P.D.,* January 29, 1898.
33. Op.Cit, December 15, 1894.
34. Op.Cit, September 24, 1898.
35. Op.Cit, January 28, 1962; *S.R. Rep.,* January 1, 1880. Tobacco was very successful, as proven by David Hetzel, at thls time. See Chapter XXX.
36. *S. D..,* April 30, 1881; August 5, 1882.
37. Op.Cit, August 11, 1883; September 15, 1883; *P.D.,* April 21, 1968.
38. *S. D.,* January 3, 1885; *R.R.F.,* October 31, 1885; *P.D.,* April 21, 1968.
39. *S. D.,* May 1, 1886, June 18, 1886; *Rep.,* September 1, 1883.
40. *P.D.,* January 28, 1962.
41. Personal interview with Gary Heck, May 22, 1984 at Santa Rosa, California. Korbel Winery insists the Korbel brothers made and fired their own bricks. There is no record in State Mining or Geology bulletins indicating any clay pits in the area except those owned by Ridenhour and Tom Brown at Hilton. There was no mention of pits or kilns being built or used by Korbels in any newspaper, interviews or other publications. The author supports the Ridenhour/Brown story.
42. *Son. Co. Hist.* 1911, p. 901.
43. *P.D.,* December 21, 1968, January 18, 1962.
44. *Ibid.*

Additional Sources:

S.D., May 29, 1886.

S.D., May 14, 1887.

S.D., August 9, 1890.

Chapter 32

GUERNEVILLE — 1896 TO 1900

The Railroad Exchange saloon, circa 1902, on the corner of Armstrong Wood Road and main Street. The last two men on the right are (left to right) Jim Morow, the town tinsmith, and J.C. "Cap" Wendt. JCS Collection

The "Gay Nineties" were in full swing. There was an influx of summer tourists about Guerneville. However, the first half of this decade was marked by fire and flood. Crime, per se, was a rare visitor to town — felonies were few, serious misdemeanors were not many, and infractions occasionally occurred. A notable offense of this second half of the decade happened when a C.E. Germann was charged with the statutory rape of his 13-year-old sister-in-law.[1]

The family was far from well-to-do and resided at Poverty Flat — named for obvious reasons — which was located across the river from town.

The preliminary examination was held in Guerneville's Redwood Judicial Court, before Judge Brown. He held Germann to answer for the crime in Superior Court at Santa Rosa.

A jury trial was held during April 1896. No verdict was returned due to a hung jury. Retrial was held in June 1896, and resulted once again in a hung jury. The District Attorney dismissed the charge on June 8, 1896.

Divorce papers were filed a year later by Germann's wife, Katie, not because of the rape charges, but because of the several beatings she suffered at the hands of her husband during their seven-year marriage. She was granted a divorce in December 1897.[2]

While Germann was being prosecuted, the townfolk proceeded with their endeavors. The Robert Coons' home was built and the final touches made. J.H. Ebers bought the Wehrspon Hotel from C.P. Sims. An inch of snow fell in March, the first snow to fall in six years.

On Sunday, March 1, another Stumptown pioneer died. James E. Batchelder, age

Inside the Raiload Exchange saloon before "Cap" Wendt bought it, 1897. Left, Jeff Banks; right, "Pa" Starrett. Alta Starrett Lutrell Collection.

61, joined other departed pioneers Murphy, Torrence and Yarbrough. Batchelder came to town in 1870 for lumber and spent nearly half his life there.

Spring arrived and school was let out. Preparations were made for tourism and the old industry — lumber.

A lot of the people spent the summer rusticating along the banks of the Russian River. It became quite the thing to do. A section in following pages is devoted to the birth of Guerneville's second industry — tourism.

On July 6, 1896, another fire occurred. It started at 10:10 p.m. in Sam S. Schloss' store. How the fire began is unknown as Sam had already closed up shop and gone home. Flames spread rapidly to H. Harms' saloon on First Street.[3] Even at this time of year — July — the reservoir was low, so water pressure was too little to be of assistance. An old method of fighting fires was employed. A span of horses was quickly hitched to a home and pulled it down. Three homes were moved in this way. This, plus buckets and wet blankets, saved adjoining houses.

Schloss' building and stock were a total loss, but they were insured for $12,000. His home, insured for $3,000, suffered the same fate, except most of the furniture and a piano were saved. Harms' saloon and dwelling experienced a similar ending, but he was insured for only $300.

The summer of 1896 was spent by some 30 to 40 men constructing a new telephone line from Sebastopol to Guerneville via Forestville.[4]

The year 1896 was also a general election year for president and other federal officers. No primary elections were held. Those were instituted in 1910. Political clubs and organizations were formed in communities around the county. These were not just the usual Democratic and Republican parties, but were comprised of people from a broad political spectrum. Voters had registered for the People's Party, the Prohibitionists, Socialists and Nationalists in the Redwood District. One organization was formed out of special interest just for this election, namely, the William Jennings Bryan Free Silver Club.[5]

The Guerneville Free Silver Club held its first meeting on the night of August 19. It was resolved by its members " . . . that the Democrats and Populists fuse together on the congressional nominee of this district." The 92 members elected Anthony McPeak chairman, J.B. Watson, John Bagley and W.H. Osborn vice chairmen, L.L. Jewett secretary, and David Hetzel treasurer. No women were represented in this group as women did not yet have the right to vote. Because the election campaign was already under way, they met once a week.

As the campaign stepped up its tempo, local politicians made their bids for local office. Guerneville merchant and former Redwood Justice of the Peace, Herbert L. Bagley, and Frank B. Glynn, current Justice, were questing for the seat of Fifth District Supervisor, of which Redwood Township was a part. They flattered, cajoled, incensed and sweettalked their ways around Bodega, Freestone, Cazadero, and places in between.

Time, the Hour of Truth, was drawing near. The polling place for Redwood East Precinct was placed at Yip Chang's (location unknown), and that for Redwood West Precinct was placed at Odd Fellows Hall in Guerneville.[6]

Much of the county was Democratic and appeared to be supporting the Bryan Free Silver Club, with the exception of the Sonoma coast and Guerneville.

The "big day" arrived. The votes cast were not by popular count for president and vice-president, but for delegates to cast electoral votes. For this reason, the candidates for those high offices preferred by Guerneville residents are not known.[7]

Even though Bert Bagley outspent Frank

Neely's Park Campground, Guerneville. JCS Collection

Glynn $98 to $69 in his campaign, the Supervisor's race ended with Glynn carrying the outlying townships of the District and winning with 539 votes, compared to Bagley's 413 votes.[8]

Election fever gave way to the impending holidays. The town put on the biggest Thanksgiving celebration in its history. The Guerneville Brass Band (all 15 pieces) performed a concert at the Union Hotel for a masquerade ball. Some 40 or more couples attended and danced into the wee hours of the next morning.[9]

Christmas and New Year's Day 1897 passed quietly. Winter was mild. School reopened. The butcher firm of Ungewitter & Palmer became Ungewitter & Torrence. Mrs. Cynthia Johnson, who had lived in the area since 1862, passed away in March at age 80. Another town improvement club was formed in April.[10]

Such routine events might leave the impression that winter and spring 1897 were fairly uneventful. But read the following column from the May 15, 1897 issue of the *Press Democrat*:

Dam on the Russian River, early 1900's. JCS Collection

Guerneville has a new jeweler, Mr. Sawyer, formerly of Santa Rosa. A new harness shop in the Connell Block. A new butcher shop, a new fruit and vegetable stand.

In the Armstrong Block, Messrs. Graham and Turner have opened a big general merchandise store.

Both the hotels will make a vigorous fight for summer people, while half dozen of our more prosperous country homes will entertain these human birds of passage.

Mr. Blair is building a fine big two story home on his ranch a mile north of town.

The Manchester home has had a thorough overhauling, a new coat of paint and a splendid new tank tower and wind mill.

Mrs. Cole has raised and painted her house and Johnnie Coon has followed suit.

That was Guerneville — a small country town.

If there is a date to be picked for the birth of the second industry of both Guerneville and the Russian River, namely, tourism and recreation, it would be July 22, 1897, the day the Guerneville Improvement Club and the town put on their first "Summer Fete." Aquatic and field events, along with a barbecue, were on the entertainment schedule offered to the public at large. But just as the logging and lumber industries did not start suddenly, neither did summer tourism and camping.

In prior years people had been visiting the river and tall timber. Various organizations — Masons, Bohemians, Methodists — had big outings around the area predominately at the Camp Grounds now called Guernewood Park. The numbers of vacationing campers (as opposed to organized groups) slowly increased during the years prior to 1896. This year the idea caught on with the people from around the county to come to the river area and rusticate. The Santa Rosa Press Democrat printed in every issue during the summer that the white tents of campers dotted the river's banks. Even Duncans' Mills was called a "summer resort."

To give support to this new local phenomenon, the Foresters of the World held their annual Big Picnic at the Camp Ground. Members from Healdsburg to San Jose — nearly

Guernewood Park, early 1900's. George E. Guerne is sitting on the chair on the porch, with family. This is looking south from the rail line. JCS Collection

4,000 people — enjoyed themselves.[11]

Duly impressed with "Vacation 1896," the Guerneville Improvement Club was born again and put on the first summer program to make 1897 and future summers more enjoyable. A dam seven feet high was planned to cross the river at Meeker's timber — today's Bohemian Grove. This would create a still-water swimming and boating pool four miles long up to Guerneville.[12]

Spring was in full reign as the first organized picnic — the Dolphin Swimming and Boating Club — took place in April at the Camp Ground. A month later the San Francisco & Northern Pacific Railroad held its outing, and 1,000 people enjoyed themselves.[13]

The Improvement Club and railroad joined forces to promote the idea of tourism. For the gain of both a pamphlet was distributed throughout the county. The dam, financed by a $200 subscription from local merchants and contributed labor, was built by June 5.[14]

To make the population at large take notice of Russian River as a summer vacation and recreation area, a water carnival was conceived. The date selected was July 22. A committee composed of James R. Watson, D.R. Bolton, J.G. Cuthill, Antoinette Lauteren, and Mrs. W.P. Ferguson was to coordinate athletic events, music and a barbecue.

As with most civic celebrations in America, Guerneville had to have a queen for its carnival. The "strut" of Guerneville girls were Cora Kuster, Vera Manchester, Gertrude Lauteren, Fanny Ansel, Gertrude Cnopius, Josie Anderson and Oda Finley. Others entered the contest later.[15]

Invitations were sent to local county high schools for competition in the carnival's athletic events. Special trains were scheduled. To make sure a crowd would be present, the round-trip fare from Santa Rosa was reduced to 50 cents.[16]

The townspeople worked hard. Lights were hung among the trees on the grounds, and platforms for bands were built. Race courses were laid out.

Camping in the redwoods at Guernewood Park. Note lanterns strung in the trees. JSC Collection

Meanwhile, a queen was selected: Miss Nellie Carr, age 19, a native of Guerneville, and "the handsomest young lady." Her popularity gave her a plurality vote of 1,200 votes over her nearest contest rival. Her choices of escort from the other contestants were Ida and Cora Kuster, Gertrude Lauteren, and Josie Anderson.[17]

Celebration time arrived.

At Santa Rosa, the train was crowded. Station agent Gill sold more than 1,300 tickets. All seats in the 13 cars were taken, aisles jammed, platforms filled, and still more wanted to get on the train. Superintendent Whiting saw the overflow and ordered up two boxcars. A dispatch from Fulton said 100 more were waiting to hop on. When the train pulled out of Santa Rosa it left some celebrants waiting for the 6 p.m. train to take them to Guerneville. There was no standing room left. The Fultonites had to wait also.[18]

Guernewood Park was decorated surpassing anything done before on the River. Bunting, streamers and Chinese lanterns were strung from tree to tree. The dance pavilion attracted large numbers of dancers. Afternoon events were track-and-field competitions. These were 50-, 100- and 200-yard dashes, along with shotput, pole vault, high jump and long jump. Swimming matches took place in Bohemian Lake, and some visitors merely went boating.

Preparations for the culinary carnival went on concurrently. Local attorney L.L. Jewett was in charge of the barbecue. The cooking pit was 20 feet long, five feet wide, and six feet deep. Two calves and three sheep were slaughtered by local butchers Ungewitter and Snow. Frank Mason did the cooking. The fire was started Thursday evening and fresh fuel was added till cooking time was near. By then the pit was a mass of hot coals. When the cooking was finished, the meats were done to "a heavenly brown." Sheriff Sam Allen took charge of the carving.

The masses enjoyed the delicious repast. After resting from the last bite, singly and in small groups the celebrants sauntered down to the beach and Lake Bohemia. At 8:30 the evening program started with the Sotoyome Band (from Healdsburg?) placed across the river from the pavilion playing various songs. Company E, Santa Rosa's National Guard unit, was bivouacked on the sand bar below the pavilion. Meanwhile, "across the river Fort Silurian gave sullen defiance."

A correspondent to the Santa Rosa Democrat wrote:

> Suddenly from a score of stations along both banks of the [River] many colored flares appeared. A bright red cast a crimson glare upon the mirror-like water, which was followed by an emerald green, changing to a clear white, then a yellow.
>
> The effect produced by this grand light sinking deep into the shadows thrown by tall and stately redwoods was simply sublime. It could not be adequately pictured with words. At a given signal a rocket was fired from the foot of Fort Silurian. Then came the stern order, "First detachment, forward!" Farther down the line echoed the order, "Second detachment, forward!"
>
> The first troop advanced twenty-five yards, fired, and were driven back, repulsed completely by the defenders. Reinforcements were called up to cover the retreat. The two sections then advanced, fired, and divided to right and left. The third and fourth divisions were brought up, the third forming the center and the fourth under Captain Haven acting as a reserve.
>
> The first section had in the meantime captured the approach to the bridge. With reinforcements they carried the bridge and made a stand at the foot of the bluff surmounted by the fort until two more detachments came to their aid. Amid an incessant cracking of rifle shots the first troop stormed the fort and attracting the fire of the [defenders] allowed the other sections of the invading force to make a flank movement. With a last volley the stern battlements were overthrown and a more beautiful tableau was never presented than the unfurling of the stars and stripes over the ruins of the fort.
>
> A bright white light illuminated the brave boys in blue as they stood on the battlements. And as the last shot was fired the band struck up that soul inspiring air so dear to patriots, "The Star Spangled Banner." As if by providence directed, just as the colors were being planted by the sergeant, a wafting breeze floated the handsome silk banner in a most effective manner.

After the attack on Fort Silurian, again rockets went off. Queen Nellie and entourage glided slowly up river in her royally decorated barge, followed by a long line of other barges, sailboats and canoes. She landed and, walking between a double row of militia forming an honor guard, mounted a carriage. The royal party, followed by the crowd, went to the Union Hall in Guerneville where the Grand Ball was held. The dance lasted through the night.

For the trip home, eight extra passenger cars were sent from Santa Rosa to the river town to handle the crowd. Thus was celebrated the birth of the Russian River Vacationland.

The summer passed fairly quietly after the festival.

An alarm was sounded one night: "The boys are lost!"[19] Men, armed with lanterns, turned out en masse. The 12-year-old son of Robert Starrett and a friend left home about dark to go to town a short distance away. The boys were still missing at bedtime, 11 o'clock. A casual search turned no clue, and the alarm was given. Over 100 men scattered along the river and around the mill pond. No sign was found.

About 1 o'clock a.m., a little girl piped up saying the boys had built a dog house and told her they were going to sleep in it. Starrett ran to the dog house and shined a light in. The two boys were fast asleep on a clean straw floor, a little pup cuddled between them. The following night the Starretts had a social gathering at their home for the search party, and the little girl had the place of honor.

Another small milestone was reached when the Carr & Bagley Company became the town's third business to incorporate. Principal stockholders were Charles F. Carr and Herbert L. Bagley. Other holders were Arthur Florence, the chairmaker; Jacob Joost, saloonkeeper; and Oliver Westcott, saloonkeeper. The amount of capital stock subscribed was $25,000.[20]

> The objectives of the company were to:
> 1. buy and sell horticulture and agriculture products;
> 2. manufacture, buy and sell all kinds of building materials;
> 3. purchase, build, charter, run, manage, etc., all kinds of railroads, river boats and crafts;
> 4. deal in real estate;
> 5. buy and sell buildings;
> 6. borrow and loan money;
> 7. do a general milling business;
> 8. purchase, run, etc. all kinds of electric plants and water works.

Carr & Bagley certainly had all aspects of the mercantile world covered.

Thanksgiving was celebrated with a dance. Christmas was celebrated in kind with a capacity crowd at Union Hall dancing to Jensen, Bagley and Prestwood's music.[21]

Guerneville's journalistic history up to this time was next to nil. The *Guerneville Blade* lasted only two months. Now, eight years later, on January 1, 1898, the *Guerneville X-Rays* made its first appearance.[22] (The x-ray was discovered by Roentgen in 1895.)

The X-Rays was published every Saturday by H.S. Bartholomew. He charged a subscription rate of $2 per year or three months for 50 cents, "paid strictly in advance." Three issues of the paper are known to exist today. The last copy was printed around the end of May 1901.[23]

The *X-Rays'* political bent was conservative concerning state and national situations, and very promotive of the local area. It was prejudiced against minority ethnic groups, compared to present times.

The *X-Rays'* subscription list and accounts receivable were bought by a new paper, the Russian River Advertiser, in May 1901. The X-Rays was the beginning of a long romance between the communites along the river and its journalism. Its successor, the Advertiser, eventually became the *Guerneville Times* in 1913. The *Times* lasted until 1966.

The *X-Rays* started its publication at a historical time: 1898 and the Spanish-American War. We saw in Chapter 15, "Chinese, Part I," how small and large communities asked the federal government for help. This resulted in the Burlingame Treaty. In 1898 the roles reversed, and the government called upon the people for help.

In February of that year the battleship Maine exploded in Havana Harbor, Cuba. Spain and the United States engaged in two months of military conflict before President McKinley declared on April 25 that war existed between the two countries. On May 1 the naval bombardment of Manila and the Philippines began in earnest. On the 25th of May McKinley called for 75,000 volunteers to serve for two years. On June 8 the start of the Cuban campaign centered on Santiago.

In Sonoma County there were two companies of the California National Guard, Company C of Petaluma and Company E of Santa Rosa, both part of the Fifth Infantry Regiment. When the President called for volunteers, the Guerneville "boys" stepped forward:

Charles F. Klein	Ben H. Klink
Frank Westcott	John C. Joost
Fred Ross	Charles & James Gilmore
C.A. Guernsey	Charles R. Price

Joost, Klein, Klink and Ross were enlisted in Company E. The Gilmores were enlisted in Company K (location unknown), Westcott in Company B of San Jose, and Guernsey in Company A (location unknown).[24]

On June 28 Company E of Santa Rosa was called to muster. Amidst marching bands, cheers and waving hankies, the boys boarded the train in Santa Rosa and left for Camp Bennett at Fruitvale, California (near Oakland).[25]

Upon arriving at camp the company set to building up its own tent area. Two weeks later, along with 15 other companies, Company E was sworn into the regular Army. They became E Company, 1st Batallion, 8th California Regiment.[26]

After a month of boot camp, Privates Klink, Klein and Joost came home for a short visit in late July, all three "looking as if they enjoy camp life."[27]

The war and boot camp went on.

On August 12, the Spanish-American War was declared over, after 3 1/2 months of conflict. What was going to happen to the Guerneville boys now? A bulletin was announced in camp that the regiment would still go to the Philippines.

"They gave a rousing cheer."[28]

So much for scuttlebutt.

Time in camp lingered on. Klink became ill, went home for a visit, and returned to camp.

Word was then passed that the regiment would split up for garrison duty stateside. This scuttlebutt was true. In mid-September the tents of Camp Barrett were struck and Companies B, C and E were assigned to Fort Point on the south side of the Golden Gate.[29]

It was cold and fog-wet at Fort Point, where the principal task was guard duty. The boys of Company E were on guard detail for one month, then transferred to the Presidio of San Francisco in mid-October for more garrison duty. It became monotonously routine.[30]

At the first of the new year, 1899, the word was passed that the Company (and regiment) were going to be released from active duty. Final inspection of the troops was held on Saturday, January 21, and they were mustered out of the Army.[31]

Two weeks were spent in returning Army equipment, packing company gear, and folding up tents.

On February 2, Company E arrived back in Santa Rosa to a cheering community. The boys marched in the "Welcome Back" parade, and were feted at parties and receptions.[32]

The people of Guerneville held a ball at the Union Hall for the ex-members of Companies A, B, E and K. The Guerneville X-Ray reported:[33]

> The banquet and reception given the boys in blue who belonged to the 8th Cal. Regiment on their return from duty was a notable occasion for Guerneville and one that will be long remembered by the participants. It was held in Union Hall on the evening of February 10th, and was attended by a rousing crowd. The hall was festooned with bunting and flags and the genial faces of McKinley, Washington, Dewey and Hancock looked serenely down upon the company. The Maine in its glory and the Maine in its ruin was also in evidence. Prof. Kahler's full orchestra furnished excellent music. At the time appointed, to the soulstirring roll of the reveille our boys came through one door into the hall and the veterans of the civil war of the 60's, the Sioux campaigns of the 70's and of the Mexican War of the 40's came in through another door and marching, met in the center of the hall where the veterans gave the youngsters their welcome. The names of those who rallied to their country's urgent call for volunteer soldiers of the past year are J.C. Joost, C.F. Klein, B.F. Klink of Co. E, Frank Wescott of Co. B, James and Charles Gilmore of Co. K. The G.A.R. representatives were W. Carr, D. Hetzel, J.H. Ansell, the navy by J.S. Bartholomew, with N. Bolton to represent the Confederate portion of the days of '61. J.W. Bagley is the only Mexican veteran now with us and he proudly wore his badge of that war and gave welcome the Native Sons back to their homes. All being seated, J.S. Bartholomew as master of ceremonies gave the following toasts and sentiments.
>
> Toast No. 1. "Our returned soldier sons and brothers." Given with all the honors, the entire audience rising to their feet.
>
> Sentiment: "The California Volunteers who never know defeat, whose motto is ever 'Onward' whose watchword's 'No Retreat.'"
>
> Music: "Star Spangled Banner."
>
> Response by Rev. Francis Lawson.

Toast No. 2. "Veterans of '61."

Sentiment: "Stand by the flag. No North, no South, no East, no West."

Music: "Dixie."

Response by David Hetzel.

Toast No. 3. "The American Army."

Sentiment: "Put none but American troops on guard."

Music: "America" or "God save the Queen," the national hymn of both the United States and Great Britain.

Response by J. H. Ansell.

Toast No. 4. "The United States Navy."

Sentiment: "We have met the enemy and they are ours."

Music: "Sailing, sailing over the bounding main."

Response by Dr. W. G. Cole.

Toast No. 5. "Mexican War Veterans."

Sentiment: Taylor's famous order: "Give them a little more grape shot Captain Bragg."

Music: Gen. Persifer F. Smith's March.

Response by J. W. Bagley.

Gen. Smith was Sergeant J.W. Bagley's old commander of the 10th and 11th Military Department of California and Oregon and the old Mexican War March was played by the band in his honor.

Toast No. 6. "Utah in the American-Spanish war."

Music: Iowa State Band March. [Composed by I. Cahler.]

Response by Lieut. J.B. Stacy of the Utah Light Battery.

Toast No. 7. "Guerneville and Russian River Valley."

Music: "When the corn is waving Annie dear."

Response by Dr. W.G. Cole.

The features of the evening were the bountiful refreshments served by the ladies committee, the elegant decoration of the hall by W.T. Kahler, Daniel B. Brian and Edward Pells, the splendid music by Kahler's full orchestra band of fourteen pieces, and lastly and greatest of all the speeches. Rev. Francis Lawson's welcome to the returning boys, was a masterpiece and everyone loudly applauded his references to their change back from the military to civil life. Mr. Lawson is a pleasing orator and everyone heartily enjoyed his response. David Hetzel's response to the toast "The veterans of '61" was in excellent taste, the music "Dixie" recalling to his memory many scenes of the Virginia campaigns under McClellan and "Fighting Joe Hooker." J.H. Ansell disclaimed against being considered an orator and followed by making a capital response to the toast "the American Army." Kahler's rendition of "Sailing, sailing over the main" incited Dr. W.G. Cole to the best effort he ever made in Guerneville in response to the toast "The United States Navy" and again in speaking to "Guerneville and our Russian River Valley" he paid the returned soldier guests a fine compliment for their soldierly conduct and bearing. Dr. J.B. Stacy responding to Utah, called the attention of the guests to the record now being made by the Mormon boys in the battles before Manila, and was heartily applauded. The Dr. is right at home as an after dinner speaker and we shall hear from him again. When the volunteers and veterans marched out to supper as guests of honor the Unionist William Carr and the Confederate Noah Bolton walked out in company there was a general outburst of applause and waving of handkerchiefs. After the reception and banquet the youngsters took possession of the large hall and tripped the light fantastic toe. Guests from all the surrounding towns were present. It was the largest and altogether the most social crowd the *X-Rays* has ever seen in Guerneville, and that it was appreciated by the soldier boys is shown by the following.

CARD OF THANKS

The undersigned volunteers of Co's E, A, K and C. of the 8th Regiment of California Volunteers most heartily thank the citizens of Guerneville for the splendid reception and banquet which greeted our return home. C.F. Mein, J.C. Joost, B.F. Mink, Frank Wescott, James Gilmore, Charles Gilmore, Charles Price, F. Ross, C.A. Guernsey.

For seven months Guerneville participated in a world event, and now she welcomed back her volunteers.

Nine months later the members of Company E were reassembled in Santa Rosa at the

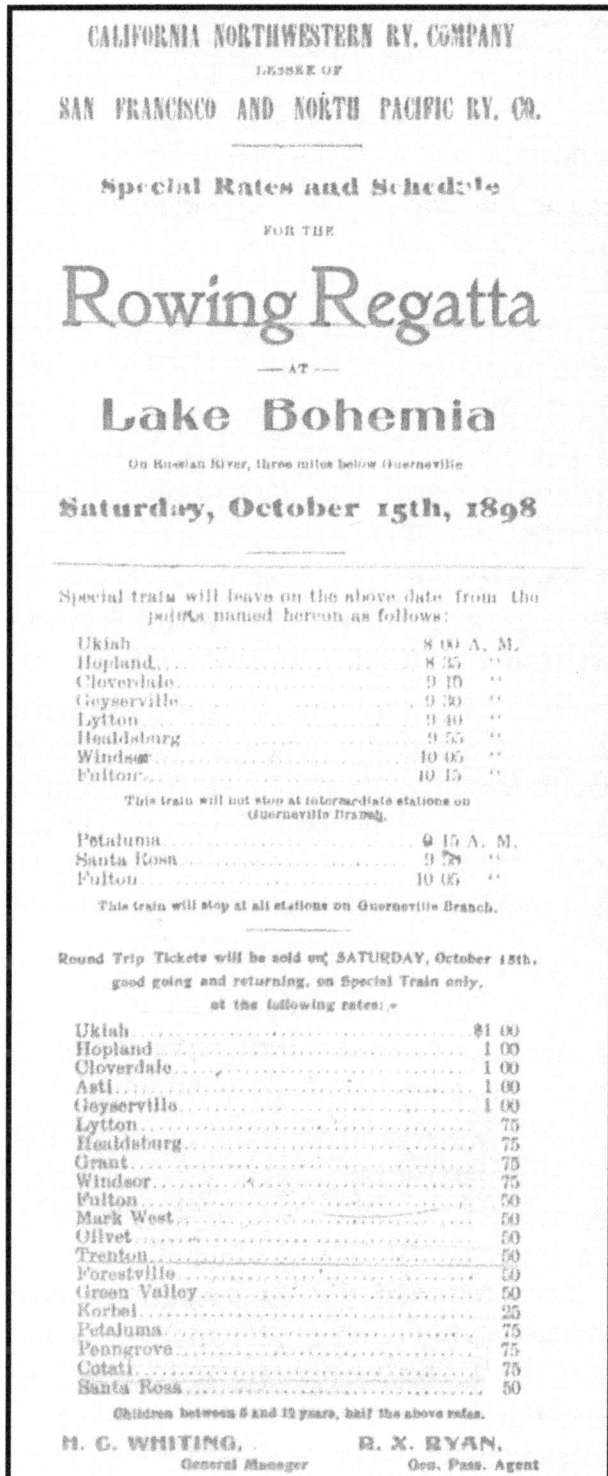

Advertisement for the Regatta in the *Santa Rosa Democrat*

Armory on Hinton Avenue. On the evening of November 10, 1899, they were all presented with campaign medals and certificates amidst pomp, ceremony and rousing cheers.[34]

Again a tragedy — this one a war halfway around the globe — served as a bond uniting a small community, giving it a stronger sense of self-identification and a feeling above all of self-righteousness.

Another event of 1898 was by design, not surprise. Because of the success of the first, a second water carnival was organized. The usual committee was drawn up in March and was comprised of H.S. Bartholomew, president, and Henry Ungewitter, secretary. Instead of having the festival in July as they did the year before, it was planned for October. More later.[35]

When Guernewood Park opened in March the dam was put in for the summer season, thus forming Lake Bohemia. There was no charge for campers or tourists to use the facilities.[36]

This year a pavilion and refreshment stand were built. The stand probably had hard liquor available as Henry Ungewitter applied to the Board of Supervisors for a license to sell such spirits at "The Guernewood Park."[37]

The few fledgling resorts that offered the basics, namely, Watson's, Gibson's and Yarbrough's, were cleaned and spruced up. At Guernewood a rustic entrance was built, and above the gate "Guernewood Park" was spelled out in redwood limbs. Horses were excluded from the grounds, but corrals and the like were located across the railroad tracks from the park.[38]

By mid-July campers and vacationers numbered in the hundreds. Many were from the Santa Rosa area. A few had camps they could "get away to" every weekend.

On the beach (at Guerneville? Guernewood?) boats and bath houses were operated by Willard Bagley.[39]

As summer progressed more campers dotted the countryside well beyond the river banks. Daily trains brought more. Guerneville was becoming crowded.[40]

The Guerneville Cornet Band gave concerts every Saturday evening. Advertisements were placed in various county newspapers to

Interior of a comfortable tent, 1904. JCS Collection

generate more tourists.

September. School was back in session and crops were ready for picking, but the vacationers kept coming. To prolong the tourist season the water carnival committee that was started in February picked the dates of October 15-16 for the event. This year's plans included a boat-down-the-chute ride, as well as competition between boat clubs from San Francisco. Financial help from the Santa Rosa area exceeded $500.[41] The program for Saturday and Sunday events were drawn up.

The railroad advertised special rates for the weekend. Close to 5,000 people were expected. A special restaurant was built to accommodate 200 at one sitting. The food was donated from different groups about the Bay Area:

    600 pounds of beans
    125 pounds of coffee
    60 pounds of sugar
    12 Alaska salmon
    8 cases of whiskey
    8 cases of wine
    3 kegs of pickles[42]

To give proper importance to this sports spectacular, all the participating clubs of the Bay Area — including Ariel, Alameda, Dolphin, Lurline, Pioneer, Southend and Triton — presented their best teams. The events were under the direct charge of the Pacific Amateur Athletic Association, of which all the clubs were members.[43]

The river bank was cleared of brush so no view of the water course was obstructed. A grandstand had a 1,000-seat capacity.[44]

The big day arrived. Attendance was in excess of 2,000, quite a bit less than the expected 5,000. The results of the races are unknown. Although the schedule called for a two-day event, it appears that the festival was held only on Saturday.

The visitors, satisfied, went home. The townfolk cleaned up, and summer finally gave way to winter.

But there were nine local boys who missed all the festivities. They were with the Army, preparing for the Spanish-American War.

The town went into deep mourning at the end of September when Crockett D. Yarbrough was killed at age 68. He was riding in his wagon when the team ran away. He was thrown to the ground and broke his neck. He first came to Big Bottom in 1861.[45]

The autumn of 1898 passed as quietly as the changing colors of the leaves.

Winter was ushered in with a rush of weddings. Three separate weddings were performed in December. Arthur Florence wed Veva Manchester, James H.W. Cooke joined Ida May Rouse, and David Bolton married as well.

The three couples, all well-known in town, got together after New Year's 1899 and rented Union Hall. The town was invited to a giant wedding reception on Thursday, January 12. Music, dancing, eats and drinks were provided through the night and into the next morning.[46]

In March another wedding of two well-known people — Fannie Ansell and Arthur Turner — took place, and again the whole town was treated: this time, to a wedding breakfast. The couple resided at Church and First Streets.[47]

The reported events for the next couple

John T. Coon, hardware and blacksmith, 1903. John on the far left; Bill Miller, second from right, is holding a horseshoe.

months were trivial: A dog bit Dr. Cole. James Renfro, Samantha McBee, Lulu Coburn, Georgia Wilson received $8 county welfare checks. Twenty-two men were making railroad ties to fill a contract for Charles Carr. A ball was held at Union Hall.

Spring of 1899 was used to prepare for the summer tourist season. W.F. Graham leased the big Wehrspon house as a place to entertain the tourists. Graham still had the Guerneville Hotel where his guests would stay.[48]

The Cornet Band, under the leadership of mill owner Frank Clar, once again gave concerts in town for the summer.

By mid-June many campers were at Guernewood. All other resorts and merchants were busy.

The dam was put in and made higher than the year before. Lake Bohemia had several new boats on it. John Bagley had four 14-foot row boats named after his daughter and daughters-in-law: "Josie," "Lulu," "Edna," and "Alice." A new steam launch was used as a water taxi from Guerneville. Fares were 10 cents to Guernewood Park, and 25 cents to Bohemian Grove.[49]

In mid-July, part of the dam gave way. It took about two weeks for the water to rise after repairs were made.[50]

At the same time Guerne and McLean ran an advertisement in the Press Democrat all summer for Guernewood Park:

> There is still plenty of room at Guerneville for 2,000 more campers. You can secure a full camping outfit (excepting bedding) from Guerne and McLean on the grounds cheaper than they can be hauled there for. If you are going to Guerneville

rent your outfits from Guerne and McLeans on the grounds.[51]

By the end of August there was still a number of campers in the area, but the town was nearly deserted. Hop picking season was starting and the schools had closed so the children could earn wages along with the adults.

There would be no water carnival this year.

Autumn arrived. A few stores and the post office were burgled one night in October. Cobb's store was hit for a take of gold and silver watches, plus some jewelry. Wadsworth & Florence had the change in their till stolen. The post office had a small amount of money swiped. Entrance to each establishment was gained by use of an iron bar. Sheriff Frank P. Grace was notified, as were all Sonoma County deputies, but after two weeks no suspects were apprehended.[52]

Winter settled in the area for its usual stay. The town's New Year's Grand Ball was held at the Union Hotel. The rains came and created two big landslides near town. The local societies, both public and private, elected new officers.

A couple of businesses changed hands during 1899. In May J.D. Wadsworth and Arthur Florence bought the Carr & Bagley store. Carr and Bagley still remained partners, though in other business ventures. Jacob Joost sold his interest in Joost & Starrett's Saloon to Alexander Wall.[53]

In December Wadsworth sold his interest in the Wadsworth & Florence store back to Charles Carr. Tom Fleming, who left town in 1895, returned and bought Oliver Wescott's saloon.

The holidays passed quietly, even though a new century was starting — the 20th Century. The year was 1900.

In February 1900, another river pioneer, Joseph Korbel, died in San Francisco at the age of 56. Joseph was 30 years old when he first arrived in the Russian River woods with his brothers.

A young man in partnership with Miller bought Dave Connell's livery from him. The young man was Robert Noel Tunstall. "Noel," as he was known, later became the town's first auto gas station owner, the town's last stage coach operator, and eventually the town's second undertaker. Connell still had his stage that ran from Guerneville to the Coast.[54]

It was the end of May. Frank Montecelli and Charlie Walls were out in the woods when they made a grisly find up Mission Canyon, north of Guernewood Park. Some brush had been laid over a body in advanced stages of decomposition. When the branches were pulled away, the men saw a badly mutilated face and a bashed-in head. The remains were brought to Guerneville and identified as those of one Joe Loccatelli, also known as "Black Joe."[55] About ten days before the discovery of his body, Black Joe and his partner, Joe Boverio, left Guerneville to cut tan bark, their usual occupation. From that time until the discovery, neither man had been seen. Since they had quarreled before their departure, "the finger of suspicion rested upon him," Joe Boverio.

A coroner's inquest was held, and the verdict of the jury formally charged Boverio with murder. The jury found,

"... that the murder was committed under circumstances pointing to Joseph Bovaria [sic] as the murderer, and, further, that the deed was done by a blunt instrument in the hands of Bovaria."[56]

After the verdict of the coroner's jury, Sheriff Grace sent the following warrant to law enforcement officers throughout the County and to Sheriff Taylor in Marin County:

Fifty dollars reward. Wanted for murder. G. Boverio, nickname "Setto Napali." Age fifty-five; height, five feet, seven inches; weight about 150 to 160 pounds; complexion rather light for an Italian; black hair, mustache and chin beard (both hair and beard well sprinkled with gray), a very noticeable old sunken scar or hole below right cheek bone, large glaring eyes, speaks broken English, wore cheap, dark-brown

Raymond Clar Collection

suit, soft black hat, dark colored shirt.[57]

A couple of days later Boverio was picked up in Black Canyon in Marin County and placed in the Sonoma County jail, charged with homicide. Speaking broken English he stoutly denied the charges, saying when he left Mission Canyon Luccatelli was asleep in his cabin. On the contrary, he said Luccatelli was a troublesome man, and to substantiate his declaration showed a scar on the right side of his forehead saying it resulted from a blow he received from the dead man two months previously.

Blood was found on Boverio's clothing at the jail, and the clothing was taken as evidence.

Jury trial was held five months later on October 11 in Superior Court No. 2, the Honorable Judge A.G. Burnett presiding. On October 13, the jury returned a verdict of guilty of second degree murder. On November 2, 1900, Boverio was sentenced to San Quentin for a term of 12 years.[58]

While Boverio was dealing with his problem, the River people were getting ready for "Tourist Season 1900." The dam was put in by mid-June. Promptly thereafter campers arrived, dotting the banks from Guerneville to the dam with their tents. However, the most popular place was Guernewood Park and its dance platform.

In mid-July, a dance was held. Music was provided by the Hawaiian Septette Club Orchestra of San Francisco. Several hundred guests "danced their shoes off."

To facilitate enjoyment of the River, Willard Bagley at Guerneville ran the boat and bath house concession.

The summer passed without a water carnival. Little was recorded in the public press about this summer or succeeding ones.

In 1903 the California Northwestern Railroad had a travel brochure published, called "Vacation 1903." The booklet described areas north of San Francisco for tourist, vacationer and visitor alike. The Guerneville River Area was represented with 24 resorts and summer boarding houses. The industry was now established quite firmly.

1. *Son. Demo.,* February 8, 1896, p. 5; Sup. Ct. Case #4114.
2. Sup. Ct. Case #4463.
3. *Son. Demo.,* July 11, 1896.
4. *Ibid.,* August 22, 1896.
5. *Ibid.*
6. *Ibid.,* September 26, 1896, p. 1; October 24, 1896.
7. *Ibid.,* November 14, 1896.
8. *Ibid.,* November 14 and 28, 1896; Bd. Supvrs. Minutes, Book 12, p. 147.
9. *Son. Demo.,* December 5, 1896.
10. *Ibid.,* February 13, 1897; March 30, 1897.
11. *Ibid.,* April 4, 1896.
12. *Ibid,* April 17, 1897.
13. *Ibid.,* April 17, 1897; May 8, 1897.
14. *Ibid.,* July 10, 1897.
15. *Ibid.,* June 26,. 1897.
16. *Ibid.,* July 17, 1897.

Tunstall's Livery on the right, looking southeast, at the intersection of Mines Road and Main Street, 1899. Engine #7 is coming into town. Note the facade on the Livery, which collapsed in the 1906 earthquake (next chapter), JCS Collection.

17. *Ibid.*

18. *Ibid.,* July 27, 1897.

19. *Ibid.,* August 14, 1897.

20. *Ibid.,* October 9, 1897; Articles of Incorporation, #467, Sonoma County Clerk's Office.

21. *Son. Demo.,* December 29, 1897.

22. *Ibid.,* January 5, 1898.

23. *Guerneville X-Rays,* September 24, 189_.

24. *Press Demo.,* June 25 and June 29, 1898; *Guerneville X-Rays,* February 11, 1899.

25. *Press Demo.,* June 29, 1898.

26. *Ibid.; Press Demo.,* July 2 and July 15, 1898.

27. *Press Demo.,* July 23, 1898.

28. *Ibid.,* August 17, 1898.

29. *Ibid.,* September 10 and September 14, 1898.

30. *Ibid.,* September 17 and September 19, 1898.

31. *Ibid.,* January 21, 1899.

32. *Ibid.,* February 2, 1899.

33. *Guerneville X-Rays,* February 11, 1899.

34. *Press Demo.,* November 11, 1899.

35. *Ibid.,* March 12, 1898.

36. *Ibid.,* May 21, 1898; Original application to Bd. of Supvrs., no number, dated March 24, 1898.

37. *Press Demo.,* July 12, 1898, p. 3.

38. *Ibid.*

39. *Ibid.,* July 23, 1898; August 17, 1898.

40. *Ibid.,* October 1, 1898.

41. *Ibid.,* p. 4.

42. *Ibid.,* October 12, 1898, p. 3.

43. *Ibid.,* October 8, 1898, p. 4.

44. *Ibid.,* October 5, 1898, p. 1.

45. *Ibid.*, October 5, 1898, p. 6.
46. *Ibid.*, January 14, 1899.
47. *Ibid.*, March 1, 1899.
48. *Ibid.*, May 17, 1899.
49. *Ibid.*, July 1 and July 5, 1899.
50. *Ibid.*, July 15 and July 22, 1899.
51. *Ibid.*, July 19, 1899.
52. *Ibid.*, July 2, 1899.
53. *Ibid.*, October 25, 1899.
54. *Ibid.*, May 13, 1899; June 17, 1899; December 9 and December 30, 1899.
55. *Ibid.*, April 18, 1900.
56. *Ibid.*, May 30, 1900.
57. *Ibid.*, June 2, 1900.
58. *Ibid.*
59. Sup. Ct. Case #206-C.

The town water wagon in front of Noel Tunstall's Livery, 1900. Alta Starrett Lutrell Collection

Damage from the 1906 quake on the west end of Tunstall's Livery, across the street from Rochdale Store. Far right: R.N. Tunstall; far left, Benjamin F. Miller, Tunstall's partner and town constable. JCS Collection

Repairing earthquake damage to the north side of the Odd Fellows building. JCS Collection

Chapter 33

EARTHQUAKE

Wednesday morning, mid-April, 1906. Just as witnesses to a crime see the scene differently, so did the following people as youngsters experience the 1906 earthquake along the River and in its communities.

Ethel (Snow) Carrier: "Our house just shook sideways with a twisting motion."[1]

George Clar: "Me and Clarence (his middle brother) were in this house (Clar Ranch) when it shook. We giggled and said it was just like riding a train."[2]

Andy Strode: "My grandmother packed me out of the house."[3]

And his sister Clara (Strode): "My mother yanked me out of bed. Walter (an older brother) was sleeping under the fireplace mantle and the clock fell off and hit him on the nose."[4]

Harold "Cap" Trine: "I was 10 at the time. I wasn't awake when the quake hit. I thought mom was getting awfully rough with me in bed trying to wake me."[5]

After the initial shock Margaret (Cole) Drake said, "We all congregated in the field in the middle of town."[6]

The after shocks were a problem.

Ina (Ellison) Stephenson: "We were so scared to stay in our house because of the ceilings and chimneys coming down that we stayed in the railroad coaches."[7]

Emergency shelter, food and medicine needed by "outside" cities — Santa Rosa, San Francisco — were not required by the River population.

Laura (Ayers) Birkhofer: "There were no hardships at that time plenty of food, water, everything."[8]

Gladys (Bagley) Goslin: "Dad (Herbert L. Bagley) wouldn't let anybody have more than one of anything in the Rochdale store (where he was manager) to prevent hoarding."[9]

Gertrude (Lauteren) Schulte: "They had a box car for a general store. We weren't allowed to burn in fireplaces or stoves because they weren't inspected (for flaws)."[10]

Laura Birkhofer (who was 17 at the time): "Reason no buildings were burned was no morning breakfast fires were started."[11]

Around the countryside, it was the little things the youngsters remember occurring at that moment.

Laura again: "At home only the clock fell off the shelf and Dad repaired it. Damage to belongings not very much."[12]

Robert Ridenhour: "We had a dug-cellar with shelves all around it. All the canned fruit on them fell in the center all broken."[13]

George Clar again: "We had a smoke house up behind here with milk pans set out on it and all the milk shook out."[14]

The older people remember the unusual events that took place during aftershocks.

Keith Neeley (then twenty years old): "Never felt an earthquake before. My father had planted some cherry trees out in our fields. I went outside and saw the trees almost bend over and touch the ground. Down on Neeley Beach (East Guernewood) it appeared that the ground opened up and came together and squirted water up. The river rose slowly about two feet and turned muddy."[15]

A young man then, Charlie Bean said, "The stumps were shaking in Laughlin's field back and forth. The water in Livreau Creek was slopping out."[16]

March 1906 view of the intersection of 1st Street (on the left) and Armstrong Road (to the right). The Guerneville Bridge lies behind the viewer; the two story brick building in center is Odd Fellows. The sin-

Though these eyewitness accounts are interesting and informative, they do not reveal the serious damage to buildings and the deaths that occurred.

Jesse (Turner) Woodcock wrote about her experiences:

> Dad had been busy every night after work excavating the basement beneath our home in Guerneville planning to start an ice cream parlor which was to be named "The Forest Ice Cream Parlor."
>
> He had been removing the underpinnings and replacing them with thin redwood trees with bark and small branches to effect the forest idea. He was about halfway through the project.
>
> On the morning of April 18, 1906, around five o'clock, the house began to shake and to tip sideways. The furniture shifted and a bureau fell on my brother's foot breaking his toes.
>
> We thought Dad had not secured the tree posts securely until the neighbors came running and told us it was an earthquake. The house was at such an angle that it might go over any minute.
>
> When we went outside, there was a wide crack down the length of the street. People had congregated in groups, afraid to go back into their homes.
>
> We had a pile of lumber, for the ice cream parlor project, in the street on which we slept for a few nights until the house was safe to enter. We ate picnic style in the street, no cooked foods, as the chimneys on most homes were down.
>
> Then, we heard about San Francisco and Santa Rosa and soon the sky was filled with red smoke as these two cities were burning. The weather was unusually warm night and day.
>
> The refugees from San Francisco were being brought to towns north and our house being made safe again, Dad decided to take in some of them, a woman, her two teenage daughters and four canaries. Mother was upset, as we were poor and she was not well, but we managed for a week.
>
> We four children (I was 10 years old), were glad when they left as they didn't take the canaries with them and we had a big time caring for them as we had never seen canaries before.
>
> "However, the Forest Ice Cream Parlor flourished for two years."[17]

The only all-brick buildings along the River were the brick kilns at Hilton, Korbel Winery, and in Guerneville. In the latter were the City Livery, the so-called Drake Block and the two-story Odd Fellows' building. Nothing is

gle-story building to its right housed the Bank of Guerneville and the Rochdale Store. Building at far right is Tunstall's Livery Stables. The vacant lot at left foreground is the result of a fire on 12 March 1906. JCS Collection

known about what happened to the kilns, if anything. At Korbel's, damage was limited to the brandy tower with cracked walls.[18]

Local newspaper, The Russian River Advertiser, reported:

> Outside of the wrecking of the Odd Fellows' building, the livery stables and other brick buildings on Main Street, the only damage in Guerneville consisted of the toppling over of nearly all the brick chimneys. The wooden buildings experienced very little damage with the exception of the old Pippin place on Second Street, occupied by Roadmaster Duncan and family. The foundations of the main building on the east end and those on the west end of the kitchen collapsed, dropping both ends about two feet to the ground and severing the building in two. The front awning and porch are detached from the house and wrecked. Throughout the whole fearful moment of shock, the family remained in bed, quietly awaiting whatever should be their fate.[19]

Some people react to life-threatening situations by laughing, others by crying. Some people panic. On the day of the quake, Rudolph Brown, cigarmaker for Dave Hetzel, left town without telling anyone — just plain disappeared. He reappeared four months later in mid-August and went back to work just like nothing had happened.[20]

The Odd Fellows' building had extensive wreckage to its second floor; the first floor damage was light in comparison. The single story Drake Block that extended to the east of Odd Fellows suffered the same extent of damage as the Odd Fellows' second floor.

Why the Odd Fellows' first floor was spared is unknown. It may have been because there was no roof over it. The same kind of damage occurred to Drake's single story block as to the second floor — they both had roofs. Or, the first floor was spared because the weight of the second story bore down and locked the lower bricks in place.

While there was damage and no fire in town, there was always the chance someone might loot or a fire (accidental or otherwise) would occur. A citizens' patrol was instituted for three weeks to prevent such happenings. It was then eliminated and Frank Harrington was selected as night watchman to guard the village.[21]

Odd Fellows' building before and after. Above: South side of Odd Fellows along 1st St. prior to the quake; standing in front of Omer O. Cobb's store re (left to right) unknown woman, Len Starett, Gertrude Shulte, unknown man, and Omer Cobb. Man on wagon is Ed "Cap" McPeak. Alta Lutrell Collection. Left: Postcard received by Amy Bagley Hatch showing the rebuilding effort. JCS Collection

The rebuilding of the brick stores and hall would take several months. The first carload of bricks arrived May 18 and work commenced the following week. The weakened sections of the walls were removed and the rest allowed to remain. The old brick was culled, cleaned and stacked for reuse. Lime was brought in also for cementing the bricks and kept in Omer Cobb's store on the first floor of Odd Fellows.[22]

Frank Harrington was put to the test on a Thursday night in May when a heavy rainstorm hit Sonoma County. The roof on Odd Fellows was still in need of repair and let the leaking water prematurely slake the lime. Harrington noticed the lime because of its sizzling and smoking so he fired his revolver for aid. Frank Perry came to his assistance and helped move the lime to a dry location. This action saved a delay of weeks in reconstruction.[23]

By June 9, the damaged walls had been torn down and the brick masons proceeded to repair. The north and west walls were completed at the end of the month. By the second of July the IOOF building was complete. The interior was cleaned and new carpet was

Quake inspection certificate. JCS Collection

Damage to the Rochdale Store's east wall, facing today's Armstrong Woods Road, next to the Odd Fellows Building. JCS Collection

installed in the fraternal hall on the second floor.[24]

The masons started work on the Drake Block, which was actually an adjoining brick structure to the east. The east wall facing Cinnabar Avenue was rebuilt from the ground up.[25]

A new civic improvement arrived with the reconstruction — a cement sidewalk! It was located in front of Drake's Block on First Street. This was probably welcomed by the youngsters about town with much regret — no longer would they be able to fish for coins dropped between the boards of the wooden sidewalk along that section. But there were other boardwalks.[26]

In September, the merchants returned to their old locations on the first floor at Odd Fellows and Drakes: Dave Hetzel's tobacco shop; O.O. Cobb's The Guerneville Department Store; Rochdale Store, Herbert Bagley, mgr.; Guerneville Drug Store; Bank of Guerneville, J.P. Overton, pres.; and the Capitol Saloon.[27]

Repairs were made at various residences to correct the toppled or cracked chimneys. The county chimney inspector, J.D. Connolly, was a busy fellow. He had to inspect all flues and chimneys in the whole fifth supervisorial district. He inspected the Guerneville area in the month of May.[28]

During the violent earth shaking, the cities were visited by death. Yet Guerneville and most of the River communities were not among them. But death did make its presence known.

At the quicksilver mine, three miles from town, three miners were riding the skip up the main shaft when the temblor hit. A large rock was shaken loose from a cliff about 30 feet to the east of the head rig. The boulder, a little smaller than the shaft, fell down the opening.[29]

The men, some 400 feet in the dark below, must have heard their death coming down, rattling against the skip's hoist cable and bouncing off the sides of the shaft. At 360 feet the rock crushed the three men. They were: George G. Hanson, age 37, Guerneville, native of Missouri, left a wife; Robert Gorsky, age 16, native of Hulbert Canyon (Guernewood), left a widowed father; and Frederick Miller, Healdsburg, left a family.[30]

When Foreman Frank Rosa and three men descended in a bucket to rescue the miners, a grisly sight greeted them. They sent up the remains of their friends.

For a while the mine continued operating, working around the plugged shaft. It was eventually cleared, but the price of mercury was dropping and eventually the mine shut down until World War I increased the demand and the mine reopened.[31]

At Duncans' Mills, the two-story El Bonito Hotel was thrown down by the quake. Since the hotel was near the train tracks, a locomotive was used to pull the wreckage apart to aid rescuers. Beneath the mass of splintered redwood and fir, Mrs. Lucille Morse and Otto Nacker were found dead.[32]

Only one local resident was killed elsewhere of the many in Santa Rosa and the Bay Area. Marshall Florence Thrasher, 15, was attending Sweet's Business College in Santa Rosa. He was staying at the Eagle Hotel when the earth shook. He apparently was trying to escape from the hotel when he was struck by falling timbers near the exit door and crushed. His body was recovered by his father and returned to Guerneville, his place of birth, for burial.[33]

1. Ethel (Snow) Carrier, interview, October 21, 1978, Guerneville.
2. George Clar, interview, July 11, 1976, Guerneville.
3. Andrew Strode, interview, August 8, 1976, Guerneville.
4. Clara Strode, interview, August 8, 1976, Guerneville.
5. Harold Trine, interview, August 29, 1978, Santa Rosa.
6. Margaret Drake, interview, October 25, 1967, Guerneville.
7. Ina Stephenson, interview, March 14, 1967, Santa Rosa.
8. Laura (Ayers) Birkhofer, interview, August 6, 1983, Sebastopol.
9. Gladys (Bagley) Goslin, interview, February 12, 1967, Healdsburg.
10. Gertrude (Joost) Schulte, interview, May 7, 1961, Guerneville.
11. Laura Birkhofer, op. cit.
12. Ibid.
13. Robert Ridenhour, interview, March 5, 1967, Hilton.
14. George Clar, op. cit.
15. Keith Neeley, interview, March 4, 1967, Guerneville.
16. Charlie Bean, interview, November 11, 1966, Guerneville.
17. Eureka Times Standard, April 20, 1979, Eureka, Calif.
18. A. Nelson, interview, May 22, 1984, Guerneville.
19. Russ. Riv. Adv., April 21, 1906, Guerneville.
20. Op. cit., August 24, 1906.
21. Op. cit., May 5, 1906
22. Op. cit., May 19, 1906
23. Op. cit. May 26, 1906
24. Op. cit., June 9 & 23, 1906
25. Op. cit., July 21 & October 20, 1906
26. Op. cit., August 18, 1906
27. Op. cit., September 8, 1906
28. Certificate dated & signed May 16, 1906, J.D. Connolly.
29. Russ. Riv. Adv., April 21, 1906
30. Ibid.
31. Keith Neeley, op. cit.
32. Russ. Riv. Adv., April 21, 1906
33. Ibid., April 21, 1906

Interior of the Rochdale Store as it looked before the earthquake. The man second fom the right is Herbert L. Bagley. JCS Collection.

Col. James B. Armstrong. California State Parks Collection

Chapter 34

ARMSTRONG PARK

Guerneville, during the first great boom of redwood lumbering (1870-1910), was second only to Eureka in production. As many as twelve mills in a five-mile radius around this town were sawing logs at the same time. It wasn't until the mid-1880's that this industry slowly realized virgin timber stands were finite.

Some mill owners were not totally averse to preserving some trees for posterity. George Guerne, mill owner (and town's namesake) made a serious attempt to set aside 15 acres of redwoods to be given to an interested government agency. No action was taken by Sonoma County or the State to acquire the land, so he had it logged off. The site is today's Guernewood Park, one mile below Guerneville on the right bank of the river. All timber there now is second growth.[1]

Another mill and timber owner in the area was Colonel James Boydston Armstrong. He bought acreage during the 1870's and in 1886 he set aside 50 acres for a park at the headwaters of Fife Creek north of Guerneville.[2]

There are suspicions as to why this 50 acres was reserved and later neighboring acres. Logging was done in the area by one of the Armstrong's managers, John French.

There was a sled road and a semi-permanent camp in the immediate area. French, also a local mill owner, logged this stumpage for him in 1883.[3] As the timber was being removed in the bottom lands and hillsides, trees showed rot in their centers.

M.C. Meeker, lumberman for 40 years in Sonoma County, was quoted saying:

> Armstrong lumbered part of his grove up to the flats, stopped. Why? Found timber on Flat rotten centered and unfit for lumber.[4]

Another man, Harold "Cap" Trine, unemployment camp foreman for the California Department of Forestry during the 1930's at Armstrong Grove, said:

> Colonel Armstrong said he was leaving the best timber for the people. But I could see that they were prospecting to see what it was like and it was all poor-rotten. That's why you see stumps in the park.[5]

In the History of Sonoma County of 1889, it was noted the grove would " . . . be the last remnant of a mighty forest before ten years."[6] How prophetic! Only one other grove of the old forest exists — Bohemian Grove — and it's under private ownership today.

J.B. Armstrong was fairly successful as a mill owner, but his other financial endeavors failed. In 1890 a banking and trust company folded and practically ruined him. To meet obligations he sold nearly all of his real estate to satisfy judgment for $11,174.[7] One item he sold was his Big Bottom Mill north of Guerneville. It was torn down and the machinery shipped to Fresno.[8] This was in the Fall of 1891. He still maintained ownership of the grove, though.

In June of '91, Armstrong made a proposal to create "a natural park and botanic garden" of 600 acres.[9] A foundation was proposed with a board of trustees to basically give the grove to the State of California. The board was composed of:

Miss Kate Armstrong – his daughter
Luther Burbank – horticulturist
E.J. Wickson – University of California professor
C. Howard Shinn – editor of Overland Monthly
Robert U. Johnson – assistant editor of Century Magazine

This last appointment was most notable at that time. Johnson was chosen for the "plucky manner" in the way he carried his part of the

Postcard of Armstrong Grove, 1919. JCS Collection

fight to secure the preservation of Yosemite and Sequoia parks.[10]

Armstrong's legal advisor said that for the state to accept the gift of the grove, a special act would have to be approved by the state legislature. No such act came to pass.

During these years, and later, the public was welcomed to use, and use they did, the grove for recreation and picnics. The status of the grove remained the same — private ownership.

On October 15, 1900, the Colonel died in his home after many strokes severely paralyzed him. His death left a question of what would happen to his estate, specifically the grove.

Lizzie Armstrong, his second daughter, by now had married Parson William L. Jones. Daughter Kate passed away at age 42, in 1898. His only son, Walter, survived him. Apparently Walter owed his father a substantial sum of money; the Colonel stated in his will he would dismiss all debts owed him by his son if Walter did not contest the will. The only property left Walter was 300 acres in Clay County, Illinois.[11]

James Armstrong also provided in his will that if the botanical garden was not created the grove would revert to his daughters as their sole and private property. Walter did not contest the will and since Kate died in 1898, Lizzie became sole owner of approximately 750 acres.

Some four years passed. Then a bizarre event occurred: Lizzie Jones sold an undivided half interest in the grove property to brother Walter and wife Nellie for $10 in gold coin.[12]

No reason for such a transaction has been found.

In 1908 another person entered this story — Harrison M. LeBaron of Valley Ford. He was a board member of the Dairymen's Bank of Valley Ford and a former assemblyman (1898-1900) to Sacramento. In July of that year Walter Armstrong sold his share to LeBaron. Within a short period of time LeBaron began some steps toward making the grove a preserve.

John McKenzie, in his paper on Colonel Armstrong, wrote:[13]

[Mr. LeBaron thought] the grove should be saved and began laying his plans. He joined forces with Mrs. Lizzie Armstrong Jones, the Colonel's daughter and on December 14, 1908 the plan was set down in a formal "Memorandum of Agreement." It was their plan to offer the entire 440 acres to the state in a bill before the State Legislature. To do this they were able to enlist the willing aid of State Senator Walter F. Price.

If the state would not accept the proposed park as a gift possibly the owner(s) could convince the state to purchase the trees. Price, State Senator from Santa Rosa, introduced Senate Bill No. 22 on January 8, 1909, an act to purchase the grove for park purposes appropriating $125,000. The bill was sent to the printers, then to the Finance Committee, on to Buildings and Grounds Committee, back to Finance, re-read to the Senate and amended to make the funds $100,000. By February 16, the act was finally passed by both houses and sent to the governor.[14]

During the bill's preparation, Senator Price (on February 7), arranged a junket of five senators and ten assemblymen to the grove to view and see what public value it had.[15] Apparently the trip worked. To quote Ray Clar in his *California Government and Forestry*:

> Their enthusiastic support caused the assembly to pass Senate Bill No. 22 unanimously on March 19. On February 23 it had been sent to them by the Senate. That house had passed it by a vote of 22 to 3 . . .
>
> Governor Gillett made no recorded statement about the Armstrong Woods State Park bill which had been transmitted to him with such obvious legislative favor. By April 28 the bill died in his pocket.[16]

It was the second setback for the grove advocates.

On May 19, 1913, Harrison LeBaron died. He had signed a will on May 29, 1908, two months before he bought the property from Walter Armstrong, six months before the drafting of the "Memorandum of Agreement." He requested his offspring to form the LeBaron Estate Company. He did not mention having any real estate as being part of Armstrong Grove and there was no codicil to the will.[17]

His six sons formed The LeBaron Estate Corporation to handle their father's bequest. They joined Lizzie Jones to try a new attack: have any governmental body — county, state, federal — purchase the land.

As witnessed above, the first approach was just to give the grove to California; the second was to convince the state to purchase it. This new method slowly developed over a period of years without much forethought.

Six years had passed since the Price Bill

The site of the future Armstrong Park is Section 18, at the top of the map. Thompson Atlas 1877

Portraits of the Armstrong daughters done in Ohio before family moved west. J.L. Williams, an unlisted itinerant painter painted Kate; John Frankenstein, whose works are in the National Collection, painted Lizzie. Private Collection.

was pocket vetoed. The public and various government agencies still did not know the trees had center-rot. Granted, if the redwoods were felled they would produce some lumber and split-stuff, i.e., shooks, shakes, posts, stakes, but not enough to make a great profit for the parties involved.

In July 1915, the *Santa Rosa Republican* headlined a column: "SONOMA'S BIG REDWOOD TREES SEEM DOOMED." It stated the LeBarons were "planning to cut the magnificent trees for railroad ties."[18] If anything would make Sonoma County rally to save the redwoods this had to be it. But the public had to be motivated.

For a year the situation didn't change: the threat of the ax hung in the air. The LeBarons and Lizzie Jones offered the Reyes Lumber Company an option on the timber.

In August, 1916, a new plan was advanced: purchase 60 acres of the grove where the largest trees stood — the "Circle," "The Encampment," "Colonel Armstrong," and "Parson Jones." This property was offered for $12,000, and would be held for the county while the rest of the timber was being cut.[19]

To raise the money a group of prominent men would ask the county at large for pledges. While that was going on Reyes Company would cut away saving the 60 acres for last.

This would be valid only if the public showed a definite interest within a reasonable length of time. If not, the trees would come down.[20]

The now ex-Senator Price read about the plan in the papers and suggested another way to raise funds — circulate an initiative petition for the proposition of a special tax.[21]

At this same time Guerneville voters were going to sign a petition to bond the county for $80,000 to purchase the entire grove.[22]

On August 14, another problem arose for the conservationists. One of the owners was Everell LeBaron, a minor. Master LeBaron's interest in his father's property was being presented in Superior Court. Would it be to the minor's benefit to sell Armstrong Grove or not?

Parson (Rev. W.L.) Jones and Lizzie Armstrong Jones on March 20, 1901, at the time of their marriage. State Parks Collection

Two days later, an alarmed Sonoma County Development Board, a committee of the Board of Supervisors, met in Santa Rosa. The opening statement to the board was made by M.J. LeBaron. He delivered an ultimatum "that either the whole grove must be saved or entirely lost forever.[23] LeBaron stated the price of the grove was $80,000, some $20,000 less than the year before.

The board promptly formed a committee of Sonoma County community leaders to plot a course of action:[24]

George P. McNear, Petaluma Merchant

Glenn Murdock, president of Santa Rosa Bank and Santa Rosa Chamber of Commerce

H.H. Elliot, president of Taxpayers' League

O.O. Cobb, merchant and president of Guerneville Chamber of Commerce

Mrs. John Thorpe, secretary of North Bay Counties Association, Guerneville

E.E. Deen, postmaster and president of Petaluma Chamber of Commerce

G.W. Hayes, president of Healdsburg Chamber of Commerce

Fred J. Duhring, president of Sonoma Chamber of Commerce

John P. Overton, banker and president of the Agricultural Association

Clarence F. Lea, District Attorney and later Congressman

Charles B. Shaw, president of Cloverdale Bank

D.L. Westover, Guerneville lumberman

Arthur B. Swain, banker and president of Sebastopol Chamber of Commerce

Peter Hansen, Sonoma County Grange

The Armstrong Grove Preservation Committee promptly elected John Overton chairman, D.L. Westover vice-chairman, Arthur Swain secretary, and Glenn Murdock treasurer.[25]

The news of the potential destruction of the grove traveled beyond the county; letters were received at the newspapers in support of purchase. The Northwestern Pacific Railroad donated $25 to help financially. To finance the campaign photographs, paintings of the grove and the like were sold. Monetary pledges were asked for.

Attorney Rolph Thompson drew up an initiative petition to have a proposition put on the general election ballot in November. These

Armstrong Woods postcard. JCS Collection

petitions were spread throughout the county. Petaluma alone secured 700 signatures in 10 days.[26]

On September 29, the *Santa Rosa Republican* reported: "Congressman Kent Endorses Armstrong Woods Campaign."

Kent wrote:

> Gentlemen: Yours of September 21, 1916, duly received. I believe that it would be the most shortsighted folly possible to destroy the Armstrong Woods. They are worth much more standing than cut, even if the matter be considered as a money making scheme.[27]

Lumbermen had estimated that it would take three years to clear off the land and allowing for all costs, the grove would yield a profit of $250,000 in three years.

The petitions made the rounds of the county and were called back by the committee. The signatures were counted; then the petitions were presented to the Board of Supervisors. The names totaled 2,432, enough to make the supervisors place the proposition on the November 7 ballot of 1916.[28]

HELP SAVE Armstrong Woods

Subscribe to the Preservation Fund, or Purchase Pictures of the Woods.

Give your active loyal support to this most worthy cause.

ARMSTRONG WOODS PRESERVATION LEAGUE
Santa Rosa Bank Building, Santa Rosa, Cal.

Vote "YES," Armstrong Woods Proposition, November 7, 1916

Campaign ad from the Santa Rosa Press Democrat, September 9, 1916.

Four weeks were left for the supporters to issue statements to the papers, knock on doors, and spread the word.

Another two weeks passed. On Halloween Day a 12-car cavalcade left Guerneville to tour the central part of the county. They went to Healdsburg, where more cars joined the parade to Santa Rosa. At the county seat more joined the procession. Members of the Guerneville band took instruments and played lively music at each stop. In Santa Rosa bugles blared and horns honked from cars covered in bunting and redwood boughs. The newspapers were visited where advertisements and posters were ordered.[29]

Sebastopol was next on the agenda; then, after a tour of town back through Santa Rosa and on to Sonoma and Petaluma. The day was rounded out by returning to Santa Rosa and heading home via Forestville.

Because of the apparent success of the motorcade of some 60 people, another was planned two days later. The second "wagon train" went further north via Windsor and Healdsburg on to Geyserville and Cloverdale. Supporters of the proposition were found wherever the travelers went.[30]

On the third of November an all-out assault on the public's conscience was made via the newspapers. An eight-page supplement was printed and inserted in the two major Santa Rosa papers, the Republican and Press Democrat, for the Friday, November 3, 1916, issues. The supplement played on nearly every human emotion:
  — don't be an outsider, join the leaders of our county
    — it's a cheap buy
    — believe our facts
    — it's a noble cause
    — the groves were God's first temples

It was the last card the advocates would play; all they could do was wait for November 7 and the election. Was this another attempt that was going to fail? This would be the fourth try to create a park. If their efforts were for naught they could resort to chaining themselves to the trees.

The election came to pass. The ballots were counted. The county total showed 11,693 votes in favor of the proposition, 6,379 against. The Supervisors were given the mandate.[31]

A notice of intention to purchase the grove was printed in the *Press Democrat* as a public notice by the Board of Supervisors to give the private citizens one last opportunity to have their say. This last chance was February 15, 1917. At least three resolutions were submitted to the board in support of purchase.[32]

In order to find out exactly what the county was purchasing, supervisors asked that "a

Edward O. Pells, who in 1917 was made the second caretaker of Armstrong County Park (later Armstrong State Park.) C. Raymond Clar Collection.

competent disinterested cruiser be appointed to cruise said Armstrong Woods" and report to them before February 15.[33]

The person nominated and approved to cruise was Enoch Percy French of Humboldt County. The motion was made by Supervisor Charles.[34] Now Enoch French was the son of John French and had been born on "the hill" in Guerneville (in a house still occupied at the time of this writing). John was previously mentioned as a logging foreman for Colonel Armstrong at the grove.

Question: Was Enoch really a disinterested cruiser considering his early days connections with Guerneville?

Question: How was his name brought up by Supervisor Charles (was there a connection between them)?

Question: At the time of appointment Enoch was a resident of long duration in Eureka, Humboldt County. Why request a "disinterested cruiser" from so great a distance?

I am not satisfied there was just coincidence having Enoch appointed cruiser, but no further evidence is available to the contrary.

E. French made his cruise report and mailed it to the Supervisors. No formal notice was made of its receipt but one map and a three-page report are in County Clerk's possession.

A second map was filed in the clerk's office on February 17, 1917.[35] It is a rather mediocre chart with none of the professional notes or signature of cartographer. This map presents Walter Armstrong's name on it.

Back to Enoch French. He wrote in his report to the supervisors:

> There is about 59 acres of Bottom Redwood timber, running small to large tall fine quality, has fine tops with very few spike or broken tops and final buts [sic] very few goose pens, but shows a great deal of spot rot in both small and large trees.
>
> About 135 acres of hill Redwood runs small to large, medium length, fine quality, with lots of spot rot and is a light stand on hills, fair in gulches.[36]

Two paragraphs later he states:

> There has been a great many of the large Redwood trees cut made into split lumber, and removed, from the bottom land.

Another two paragraphs further:

> All the Tan Bark has been cut, peeled, and re-

The Parson Jones Tree, circa 1910. Burton Travis collection.

moved from this land some years ago.

In September, 1980, this writer took a count of old redwood stumps in a rough triangle area formed by the roads between Parson Jones Tree and Burbank Circle. The total is approximately 51. There are other numerous redwood stumps outside this triangle in the park.

Some two months passed. On March 16, 1917, the supervisors voted to purchase the grove from the LeBarons and Lizzie A. Jones for $80,000, while the two parties agreed to donate $5,000 each.[37] Regardless of French's cruise report, the reputation of Armstrong Grove was great enough to overcome any factual detraction of it.

To insure and protect their potential acquisition the supervisors on July 1 appointed Robert S. Coon as caretaker of the grove at a salary of $60 per month.[38]

The "rotten" grove officially changed ownership on December 5, 1918.[39]

Robert Coon left for World War I and in his place for the duration of the war was Ed Pells of Guerneville. Coon returned and took charge again.

It was during the Depression of the 1930's when some major changes and additions were made to the grove.

The California Division of Forestry received permission in July 1933 to establish a reforestation camp and an assistant ranger station. In December they were granted permission to build offices, a garage, and fire crew house in the park lands.[40]

This apparently was all in preparation for the state to acquire the park in 1934, for on January 8 that year the Sonoma County Board of Supervisors voted to deed the grove to the state. As we all know, the state does not move swiftly. It was finally accepted by California on April 8, 1934.[41]

The state, like the federal government, had various programs to keep people working during those trying years and help build the country's economy. Harold "Cap" Trine was working for the California State Forestry at this time.

Bill Kenyon, Henry Brown, and "Cap", all of Guerneville, had an idea to make the park more attractive to the public — a forest theatre. In Cap's words:[42]

> We got some big shots [from Guerneville] up there but they didn't see it. I cleaned up the brush, leaves, and stuff and hid it under the brush around on the slopes. After I cleaned it up some University of California professors, about four, six from the Guerneville Chamber of Commerce, and two from the Division of Forestry, (they were notified of the meeting), came up. A professor stood where the stage is now and spoke to the rest at the back. It went over big and the theatre was built.

But other work had priority.[43] The first construction undertaken (probably 1933) was the crew house and garage located at the north end and to the right (east) of the picnic grounds.

The second to go up was the park administration building, a log cabin/lodge-like structure at the south boundary of the park.

At nearly the same time formal work was creating the Forest Theatre. This was during 1934 to 1936.

The plans for the lodge came from Sacramento. Nobody asked for them, they were just sent. The redwood logs for the lodge were brought from Guernewood Park Resort alongside Russian River. The money to buy the logs was put up by the Guerneville Chamber of Commerce and the Work Projects Administration (WPA).

Trine (from state forestry) was projects foreman over the WPA crew. He blazed the trees in Guernewood, the crew felled them, and they were hauled to the state park.

It was through state park superintendent Robert Coon that the forestry got a small mill to help with the work. This operation was put up near the Parson Jones Tree and was used to cut off two sides of the logs so there would be a snug fit on the walls.

The roof trusses were built on the ground and were lifted into place on the building by a gin-pole.

At the same time, the Forest Theatre was being formed. The logs that were too big for use on the administration building were used as seats, laid in rows. At the stage other large logs were cut six feet long and placed on end to hold up the front end of the stage. The lumber for the stage floor was cut on the small mill.

There were two small buildings on the slopes, left and right, behind the trees and to the rear of the stage. The left one was the power transformer for stage lighting. The house to the right was the dressing room. The labor for these projects was provided by a whole alphabet of bureaucratic agencies: C.W.A., G.R.A., S.E.R.A., W.P.A.

Trine said:

> I never had Civilian Conservation Corps. These were "wino" forestry camps — guys from off Second Street in Sacramento and Third Street in San Francisco. I ran [through] the alphabet.

Every time we changed letters, we closed camp and opened a couple of days later.

Other labor was provided by local people like carpenter George Ayers. The theatre was formally dedicated on a Sunday, September 27, 1936. Some 3,000 people attended.

The last major changes to the park (this does not include the neighboring Austin Creek Recreation Area) were the demolitions. The log administration building at the grove entrance was razed in 1966. Termites and rot made it unsafe for public use. The cabins at the theatre were removed in early 1978. The other change in the theatre was the replacement of the logs as seats with bolted planks on cement piers in 1951.[44]

1. *P.D. [S.R.Rep.]* Letter, February 20, 1909 by G. E. Guerne.
2. *S.D.*, Santa Rosa, November 27, 1886.
3. John French, *Memories of John French*, (1918?).
4. *San Francisco Call*, March 26, 1909, p. 3.
5. Harold "Cap" Trine, interview. Santa Rosa, December 1, 1976.
6. Lewis Co., *History of Sonoma County;* Chicago, Illinois; 1889, p. 190.
7. Sonoma County Recorder's Office, Book of Deeds, Vol. 127, p. 530.
8. *S.D.*, Santa Rosa, October 24, and November 22, 1894.
9. [James B. Armstrong?], *Armstrong's Woods*, Cloverdale Reveille Print, Cloverdale, 1891.
10. Ibid; and S.D., March 26, 1892.
11. John C. McKenzie, *Colonel James B. Armstrong and His Redwood Park.* Cazadero, California, May 11, 1950. MSS p. 16.
12. Sonoma County Clerk's Office, Will #5350, April 10, 1893.
13. Sonoma County Recorder's Office, Book of Deeds, Vol. 219, p. 218.
14. Op. Cit., p. 219.
15. Senate Bill Number 22, 1909.
16. C. Raymond Clar, California Government and Forestry. Sacramento; California State Printing, 1959, pp. 284-86.
17. Sonoma County Clerk's Office, Will #5547.
18. *S.R.Rep.*, June [?], 1915, page [?].
19. *S.R.Rep.*, August 1, 1916, page 3.
20. *P.D.*, August 2, 1916, page 3.
21. *S.R. Rep.*, August 3, 1916, page 8.
22. Op. cit., p. 4.
23. *S.R. Rep.*, August 16, 1916, p. 1.
24. *P.D.*, August 17, 1916, p. 2.
25. *P.D.*, August 19, 1916, p. 5.
26. *P.D.*, September 1 and 20, 1916.
27. *S.R. Rep.*, September 29, 1916, p. 5.
28. *P.D.*, October 7, 1916; *S.R. Rep.*, October 10, 1916, Board of Supervisors Minutes, Vol. 20, October 11, 1916.
29. *P.D.* and *S.R. Rep.*, both October 31, 1916.
30. *P.D.* and *S.R. Rep.*, both November 2, 1916.
31. Board of Supervisors Minutes, Vol. 21, page 5 1/2, 1917.
32. Pomona Grange Taxpayers Assn; Sonoma County Development Assn.
33. Board of Supervisors Minutes, Vol 21, p. 5.
34. Op. cit., p. 6, January 16, 1917. E. French was hired at $10 per day with $4 per day expenses.
35. Map of Walter Armstrong Division, Armstrong Grove; unsigned; undated; blueprint copy, County Clerk's Office.
36. Enoch P. French, Armstrong Grove, 1 page undated cover sheet. Cruise made January 18-26, 1917.
37. Board of Supervisors Minutes, Vol. 21, p. 24.
38. Op. cit., p. 44.
39. County Recorder's Office; Book of Deeds, Vol. 366, p. 167.
40. Ernest Finley, History of Sonoma County, Press Democrat Printing Company, Santa Rosa, 1927, p. 200
41. County Recorder's Office, Book of Deeds, Vol. 361, page 442 and Board of Supervisors Minutes, Vol. 30, p. 270, 1920.
42. Harold "Cap" Trine interview, August 12, 1978, Santa Rosa.
43. Ibid. [Trine~interview]. All statements about construction in the park are from this interview.
44. Derrick Andrews, interview, September 27, 1980.

Postcard of the lodge just after its completion in 1935. In later years it served as park headquarters. JCS Collection

J.W. Bagley in 1902. JCS Collection

JOHN WASHINGTON BAGLEY

Every town, city, and settlement has one individual in its early history who laid down the foundations of the community. Guerneville's keystone, the person who put the pieces of a small scattered society and held them in place, was John Washington Bagley.

John was born near the town of Metz (or Mentz) in Cayuga County, New York, on October 2, 1827. His father was David Bagley of Catham, Middlesex County, Connecticut. His mother, David's second wife, was Louisa Pennoyer of Fishkill, Duchess County, New York. John was the oldest of five siblings of the marriage.

When he was nine, his parents moved to North Adams in southeastern Michigan, where he received his basic education. Sometime later he found work driving horses on the Erie Canal during the summer months.

On May 15, 1848, during the Mexican-American War, 20-year-old John Bagley enlisted in Company G, 2nd Infantry of the U.S. Army for five years. His regiment was ordered to Mexico. He got as far west as Jefferson Barracks, Missouri when the regiment was ordered to New York. The unit sailed for California via Cape Horn on the transport Iowa, arriving in Monterey on April 12, 1849, after a six month voyage. After peace was declared, Bagley spent the remainder of his enlistment at the Benicia Arsenal. He was honorably discharged on May 15, 1853, with the rank of sergeant.

Bagley first went into the lumber mill business in the Moraga redwoods of Contra Costa County, then moved to Sonoma County, locating on Mill Creek. A year or two later he had a planing mill in Healdsburg. During this time he met Ellen A. Downing, a Healdsburg schoolteacher, and they were married on Nov. 14, 1858.

During the squatters troubles, the former Army sergeant joined the Russian River Rifles, Company B, 1st Battalion, 4th Regiment, 2nd Brigade, 1st Division of the California State Militia. During the Civil War, he was the enrolling officer for upper Sonoma County—a dangerous assignment, as the county had a large population of Southern sympathizers. Although enlisted as a sergeant, Bagley was quickly promoted to lieutenant of the Healdsburg Co. and remained so until July 4, 1863. He was then transferred to the 2nd brigade in Petaluma as adjutant, a position he kept until he retired sometime in 1866.

Besides being in the militia (similar to today's reserves), he was roadmaster of Mendocino Township, which comprised all of northern Sonoma County, from early 1862 to late 1863. In 1864 he surveyed the original Dry Creek Rd. out of Healdsburg. In 1865 he also campaigned for the post of Justice of the Peace; alas, the electorate thought otherwise.

The year 1865 was a pivotal one in Bagley's life. He was married, had children, and lived in Healdsburg, where he was a mill owner. At this point he joined William Willets, who had a quarter section of land farther down the Russian River, a tract that possessed the densest stand of redwoods of record. A third party also joined their venture: Thomas Heald, brother of Harmon Heald, the town's name sake.

Bagley and Heald disassembled Bagley's lumber mill and started hauling it down river to Willets' claim to Big Bottom (the first name given to the Guerneville area). Along with a new fourth partner, George Guerne, they literally carved a road in places where only a path existed along the trace. There Bagley reassembled his mill on the east bank of Fife Creek, southwest of today's intersection of Main and Mill Streets in Guerneville.

In 1866 Bagley withdrew from the partnership, but stayed on as a sawyer until 1869. Sawing the first board at the mill in 1865, he also sawed the mill's last cut in 1901. In 1869, after considering how many people were now residing and working in the area, Bagley quit the lumber business and erected Big Bottom's first store, with a meeting hall on the second floor. In 1870 he figured there were now enough people to warrant a post office. He petitioned Washington, D.C., and was granted the job of postmaster of "Guerneville" at $26 per year.

The Bagley store was the de facto city hall. All tax collections were made there, voting polls were conducted there, and the upper hall was used at times as a funeral parlor. Bagley had yet another trade: local sexton. He retrieved the dearly departed, made the coffin, and transported same to the local cemetery — one that he himself plotted out formally in 1876. He retained the dual roles of surveyor and undertaker until his death.

Bagley's reputation as surveyor was well known and was supported in later decades by the courts. He honed his surveying skills during the 1870s, while conducting a multitude of other enterprises. Sorely needed lines were run along timber claims for various contracts between timber owners and mill operators. Many county roads were first documented by Bagley's work. In 1872, mining claims were laid out during the "quicksilver rush" on the west slope of Mount Jackson.

As his reputation spread, his expertise was in demand. When the county Board of Supervisors created a new school district, they hired Bagley to mark out the boundary and also called on him to survey new bridge sites over the Russian River.

In the mid-1880s, two local railroads were incorporated, one by Col. James Armstrong (of State Park fame) and the other by George Guerne. Both hired Bagley to survey potential rights-of-way. The Armstrong and Big Bottom Railroad never got off paper, but the Guerneville and Russian River Railroad eventually laid rail up Hulbert Creek west of town, using Bagley's survey. This short line eventually became a small section of the Guerneville Branch of the Northwestern Pacific Railroad.

On several occasions Bagley would take note of previous surveyors' errors and write his comments in a journal. "This corner is false as hell...as he was never at the corner nor at the section corner's E W S N of it," Bagley wrote of one site. Of another he noted, "Between Sections 26 & 27 the following notes by the original surveyor V. Walkenrider shows the fraud committed by him to leave the brush & take the timber."

Among Bagley's many repeat clients were the Korbel brothers, Bohemian Club of San Francisco, Great Eastern Mining Co., and Duncan Mill Land & Lumber Co. He worked continually through the 1890s and into the 20th century.

In private life, Bagley was a dedicated Union supporter. He joined the Working Man's Party, an anti-Chinese organization of the 1870s that called for all Asians to return to their homeland. His attitude seems to have moderated, since he hired Chinese to work in 1875-77, when he was road overseer to Redwood Township. Bagley was also a member of the Independent Order of Good Templars, a temperance group.

The Bagley home, built in 1866, always stood next to the intersection of First and Mill Streets. Five of the Bagley's six children was born there; only Herbert L. was born in Healdsburg. Two daughters died in infancy. Frank T., Alice C. and Carl E. Bagley lived on.

Bagley's final survey was run on Feb. 11, 1906. A week later, he was returning from Duncan's Mills where he had been called as undertaker. It was raining heavily and Bagley was driving a buggy back to the stables in Guerneville. The horses, anxious to get to their stalls, slipped on the wet planks at the entrance to the stables. The quick stop pitched Bagley forward and he struck his face on the brick entrance. His face was crushed and his left side paralyzed. He lingered until February 22, the birthday of his name sake.

The *Russian River Advertiser* announced the community's loss by printing his biography on the front page and edging the four full columns of print in black: John Washington Bagley. First millwright, first surveyor, first businessman, first sexton, first postmaster, a pillar of the town and countryside. Age 78 years, 4 months, 20 days.

In Closing

Congratulations! You finished wading through several hundred pages of a small town's "biography."

The attitude and appearance of Guerneville and the River Area had changed from a small lumbering village to a major lumbering center to a country town with its economy based on agriculture and tourism.

Eventually agriculture, a major industry, would fade from the area. Olive production faltered and ceased after 1910; tobacco, after David Hetzel retired, was not continued; hop fields in part were put to other uses and the remainder succumbed to a hop disease that was fatal to the hop industry throughout the county in 1950. Only apples remain of all the horticultural products grown by individuals (Andy Strode and Roscoe Drake, the last two).

The village once known as Stumptown or Heald's Mill is now called locally as "town" or Guerneville and known around the county as The River or the River Community.

It is today the only unincorporated community in Sonoma County that has all the elements of a municipality: fire department, sheriff's office sub-station, library, veterans hall, two water companies, mortuary, three grocery stores (one a chain store), banking institution, four year-round restaurants, six year-round saloons, auto shop, a sewer system, etc.

The pioneer community is nearly gone. Only three pre-1894 buildings exist: the French house (1881) on the hill east of town, and the Lundsford home (1871) on the southwest corner of Church and First Streets. Marshall House (1880) was moved from the northwest corner of Fifth and Church Streets one mile north of town at the corner of Armstrong and Watson Roads in 2010.

The "good old days" were, granted, pretty good because we remember only the good times of our youth. Even the stories and tales of our grandparents and old timers are of the good times past — if occasionally peppered with comments about how things are easy now.

The perils to human life one hundred years ago have been halved; a child born these days has three times the chance of surviving infancy and childhood and reaching adulthood. Even as an adolescent a youngster had no guarantees of reaching adulthood. Diseases would run rampant in small sections of the country, or even localized to single families.

As for adults, industrial accidents were common place, on the railroad, in the woods, at the mines; one would pay for his thoughtlessness with an arm, a leg, or a life. But some people "came from good stock" and were long lived.

Mother Nature has provided the master calendar for human memories of notable events and not the human calendar of 365 days. Historical events marked irregular chapters of the town's story in people's minds: the Big Flood of ____, the Fire of 18_, the shooting of ____, the Last Train.

This story of Guerneville combines (and clarifies) the two calendars, Natural and Human.

Though this volume ends roughly at 1910, there are another 90 years and more of history to investigate, to substantiate, and to rectify.

Some events repeat themselves — fire, flood, crime, etc. Some events are one of a kind — arrival of the first aircraft, the only junior high school and the like.

I pass on the heavy yet exciting job of Russian River Historian to those who accept the challenge of finding these stories and others yet to be uncovered. I stated at the start: prove me wrong — I mean it. Correct any story or chapter I have written.

At the beginning of this book I said "Welcome." Since then I hope you have found some enjoyment traveling these pages and found answers to any of your questions about yesteryear.

This closes the story of "Guerneville Early Days."

— J.C.S.

Guerneville, Ca - circa 1920, JCS Collection

Appendices

Appendix One
Pioneers & Early Settlers to 1870

NAME	OCCUPATION	AGE	EARLIEST YEAR KNOWN IN AREA
Alden, B.F.	Farmer	—	1860
Alley, Thomas J.	Teacher	—	1867
Armstrong, James	Laborer	39	1869
Ayers, William Henry M.	Son	5	1866
Ayers, Rebecca M.	Mother	—	1866
Ayers, Ben J. Franklin	Son	6	1866
Bachelder, James Eaton	Lumber	46	1870
Bachelder, Mary Louise	Wife	53	1870
Bagley, John Washington	Lumber	37	1865
Bagley, Ellen Antoinet (Downing)	Wife	31	1870
Bagley, Frank	Son	11	1870
Bagley, Josephine	Daughter	10	1870
Bagley, Mary L.	Daughter	7	1870
Bagley, Herbert L.	Son	5	1870
Batey, William	Farmer	32	1866
Bayler, John	Lumber	33	1868
Bayler, Caroline	Wife	—	1870
Beaver, Henry	—	40	1864
Beaver, Mary	Wife	—	1863
Beaver, William	Son	Born	1863
Bell, Bradford	—	—	1863
Bellah, Samuel	—	—	1865
Bidwell, J.	—	—	1867
Blakely, James M.	—	Born	1851
Blakely, Samuel	—	—	1862
Blakely, Sarah	Wife	Born	1858
Blakely, T	—		1886
Bledsoe, Linn	—	—	1870
Bohn, Frederick	—	22	1866
Bowers, William	Farmer	46	1870
Brown, Charles	Laborer	34	1868
Blakely, Sarah	Wife of		1868
Campbell, William	—	36	1868
Cargile, John B.	—	—	1868
Cargile, Johanna L.	Wife	24	1868
Carter, Edward D.	Lumber	45	1868
Carter, Susan R.	Wife	47	1870
Chapman, J.N.	Surveyor	—	1869

Name	Role	Age	Year
Chormicle, William C.	—	—	1862
Chormicle, M.	Wife	15	1862
Chormicle, Nancy S.	Daughter	Born	1862
Clover, Milton	Teacher	38	1870
Coon, Robert W.	—	28	1861
Cowen, James H.	—	30	1868
Crow, James Ranking	Farmer	29	1868
Dagget, Henry	Laborer	28	1870
DePencier, S.L.	Teacher	—	1870
Deychert, J.	—	—	1868
Dudley, Hattie J.	Teacher	—	1866
Duncan, Samuel	—	55	1868
Dunhill, F.S.	Teacher	—	1861
Dunwordey, George Washington	—	26	1868
East, William	Laborer	37	1870
Elliot, William Ross	Lumber	33	1868
English, David Barton	Farmer	18	1855
English, Charles	School Trustee	—	1861
English, Leonora E	—	18	1870
Faudre, Stewart Wm.	Chairmaker	51	1860
Faudre, Martha C. (Jose)	Wife	—	1860
Faudre, Sylvester Florence	Son	Born	1860
Ferguson, Harvey	Laborer	24	1868
Ferguson, Thomas	Laborer	32	1868
Fife, Andrew	—	—	1860
Florence, Marshal	Chairmaker	24	1866
Florence, Louanna	Wife	18	1870
Florence, Cami B.	Daughter	9 mo.	1870
Foster, Charles	Lumber	29	1866
Foster, Sarah A.	Wife	21	1870
Freeborn, John Greene	Farmer	42	1868
Freshour, A.	—	—	1860
Freshour, Columbus	—	—	1866
Freshour, L.H.	—	—	1866
Freshour, William	—	—	1868
Frost, Thomas	School Trustee	—	1862
Fry, William	Laborer	28	1860
Fry, Mary	—	15	1870
Gabler, Chauncy R.	Farmer	29	1868
Gibson, John H.	Farmer	24	1868
Gilbert, John	Laborer	38	1870
Gilbert, Elizabeth	Wife	37	1870
Gilbert, E.	—	14	1870
Gilbert, Donida	—	15	1870
Goddart	—	—	1868
Gordon, Joseph	Lumber	43	1868
Greenwood, James	—	—	1863
Guerne, Augustus	Laborer	30	1870
Guerne, George E.	Lumber	28	1865
Guerne, Elizabeth Gibson Montgomery	Wife	21	1865
Guerne, Jonathon Henry Louis	Son	3	1865
Guerne, Marie Louise	Daughter	Born	1865

Name	Role/Occupation	Age	Year
Guerne, Alfred A.	Son	Born	1867
Guerne, Julia Alfrette	Daughter	Born	1870
Gutridge, T.H.	–	–	1867
Ham, Thomas	Lumber	53	1868
Ham, Rebecca	Wife	57	1870
Ham, Mariah	Daughter	13	1870
Ham, William	Son	11	1870
Ham, Charles A.	Son	5	1870
Hayes, R.H.	–	–	1860
Heald, Thomas Tobin	Lumber	41	1865
Helm, S.W.	–	–	1861
Herriot, Hiram	Survey Axeman	–	1866
Hewlett, P.B.	–	–	1863
Higson, Alexander	–	–	1867
Hill, James M.	School Trustee	50	1860
Hudspeth, J.C.	Surveyor	–	1855
Hulbert, Henry	Lumber	21	1856
Hulbert, Mary A.	Wife	24	1856
Hulbert, Mary Belle	Daughter		1857
Hulbert, Hiram Perry	Son	3	1856
Hulbert, Harry	Son	Born	1865
Johnson, Cynthia	Wife	45	1862
Johnson, James	–	–	1870
Jones, ??	–	–	1868
Jose, H.K.	–	–	1869
Jose, Michel Worth	Painter	21	1868
Jose, Michel Henry	Farmer	59	1868
Kanajah, John	Laborer	35	1870
Keith, James	Teacher	–	1867
Keith, Jennie	–	–	1867
Keran, J.N.	Teacher	–	1870
King, John McLean	Boat Captain	38	1868
Klein, Gottlieb Henry	Laborer	24	1866
Klein, Sarah C. (Ayers)	Wife (at 15)	11	1866
Langley, James	Lumber	53	1866
Laud, A.C.	Timber	–	1867
Lewis, R.E.	–	–	1860
Line, J. Able	Laborer	58	1869
Line, Emily	Wife	41	1869
Line, William	Son	11	1869
Line, Nancy E.	Daughter	9	1869
Line, Sarah E.	Daughter	7	1869
Line, Eva	Daughter	5	1869
Line, Abraham	Son	4	1869
Line, Mary A.	Daughter	2	1869
Line, Hattie	Daughter	1	1869
Livreau, Joseph	Lumber	46	1869
Longley, Roscoe Green	Logger	19	1855
Longley, Edwin Roscoe	Son	born	1869
Longley, Mary Adelia	Wife	18	1868
Looney, William Denton	Farmer	25	1868
Looney, Francis Marion	Farmer	24	1868

Lundsford, Robert Burton	Wheelwright	40	1860
Maddox, William H.	—	—	1866
Mahan, John	School Trustee	—	1859
Mahan, R.E.	Wife	—	1859
Mahan, Eva	Daughter	—	1859
Mahan, Alison	Son	Born	1859
Mahan, Mary Ellen	Daughter	Born	1867
Marsh, John Shelby	Blacksmith	29	1866
Mershon, Cornelius	Farmer	71	1868
Miller, Beate	Farmer	32	1868
Miller, Henry	Laborer	30	1868
Miller, Henry W.	Laborer	56	1870
Miller Jacob Madison	Painter	51	1866
Miller Lydia E.	—	28	1870
Miller, R.H.	Pastor	—	1869
Millington, Seth	Surveyor	—	1866
Morton, W.W.	—	—	1860
Murphy Rufus	Lumber	—	1869
McCush, Sarah	Teacher	—	1868
McFaydn,	Laborer	24	1870
McGill, Isaac	—	24	1868
McGill, Patrick	Farmer	66	1868
McKee, Joseph	Farmer	24	1868
McPeak, Anthony M.	Farmer	20	1856
McPeak, Melissa E.	Wife (of A.M.)	19	1867
McPeak, Lanora Florence	Daughter		1867
McPeak, Eugene	—	—	1861
McPeak, Matthew Addison	—	31	1870
McPeak, Mary H.	Wife (of M.A.)	—	1870
Osborn, John Thomas	Farmer	48	1868
Patterson, James T.	Carpenter	39	1868
Patterson, Mary	—	17	1870
Pearson, Charles Hunter	Farmer	27	1868
Pell, James	Engineer	42	1870
Pell, Mary	Wife	27	1870
Pell, Mary E.	Daughter	10	1870
Pell, Hannah S.	Daughter	7	1870
Pell, Catherine E.	Daughter	4	1870
Pell, Agness B.	Daughter	1	1870
Peterson, George W.	Teacher	—	1862
Phillips, Alexander Sechraise	Blacksmith	28	1868
Phillips, Archibald	Farmer	42	1868
Phips, E.	—	—	1867
Phips, J.C.	—	—	1867
Pinson, Chrles	—	—	1867
Pippin, Thomas C.C.	Teamster	37	1866
Pippin, Josephine	Daughter	5	1866
Pippin, John	Son	2	1866
Pippin, Benjamin	Son	Born	1866
Pippin, George W.	Son	Born	1868
Pippin, Margaret Frost	Wife	23	1866
Pool, A.	—	—	1868

Pool, John	Farmer	42	1868
Pool, Lydia Hitchcock	Wife	34	1868
Pool, Jonnie R.	Son	15	1868
Pool, Lucinda	Daughter	13	1868
Pool, Margaret	Daughter	11	1868
Pool, Lee	Son	6	1868
Pool, John	Son	4	1868
Pool, Francis E.	Son	3	1868
Pool, James	Son	16	1868
Power, L.T.	–	–	1863
Rainey, Henry Clay	Farmer	26	1868
Ramey, James	Physician	45	1856
Renfroe, James Fielding	Farmer	33	1866
Rich, James	Carpenter	58	1868
Ridenhour, Louis William	Farmer	33	1853
Ridenhour, Mary	Wife	28	1870
Ridenhour, William R.	Son	13	1870
Ridenhour, Emily	Daughter	11	1870
Ridenhour, Edward Louis	Son	9	1870
Ridenhour, Louisa A.	Daughter	8	1870
Ridenhour, Ellen	Daughter	5	1870
Ridenhour, Hilton	Son	2	1870
Ripley, Jacob	–	–	1863
Robinson, John	Laborer	21	1868
Robinson, Mary	Wife	19	1870
Robinson, Mabel	–	1	1870
Russell, J.C.	–	–	1860
Sacsy, D.S.	Teacher	–	1863
Sedgley, Joseph Lorm	Lumber Mill	–	1857
Seward, James	School Trustee	–	1861
Seward, Jared	Farmer	45	1868
Simmons, William N.	Timber	–	1869
Smith, J.L.P.	Survey Chainman	–	1866
Smith, John	Landowner	–	1868
Stevens, Ward S.	School Trustee	–	1870
Stone, Thomas H.	Timber	–	1867
Strode, Charles E.	–	–	1864
Strode, Margaret (Goddard)	Wife	–	1864
Strode, John Morgan	Son	Born	1864
Sutton, Levi	–	45	1868
Sutton, Elizabeth	Daughter	11	1870
Thompson, Leonard	Teamster	39	1870
Thompson, Charlotte	Wife	28	1870
Thompson, Lambert P.	Son	12	1870
Thompson, Victoria L.	Daughter	10	1870
Thompson, Sarah T.	Daughter	8	1870
Thompson, Hermit T.	Son	3	1870
Thompson, George W.	Son	3 mo.	1870
Torrance, Shubel H.	Lumber	25	1856
Torrance, Samuel H.	Son	13	1866
Turner, Noah Hatton	Rancher	34	1868
Ungewitter, John	Teamster	34	1864

Name	Role	Age	Year
Ungewitter, Sarah	Daughter	15	1870
Ungewitter, William	Son	10	1870
Ungewitter, John	Son	8	1870
Ungewitter, Henry West	Son	7	1870
Vaughan, Lewis	Farmer	33	1868
Wackenvueder, L.	Surveyor	—	1868
Walker, John King	Pastor	73	1870
Walker, Pauline Buel	Wife	67	1870
Walker, Lycurgus	Son	born	1870
Wall, Christian	Surveyor	—	1867
Watson, James	—	45	1868
Weldmann, Nettie	Teacher	—	1868
Welms, J.W.	School Trustee	—	1863
Westcott, Oliver	Lumber	25	1865
Wheeler, E.W.	—	—	1868
Whelms, Shelby	—	—	1861
White, Henry Lawrence	Farmer	21	1868
Wilfley, Samuel	Farmer	61	1868
Williams, Johnson	Farmer	35	1868
Williams, Ruben	Saloonkeeper	27	1868
Williams, Caroline	Wife	27	1868
Williams, Samuel	Son	9	1868
Williams, Mary J.	Daughter	8	1868
Williams, Laura	Daughter	6	1868
Williams, Leona	Daughter	4	1868
Williams, Fannie	Daughter	1	1868
Willits, William Henry	Lumber	41	1858
Wilsie, Owen	Farmer	36	1868
Wilson, Johnny	—	48	1862
Wilson, Cynthia Horilla (Pippin)	Wife	42	1862
Wilson, Lewis	Laborer	23	1870
Wilson, S.W.	Teacher	—	1864
Wilson, William	—	—	1861
Wood, John Kinsley	Timber Contractor	34	1870
Wooley, T.D.	—	—	1867
Yarbrough, Crocket D.	Farmer	31	1861
Yarbrough, Jemima A.	Wife	18	1861
Yarbrough, Adelia E.	Daughter	—	1861
Yarbrough, Thomas J.J.	Son	Born	1866

APPENDIX TWO

ASIAN RESIDENTS TO 1900

NAME	LOCATION	OCCUPATION	YEAR[3]
Ah, Ait	—[1]	—	1874
Ah, Bong	—	—	1875
Ah, Charley	—	—	1875
Ah, Cheen	—	—	1875
Ah, Chei	QSM[2]	Miner	1880
Ah, Chin	QSM	Miner	1874
Ah, Ching	QSM	Miner	1880
Ah, Chook	—	Farm Laborer	1880
Ah, Chow	QSM	Miner	1880
Ah, Chung	QSM	Miner	1880
Ah, Cohy	—	—	1875
Ah, Cong	QSM	Miner	1880
Ah, Coon	—	—	1874
Ah, Cue	—	—	1874
Ah, Fah	—	—	1875
Ah, Fong ("Pan")	QSM	Cook	1893
Ah, Fow	—	Farm Laborer	1880
Ah, Gin	—	—	1875
Ah, Gon	—	Road Work	1874
Ah, Goon	—	—	1874
Ah, Guy	Duncans' Mills	Timber	1869
Ah, Hee	QSM	Miner	1880
Ah, Henry	—	—	1875
Ah, Jen	—	Farm Laborer	1880
Ah, Jim	Guerneville	Cook	1879
Ah, Jim	—	Farm Laborer	1880
Ah, Jim	QSM	Miner	1880
Ah, Ki	—	—	1875
Ah, Lee	—	Miner	1880
Ah, Low	—	Farm Laborer	1880
Ah, Lui	—	—	1875
Ah, Luin	—	Road Work	1874
Ah, Mung	—	—	1875
Ah, Poi	—	—	1875
Ah, Poo	—	—	1875
Ah, Quan	---	---	1875
Ah, Quin	---	---	1875
Ah, Sam	QSM	Miner	1880
Ah, See	---	Road Work	1874
Ah, Soo	---	---	1875
Ah, Tae	QSM	Miner	1880
Ah, Sam	QSM	Miner	1880
Ah, Ten	—	—	1875
Ah, Tere	—	—	1875

Name	Location	Occupation	Year
Ah, Thae	—	Cook	1880
Ah, Thai	—	Farm Laborer	1880
Ah, Tia	—	—	1874
Ah, Tien	—	—	1875
Ah, Tong	QSM	Miner	1880
Ah, Tsen	QSM	Miner	1880
Ah, Wah	—	—	1875
Ah Woo	QSM	Miner	1875
Ah Yee	—	Road Work	1874
Ah, Yet	—	Miner	1880
Ah, Zin	—	—	1875
Ah, Zone	—	—	1874
Cheo	—	—	1875
Chow Sune	—	Cook	1880
Chuin	—	—	1875
Chung Fat	—	—	1878
Cong	—	—	1875
Chong, Chung*	Merchant	Owner	1876
Foug Zu	—	—	1874
Hop Kee	—	Road Work	1873
"Jim Mahoney"	Guerneville	Gambler	1885
Jung	—	—	1875
Ki, Mai	—	—	1874
Ki, Not	—	—	1875
Kin	—	—	1875
Kong, Chun	QSM	Furnaceman	1880
Kong, Hung Ah*	QSM	Daughter	1880
Kong, Sing	QSM	Wife	1880
Kong, Sun Ah	QSM	Son	1880
Lang	—	—	1875
Lee, Sam	—	Road Work	1873
Lo	—	—	1873
Lo, Woo	—	—	1874
Lui, Ah Chow	—	—	1875
Lui, Ah Con	—	—	1875
Luk, Quon	—	—	1875
Po	—	—	1875
Sam, Sing	—	—	1875
Sam, Song	—	—	1875
Sing, Ah	—	Washer	1880
Sing, Sam	—	Cook	1880
Sing, Wo	—	Laundry	1901
Tong	—	—	1875
Tong, Chung	Guerneville	Store Owner	1876
Tong, Cue	—	—	—
Tong, Gin	Guerneville	Store Owner	1876
Tuin	—	—	1875
Wi	—	—	1875
Wong, Tau	—	Road Work	1874
Yip, Ching	Guernevllle	Store Owner	1896
Yuin	—	—	1875
Yu Lin	—	—	1875

1. Dashes in this column mean location unknown but probably in the Guerneville area.
2. QSM — Quicksilver Mines
3. Earliest date found of the person's appearance in the River area.

* Indicates Native Californian

APPENDIX THREE

POSTMASTERS OF GUERNEVILLE

DATE APPOINTED	NAME
July 28, 1870	John W. Bagley
June 21, 1880	Gerhard Dietz
1eptember 17, 1886	Mrs. Amelia R. Thompson
October 24, 1889	Gerhard Dietz
January 17, 1895	Mary L. Ungewitter
December 21, 1898	William A. Turner
February 4, 1908	Thomas T. Duncan
March 9, 1915	Elizabeth Clar
February 9, 1923	George L. Clar
March 31, 1964	Albert Markarian*
October 23, 1964	Harold B. James
November 1975	Dick Mazzanti*
January 1976	Carl Helman
May 1980	Regina Harlon-Taber*
October 1980	Don Hunerlach*
December 1980	Howard Wright
July 1983	John Maier*
January 1984	Dan Danieli*
March 1984	Gregory Pace
July 2004	Federico Solorio*
August 30, 2004	Joe Mills

* Denotes officer in charge, not Postmaster.

APPENDIX FOUR

REDWOOD TOWNSHIP POST OFFICES

NAME	DATE ESTABLISHED OR DATE NAME CHANGED
Austin	August 5, 1881
Austin changed to Ingram's	June 23, 1886
Cazadero changed from Ingram's	Aprll 24, 1889
Duncans' Mills	December 20, 1862
Eaglenest	May 26, 1908
Eaglenest changed to Rionido	May 23, 1910
Grandville	June 25, 1907
Grandville changed to Villagrande	March 24, 1921
Guerneville	July 28, 1870
Guernewood Park	July 17, 1925
Guernewood Park susbtation of Guerneville	July 31, 1946
Guernewood discontinued	August 19, 1985
Hilton	October 17, 1894
Hilton discontinued	June 30, 1953
Ingram's	June 23, 1886
Ingram's changed to Cazadero	April 24, 1889
Jenner	April 4, 1904
Korbel Mills	June 23, 1886
Korbel Mills discontinued	March 25, 1881
Markhams	November 8, 1883
Markhams discontinued	June 15, 1900
Markhams	December 23, 1903
Markhams discontinued	July 15, 1910
Mercury	July 5, 1898
Mercury discontinued	September 15, 1898
Mercury	January 6, 1899
Mercury discontinued	April 30, 1909
Montrio	May 26, 1902
Montrio changed to Monte Rio	August 1, 1924
Northwood	July 25, 1929
Northwood discontinued	December 31, 1938
Rionido changed from Eaglenest	May 23, 1910
Tyrone	July 18, 1877
Tyrone discontinued	June 30, 1881
Tyrone reestablished	November 28, 1882
Tyrone discontinued	October 15, 1883
Vacation	January 29, 1904
Vacation discontinued	August 30, 1941
Villa Grande changed from Grandview	March 24, 1921

APPENDIX FIVE

REDWOOD TOWNSHIP JUSTICES OF THE PEACE
(Including Judges of the Justice Court)

Year	Name
1871	J. Pool; C.A. Brackett
1873	M.S. Clover; N.E. Manning
1875	M.S. Clover; M. McPeak
1876	J.M. Miller; S.H. Hudson
1877	J.M. Miller; Fred Bohn
1878	J.M. Miller; B.F. Murphy
1879	J.M. Miller; Thomas Cramer
1880	J. M. Miller; Marshall Florence
1886	L.L. Jewett; Marshall Florence
1888	L.L. Jewett; Marshall Florence
1890	W.H. Bagley; H.L. Bagley
1892	W.B. Turner, Jr.; Marshall Florence
1894	W.V. Cole; W.F. Graham
1898	R.B. Brown
1902	R.B. Brown
1906	A.P. Mosley
1910	M. Florence
1914	E.F. Manchester
1918	Walter Olney
1922	Robert S. Coon
1926	Robert S. Coon
1930	E.J. Guidotti
1934	E.J. Guidotti
1938	Rand Starret
1939	Leland H. Fleming
1942	Ellen Fleming
1944	Ellen Fleming
1945	Leland Fleming
1946	Leland Fleming
1950	A.F. "Gus" Tompkins
1952	Jesse J. Robertson
1956	Jesse J. Robertson
1960	Jesse J. Robertson

APPENDIX SIX

REDWOOD TOWNSHIP CONSTABLES

Year	Name
1871	Ruben Williams, Ward S. Stevens
1873	T.C. Pippin, William Maddox
1875	T.C. Pippin; J. Pool
1877	T.C. Pippin; J. Taggert
1879	T.C. Pippin, Jacob Acor
1879	Lew M. Elison; John Robertson
1880	Lew M. Ellison
1882	John Keaton; Roscoe McKinney
1884	John Keaton; Charles Hill
1886	George W. French, William Bartley
1888	John Pool; William Bartley
1890	John Pool; T.A. Griffin
1892	B.G. Pippin; George Brow
1894	B.G. Pippin; O.O. Cobb
1898	D.E.L. Pool
1902	O. Westcott
1906	W.L. Cole
1910	Charles Door
1914	Clyde Ayers
1918	Clyde Ayers*
1922	John R. Starrett
1926	Charles W. Evans
1930	Charles Tibbots
1934	Otis L. Knight
1938	Otis L. Knight
1942	Otis L. Knight
1946	Otis L. Knight
1950	Joseph L. Kerr
1954	George Guerne
1958	George Sproul

* On June 14, 1916 Ayers resigned. His vacancy existed until February 14, 1917, at which time Charles Tibbit was appointed by the Board of Supervisors to finish Ayers' term.

APPENDIX SEVEN

Roadmasters of Redwood Road District

YEAR	NAME(S)
1868	Joseph H.P. Morris
1869-1872	—
1874-1874	Crocket D. Yarborough
1875-1877	John W. Bagley
1886	J.R. Simmons
1887-1888	William Garrison
1889-1890	Sam Varner
1891-1893	D.B. Peugh
1894-1896	—
1897-1906	O.B. Glynn

* The name was changed from Miriam to Redwood with the creation of Redwood Township in 1871.

APPENDIX EIGHT

Agents of Wells, Fargo & Co. Express at Guerneville

1877	Jacob Selling
1878	S. Schloss
1879	Heald & Guerne
1880-1891	Gerhard Dietz
1892-1897	W.P. Ferguson
1897-1902	C.W. Barker
1902-1904	—
1904	C.T. Rhodes
1904-1910	L.M. Martin

APPENDIX NINE

INCORPORATIONS

SONOMA COUNTY

CLERK #	NAME	DATE
95	Guerneville Literary & Social Co.	April 8, 1874
105	Mount Jackson Quicksilver Mining Co.	Jan. 26, 1875
113	Great Eastern Quicksilver Mining Co.	March 29, 1875
178	Mount Jackson Quicksilver Mining Co.	June 29, 1875
249	Guerneville Loan Association	May 3, 1882
280	Guerneville & Russian River Railroad	March 6, 1886
284	Big Bottom Railroad Co.	Oct. 26, 1886
342	Sonoma Lumber Co.	April 12, 1890
467	Carr & Bagley Co.	Oct. 7, 1897
602	Guerneville Rochdale Co.	May 19, 1903
669	Redwood Water & Improvement Co.	Aug. 18, 1904
670	F. Korbel & Bros.	Aug. 24, 1904
676	Guerneville Light Co.	Oct. 7, 1904
721	Bank of Guerneville	Oct. 19, 1905

APPENDIX TEN

REGISTERED PARTNERSHIPS

SONOMA COUNTY

CLERK #	NAME	DATE
18	Selling & Son (Jacob & John)	Aug. 26, 1874
29	F. Korbel & Bros. (Antone, Francis & Joseph)	Sept. 15, 1884
91	G.R. Skinner & Co. (General Merchant)	Sept. 3, 1886
121	A. Duncan & Co. (Sawmilling)	Sept. 18, 1878
123	Bradford Bell & John J. Keaton (Wholesale & Retail Meats)	Nov. 15, 1875
138	Guerne, Murphy & Ludwig (Sawmilling)	March 15, 1880
213	Big Bottom Mill Co. (James B. Armstrong & Albert Brown)	Dec. 15, 1885
262	Sonoma Lumber Co. (Westover & Dollar)	Jan. 9, 1889
268	French & Turner (John H. French & Napolean B. Turner)	May 18, 1889
274	Wescott, King & Co. (Oliver Wescott, William King & Charles Carr)	Aug. 20, 1890
289	John Ansell, Jeremiah Hunt & John Cunningham (Sawmilling & Contracting Lumber Lands)	Sept. 15, 1882
346	Central Supply Co. (Antoinette Cobb & Antone J. Lauteren)	Feb. 2, 1909

APPENDIX ELEVEN

BIOGRAPHIES

The following biographies are found in the standard histories of Sonoma County under the years of publication indicated. In some cases only passing mention is made of Guerneville or the Russian River Area.

A. History of 1880:

Name	Page
Bell, Bradford	609
Florence, Marshall	609
Hasset, J.D.	508
Heald, Thomas T.	609
Manning, N.E.	610

B. History of 1889:

Name	Page
Anderson, Leroy S.	675
Bayler, John	511
Dietz, Gerhard	725
Hall, James M.	451
Lewis, R.E.	380
Morris, Joseph H.P.	353
Torrance, S.H.	573

C. History of California Coast Counties — 1904 Vol 2

Name	Page
Cobb, Omer o.	1471
Guerne, George E.	641
Healde, Thomas T.	458
McPeak, E.	922
Meeker, M.C.	353

D. History of 1911:

Name	Page
Austin, G.J.	728
Ayers, W.H.	836
Birkhofer, C.	880
Dinucci, A.	1064
Eckman, J.	451
English, D.B.	861
Fowler, J.G.	530, 533
Gisel, H.	884
Korbel, Inc.	900
McPeak, A.	523
Morris, H.B.	341
Ridenhour, L.W.	869
Stagg, A.A.	623
Strode, J.	903

E. History of 1926:

Name	Page
Butt, T.V.	488
Carr, W.H.	907
Downie, D.D.	839
Easdale, John	537
Graham, W.F,	77
Guerne, Bert	766
Hicks, George	354
Keaton, J.J.	891
Morelli, J.B.	889
Peugh, Edward	42
Robertson Bros.	228
Starrett, Robert	811
Stoffal, Phillip	552

F. History of 1937:

Name	Page
Belden, Ralph	333
Guerne, Bert	202
Guidotti, E.G.	27
Herling, Max	325
Hotle, Harold	170
Laughlin, Glen	161
Lopus, Veva	3
Read, George	340
Stoffal, Ida	89
Trombetta, Floyd	28

GRAND ARMY OF THE REPUBLIC
J.W. MOREY POST, NO. 81
GUERNEVILLE, CAL.

OFFICERS, 1886

SAMUEL VARNER	Commander
DAVID HETZEL	Senior Vice-Commander
G.L. COBB	Junior Vice-Commander
G. DIETZ	Adjutant
W.V. CARR	Quartermaster
J.J. ANTHONY	Surgeon
JOSEPH SMITH	Chaplain
J.J. KEATON	Officer of the Day
J.A. CROSBY	Officer of the Guard
JAMES NEAL	Sergeant Major
W.V. COLE	Quartermaster Sergeant

Meeting, First Monday

BIBLIOGRAPHY

I. BOOKS

Anthony, C.V. *50 Years of Methodism.* San Francisco: Methodist Book Concern, 1901.

[Armstrong, James B.] *Armstrong's Woods*; Cloverdale, CA: Cloverdale Reveille Print, 1891.

Bagley, Ellen D. *[Scrapbook].* Guerneville, CA, 1874-1890.

Bagley, John W. *Survey Book No. 1.* Guerneville, CA, MSS., 1880(?)

Bancroft, H. H. *Bancroft Scraps,* Set "W," Vol. 5. San Francisco: H. H. Bancroft,

_____. *History of California,* Vol. I -VII. San Francis co: H. H. Bancroft, (year??)

_____. *Native Races,* Vol. I. San Francisco: H. H. Bancroft, 1885.

Barrett, S. A. *The Ethno-Geography of the Pomo Indians.* Berkeley: University Press of Califomia, 1908.

[Cassidy, Sam] *An Illustrated History of Sonoma County.* Chicago: Lewis Publishing Com pany, 1889.

Conner, A. M. *The Church Built from One Redwood Tree.* Reprint. Coronado, CA, 1971.

Coolidge, Mary R. *Chinese Immigration.* New York: Henry Holt Company, 1909.

DuFlot de Mofras, Eugene. *Travels on the Pacific Coast.* Trans. Marguerite Wilbur. Santa Ana, CA: The Five Arts Press, 1937.

Engleson, Lester. *Interests & Activities of the Hudson's Bay Company in California.* Master's Thesis. Berkeley: University of California Press, 1939.

Finley, Ernest L. *History of Sonoma County.* Santa Rosa, CA: Press Democrat Publishing Company, 1937.

Gregory, Tom. History of Sonoma County, California. Los Angeles: Historic Record Company, 1911.

Guerne, Julia. *[Personal Notebook.]* Guerneville, CA: MSS. undated.

Guinn, J. M. *History of the State of California Biographical Record of Coast Counties.* Chicago: Chapman Publishing Company, 1904.

Hetzel, Jack. *History of David Hetzel.* Guerneville, CA., MSS., 1975.

Holoway, R. S. *The Russian River. A Characterisitic Stream of the California Coast Ranges.* Univer sity of California Publication in Geography. Berkeley: University of California Press, 1913.

Kroeber, A. L. *Handbook of Indians of California.* Berkeley: California Book Company, 1953.

Loeb, E. M. *Pomo Folkways.* University of California Publications in American Archeology and Ethnology, Vol. 19. Berkeley: University of California Press, 1926.

McKenzie, John C. *Colonel James B. Armstrong and His Redwood Park.* Cazadero, CA., MSS., 1950.

Nordhoff, Charles. *Northern California, Oregon and The Sandwich Islands.* New York: Harper Brothers, 1874.

Olsen, Pauline, and Edith Olsen Merritt. *Sonoma County Cemetery Records.* Santa Rosa, CA., MSS. ,1950.

_____. *The Origin of the Russian-American Com pany.* St. Petersberg, 1863.Russian-American MSS. Trans. Dmitri Krenov and Michael Dobrynin. Berkeley: University of California, Bancroft Library.

Oswalt, Robert L. *Kashaya Texts.* University of California Publications in Linguistics, Vol. 36. Berkeley: University of California Press, 1964.

Pearsall, Clarence E. *The Quest for Qual-A-Wa-Loo.* Oakland, CA: Holmes Book Company, 1966.

Register of Burial, Guerneville Cemetery. Guerneville, CA: Redwood Memorial Chapel & Mortuary (Note: This ledger was stolen in 1980.)Scribner's *Log & Lumber Book of 1882.* New York: Scribner & Sons, 1882.

_____. *Sonoma County & Russian River Valley.* San Francisco: Bell & Heymans, 1888.

Thompson, *R.A. Atlas of Sonoma County.* Oakland, CA: R. A. Thompson, 1877.

Tuomey, Honoria. History of Sonoma County. San Francisco: Clark Publishing Co., 1926.

Watson, James R. *Guerneville.* MSS., Guerneville, CA., [undated].

II. GOVERNMENT SOURCES:
A. Federal Government

United States Bureau of Census, Reports of

1860, 1870 and 1880. Washington: Government Printing Office.

B. State of California:

Bureau of Mines: *Mines and Mineral Resources of Colusa, Glenn, Lake, Marin, Napa, Solano, Sonoma, Yolo Counties.* Sacramento: State Printing Office, July 1915.

Department of Forestry: Clar, C. Raymond. *California Government and Forestry.* Sacramento: State Printing Office, 1959.

Penal Code. Sacramento: State Printing Office, 1880

Statutes of California. Sacramento: State Printing Office, 1870, 1873, 1874.

Reports [of the California Supreme Court]. Vol. 48. San Francisco: Bancroft-Whitney, 1874.

Appendix to Journals of Senate and Assembly, 21st Session. Sacramento: State Printing Office, 1874.

C. County of Sonoma:

Recorder's Office:

Map Book. No. 8.

Land Patents. Book A.

Promiscuous Records. Book B.

Book of Deeds. Vols 127, 219, 361, 366.

Board of Supervisors:

Road Records. Books A, 1, 3.

Minutes. Vols. V, VI, IIX, 20, 21, 30.

Assessor's Office:

Records. 1873, 1877 (in possession of Sonoma County Library, Santa Rosa).

County Clerk's Office:

Register of Voters. 1903, 1908, 1910, 1914, 1916, 1918.

Incorporation Papers

Index to Civil Actions

Index to Criminal Actions

Register of Limited Partnerships. Vol. I

III. PERIODICALS:

A. Newspapers:

Democrat Standard [Healdsburg, CA.], 1866- 1869.

Guerneville Times [Guerneville, CA.], 1933.

Guerneville Xrays [Guerneville, CA.] ,1898.

Healdsburg Enterprise [Healdsburg, CA.], 1891.

HealdsburgTribune [Healdsburg, CA.], 1889.

Oakland Tribune [Oakland, CA.] ,1966.

Petaluma Argus [Petaluma, CA.], 1882.

Russian River Advertiser [Guerneville, CA.],1904-1906.

Russian River Flag [Healdsburg, CA], 1869- 1894.

San Francisco Call [San Francisco], 1909.

San Francisco Chronicle [San Francico],1894.

San Francisco Examiner [San Francisco], 1899.

Santa Rosa Press Democrat [Santa Rosa, CA.],1894-1901.

Santa Rosa Republican [Santa Rosa, CA.],1880-1916.

Sonoma Democrat [Santa Rosa, CA.] ,1870- 1895.

Ukiah Daily Journal [Ukiah, CA.],1958.

B. Magazines:

California Historical Society Quarterly [San Francisco],1929.

Harper's New Monthly Magazine [New York], 1871.

Pacific Rural Press [San Francisco], 1875.

**Snowfall in Guerneville, looking south along Fife Creek, January 19, 1907.
JCS Collection**

www.ingramcontent.com/pod-product-compliance
Lightning Source LLC
Chambersburg PA
CBHW081345080526
44588CB00016B/2382